50
People Every
Christian
Should Know

50
People Every
Christian
Should Know

*Learning from Spiritual
Giants of the Faith*

Warren W. Wiersbe

BakerBooks
a division of Baker Publishing Group
Grand Rapids, Michigan

© 2009 by Warren W. Wiersbe

Published by Baker Books
a division of Baker Publishing Group
P.O. Box 6287, Grand Rapids, MI 49516–6287
www.bakerbooks.com

Combined edition published 2009
Third printing, August 2009

Previously published as two separate titles
Living with the Giants, © 1993 by Warren W. Wiersbe
Victorious Christians You Should Know, © 1984 by Good News Broadcasting Association, Inc.

Printed in the United States of America

Library of Congress Cataloging-in-Publication Data
Wiersbe, Warren W.
    50 people every Christian should know : learning from spiritual giants of the faith /
Warren W. Wiersbe.
        p.   cm.
    Includes bibliographical references.
    ISBN 978-0-8010-7194-2 (pbk.)
    1. Christian biography. I. Title. II. Title: Fifty people every Christian should know.
BR1700.3.W54 2009
270.092'2—dc22
    [B]   2008045366

Chapters 2, 9, 12, 15–21, 23, 25–29, 31, 33–39, 41, 42, 44, 48–50 © 1971–1977 by the Moody Bible Institute, reprinted by permission of *Moody Monthly*. Chapter 24 © 1984, 1985 by Back to the Bible. Reprinted by permission.

Chapters 1, 3–8, 10, 11, 13, 14, 22, 30, 32, 40, 43, 45, 46 originally appeared as articles in *Good News Broadcaster*, copyright by The Good News Broadcasting Association, Inc., Lincoln, NE 68501. Used with permission.

16   17   18   19   20   21   22   24   23   22   21   20   19   18

Contents

Preface   7

1. Katherine von Bora (1499–1552)   9
2. Samuel Rutherford (1600–1661)   16
3. Matthew Henry (1662–1714)   24
4. Jonathan Edwards (1703–1758)   30
5. George Whitefield (1714–1770)   38
6. Charles Simeon (1759–1836)   46
7. Christmas Evans (1766–1838)   53
8. John Henry Newman (1801–1890)   59
9. Richard Trench (1807–1886)   67
10. Andrew Bonar (1810–1892)   74
11. Robert Murray McCheyne (1813–1843)   81
12. F. W. Robertson (1816–1853)   86
13. John Charles Ryle (1816–1900)   95
14. Fanny Crosby (1820–1915)   101
15. Alexander Maclaren (1826–1910)   106
16. J. B. Lightfoot (1828–1889)   112
17. R. W. Dale (1829–1895)   119
18. Joseph Parker (1830–1902)   125
19. J. Hudson Taylor (1832–1905)   133
20. Charles H. Spurgeon (1834–1892)   141
21. Phillips Brooks (1835–1893)   149

22. Frances Ridley Havergal (1836–1879)   157
23. Alexander Whyte (1836–1921)   164
24. Dwight L. Moody (1837–1899)   177
25. George Matheson (1842–1906)   197
26. C. I. Scofield (1843–1921)   203
27. F. B. Meyer (1847–1929)   209
28. W. Robertson Nicoll (1851–1923)   219
29. Henry Drummond (1851–1897)   226
30. R. A. Torrey (1856–1928)   234
31. Thomas Spurgeon (1856–1917)   240
32. Samuel Chadwick (1860–1932)   246
33. Charles E. Jefferson (1860–1937)   253
34. W. H. Griffith Thomas (1861–1924)   259
35. A. C. Gaebelein (1861–1945)/ B. H. Carroll
    (1843–1914)   265
36. G. Campbell Morgan (1863–1945)   273
37. John Henry Jowett (1864–1923)   281
38. J. D. Jones (1865–1942)   287
39. George H. Morrison (1866–1928)   294
40. Amy Carmichael (1867–1951)   299
41. Frank W. Boreham (1871–1959)   307
42. Joseph W. Kemp (1872–1933)   315
43. Oswald Chambers (1874–1917)   320
44. H. A. Ironside (1876–1951)   327
45. Clarence Edward Macartney (1879–1957)   332
46. William Whiting Borden (1887–1913)   340
47. Alva Jay McClain (1888–1968)   346
48. A. W. Tozer (1897–1963)   352
49. W. E. Sangster (1900–1960)   359
50. William Culbertson (1905–1971)   366

Notes   373
Further Reading   381

Preface

These brief biographies originally appeared as magazine articles, thirty-two of them in *Moody Monthly* magazine (1971–77) and sixteen in *The Good News Broadcaster,* published by Back to the Bible Broadcast. The *Moody Monthly* articles were compiled into *Walking with the Giants* and *Listening to the Giants,* both published by Baker; and the others into *Victorious Christians You Should Know,* co-published in 1984 by Back to the Bible and Baker. The biographies from the two *Giants* books later became *Living with the Giants,* which was published by Baker in 1993.

At the request of the publisher, I wrote the chapters on Clarence Edward Macartney and Alva Jay McClain especially for this volume.

It pleases me that there is still an interest in Christian biography. One of the goals in my writing ministry has been to encourage Christians—especially pastors—to "dig again the old wells" (see Gen. 26:18) and get acquainted with the godly leaders of the past who kept the light shining long before we were ever on the scene. I have heard from people in different parts of the world who have read these studies and been helped by them. Many of my readers have especially appreciated the bibliographical information and have searched for these forgotten books. I hope they found them!

Many Christians today are so fascinated with the latest religious fads and celebrities that they forget that all of us are "like dwarfs on the shoulders of giants," to quote the French philosopher Bernard of Chartres (d. c. 1130). In his essay "History," Emerson reminds us, "There is properly no history; only biography." I rejoice that in recent years, at least in the United States, there have been an increase in published biographies, both popular and academic, and I hope this continues. We must remember the warning issued by George Santayana, "Those who cannot remember the past are condemned to repeat it."

The past is not an anchor to drag us back but a rudder to help guide us into the future. I have been helped greatly in my own life and ministry by reading the hundreds of biographies, autobiographies, and histories that have enabled me to write these chapters, and I trust you will benefit from reading them. When I started the *Moody Monthly* series, I was pastoring Calvary Baptist Church in Covington, Kentucky, near Cincinnati. Then we moved to Moody Church in Chicago (1971–78) and then to Back to the Bible Broadcast in Lincoln, Nebraska (1979–89).

The magazines I once wrote for are no longer being published. I'm grateful that these articles can be conserved in this volume, and I trust they will inform and inspire you.

Warren W. Wiersbe

1

Katherine von Bora
1499–1552

November 10, 1983, marked the five hundredth anniversary of the birth of Martin Luther. We have heard a great deal about this courageous reformer and his ministry. But I want to focus our attention now not on Luther the preacher and leader, but on Luther the husband and father; for I want you to meet Katherine von Bora, the nun who became Martin Luther's devoted wife. He called her "Kitty, my rib," and he loved her dearly.

Katherine was born January 29, 1499, at Lippendorf, Germany, about six miles south of Leipzig. When her mother died five years later, her father put Katherine into a boarding school, and then, when she was nine, placed her in the Cistercian convent at Nimbschen in Saxony. It was not an easy place for a little girl to grow up, but at least she had protection, food, and friends. On October 8, 1515, she was "married to Christ" and officially became a nun. Little did she realize that, two years later, a daring Wittenberg professor named Martin Luther would nail his ninety-five theses to the church door and usher in a religious movement that would change her life.

As the Reformation doctrine spread across Germany, numbers of monks and nuns became believers and sought to escape from their convents and monasteries. Some of the nuns who sought freedom were severely punished, and some who escaped were brought back into even worse bondage. Twelve nuns at the Nimbschen convent somehow got word to Luther that they wanted to get out, and he arranged for their escape.

On Easter evening, April 5, 1523, a brave merchant and his nephew, Henry and Leonard Koppe, drove a wagonload of barrels into the convent, put each of the twelve nuns into a barrel, and drove away. When a suspicious man asked Koppe what he was carrying in the barrels, he replied, "Herring." Three of the girls were returned to their homes, but the other nine were taken to Wittenberg where husbands would be found for them. Two years later all of them had husbands—except Katherine von Bora.

Luther did his best to match her with a godly husband, but all his attempts failed. The one man she really fell in love with ran off and married another girl. Luther urged her to marry Pastor Casper Glatz, but she refused. She was living with some of the leading citizens in Wittenberg and learning how to be a lady and manage a household, so those two years of waiting were not wasted. Finally, she let it be known that if Doctor Luther were to ask her to be his wife, she would not say no.

It was not that Luther was against marriage, but he knew that he was a marked man and that, if he married, he would only put his wife and family into great danger. He urged others to marry, if only to spite the devil and his teaching (the policy of Rome concerning married clergy). How could a man who was declared a heretic by the pope and an outlaw by the Kaiser take a wife and establish a home?

But as the months passed, Luther weakened. He wrote to a friend, "If I can swing it, I'll take my Kate to wife ere I die, to spite the devil." Not the least of Luther's concerns were the economic factors involved in marriage. He accepted no payment or royalties for his books, his own income was unsteady and meager, and he was known for his generosity to anybody in need. If he wanted to deprive himself that was one thing, but did he have the right to force his wife to make such constant sacrifices?

On June 13, 1525, Dr. Martin Luther and Katherine von Bora were married in a private ceremony at the Black Cloister, the "converted monastery" where Luther lived. As per the custom, two weeks later there was a public ceremony at the church. A host of friends attended, and the couple received many choice gifts. Of course, the enemy immediately circulated slanderous stories about the couple, but few people believed them. One man even said that their first child would be the Antichrist.

Luther was forty-two years old and Katherine was twenty-five. Would the marriage succeed? History records the glorious fact that the marriage not only succeeded, but set a high standard for Christian family life for centuries to come. The church historian Philip Schaff wrote:

> The domestic life of Luther has far more than a biographical interest. It is one of the factors of modern civilization. Without Luther's reformation clerical celibacy, with all its risks and evil consequences, might still be the universal law in all Western churches. There would be no married clergymen and clerical families in which the duties and virtues of conjugal, parental, and filial relations could be practiced. . . . Viewed simply as a husband-father, and as one of the founders of the clerical family, Luther deserves to be esteemed and honored as one of the greatest benefactors of mankind.

While we are at it, let's give some bouquets to Katherine too. It was not easy to convert a rundown cloister into a comfortable home. Nor was it easy to convert a hyperactive professor-preacher into a patient husband and father. She always called him Doctor Luther, but Luther had a number of pet names for his Katherine. "Kitty, my rib" is perhaps the best-known nickname, but he also called her *Selbander*, which is German for "better half." It was not unusual for him to refer to her as "my Lord Kate" or even "Doctor Katherine" (she was an excellent nurse and dispenser of herbal medicines). When he felt she was giving too many orders, he quietly called her *Kette*, the German word for "chain."

"There is a lot to get used to in the first year of marriage," said Luther, and no husband knew this better than he. Accustomed to planning his own day, Luther had to learn that another mind and heart were now involved in his schedule. "Wives usually know the art to ensnare a man with tears and pleadings," he wrote. "They can turn and twist nicely and give the best words."

But he had nothing to fear, for nobody was a better manager of a house or a home than Katherine Luther. She transformed the old cloister into a fairly comfortable house, and, like the energetic woman of Proverbs 31, she launched into various enterprises to feed and sustain her household. She kept cows for milk and butter and for making cheese that, said her guests, was better than what they purchased at the market. She started a piggery because her husband liked pork, and this gave Luther a new name for his wife: My Lord Kate, Mistress of the Pigsty.

She turned a neglected field into a productive garden and even planted an orchard. What produce she did not use herself, she sold or bartered at the market and used the income to purchase items for the home. She even stocked a pond with fish! "Have I not at home a fair wife," Luther said proudly, "or shall I say *boss?*"

It was not long before the Black Cloister became a crowded and busy place. Katherine had not only her own children to care for— six of them—but also (at various times) her own niece and nephew, eleven of Martin's nieces and nephews, various students who boarded with them, and ever-present guests who came to confer with her famous husband. Before the Reformation, forty monks had lived in the Cloister; now, nearly as many joyful Christians lived there, learning to serve one another.

Luther wisely permitted his wife to be in charge of the management of the home. To begin with, he was far too busy to worry about such things, and, he had to admit, she did a far better job than he could do. Katherine not only cared for him and the household, but she ministered to the needs of people all over Wittenberg. She listened to their problems, gave them care and medicine in their sicknesses, counseled them in their sorrows, and advised them in their business affairs. The town recognized that the Luther household was an exemplary Christian home, and much of that success was due to Katherine.

It was not easy being married to Martin Luther. He would let his food get cold while he debated theology with his guests or answered the questions of students. "Doctor," said Katherine one day as the dinner grew cold, "why don't you stop talking and eat?" Luther knew she was right, but he still snapped back, "I wish that women would repeat the Lord's Prayer before opening their mouths!" One day he said, "All my life is patience! I have to have patience with the pope, the heretics, my family, and Kate."

But out of those mealtime conversations came one of Luther's finest books, *The Table Talk of Martin Luther*. Baker Books has reprinted the edition edited by Thomas S. Kepler, and I recommend it to you. As you read it, keep in mind that it was Katherine Luther who really made the book possible. It was at her table that these sparkling conversations were recorded--while the food grew cold.

Luther called marriage "a school for character," and he was right. He realized that his own life was enriched because of the love of his wife and family. When I was teaching the history of preaching to seminary students, I reviewed Luther's philosophy of ministry and read many of his sermons, and I was impressed with the many allusions and illustrations drawn from the home. I was also impressed with Luther's Christmas sermons, and I wonder if they would have been as effective had he remained an unmarried man.

As in every home, there were times of trial and sorrow. The Luthers had six children: Hans (b. 1526), Elizabeth (b. 1527, d. 1528), Magdalene (b. 1529, d. 1542), Martin (b. 1531), Paul (b. 1533), and Margaret (b. 1534). Luther would arise at six each morning and pray with the children, and they would recite the Ten Commandments, the Creed, and the Lord's Prayer, and then sing a psalm (Luther himself was an excellent musician). He would then hurry off to preach or to lecture and would be busy the entire day.

But Luther was not a robust man, and he had many ailments that often struck him without warning. On several occasions, Katherine prepared to become a widow, but the Lord graciously healed her husband and restored him to her. In 1540, it was Katherine who was despaired of, her condition considered hopeless. Day and night her husband was at her side, praying for God's mercy on her and the children, and the Lord graciously answered. Six years later, it was Martin who was being nursed by Katherine, but his recovery was not to be, and on February 18, 1546, he entered into glory. I am sure that one of his first acts of worship in heaven was to thank God for Katherine.

Let me share two of my favorite stories about Katherine Luther.

At family devotions one morning, Luther read Genesis 22 and talked about Abraham's sacrifice of Isaac. "I do not believe it!" said Katherine. "God would not have treated his son like that!"

"But, Katie," Luther quietly replied, "He did!"

During one very difficult period, Luther was carrying many burdens and fighting many battles. Usually jolly and smiling, he was instead depressed and worried. Katherine endured this for days. One day, she met him at the door wearing a black mourning dress.

"Who died?" the professor asked.

"God," said Katherine.

"You foolish thing!" said Luther. "Why this foolishness!"

"It is true," she persisted. "God must have died, or Doctor Luther would not be so sorrowful."

Her therapy worked, and Luther snapped out of his depression.

It is interesting to read Luther's letters to his wife and note the various ways he addressed her: "To the deeply learned Mrs. Katherine Luther, my gracious housewife in Wittenberg"; "To my dear housewife, Katherine Luther, Doctress, self-martyr at Wittenberg"; "To the holy, worrisome Lady, Katherine Luther, Doctor, at Wittenberg, my gracious, dear housewife"; "Housewife Katherine Luther, Doctress, and whatever else she may be"!

After Luther's death, the situation in Germany became critical and war broke out. Katherine had to flee Wittenberg, and when she returned, she found her house and gardens ruined and all her cattle gone. Then the plague returned, and Katherine and the children again had to flee. During that trip, she was thrown out of a wagon into the icy waters of a ditch, and that was the beginning of the end for her. Her daughter Margaret nursed her mother tenderly, even as her mother had nursed others, but there was no recovery. Katherine died on December 20, 1552, at Torgau, where she is buried in St. Mary's Church.

On her monument, you will read: "There fell asleep in God here at Torgau the late blessed Dr. Martin Luther's widow Katherine von Bora."

They could have added: "Many daughters have done virtuously, but thou excellest them all" (Prov. 31:29).

I suggest that we make either January 29 or June 13 "Pastors' Wives' Day," not only in honor of Katherine von Bora, but in honor of all pastors' wives everywhere—that great host of sacrificing women of God who make it possible for their husbands to minister. I salute these women who must often turn houses into homes, who carry the burdens of their people as well as their own, who do without that others may have, who cheerfully bear criticism, and who do it all to the glory of God.

By the way, what have *you* done lately to encourage *your* pastor's wife?

Samuel Rutherford
1600–1661

An English merchant, traveling in Scotland in the seventeenth century, made this entry in his journal:

> In St. Andrews I heard a tall, stately man preach, and he showed me the majesty of God. I afterwards heard a little fair man preach, and he showed me the loveliness of Christ. I then went to Irvine, where I heard preach a well-favoured, proper old man, with a long beard, and that man showed me all my heart.

The first preacher was Robert Blair, who ministered at St. Andrews in Edinburgh for more than a quarter of a century. The third preacher was the great Covenanter and professor of theology, David Dickson, whose commentary on the Psalms has been reissued by Banner of Truth and is worth owning. The "little fair man" was Samuel Rutherford, one of the most paradoxical preachers Scotland has ever produced.

"For generations Rutherford has inspired the best preaching in Scotland," wrote Alexander Whyte in 1908; and yet today this man is almost forgotten. He should be known as the saintly writer of *The Letters of Samuel Rutherford*, but most people associate the name with Mrs. A. R. Cousin's song "The Sands of Time Are Sinking," which was inspired by statements found in his letters. (This happened to be D. L. Moody's favorite song.)

Rutherford was born in the little village of Nisbet, in the shire of Roxburgh, about 1600. Apparently he lived a rather careless life during his youth. "I must first tell you that there is not such a glassy, icy, and slippery piece of way betwixt you and heaven, as Youth," he wrote to his friend William Gordon. "The old ashes of the sins of my youth are new fire of sorrow to me." To another friend he wrote, "Like a fool, as I was, I suffered my sun to be high in the heaven, and near afternoon, before ever I took the gate by the end." He entered the university in Edinburgh in 1617, began his theological studies in 1626, and in 1627 was licensed to preach. That same year he was called to Anwoth. His life and ministry there put that little village on the map.

Thirty years before, the congregation at Anwoth had enjoyed the ministry of another man of God, John Welsh, the son-in-law of the famous John Knox. Welsh often left his bed in the middle of the night, wrapped himself in a warm plaid, and interceded for the people of his parish. When his wife would beg him to go back to sleep, he would say, "I have the souls of three thousand to answer for and I know not how it is with many of them." It is interesting that both Welsh and Rutherford were exiled because of their preaching and their opposition to the king's encroachments upon the church. When he was on his deathbed, Welsh received word that the king had lifted the ban; so he arose, went to the church, and preached a sermon. He then returned to his bed and died two hours later!

I visited Rutherford's church at Anwoth and was surprised to find the ruins of a barn-like building, sixty by twenty feet. It could not have seated more than 250 people; and yet Rutherford faithfully ministered there for nine years. "I see exceedingly small fruit of my ministry," he wrote after two years at Anwoth. "I would be glad of one soul, to be a crown of joy and rejoicing in the day of Christ." Mrs. A. R. Cousin put it this way in her song:

Fair Anwoth by the Solway,
    To me thou still art dear!
E'en from the verge of Heaven
    I drop for thee a tear.
Oh, if one soul from Anwoth
    Meet me at God's right hand,
My Heaven will be two Heavens,
    In Immanuel's land.

The people of the congregation knew that God had sent them a dedicated pastor. They said to their friends, "He is always praying, always preaching, always visiting the sick, always catechizing, always writing and studying." Often he fell asleep at night talking about Christ, and often he spoke of Christ while sleeping. (Spurgeon once preached a sermon in his sleep. His wife wrote down the main points and gave the outline to him the next morning—and he went to the tabernacle and preached it!)

In 1630 Rutherford's wife died; he was also to lose two children during his Anwoth ministry. But in spite of difficulties and the smallness of the place in which he ministered, Rutherford never sought to put himself into a larger place. "His own hand planted me here," he wrote in 1631. "And here I will abide till the great Master of the Vineyard think fit to transplant me." "Transplanted" he would be, but not in the manner he anticipated. For in 1636 Rutherford published *An Apology [Argument] for Divine Grace,* a book that assailed the weak theology of the day and aroused the opposition of Archbishop Laud's party. Rutherford was tried in Edinburgh on July 27, 1636, and was banished to Aberdeen and warned never to preach in Scotland again. He remained in Aberdeen from August 20, 1636, to June 1638, where he was known as "the banished minister." It is important to note that Rutherford was not imprisoned or made to suffer physically. He was exiled from his ministry and made to suffer in an even greater way by being forbidden to preach.

But history repeated itself, for out of the exile came one of the most spiritual devotional books ever written. Out of Paul's imprisonment came Ephesians, Philippians, and Colossians; out of Bunyan's

18

imprisonment came *Pilgrim's Progress*; and from Rutherford's exile in Aberdeen came *The Letters of Samuel Rutherford*. Of course, Rutherford did not write these letters with any thought of publication.

He died on March 29, 1661; and in 1664 an edition of 284 letters was published in Rotterdam, edited by his former student and secretary, Robert McWard. The title of this first edition was *Joshua Redivivus, or, Mr. Rutherfoord's Letters. Joshua Resurrected* seems at first to be a strange title; but if you think about it and read some of his letters, it begins to make sense. McWard considered Rutherford to be a second Joshua, who spied out the spiritual land of Canaan and came back to share the precious fruits with others. The third edition of the book, issued in 1675, contained 68 additional letters; the 1848 edition added 10 more. By the 1863 edition there were 365 letters, one for each day of the year.

Why would anyone want to preserve and read these letters? After all, they were never written for the public eye: they were intimate letters, written from a pastor's heart, to help people he could no longer minister to publicly. Two-thirds of the letters were written during Rutherford's years of exile, when his ministerial burden for his people was especially heavy. But here, I think, is the value of the letters: they are "heart to heart," and focus on the specific needs of real people. Rutherford's encouragement and spiritual counsel are just as helpful today as they were three centuries ago.

Let me confess that there are times when Rutherford's writing is a bit too effeminate for me. I am sure the problem is with me and not with the saintly author. Rutherford, of course, steeped his writing in Scripture, quoting primarily from Isaiah and the Song of Solomon. I started keeping a list of references and allusions while reading the letters, but I finally gave up. There were just too many of them.

Rutherford had three favorite images of the church in his letters: the bride of Christ, the vineyard of the Lord, and the ship. There are hundreds of references to the bride, and Mrs. Cousin included a few of them in her song. There is no question that Samuel Rutherford had an intimate communion with his Lord and was not afraid to talk about it.

The Bride eyes not her garment,
　　But her dear Bridegroom's face;
I will not gaze at glory,
　　But on my King of Grace—
Not at the crown He giveth,
　　But on His pierced hand:
The Lamb is all the glory
　　Of Immanuel's land.

The allusions to the vineyard are not surprising since Anwoth was situated in farming country, and the nautical image stems from Anwoth's proximity to the Solway on the River Fleet. "Have all in readiness against the time that ye must sail through the black and impetuous Jordan," he wrote to John Kennedy in 1632, "and Jesus, Jesus, who knoweth both those depths and the rocks, and all the coast, be your pilot." He wrote to his close friend Lady Kenmure, "Look for crosses, and while it is fair weather mend the sails of the ship."

Rutherford's letters were not written for speed readers or frantic pastors looking for sermon outlines. These letters must be read slowly, meditatively, prayerfully. This perhaps explains why this priceless collection is almost ignored today: we are too busy and too pragmatic. If a book today can be read quickly and easily, without demanding too much thinking, and if it contains two or three outlines or promotional ideas, then it is well on its way to popularity. However, if a book like *The Letters of Samuel Rutherford* can only minister to the interior life, make Jesus Christ very wonderful, and create in the reader a deeper love for God and the souls of men, then it may have to fight for survival.

Before you dismiss Rutherford as an impractical mystic, let me share with you the other side of his life and ministry, which prompted my earlier reference to him as "one of the most paradoxical preachers Scotland ever produced." Rutherford was not only the writer of devotional letters; he was also the author of a number of theological works that placed him among the leading thinkers and apologists of his day. In addition to *An Apology for Divine Grace*, the book that precipitated Rutherford's exile, he also helped write the famous

Westminster Confession of Faith, and tradition states that he wrote the famous Shorter Catechism based on that great confession. The story is worth telling.

In March 1638 it was possible for Rutherford to leave Aberdeen and return to Anwoth. His last letter from exile is dated June 11, 1638, and his first letter from Anwoth is dated August 5, 1638. In November of that year, he was officially "vindicated" by the Assembly, and he settled down to minister again to his beloved flock. But in 1639 he was commissioned to take the chair of divinity at St. Mary's College, Edinburgh, and reluctantly he obeyed. Then in 1643 he was sent to London to represent the Scottish church at the Westminster Assembly. He took Robert McWard, one of his students, to be his secretary—little knowing that one day McWard would give the world the classic book of letters. He remained in London until November 1647, when he returned to Edinburgh to become principal of St. Mary's.

However, while in London in 1644 he had published a book that was to take Great Britain by storm, a book that almost led Rutherford to the gallows. It was called *Lex Rex* (Latin for "The Law and the Prince"). In that day, anybody who wrote about the monarchy had better be loyal or prepared to make a quick getaway; Rutherford was neither. When he was involved in controversy, his stubbornness and devotion to truth could be as strong as the mysticism of his letters. He was an ardent apologist, and he could wield the sword with deadly blows. No doubt his deep love for Christ and the church gave him courage and daring in the theological arena.

What he wrote in *Lex Rex* would cause little excitement today because we are accustomed to democracy and civil rights; but in the days of Charles I and Charles II, a call for democracy and constitutional rights was a summons for the hangman. In fact, when Charles II was crowned in Scotland in 1651, Rutherford opposed his policies and, because of his convictions, broke with his two close friends, Blair and Dickson. Rutherford wrote to Lady Kenmure, "The Lord hath removed Scotland's crown, for we owned not His crown." On October 16, 1660, the common hangman burned *Lex Rex* at the cross of Edinburgh, and on March 28, 1661 the "Drunken Parliament" indicted Rutherford and three other Christian leaders. But by that time, the author of *Lex Rex* was on his deathbed; his reply to the official summons was: "I behoove to answer my first summons, and ere your day come, I will be where few kings and great folk come." He died on March 29, 1661. His last words were, "Glory, glory dwelleth in Immanuel's land!"

Should you wish to get acquainted with Rutherford, I suggest you begin with the excellent essay by Marcus Loane in his *Makers of Religious Freedom in the Seventeenth Century*. You might also read the chapter on Alexander Henderson, another "man of the Covenant." Then secure the edition of *Rutherford's Letters* edited by Andrew Bonar, because this is by far the best: it is complete. The biographical and historical notes help the reader identify people, times, and places; the glossary of Scottish terms is invaluable; and the letters are arranged in chronological order. Do not plan to read this book in one sitting; read a letter or two a day and let the Spirit of God quietly speak to your heart. Granted, Rutherford is not for everyone; but if he is for you, then enjoy this first meeting as long as you can.

Alexander Whyte preached a series of sermons from *Rutherford's Letters*, and they were published under the title *Samuel Rutherford and Some of His Correspondents*. You should read the first two sermons before you begin the *Letters* themselves; they are an excellent introduction to the book and its author. After reading several of the letters, you can see how Whyte interprets them in his sermons. By the way, Whyte also brought out an edition of the Shorter Catechism in his *Handbooks for Bible Classes* series. And in the same series is John Macpherson's fine history of the Westminster Confession entitled *The Westminster Confession of Faith*.

One of the best studies of Rutherford's life and character is that by A. Taylor Innes in *The Evangelical Succession* series. It is called simply *Samuel Rutherford*, and Alexander Whyte himself called it "the finest thing that has ever been written on Rutherford." Alexander Smellie's classic volume *Men of the Covenant* should also be consulted.

"I look not to win away to my home without wounds and blood," Rutherford wrote in 1630; shortly before his death thirty-one years later, he wrote, "For me, I am now near to eternity. . . . Fear not men, for the Lord is your light and your salvation."

It is best that we remember Samuel Rutherford not as the courageous apologist or the dogmatic theologian but as the man who lived so close to the Savior's heart. His pen was always ready to write of the things "touching the King." In this day of headache and haste, perhaps it is good for us to heed his invitation to a closer communion with our Lord. Then we can join the testimony Mrs. Cousin put on his lips:

> With mercy and with judgment
> My web of time He wove,
> And aye the dews of sorrow
> Were lustred with His love.
> I'll bless the hand that guided,
> I'll bless the heart that planned,
> When throned where glory dwelleth
> In Immanuel's land.

3

Matthew Henry
1662–1714

Suitable to everybody, instructive to all" is the way Charles Spurgeon described what is probably the best-known commentary on the Bible written in the English language, *Matthew Henry's Commentary*.[1] Since it was first published more than two hundred and fifty years ago, this commentary has appeared in many different editions, including a condensation in one volume.

Spurgeon recommended that every minister of the gospel read straight through *Matthew Henry's Commentary* at least once during his lifetime. Perhaps he got this idea from his model, George Whitefield, who carried his set of Matthew Henry on all of his travels and read it daily on his knees.

Matthew Henry was born at Broad Oaks, Shropshire, England, on October 18, 1662. His father, Philip Henry, was a Nonconformist minister who, along with two thousand other clergymen, had been ejected from his church by the Act of Uniformity issued that year by Charles II. These courageous men had refused to compromise their convictions and give "unfeigned consent and assent" to the Prayer Book. They also refused to submit to Episcopal ordination.

Philip Henry had married an heiress of a large estate in Broad Oaks named Catherine Matthews. Her father was not in favor of the match and told his daughter, "Nobody knows where he came from." But Catherine wisely replied, "True, but I know where he is going, and I should like to go with him!"

Matthew was physically weak, but it was not long before his strength of intellect and character made themselves known. At the age of three, he was reading the Bible; by the time he was nine, he was competent in Latin and Greek. He spent his first eighteen years being tutored at home, in an atmosphere that was joyfully and lovingly Christian.

He loved to hear his father preach. A sermon on Psalm 51:17 first awakened in young Matthew a desire to know the Lord personally. He was only ten years old at the time, but the impression was lasting. When he was thirteen, Matthew wrote an amazingly mature analysis of his own spiritual condition, a document that reads like an ordinary paper. Often, after hearing his father preach, Matthew would hurry to his room and pray that God would seal the Word and the spiritual impressions made to his heart so that he might not lose them. God answered those youthful prayers.

In July 1680, Matthew was sent to London to study with "that holy, faithful minister," Thomas Doolittle, who had an academy in his home. Unfortunately, the religious persecutions of the day forced Doolittle to close his academy; Matthew returned to Broad Oaks. In April 1685, he returned to London to study law at Gray's Inn. He was a good student, but he never lost the burning desire to be a minister of the gospel.

A year later he returned to Broad Oaks and began to preach whenever opportunity presented itself, and on May 9, 1687, he was ordained. Before his ordination, he put himself through a heart-searching self-examination in which he seriously studied his own Christian experience, motives for ministry, and fitness for service. The paper contains both confession of faith and confession of sin. He concluded that he was not entering the ministry "as a trade to live by" or to make a name for himself. He also concluded, "I have no design in the least to maintain a party, or to keep up any schismatical faction."

Throughout his ministry, Matthew Henry loved and cooperated with all who trusted Christ and wanted to serve him, no matter what their denominational connections. Even the leaders of the Episcopal Church admitted that Matthew Henry was a good and godly man. This document ought to be read by every prospective minister before he comes to ordination, and it would not hurt those of us who are already ordained to review it on occasion.

A group of believers in Chester invited Matthew Henry to become their pastor, and on June 2, 1687, he began twenty-five happy years of ministry among them. Though he was in demand to preach in other churches in the area, he was rarely absent from his own pulpit on the Lord's Day.

He was married in August of the same year. On February 14, 1689, his wife died in childbirth, although, by the mercy of God, their daughter lived. Matthew married again on July 8, 1690, and God gave him and his wife nine children, eight of them girls, three of whom died during their first year. His only son, Philip, was born May 3, 1700, but he did not follow his father's faith, or his grandfather's. His interests lay in this world and not in the world to come.

God blessed the ministry in Chester so that a new sanctuary was erected and was dedicated on August 8, 1700. The effectiveness of Matthew Henry's pulpit ministry reached even to London, and several churches there tried to secure his service. But he loved his people at Trinity Church in Chester, and refused each invitation.

Matthew was usually in his study before five o'clock each morning, devoting himself to the preparation of his exposition of the Word. He had breakfast with his family and always led them in worship, reading and expounding some passage from the Old Testament. He then returned to his study until afternoon, when he would set out to visit his people. After the evening meal, he would again lead the household in worship, using a New Testament passage for his meditation. He often questioned the children and the servants to make sure they had understood the teaching.

Often in the late evening, he would put in a few more hours of study before retiring. "Take heed of growing remiss in your work," he warned fellow pastors. "Take pains while you live. . . . The Scripture still affords new things, to those who search them." It was not unusual for him to preach seven times a week, and yet he was always fresh and practical. "No place is like my own study," he said. "No company like good books, especially the book of God." We wonder what Matthew Henry would think of those ministers who rush about all week, wasting time, and then "borrow" another man's sermon for the Lord's Day.

The key date in Matthew Henry's life is November 12, 1704; on that day he started writing his famous *Commentary*. On April 17, 1714, he completed his comments on the Book of Acts; but two months later, on June 22, he suddenly took ill and died.

Matthew Henry was not pastoring in Chester when he was called home. On May 18, 1712, he had begun his new ministry in Hackney, London. One of the factors motivating his move was his desire to be closer to his publisher as his *Commentary* was being printed. He had ministered twenty-five years at Trinity Church, Chester, and only two years in London. The funeral service was held on June 25, and he was buried at Trinity Church.

Much of the material in Henry's *Commentary* came from his own expositions of Scripture given at family worship and from the pulpit. There is also a great deal of Philip Henry in these pages, especially the pithy sayings that season the exposition. Matthew's purpose in writing the *Commentary* was practical, not academic. He simply wanted to explain and apply the Word of God in language the common people could understand.

Several of his pastor friends gathered up his notes and sermons and completed the *Commentary* from Romans to Revelation. When you read their expositions, you can see how far short they fall of the high standard set by the original author. In true Puritan fashion, Matthew Henry had the ability to get to the heart of a passage, outline the passage clearly, and then apply its truths to daily life. True, there were times when he spiritualized the text and missed the point; but generally speaking, he did his work well. One does not have to agree with all of his interpretations to benefit from his observations.

In 1765, John Wesley published an edited version of the *Commentary*, hoping to bring it within the reach of the average Christian reader. He felt the current version was too large and too expensive. But, at the same time, Wesley also deleted all that Matthew Henry had to say about election and predestination. He also omitted an "abundance of quaint sayings" and thus took the seasoning out of the dinner. In his preface, Wesley remarked that he used to wonder where some preachers "whom I greatly esteem" obtained the "pretty turns in preaching" that he heard in their sermons; but, after reading Matthew Henry, he discovered their source. I have a suspicion that this was a gentle criticism of his estranged friend, George Whitefield, who used to read Matthew Henry before going into the pulpit.

You will not find Matthew Henry grappling with big problems as he expounds the Word, or always shedding light on difficult passages in the Bible. For this kind of help you must consult the critical commentaries. He did not know a great deal about customs in the Holy Land, since travel to the East was quite limited in that day. Again, the student will need up-to-date commentaries and Bible dictionaries to help him in that area. However, for a devotional and practical approach to Bible exposition, this commentary leads the way.

I must confess that I have not followed Spurgeon's advice to read straight through *Matthew Henry's Commentary*, but I have used it with profit over the years. I think Henry is especially good in Genesis, Psalms, and the four Gospels. I have never consulted his *Commentary* early in my sermon preparation, but rather have left him (and Maclaren and Spurgeon) until after I had done my own digging and meditating. Often just a sentence from Matthew Henry has opened up a new area of thought for me and helped me feed my people.

I was surprised to discover that Matthew Henry is quoted in our two leading books of quotations. *Bartlett's Familiar Quotations* has fourteen Henry quotations and *The Oxford Dictionary of Quotations* (3rd edition) has six. Apparently Matthew Henry is the originator of the phrase "creature comforts" as well as the popular saying "All this and heaven too." Perhaps some enterprising reader could mine some of Matthew Henry's pithy sayings and put them into a book for us.

If you want to get to know this expositor and his father better, secure *The Lives of Philip and Matthew Henry*, published by Banner of Truth. Matthew Henry wrote the biography of his father, and it is a classic. J. B. Williams wrote the son's life, but it is not as exciting.

When he was on his deathbed, Matthew Henry said to a friend, "You have been asked to take notice of the sayings of dying men—this is mine: that a life spent in the service of God and communion with Him is the most pleasant life that anyone can live in this world."

4

Jonathan Edwards
1703–1758

It is unfortunate that many people imagine Jonathan Edwards as a ranting Puritan preacher, pounding the pulpit and trying to frighten sinners into heaven. Of course, most of these people have probably never read his famous sermon "Sinners in the Hands of an Angry God" or even examined the life of this godly man. For Jonathan Edwards was a quiet scholar, a loving father, a concerned pastor, a burdened missionary, and a man who loved God and longed more than anything else to glorify him.

Edwards was born into the home of Reverend Timothy Edwards in East Windsor, Connecticut, on October 5, 1703. He was the only son in the family; he had ten sisters. He came from good Puritan stock, especially on his mother's side of the family. Her father was Reverend Solomon Stoddard, revered pastor of the Congregational Church at Northampton, Massachusetts.

Stoddard was the accepted spiritual leader of the churches in the Connecticut Valley; in fact, some people called him "Pope" Stoddard. He pastored there for fifty years, and under his ministry at least five special spiritual awakenings had been experienced.

Jonathan Edwards received his schooling at home; at an early age he learned Latin, and later he took on Greek and Hebrew. He had two passionate interests in those early years—science and religion. He watched spiders and wrote an amazing essay about them. He saw the mind and heart of God in creation; everything in nature revealed to him something about God.

But his interest in spiritual things was remarkable for a boy so young. He prayed five times each day. With some of his friends he built a "booth" in the swamp, and there they would gather together to discuss spiritual matters and pray. I must confess that the boys' clubs my friends and I formed in our youthful years centered more around fun and games.

In 1716, when he was thirteen, Edwards entered Yale college, where he invested four years in undergraduate study and then two more years studying theology. It was while he was at Yale that he had two life-changing experiences. The first was his conversion when he was about seventeen years old. Since childhood he had revolted against the doctrine of the sovereignty of God. But as he read 1 Timothy 1:17, he had a remarkable experience of the sense of God's greatness and glory, and all his theological objections disappeared.

"As I read the words," he wrote in his personal account, "there came into my soul, and was as it were diffused through it, a sense of the glory of the divine Being; a new sense, quite different from anything I ever experienced before. . . . From about that time, I began to have a new kind of apprehensions and ideas of Christ, and the work of redemption, and the glorious way of salvation by Him."

Edwards was never content to have only book knowledge of God. He sought to experience God in his own life in a personal way. He was not an ivory-tower theologian, spinning webs of words. He always centered on the experience of the heart; it was this conviction that brought him many spiritual blessings as well as many spiritual battles.

His second crisis experience was more intellectual than spiritual, although Edwards would never divorce the mind and the heart. He read John Locke's *Essay Concerning Human Understanding* and made an about-face in his approach to the problem of how people think and learn. He came to the conclusion that "knowledge" was not something divorced from the rest of life, but that a man's senses helped to teach him truth. In other words, sensory experience and thinking must go together. Again, Edwards saw the importance of uniting the mind and the heart.

This approach would govern his philosophy of preaching for the rest of his life. He would first aim for the heart and move the affections before trying to instruct the mind. In one of his most important books, *A Treatise Concerning Religious Affections*, Edwards wrote, "True religion, in great part, consists in holy affections."[1] However, he opposed emotion for emotion's sake. He carefully explained the difference between shallow emotionalism and true affections that prepare the way for men and women to receive God's truth.

On January 12, 1723, Jonathan Edwards solemnly dedicated himself to God. Earlier he had made a list of resolutions that he read once each week and sought to obey daily. From time to time, he added to this list as he saw special needs in his life. He used it not as a law to bind him, but as a compass to guide him and as a mirror to help him examine his progress in his spiritual walk.

On February 15, 1727, Jonathan Edwards was ordained and became assistant to his grandfather, Solomon Stoddard. On July 20 of that same year, he married Sarah Pierrepont, an exemplary Christian lady who bore him eleven children. It is worth noting that Jonathan Edwards used to spend at least one hour each evening with his children before they went to bed. He often studied thirteen hours a day, yet he took time for his family. He and his wife were very happy together; their marriage and their home were a testimony to the goodness and grace of God.

In February 1729, Solomon Stoddard died, and Jonathan Edwards became the pastor of his church, perhaps the most important congregation outside Boston. Spiritual life in the American colonies was very low, and there was a desperate need for revival. Preachers were generally well-educated, but they lacked a burden for souls and power in preaching. Some of them were not even converted themselves!

"I am greatly persuaded," wrote George Whitefield when he visited New England, "that the generality of preachers talk of an unknown, unfelt Christ. And the reason why congregations have been so dead is because dead men preach to them."

But the preachers were not the only ones to blame. While the founders of the churches had, for the most part, been converted people who feared God, their children and grandchildren were too often unconverted but baptized church members.

The churches operated under what was known as the Half-Way Covenant. This permitted people to unite with the church if they had been baptized but had not made a profession of faith in Christ (they were baptized as infants, of course). Their children were then baptized as "half-way members," but they were not permitted to share the Lord's Supper or vote in church elections.

But Solomon Stoddard had gone even further in opening the doors of the church to unsaved people. He decided that the Lord's Supper was a saving ordinance and that unconverted people should not be barred from the table. The result, of course, was a church composed largely of unconverted people who gave lip service to the doctrine but who had never experienced the life of God in their own hearts.

Obviously, the new pastor and his flock were on a collision course. Edwards had experienced eternal life in an overwhelmingly personal way. It was his conviction that truth must be experienced in the heart as well as understood in the mind. In his study of the Word, he concluded that church membership and the Lord's Supper were for saved people alone. He realized that many of the "children of the covenant" in the colonies were living in sin, apart from God, and destined for eternal destruction.

In 1734 he preached a series of sermons on justification by faith. The time was ripe, and the Spirit began to move. In the next year, Edwards saw more than three hundred people unite with the church. Some notable sinners in the town were converted, and some remarkable events took place. This was one of the early phases of the spiritual movement in America historians call the Great Awakening, which covered a period from about 1725 to 1760.

Whenever the Spirit works, the flesh and the devil start to work to counterfeit God's blessing; and it was not long before excesses appeared in the revival movement. George Whitefield had joined the movement in 1740, and in some of his meetings people fainted, cried out with fear, and even experienced fits of shaking. Whitefield, like Edwards, did not encourage these activities, but had no control over them. Ministers who opposed religious enthusiasm openly criticized Edwards and accused him of leading the people astray, so Edwards wrote and published a book on how to discern a true working of God's Spirit: *The Distinguishing Marks of a Work of the Spirit of God.* It is still today one of the best studies of religious psychology available.

That same year (1741), Edwards was invited to preach at Enfield, Connecticut, and on July 8, he preached "Sinners in the Hands of an Angry God," perhaps the most famous sermon ever preached in America.

The text was Deuteronomy 32:35: "Their foot shall slide in due time." There is no question that Edwards had one purpose in mind: to shake the people out of their religious complacency and into the saving arms of the Lord. Edwards was always quiet in his delivery; he read from a manuscript and rarely looked at the people. He did not pound the pulpit or shout. He simply opened up the Scriptures and warned lost sinners to flee from the wrath to come.

The Spirit of God broke into the meeting, and many people came under conviction. Some cried out in fear. A minister sitting on the platform pulled at the preacher's coattails and said, "Mr. Edwards! Mr. Edwards! Is not God also a God of mercy!" Edwards had to stop preaching and wait for the congregation to become quiet. He concluded the sermon, led in prayer, and closed the meeting. Those who remained afterward to talk to the preacher were not necessarily upset or afraid. In fact, people were impressed with the cheerfulness and pleasantness of the expressions on others' faces.

Concerned with the salvation of the lost, Jonathan Edwards could not continue to live with the compromising situation that he had inherited at Northampton. In 1748, he informed the church that he would not receive as new members persons who had not given evidence of salvation, nor would he permit unconverted people to come to the Lord's table. Even though ministers in that day had far more authority and respect than they do today, this step was daring and was violently opposed by most of the other church leaders.

There followed nearly two years of debate and discussion, and the result was the dismissal of the pastor. Edwards preached his farewell sermon on July 1, 1750, a pastoral message that showed no animosity or bitterness, although certainly the preacher was a man with a broken heart. His text was 2 Corinthians 1:14, and his emphasis was on what would happen when ministers meet their congregations at the future judgment.

History has proven that Edwards was right and his congregation wrong. The colonial churches that rejected the working of God and refused to examine people as to their spiritual experience eventually turned from the faith and became liberal. The churches that followed Whitefield and Edwards continued to win the lost, send out missionaries, and train ministers who were true to the faith. An unconverted ministry and an unconverted membership are the devil's chief weapons in opposing the work of God.

Jonathan Edwards moved his wife and large family to Stockbridge, Massachusetts, where he ministered as a missionary to the Indians. His income was reduced, of course, and yet God provided all their needs. Freed from pastoral duties and church problems, Edwards now had more time to study and write; during those Stockbridge years (1751–58) he wrote several of his most important works, some of which were published after his death. In 1757 he was named president of Princeton College, an office that his son-in-law Aaron Burr later held. He took office in 1758 when a smallpox epidemic was invading the area; he caught the infection through an inoculation that backfired, and on March 22 he died.

We have had more than two hundred years to evaluate the life and ministry of Jonathan Edwards. He was perhaps the greatest thinker that America ever produced, and yet he had the heart of a child. He was a great theologian, and yet his books and sermons touch life and reach into the heart. He was a rare blend of biblical scholar and revivalist. He had a longing to see people know God personally, but he refused to accommodate his theology just to get results. He was also a man concerned about missions. Even the *Encyclopedia Britannica* admits, "By his writings and example, he gave impetus to the infant evangelical missionary movement."

Edwards was not afraid to give his people solid doctrine. His Resolution 28 reads: "Resolved to study the Scriptures so steadily, constantly, and frequently, so that I may find, and plainly perceive myself to grow in the knowledge of the same." Some preachers today seem to have time for everything else but Bible study and the preparation of spiritual nourishment for their people. It is easy to borrow a sermon from a book or listen to a recording of another preacher's message.

Edwards used imagination in his preaching. Like every good teacher and preacher, he turned the ear into an eye and helped people to *see* spiritual truth. He knew that the mind is not a debating chamber—it is a picture gallery.

He was a courageous man who held to his biblical convictions even though they cost him his church and the loss of many friends. He stood with George Whitefield when many were opposing him. Edwards encouraged spiritual awakening even though he knew there would be excesses and abuses. He would have enjoyed Billy Sunday's reply to the critic who said that revivals did not last: "Neither does a bath," said Sunday, "but it's good to have one once in a while!" Edwards preached for decisions in an era when ministers were not supposed to disturb the congregation.

The Works of President Edwards, a single volume, may be available in your local library. Ola Elizabeth Winslow has written one of the best biographies, *Jonathan Edwards*, published by Macmillan in 1940. She also edited a helpful anthology of his most important sermons and writings, *Jonathan Edwards: Basic Writings* (New American Library).

Jonathan Edwards on Heaven and Hell by Dr. John Gerstner (Baker Books) is a fascinating and very readable study of this important subject. Dr. Gerstner is perhaps our leading evangelical scholar when it comes to the life and theology of Jonathan Edwards. For a satisfying but readable study of Edwards's theology, read *Jonathan Edwards, Theologian of the Heart*, by Harold Simonson (Eerdmans).

Our nation is desperately in need of spiritual awakening. But our emphasis on evangelism apart from doctrine will certainly not do it. The Great Awakening was the result of solid doctrinal preaching that addressed itself to both the heart and the mind. It was preaching that dared to expose sin in the church. And God used it to sweep thousands into his family.

Perhaps it is time that we dug again these old wells and learned why their waters flowed with life so fruitfully and so bountifully.

5

George Whitefield
1714–1770

O Heavenly Father," prayed a twenty-two-year-old preacher in London, "for Thy dear Son's sake, keep me from climbing."

That young preacher was George Whitefield, and he had every reason to fear popularity and promotion. Great crowds were coming to hear him preach the gospel, and hundreds were being converted to faith in Christ. He was the boy wonder of London. His preaching shook both Great Britain and the United States, and the results are still with us.

Historians tell us that Whitefield preached from forty to sixty hours a week, a total of more than eighteen thousand sermons during thirty-four years of public ministry. He crossed the Atlantic thirteen times and ministered extensively in the American colonies. He preached to thousands throughout Great Britain, and this included three trips to Ireland and fourteen visits to Scotland.

"I had rather wear out than rust out," he told a friend who protested that he preached too often. He often quoted the adage, "We are immortal until our work is done." When it is learned that Whitefield was not a healthy man, that he often had severe spells of vomiting, and that he arose each morning at four o'clock, this record of ministry becomes even more amazing.

We need to meet this boy preacher whom Dr. D. Martyn Lloyd-Jones called the greatest preacher that England has ever produced.

George Whitefield was born in Gloucester on December 16, 1714, into a respectable family that owned and managed the Bell Inn. Whitefield was but two years old when his father died, and when his mother remarried eight years later, the match was an unhappy one.

Young George had a good memory and a glib tongue, so he excelled in making speeches in school and acting in plays. Little did he realize that his youthful public appearances would help to prepare him for his pulpit ministry.

Of course, as a youngster, he got involved in the usual sins of youth, even to the point of stealing money from his mother. But even in the midst of his childhood corruption (as he termed it), he had the conviction that he would one day be a clergyman. "I was always fond of being a clergyman," he wrote in his *Journals*, and "used frequently to imitate the ministers reading prayers, etc."[1]

When he was about fifteen, he left school to assist his mother in the work of the inn. He continued to read the Bible even though he was not a professed Christian, and during a visit with his brother in Bristol he found great delight in attending church. He made vows and apparently had some adolescent emotional religious experiences; but no sooner had he returned to Gloucester than the old life overtook him again.

By the providence of God, Whitefield did return to school and then entered Oxford, where he met John and Charles Wesley and became a part of their Holy Club. While the Wesley brothers and their friends were moral and religious people, they did not as yet know much about the new birth. Their Christianity consisted mainly of religious exercises, mutual exhortation, and ministry to the poor and needy.

John Wesley gave Whitefield a copy of Henry Scrougal's spiritual classic, *The Life of God in the Soul of Man*; and the reading of that book opened Whitefield's eyes to the miracle of the new birth (at that time, Wesley himself knew nothing of a regeneration experience). Whitefield did not enter into true life and liberty immediately, but at least he was moving in the right direction. Finally, in the spring of 1735, he cast himself on God's mercy and experienced new life in Christ.

He then returned to Gloucester, where he lived with friends for several months. He began his lifelong practice of reading the Bible on his knees and studying his Greek New Testament (Whitefield was a competent Greek and Latin student). He also purchased the famous *Matthew Henry Commentary* and read it carefully. In fact, the set became his constant companion in all his travels.

He gathered around him a small group of new believers, many of them his old "partners in crime," and they met weekly for Bible study, prayer, and mutual edification. This was the first Methodist Society ever to be organized. It comes as a surprise to many people to learn that it was George Whitefield, not John and Charles Wesley, who founded the Methodist Church. The Wesleys entered into Whitefield's labors, and eventually were given the leadership of the movement by Whitefield.

Whitefield returned to Oxford in March, 1736. The Wesleys had already sailed to Georgia to work with General Oglethorpe in the new colony. On June 10, 1736, George Whitefield was ordained as a deacon by Bishop Martin Benson in Gloucester; and on June 26, he preached his first sermon. The curious congregation—many of them relatives and friends—were amazed at the power and spiritual wisdom of the young preacher. In fact, someone reported to the bishop that Whitefield's sermon "drove fifteen people mad." The bishop said he hoped the madness would not be forgotten by the next Sunday.

That was the beginning of a miracle ministry. In July, Whitefield graduated from Oxford; for the next two months, he ministered in London as a supply preacher for a friend. He then preached for four months in Oxford, followed by a marvelous ministry in Gloucester, Bristol, and London. Thousands came to listen, and hundreds were brought to the Savior. He personally counseled with hundreds of seeking souls. Wherever he preached, the crowds were great and the benefits were lasting.

On February 1, 1738, John Wesley returned from Georgia, a weary and defeated man. His ministry in the colony had been a failure; and, unfortunately, he had left behind a bad name and a number of determined enemies. Whitefield had felt a call to serve in Georgia, and he was ready to sail when Wesley's ship arrived in England.

For some reason, Wesley did not try to see Whitefield personally; but he did try to persuade him not to go to Georgia. In his earlier years, John Wesley believed in casting lots to determine God's will for himself and for his friends. Had Whitefield listened to Wesley at that time, what a loss it would have been to the people of the United States. On February 2, 1738, Whitefield set off on the first of seven visits to the colonies, visits that were greatly blessed by God and helped to spearhead the Great Awakening.

Whitefield arrived in Savannah, Georgia, on May 7. The very next day, in London, John Wesley "very unwillingly" attended that meeting in Aldersgate Street where his heart was "strangely warmed," and he found the assurance of personal salvation through faith in Christ. He then began to preach the Word and gradually entered into the ministries that Whitefield had left behind.

Whitefield returned to London in December and found himself excluded from all but four London churches. He preached again to thousands and experienced a mighty working of the Spirit. He and the Wesleys joined forces in the sharing of the gospel. On January 14, 1739, Whitefield was ordained as a priest of the Church of England; throughout his ministry, he remained true to those ordination vows. Though his ministry was interdenominational, he was always a faithful son of the Church of England.

Finding that he was excluded from the established churches, Whitefield decided to take to the open air; on February 17, he began his outdoor preaching at Kingswood near Bristol. "It was a brave day for England when Whitefield began field preaching!" Charles Spurgeon told his students. Whitefield collected the miners and their families, about two hundred people, and preached the gospel to them. "Blessed be God!" said the evangelist, "I have now broken the ice!"

From that day on, huge crowds gathered wherever Whitefield set up his portable pulpit, from among both the poor and the upper strata of English society. Even the little children crowded close to the preacher to hear him. Whitefield followed this practice both in Britain and in America. Benjamin Franklin calculated that Whitefield's message could be heard *clearly* by thirty thousand people at one time.

Whitefield began to organize societies and place mature believers over them to supervise the growth of the converts. By this time John Wesley was also preaching in the open air, following Whitefield's example; the movement took on the name Methodist, from the Holy Club that had been founded at Oxford.

Both the preachers and the converts were persecuted by unbelieving rabble, sometimes with the approval of the resident clergy. It was not unusual for Wesley and Whitefield to be pelted with stones and dirt—or worse, to have a dead cat hurled at their heads. But, like the apostles of old, none of these things moved them, and they continued to preach the Word and organize societies.

Whitefield had two reasons to be interested in America. One was the preaching of the Word, and the other was the founding and managing of an orphan's home in Georgia. While preaching in Britain, he often took an offering for the home; and he also encouraged his many American friends to support it. For a long time, the home was a heavy burden on the evangelist, and it probably cost him more in health, time, and energy than it was worth. At one point he was afraid of being arrested for the debts incurred by the home. Whenever he visited the colonies, he always made his way to Georgia to check on the work, supervise construction, and encourage the workers. The spiritual influence of George Whitefield on colonial America can never be fully estimated.

It is no secret that John and Charles Wesley were Arminian in doctrine, while Whitefield was more Calvinistic. The Wesleys opposed the doctrines of election, predestination, and the security of the believer. One day, Charles Wesley even called John Calvin "the firstborn son of the Devil!" Whitefield begged the Wesleys not to bring their doctrinal differences into the pulpit, but the men refused to listen. While Whitefield was ministering in America, John Wesley published his sermon on "Free Grace" in which he openly attacked Whitefield's theology.

This painful conflict ultimately divided the Methodists and led to the founding of a Calvinistic Methodist branch, which was particularly strong in Wales. Like most disputes, there were faults and mistakes on both sides, because even the most saintly men are made of clay. Wesley's emphasis on Christian perfection irritated Whitefield; and Whitefield's proclamation of the doctrines of grace upset Wesley.

However, it is to Whitefield's credit that he strenuously sought reconciliation and fellowship with the Wesleys. He did his utmost to keep the controversy private. Finally, Whitefield did the one thing his friends had hoped he would not do: he turned the entire ministry over to Wesley and stepped aside as leader. "I have no party to be at the head of," he wrote, "and through God's grace I will have none; but as much as in me lies, I will strengthen the hands of all of every denomination that preach Jesus Christ in sincerity."

When his followers protested his decision, he said, "Let my name be forgotten, let me be trodden under the feet of all men, if Jesus may thereby be glorified. . . . Let us look above names and parties; let Jesus be our all in all. . . . I care not who is uppermost. I know my place . . . even to be the servant of all."[2]

He sent a letter to the godly Lady Huntingdon in which he said, "Oh, that I may learn from all I see to desire to be nothing and to think it my highest privilege to be an assistant to all but the head of none."

Whitefield spent the rest of his days as "an assistant to all." The more popular he became, the more the opposition grew and the slander increased. He was even mimicked on the London stage, and obscene songs were written about him. He ignored them all and continued to magnify Jesus Christ. The opposition of the unbelievers did not pain him as much as the division of the believers. "But, oh! That division!" he wrote. "What slaughter it has made!"

Early in his Christian life and ministry, Whitefield developed a love for all God's people who held to the fundamental doctrines of the faith. When he was only twenty, he wrote in his *Journals*: "I bless God, the partition wall of bigotry and sect-religion was soon broken down in my heart; for, as soon as the love of God was shed abroad in my soul, I loved all, of whatsoever denomination, who loved the Lord Jesus in sincerity of heart."[3]

It was during his seventh visit to America, on September 30, 1770, that George Whitefield died, in the Presbyterian parsonage at Newburyport, Massachusetts. He is buried there at the church.

The fact that Whitefield preached in the open air to crowds of thirty thousand and even forty thousand people is of itself astounding. He was the true founder of the Methodist Church, and yet he handed his leadership to another in order to preserve "the unity of the Spirit in the bond of peace." He raised great amounts of money for the care of orphans and the poor, and he helped to establish several educational institutions.

But perhaps greater than all these accomplishments is the life of the man himself. Spurgeon commented:

> Often as I have read his life, I am conscious of distinct quickening whenever I turn to it. *He lived.* Other men seem to be only half alive; but Whitefield was all life, fire, wing, force. My own model, if I may have such a thing in due subordination to my Lord, is George Whitefield; but with unequal footsteps must I follow in his glorious track.[4]

I suggest that you secure the recent two-volume biography of George Whitefield written by Arnold A. Dallimore. Do not permit the size of the books to frighten you. These volumes read like an exciting tale of adventure; they are not in the least dull and academic. This is probably the most scholarly, and yet the most readable, biography of an evangelical preacher to appear in many years. You will learn a great deal of church history, and have a better grasp of the situation today, after reading these volumes.

Then, secure Whitefield's *Journals*, published by Banner of Truth Trust. You may even want to read the *Journals* as you read the biography. Its pages are filled with spiritual nuggets that cannot help but enrich your own spiritual life.

6

Charles Simeon
1759–1836

The year 1759 was a good one for producing leadership in Great Britain. William Pitt the younger was born in that year and became the great political leader during the Napoleonic wars. That same year also gave Britain William Wilberforce, the Christian statesman who led the fight against slavery. But the man of that year who fascinates me the most is Charles Simeon, a neglected evangelical leader in the Anglican Church, an aristocrat who used his money and position to further the cause of the gospel at a difficult time in church history.

He was born on September 24 into a well-to-do family in Reading, England. His father, Richard Simeon, was a wealthy lawyer, and Charles grew up accustomed to affluence. He entered Cambridge in 1779, enrolling at King's College. Extravagant in his dress and rather handsome in features, Simeon attracted attention and took advantage of it.

Although he was not an outstanding student, classes were not particularly difficult for him, and he always managed to enjoy a good time. His first real problem arose when he discovered that, at Lenten season, he would have to join the other students in Holy Communion. Religious life at Cambridge was very low, but the traditions were carried on routinely, and the young men were expected to cooperate. "Satan himself was as fit to attend as I!" Simeon remarked in later years. He was an unconverted sinner, and he knew it.

Although he fasted and prayed and even read books on Christianity, the heavens were brass and he received no light. He knew that most of the other men were also unconverted and would, like him, bluff their way through; but even this did not give him peace.

At some point early in Holy Week, Simeon ran across the statement, "The Jews knew what they did when they transferred their sin to the head of their offering." Instantly, Simeon grasped the idea of a substitute dying for his sins; and he began to have hope.

By faith, he laid his sins on Jesus Christ; but it was not until Easter Sunday morning that the full assurance of salvation gripped him. It was April 4, 1779, and he awoke with praise on his lips. He attended chapel, shared in the Communion service, and felt a nearness to the Savior.

His conversion did not excite his family; in fact, they resisted his attempt to witness to them. He found no Christian fellowship at the university, yet he managed to keep growing and living faithfully during his student years. His evangelical zeal made him not a few enemies. He was still an aristocrat and had much to learn about humility and service.

He was ordained a deacon of the church in 1782 and began preaching whenever he had opportunity. During the summer, he filled the pulpit at a friend's church and soon saw the building packed with attentive listeners. The zealous young man with the clear gospel message was attracting attention. In fact, so filled was the church building that the illustrious parish clerk even lost his reserved seat. The angry clerk rejoiced when the regular pastor returned after his summer holiday, saying to him, "I am so glad you are come! Now we shall have some room!"

Simeon was appointed minister of Holy Trinity Church, Cambridge, on November 9, 1783, in spite of opposition from people who did not appreciate the young man's evangelical zeal or doctrine. The next day, Simeon preached his first sermon at the church.

The building held about nine hundred people, but most of the members stayed home in protest. Simeon preached to the visitors who came to hear him. Then the pewholders locked the doors of the pews to prevent visitors from using them. So, Simeon placed benches in the aisles; but the church officers threw the benches into the churchyard. Simeon started a Sunday evening service to reach the needy sinners, and the officers locked the church doors.

It is difficult to believe that Charles Simeon remained at Holy Trinity Church for fifty-four years, the first thirty of which were filled with constant opposition, persecution, and harassment. He had been ordained September 28, 1783, and he took his ordination vows seriously. Simeon had a very high view of the ministry and was determined to do his best to be faithful, no matter what the university, the church officers, or the townsmen might do. During the first fourteen years of his ministry he labored alone, but then he was allowed to have assistants who shared the load with him.

One of his young assistants was Henry Martyn, one of the first missionaries to India. Some years ago Henry Martyn's namesake, Dr. D. Martyn Lloyd-Jones, gave my wife and me a guided tour of Cambridge, centering on Holy Trinity Church. He enjoyed showing us the "upper room" where Martyn gave himself to Christ for service, as well as the famous pulpit from which Simeon faithfully preached the Word.

Simeon realized that it was the preaching of the Word of God alone that could change lives and change the church. In 1792, he started sermon classes for the young men who were training for ministry at the university. Since there were no special ministerial courses for students training for the church, Simeon's lectures met a real need. It was not easy for these young men to associate with Simeon, because he was an object of scorn and ridicule. They were known as "Simeonites" or "Sims" to the other students.

But God blessed Simeon's ministry, and the church began to prosper. The zealous pastor used to rise at four each morning so that he might devote hours to prayer and study of the Bible. He himself had received no training in Bible study, sermon preparation, or pastoral ministry. He was teaching himself that he might be able to teach others, and God met his needs. His convictions about the ministry and preaching are still worth considering today.

"My endeavor," he wrote, "is to bring out of Scripture what is there and not to trust in what I think might be there." He also said, "Take the Word as little children without enquiring what human system it appears to favor."[1] Simeon made it clear that he was neither a Calvinist nor an Arminian, but rather a Bible Christian. "Be a Bible Christian and not a system Christian," he advised his students.

Of course, in Simeon's day, the great controversy over doctrine centered around John Wesley the Arminian and George Whitefield the Calvinist. Simeon had a delightful personal meeting with Wesley on December 20, 1748. Wesley recorded in his journal: "I went to Hinxworth, where I had the satisfaction of meeting Mr. Simeon. . . . He gave me the pleasing information, that there are three parish churches in Cambridge, wherein true scriptural religion is preached; and several young gentlemen who are happy partakers of it."[2] But Simeon has left us with a more complete record of the conversation.

"Sir," said Simeon to Wesley, "I understand that you are called an Arminian; and I have been sometimes called a Calvinist; and therefore I suppose we are to draw daggers. But before I consent to begin the combat, with your permission I will ask you a few questions, not from impertinent curiosity, but for real instruction. Pray, Sir, do you feel yourself a depraved creature, so depraved that you would never have thought of turning to God if God had not first put it into your heart?"

"Yes, I do indeed," Wesley replied.

"And do you utterly despair of recommending yourself to God by anything you can do; and look for salvation solely through the blood and righteousness of Christ?"

"Yes, solely through Christ."

"But, sir, supposing you were first saved by Christ, are you not somehow or other to save yourself afterwards by your own works?"

"No, I must be saved by Christ from first to last."

"Allowing then that you were first turned by the grace of God, are you not in some way or other to keep yourself by your own power?"

"No."

"What, then, are you to be upheld every hour and every moment by God, as much as an infant in its mother's arms?"

"Yes, altogether."

"And is all your hope in the grace and mercy of God to preserve you unto his heavenly kingdom?"

"Yes, I have no hope but in him."

"Then, sir, with your leave, I will put up my dagger again; for this is all my Calvinism; this is my election, my justification by faith, my final perseverance: it is, in substance, all that I hold, and as I hold it: and therefore, if you please, instead of searching out terms and phrases to be a ground of contention between us, we will cordially unite in those things wherein we agree."

Always burdened to help others preach the Word, in 1796 Simeon published a book of one hundred "skeletons" of expository sermons, and increased it to five hundred outlines five years later (he claimed that he had put over seven thousand hours of work into those five hundred outlines). He had discovered *An Essay on the Composition of Sermons* by the French preacher Jean Claude, and had received great help from it; so he translated it and made it available to English readers.

Eventually, this little book of sermon skeletons grew into a large set of books containing 2,536 outlines and covering the entire Bible.[3] His critics called these skeletons nothing but a valley of dry bones, but Charles Spurgeon recommended them. "Be a prophet," he said, "and they will live!"

As he grew in grace and in his ministry, Simeon had to battle his aristocratic nature and learn love and humility. In his early years he was demanding and autocratic, but the Holy Spirit prevailed, and he learned to minister in love. He was orthodox in his doctrine, but he knew that orthodoxy alone was not sufficient for an effective ministry. He wrote: "True, you are not to keep back the fundamental doctrines of the gospel: but there are different ways of stating them; and you should adopt that which expresses kindness and love, and not that which indicates an unfeeling harshness."

He saw the pastor as a combination of spiritual father, heavenly ambassador, and watchman on the wall. He often quoted Ezekiel

33:8 and reminded his people that the minister must warn as well as encourage. The text he chose for his own epitaph was 1 Corinthians 2:2, and it accurately describes his ministry. "My aim in the style of preaching," he said, "is to do it so plainly and simply that all may understand and be ready to say, 'I could have made as good a sermon myself.'"

Simeon was concerned that evangelical men be assigned to the various churches, so he used his wealth to "buy up" benefices and give them to qualified men. In those days, in the Anglican Church, the buildings and ministry of various churches were actually owned by wealthy patrons, and the right to appoint the pastor could be purchased. Simeon set up a Patronage Trust to oversee this special ministry, and as a result, godly evangelical men were put into the churches, much to the regret of the liberal opposition.

Simeon traveled widely in Great Britain, preaching wherever the doors were open to him. He was always true to the Anglican Church, but he was open to sincere believers everywhere. He had a special burden for missions and helped to found the Church Missionary Society. He also had a burden for the Jews and came very close to a premillennial view of the future of Israel. He founded a chapel in Amsterdam for witness to the Jews there.

In 1813, Simeon instituted what he called "conversation parties," informal Friday evening fellowships at which he would answer questions relating to the spiritual life. These parties were the means of encouraging many young Christians in the faith. He also started summer "house parties" for clergymen and their wives, to give them opportunity for relaxation combined with spiritual fellowship and encouragement. Simeon might well be considered the father of the summer pastoral institute program.

In 1832, Simeon commemorated the fiftieth anniversary of his ministry, and by this time he had either silenced or outlasted all of his enemies. He gave a dinner for several hundred of the poorer churchgoers, received congratulations from many famous people, and preached a stirring sermon from 2 Peter 1:12–15. There was harmony in the church, the buildings were being renovated, and the gospel was going forth with clarity and power. He had come a long way from those days when his church officers had locked him out of his own church.

It was the courageous preaching of the Word of God that had brought about the change. Simeon wrote that his test for preaching was: Does it humble the sinner? Does it exalt the Savior? Does it promote holiness? Critics might call his twenty-one volumes of outlines dead skeletons, but they throbbed with life when he preached them. At one service, a little girl asked her mother, "Mama, what is the gentleman in a passion about?" The answer: he was in a passion to proclaim Jesus Christ and him crucified.

Charles Simeon died, honored and full of days, on November 13, 1836. Even though it was market day, the town closed all the shops for his funeral, and the university canceled all lectures. Nearly two thousand people, including the robed academic community, paid tribute to the man who had remained true to the Word during fifty-four years of difficult ministry. The people would not hear his voice again, but the word that he preached would go on, and the men he had influenced and trained would continue the ministry.

Charles Simeon by Handley Moule (InterVarsity Press), is a warm biography written by a Bible scholar sympathetic to Simeon's position. A more recent work is *Charles Simeon of Cambridge* by Hugh Evan Hopkins (Eerdmans). If you want to read some of his university sermons, secure *Let Wisdom Judge*, edited by Arthur Pollard and published by InterVarsity Press. Simeon's Bible outlines were reprinted some years ago by Zondervan, but are now out of print.

What does Charles Simeon say to us today—even those of us who might not totally agree with his views of the church? For one thing, preach the Word. For another, stay with the job in spite of opposition. He would also urge us to reproduce ourselves in others so that the ministry might continue and grow. Finally, he would set the example for disciplined prayer and study. He spent the first four hours of every day with God, and he grew because of it.

The aristocrat in the pulpit was truly an ambassador from God.

7

Christmas Evans
1766–1838

Johanna Evans gave birth to a son on December 25, 1766; she and her husband, Samuel, decided to name him Christmas. Their humble home was in Llandyssul, Cardiganshire, Wales, a land of wild scenery and fiery preaching. Little did they know that their boy would grow up to become one of the greatest pulpit masters Wales would ever produce.

Samuel died while Christmas was a child, so his mother sent him to the farm of her brother, James Lewis. Christmas remained there for six miserable years. Lewis was a cruel man and a drunkard. Christmas received no education—at seventeen he could neither read nor write—and no moral or religious training. He was repeatedly involved in fights; only the providence of God kept him from being killed. Once he was stabbed, and once he nearly drowned. In one of these brawls he lost his right eye; for the remainder of his life he had to daub the empty socket with laudanum to ease the pain.

When Christmas was seventeen, he left the farm and went to work for a Presbyterian minister. He was caught up in a revival in the church and was soundly converted. Within a short time he learned to read and write, and he even began to minister in a small way. In those days it was customary to hold cottage meetings for the poorer people, and Evans used to occasionally preach or pray. He later admitted that he memorized sermons and prayers that he found in books.

As he studied his Bible, his religious convictions changed, and in 1786 he joined the Baptist church. So effective was his ministry of the Word that the church ordained him in 1790 and sent him to an area where the work was small and struggling. He took his bride to Lleyn, trusted God, and saw a time of rich blessing.

The preaching tradition in Wales is a very strong one. In those days, huge crowds of people attended preaching festivals to hear men declare the Word of God. These annual gatherings would draw as many as twenty-five thousand people into the natural amphitheaters. The Welsh people have poetry, song, and preaching in their blood. And the more dramatic and imaginative the preaching, the better they like it.

Christmas Evans first came into prominence at a Baptist Association preaching festival. The crowd was waiting for two of their spellbinding preachers to show up when someone suggested that it would be a good thing to warm up the crowd so they would be ready. One of the ministers suggested, "Why not ask the one-eyed lad from the North? I hear he preaches quite wonderfully." Christmas Evans instantly agreed to preach and took Colossians 1:21 as his text.

One of the traditions of Welsh preaching is "catching the *hwyl*." I once discussed this subject with the late Dr. D. Martyn Lloyd-Jones, himself a Welshman and a master preacher. He explained that the Welsh word *hwyl* means "the canvas of a ship." In preaching it refers to "catching the wind of the Spirit" and being carried along with great spiritual power. Often the preacher would move the crowds by raising his voice to a high-pitched falsetto—"oratory on fire"—as he was caught up in the power and unction of the Spirit.

Christmas Evans caught the *hwyl* that day. The people began to move closer to the preacher, amazed that the tall, bony, ill-dressed farm youth had such power with words and over people. He was the talk of the festival, the newest preaching sensation in Wales.

In 1792 Evans and his wife moved to the Island of Anglesea (or Anglesey) in northwest Wales; there he ministered for twenty years. When he arrived there were ten small Baptist societies meeting, some of them torn apart by controversy. Evans rode his horse from meeting to meeting and eventually developed twenty preaching places where people eagerly assembled to hear him. Within a few years, he saw more than six hundred people trust Christ and enter the family of God.

Twice in his long life, Christmas Evans made a special covenant with God. The first time was on April 10, 1802. It was a solemn covenant of dedication, with thirteen paragraphs spelling out his personal commitment to Jesus Christ. He signed each paragraph "Amen. C.E." It is touching to read this covenant and to realize that God honored his faith and dedication.

Christmas Evans was a self-taught man. He taught himself Hebrew and Greek, and he read the meaty works of men like John Owen and John Gill. Though he had but one eye, he was a constant reader, either in his simple home or while riding to a preaching appointment. He often preached daily and twice on Sunday, and while he was riding, he meditated and wrote his eloquent sermons.

Mrs. Evans died in 1823, and in 1826 Christmas Evans remarried, resigned from the Anglesea ministry, and accepted a small Baptist church in Tonyvelin, Caerphilly. Unfortunately, the jealousy of younger ministers and the barbs of theological controversy were damaging to the work in Anglesea, and Evans felt it was time to move. These problems are reflected in the second covenant that Evans made with the Lord on April 24, 1829.

As he was returning home from a preaching mission, a spirit of prayer came upon him, and he stopped to commune with God, weep, and pray. He wrote fifteen requests of God and signed each one "Amen. C.E." Here are a few quotations:

> Grant Thy blessing upon bitter things, do brighten and quicken me, more and more, and do not depress and make me more lifeless.
>
> Suffer me not to be trodden under the proud feet of members, or deacons, for the sake of Thy goodness.

Help me to wait silently, and patiently upon Thee, for the fulfillment of these things, and not to become enraged, angry, and speak
unadvisedly with my lips, like Moses, the servant of the Lord. Sustain
my heart from sinking, to wait for fresh strength from Zion.[1]

God gave him a new experience of faith and power, even though
the enemy opposed the preaching of the Word. In 1832, Evans made
his final move and became pastor of a dying church at Caernarvon,
where thirty members were struggling under the weight of a debt
they could not pay.

Evans wrote in his journal: "I have been thinking of the great
goodness of the Lord unto me, throughout my unworthy ministry;
and now, in my old age, I see the work prospering wonderfully in
my hand, so that there is reason to think that I am, in some degree,
a blessing to the Church."

When he had been at the chapel six years, Evans, his wife, and a
young pastor set out on a preaching mission to raise funds to pay
off the crippling debt. He put a notice in the *Welsh Magazine* asking his brethren to pray for and support this special endeavor. "This
is my last sacrifice for the Redeemer's cause," he wrote, and it was.
But God prospered the mission and great crowds heard him preach;
even when the meeting house was filled, crowds stood outside and
listened.

But the undertaking was too difficult for the old preacher. On
Sunday, July 15, he preached two sermons in Swansea—in the morning on the Prodigal Son, and in the evening on Romans 1:16. He
preached again on Monday on a favorite text, "and beginning at Jerusalem." When he concluded the message, he said in a quiet voice,
"This is my last sermon." He became ill the next day; and on Friday,
July 20, 1838, Christmas Evans was called to Glory. His last words
were, "Goodbye! Drive on!"

Christmas Evans often counseled younger pastors, and his philosophy of ministry is worth sharing today. He wrote to one: "Consider,
in the first place, the great importance, to a preacher, of a blameless
life." Then he added, "I remember the words of Luther, that *reading,*

prayer, and *temptation* are necessary to strengthen, and to purify the talents of a minister."

We expect him to give this advice: "Always have a book to read, instead of indulging in vain conversations. Strive to learn English. . . . Remember this, that you cannot commit some loved sin in private, and perform the work of the ministry in public, with facility and acceptance."

Evans could preach with power both in English and Welsh, and in both languages his aim was to honor Christ. "The gospel, as a glass [mirror], should be kept clean and clear in the pulpit," he wrote, "that the hearers may see the glory of Christ and be changed to the same image."[2]

When asked about style and delivery, Evans said, "Preach the gospel of the grace of God intelligently, affectionately, and without shame— all the contents of the great box, from predestination to glorification. . . . Let the preacher influence himself; let him reach his own heart, if he would reach the hearts of others; if he would have others feel, he must feel himself."

Evans liked to compare the ministry of the Word to that of a miner, who takes the ore from the earth, melts it, and puts it into the mold. "The gospel is like a form, or mold, and sinners are to be melted, as it were, and cast into it." He urged young preachers to be faithful to "the form of sound words" that Paul wrote about (2 Tim. 1:13).

With all of his reputation for pulpit eloquence and evangelistic zeal, Evans should perhaps be remembered most as a man of prayer. He never worried about the theology or philosophy of prayer; he simply prayed, and God answered. He had three stated times for prayer during the day, and he regularly arose at midnight to seek the face of God. He enjoyed the solitude of his long journeys, when he could pray and meditate on the deep things of God. The passion in his preaching arose from the burning in his heart.

From a human point of view, Christmas Evans seemed an unlikely candidate for becoming a spiritual giant. Born and raised in poverty, subjected to brutality, deprived of formal education, lacking in the physical graces that usually attracted others, this child of Wales was certainly a trophy of the grace of God. Deaf to the slanders of his enemies and blind to the obstacles around him, he courageously and sacrificially carried the gospel throughout the land, and many found salvation because of his ministry.

During his long and difficult ministry, he never received a large salary. He could have carved out a religious empire for himself, but he preferred to follow the Lord into the small and difficult places where men needed the bread of life. Instead of embroiling himself in the hairsplitting theological discussions and controversies of the day, he gave himself to the preaching of the gospel and the great truths that undergird that saving message.

In short, Christmas Evans was a man of God who gave himself unsparingly to the work of the ministry. God used him to bring life to dead sinners, to dead churches, and to Christians whose spiritual experience was dead.

"Life is the only cure for death," he said, "not the prescriptions of duty, not the threats of punishment and damnation, not the arts and refinements of education, but new, spiritual, Divine *Life*."[3]

Perhaps that is the prescription we most need today.

8

John Henry Newman
1801–1890

If people today think at all of John Henry Newman, it is probably as the author of the familiar hymn "Lead, Kindly Light." Those who are somewhat acquainted with church history will identify him as one of the leaders of the Oxford Movement, which shook the Church of England and eventually led Newman himself into the Church of Rome. But it is Newman the preacher I want to examine in this chapter, the man whom W. Robertson Nicoll called "the most influential preacher Oxford has ever known,"[1] and whom Alexander Whyte admired so much that he wrote *Newman: An Appreciation*.

Newman was born in London on February 21, 1801. His family would be identified with the moderate evangelicals in the Church of England. At age fifteen, Newman experienced conversion. He was educated at Trinity College, Oxford, where he fell under the influence of Richard Whately. "He, emphatically, opened my mind, and taught me to think and to use my reason," Newman later wrote in his famous autobiography, *Apologia pro vita sua*. This was probably the beginning of Newman's drift from the evangelical emphasis and into the High Church party, and eventually to the Church of Rome.

However, it was his dear friend Richard Hurrell Froude who influenced Newman the most. "He taught me to look with admiration towards the Church of Rome," Newman wrote, "and in the same degree to dislike the Reformation." Froude did more than this: he introduced Newman to John Keble—brilliant Oxford scholar, humble Anglican pastor, and a man utterly devoted to the Church of England. Keble is remembered today as the writer of "Sun of My Soul, Thou Savior Dear," taken from his once-popular book of religious poetry, *The Christian Year*.

In 1824 Newman was ordained, and in 1828 he began his ministry as vicar of St. Mary's, Oxford. I can never forget stepping into that historic church one summer day and actually climbing the stairs into Newman's pulpit. As I stood there, I could hear faintly the Oxford traffic outside; but I quickly found myself carried, via imagination, to a Sunday afternoon service at which Newman was preaching. The church was filled with worshipers, mostly the younger fellows of the colleges and the undergraduates. Newman came in—"gliding" is the way one observer described it—and made his way to the pulpit, where he adjusted the gas lamp, laid his manuscript before him, and then in a musical voice that haunted, began to preach in a way that penetrated one's very being. "It was from the pulpit of St. Mary's that he began to conquer and to rule the world," wrote Alexander Whyte, one of Newman's most ardent Protestant admirers.

The rest of the story need not delay us. On July 14, 1833, Keble preached the "assize sermon" at St. Mary's, and his theme was "national apostasy." It was this sermon that gave birth to the concern that eventuated in what we know as the Oxford Movement (not to be confused with the Oxford Group Movement begun by Frank Buchman and later renamed Moral Re-armament). The burden of the movement was spiritual renewal in the Church of England. Newman, Keble, Froude, E. B. Pusey, and their associates sought to restore the spiritual authority of the church and to return the church to its ancient moorings. Their motives were commendable; their methods perhaps left something to be desired.

One of their chief ministries was the publication of "tracts for the times." Various men—not all as gifted as Newman—wrote on subjects pertaining to the Church of England. The critics noticed a Rome-ward trend in the tracts, but the writers persisted. It was *Tract Ninety* that wrote *finis* to Newman's leadership in the movement and his ministry at St. Mary's. In this famous pamphlet, Newman tried to prove that the Thirty-nine Articles of the Church of England could be honestly interpreted from a Roman Catholic point of view. The result was official censure—the politics of the controversies from 1833 to 1845 are worthy of study—and Newman could do nothing but either step aside or recant. Deeply hurt by the church leaders he had thought would encourage him, Newman left Oxford; and on October 8, 1845, he was received into the Roman Catholic church.

I find the history of the Oxford Movement fascinating. In it one finds events and leaders that parallel situations we have today. There is really nothing new under the sun. People today who want to "purify" or "renew" the church would do well to read up on the Oxford Movement and then avoid its mistakes. *The Oxford Movement* by R. W. Church, dean of St. Paul's, is the best introduction. A more modern study is *The Oxford Conspirators* by Marvin R. O'Connell. It is desirable to read Newman's own account in *Apologia pro vita sua*, and keep in mind that he wrote this some twenty years after these events.

But now to Newman's preaching.

Between 1824, when he was ordained, and 1845, when he left Oxford, Newman preached over one thousand sermons, ten volumes of which are available today. His eight volumes of *Parochial and Plain Sermons* represent the best of his pulpit ministry at St. Mary's. *Sermons Bearing on Subjects of the Day* and *Fifteen Sermons Preached Before the University of Oxford* are two volumes that complete the Protestant years. *Discourses Addressed to Mixed Congregations* and *Sermons Preached on Various Occasions* come from his Roman Catholic years.

I was amazed when I learned that Whyte had been such an admirer of Newman; for if any preacher emphasized the grace of God and the gospel of Jesus Christ, it was Whyte. Yet Whyte told a friend that he valued Newman's sermons more than those of F. W. Robertson! On March 14, 1876, Whyte and some friends visited Newman at the oratory in Edgbaston and were received graciously. Whyte even incorporated in his *Catechism* a revision from Newman that clarified the doctrine of transubstantiation. There is no escaping the fact that Alexander Whyte admired John Henry Cardinal Newman.

Let us begin with the obvious reason: Newman's sermons, not unlike Whyte's, were directed to the conscience. "The effect of Newman's preaching on us young men," wrote William Lockhart, "was to turn our souls inside out!" In this, Whyte was a kindred spirit of Newman, for few evangelical preachers can expose sin and "perform spiritual surgery" like Alexander Whyte! But another factor was Newman's "other-worldliness." He, like Whyte, had an utter disdain of earthly things. Whyte reveled among the mystics and constantly called his congregation to a life of reality in the things of the Spirit. While Whyte would point sinners to the Lamb of God, however, Newman would find this life of the Spirit in a sacramental system.

Newman's ability to examine a text and then develop it into a sermon was something Whyte greatly admired. "For, let any young man of real capacity once master Newman's methods of exposition, discussion, and argumentation; his way of addressing himself to the treatment of a subject; his way of entering upon a subject, worming his way to the very heart of it, working it out, and winding it up," wrote Whyte in his *Appreciation*, and that man would "soon make his presence and his power felt in any of our newspapers or magazines."[2]

Add to this Newman's pure English style—"the quiet perfection of his English style," wrote Whyte's biographer—and you can understand why the old Covenanter so much appreciated the preaching of Cardinal Newman.

Whyte was careful to point out his disagreements with Newman, not the least of which was Newman's neglect of preaching the good news of salvation through faith in Jesus Christ. When Newman's sermons are "looked at as pulpit work, as preaching the Gospel," wrote

Whyte, "they are full of the most serious, and even fatal, defects. . . . They are not, properly speaking, New Testament preaching at all. . . . As an analysis of the heart of man, and as a penetrating criticism of human life, their equal is nowhere to be found. But, with all that, they lack the one all-essential element of all true preaching—the message to sinful man concerning the free grace of God. . . . Newman's preaching—and I say it with more pain than I can express—never once touches the true core, and real and innermost essence, of the Gospel."[3]

Why bother to read the sermons of a man who did not preach the gospel, a man who eventually preached himself right out of an evangelical tradition and into a sacramental system? Because Newman can help teach us how to preach to a man's conscience, how to get beneath the surface and apply spiritual truth where it is needed. Newman was a better diagnostician than a dispenser of healing medicine ("I never take down Newman's sermons for my recovery and my comfort," admitted Whyte); but it is easier to apply the medicine after you have convinced the patient of his need.

It is worth noting that Newman warned against magnifying preaching above the other ministries of the church. In this, I think, he was reacting against the tendency on the part of some evangelicals of the day to turn their preachers into celebrities. Newman believed strongly in the continuity of the church and the need for sermons to minister to the body collectively. He himself shunned and even fled from becoming "a popular preacher," and he had little confidence in men who used the pulpit to promote themselves.

It is unfortunate that Newman did not know the better evangelical men of that day. He saw only (or perhaps only wanted to see) a ministry that emphasized correct doctrine and dedicated zeal, but lacked Christian character and true spiritual power. R. W. Church described evangelicals as people with "an exhausted teaching and a spent enthusiasm." The evangelical churches were "respectable" and popular with men of position, but (added Church) "they were on very easy terms with the world."[4] If there was one thing Newman hated with a holy zeal, it was a religion of words without reality, words that described an experience but failed to effect it in the lives of people.

Newman desired to elevate worship in the church. While I do not agree with his sacramentalism, I do applaud his purpose; it is my conviction that true worship is the greatest need in our churches today. How easy it is to have words without power (Paul was aware of this—read 1 Thessalonians 1:5) and program without substance, especially in an evangelical church. Newman would have agreed with William Temple's definition of *worship*: "to quicken the conscience by the holiness of God, to feed the mind with the truth of God, to purge the imagination by the beauty of God, to open up the heart to the love of God, to devote the will to the purpose of God." We do not experience this kind of worship in many churches today, and often the preacher is to blame. Newman spoke about the "rudeness, irreverence, and almost profaneness . . . involved in pulpit addresses, which speak of the adorable works and sufferings of Christ, with the familiarity and absence of awe with which we speak about our friends."

Next to irreverence and the "unreality of words," Newman abhorred preaching that tried to cover "three or four subjects at once." He insisted that each sermon have a definite purpose expressed in a concrete statement. "Definiteness is the life of preaching," he wrote in *Lectures and Essays on University Subjects*, "a definite hearer, not the whole world; a definite topic, not the whole evangelical tradition; and, in like manner, a definite speaker. Nothing that is anonymous will preach."[5] Of course, the ultimate aim of all preaching is the salvation of the hearer, but this can be accomplished only when the preacher is prepared and knows what his aim is. We preach to persuade, and we must preach to the emotions as well as to the intellect, always using simple and concrete language.

The thing that impresses me about Newman's sermons is their freshness of spiritual expression. He did not preach on the "topics of the day." He carefully explained some first principle of the Christian life, some doctrine of the Christian faith, and wedded it to the practical life of the worshiper. He shunned oratory and sought to make the message of the Word the most important thing and the messenger the least important. He did not even debate the great issues involved in the Oxford Movement. Rather he strengthened and extended the movement by avoiding the issues and dealing with the fundamental truths that gave rise to these issues.

There are men called by God to preach on the issues of the hour, and we need their ministry. But for permanent strengthening of the church, we also need preachers who will dig again the old wells and lead us intelligently down the old paths and who, renouncing cheap pulpit rhetoric, will focus the white light of revelation on the human heart and examine us in that light. In short, today we need preaching that appeals to the conscience, penetrating preaching, clinical preaching, preaching that moves men to cry, "Men and brethren, what shall we do?" Newman's preaching did this.

But let us go one step further: let us apply the blessed medicine of the gospel (something Newman did not do) and reply to those under conviction, "Believe on the Lord Jesus Christ, and you shall be saved!" Newman would run to the beaten man at the side of the road and pour in the wine; but he could not pour in the oil.

If you want to get acquainted with Cardinal Newman, start with *Newman: An Appreciation* by Whyte. Then secure *The Preaching of John Henry Newman*, edited by Newman scholar W. D. White. White's scholarly introduction will acquaint you with Newman's world and his philosophy of preaching. I think both Newman and White were too hard on the evangelicals, but this is a minor fault in an otherwise capable essay. White included thirteen sermons that Newman considered his best. If you are interested in owning more of Newman's sermons, visit your local Catholic bookshop or watch the used-book stores in your area.

The best modern biography of Newman is Meriol Trevor's two-volume *Newman*. The first volume is subtitled *The Pillar of the Cloud*, the second *Light in Winter*. The author has also abridged this work into a one-volume edition titled *Newman's Journey*.

Newman wrote materials other than sermons, some excellent and some not so good. *A Newman Reader*, edited by Francis X.

Connolly, will give you a rich sampling of his writings. My favorite edition of his autobiography, *Apologia pro vita sua*, is the one edited by David J. DeLaura. It contains all the necessary texts of Newman's controversy with Charles Kingsley, plus helpful notes that clarify material in the text.

One final observation: When I read Newman's sermons, I find myself examining not only my heart but also my preaching. I find myself asking: Am I a faithful physician of the soul? Am I preaching to the conscience? Am I faithful to declare *truth*, not simply my "clever ideas" about truth? Do I offer Christ as the only Redeemer? Do I get beneath the surface and help my hearers where they need it most? While I disagree with Newman's theology, I appreciate his preaching and have learned from it.

9

Richard Trench
1807–1886

The life of Richard Chenevix Trench contained ingredients so diverse as to seem almost contradictory. A scholar by nature, his position in the Anglican church forced him into prominence, where he fought and lost unpopular battles. Born into a comfortable and cultured family, he recklessly identified with an abortive "student invasion" to free the oppressed people of Spain, a venture that could have cost him his life. When he returned to Cambridge in 1831 to prepare for the ministry, he admitted to a friend that he had forgotten "well-nigh all" his Greek. Yet he wrote *Synonyms of the New Testament*, a classic in Greek studies that is still valuable today. Trench was not recognized as a good preacher. But his two monumental works, *Notes on the Parables of Our Lord* and *Notes on the Miracles of Our Lord*, have helped many preachers prepare better messages.

Trench would have rejoiced to stay out of the public arena and in his study, but circumstances dictated otherwise. He became dean of Westminster Abbey and eventually archbishop of Dublin. Perhaps it was the outworking of the "Peter Principle" (each person rises to his level of incompetence), because Trench was not cut out to fight church battles. He was born to study and to write.

Words were his passion. Two of his classics, though a bit out-dated, are still helpful and most enjoyable: *On the Study of Words* and *English, Past and Present.* One of the greatest things Trench did was to propose to the Philological Society on January 7, 1858, that "a new and independent dictionary should be prepared." The result was the monumental *Oxford English Dictionary* (OED), originally published in ten huge volumes and now available (micrographically reproduced) in one. One of the assistants who worked with James Murray on the great OED was George H. Morrison. In later years he would be known as Morrison of Wellington, one of Scotland's greatest preachers. Whenever I use my OED, I think of Trench and Morrison and give thanks.

Richard Trench was born on September 5, 1807, in Dublin, Ireland. His father belonged to the Anglo-Irish aristocracy, and his mother, a cultured Christian, had traveled widely. She greatly influenced him in his love for books and poetry and in his desire to write. Early in his school career he displayed his love for linguistic studies. When her son was only fifteen, Mrs. Trench wrote to a friend: "My son Richard has a craving for books. . . . He cannot take an airing without arming himself against ennui by one or more volumes. . . . He wishes much we should purchase a certain Polyglot and luxuriates in the idea of finding fifteen readings of the same passage in Scripture."[1]

Trench entered Trinity College, Cambridge, in October 1825. He became a member of an elite group known familiarly as the Apostles. In this group were men who would one day greatly influence England: F. D. Maurice, the Christian socialist; Alfred Tennyson, future poet laureate; Arthur Hallam, a friend of Tennyson whose death inspired "In Memoriam"; and others.

Trench received his BA in 1829 and then spent the next year traveling. In Spain he saw the desperate need of the people. When he returned to England, he threw himself in with a group of ideal-istic young men who planned to invade Cadiz and set the masses free. Why would a scholar get involved in such a daring venture? Partly from heredity: his mother's family was of Huguenot origin, and Trench was attracted to anything that smacked of chivalry. While a student at Cambridge, Trench had been fascinated by Spanish history and culture. But perhaps the main reason was his own need for a challenge. He was living rather aimlessly, which made him somewhat depressed. The liberation of Spain was just the tonic he needed. However, the whole enterprise aborted. Some of the men involved were arrested and shot. Trench never spoke about the event in later years, nor did he ever visit Spain again. The experience soured him on all revolutionary movements, a fact that played an important role when he became archbishop of Dublin.

Trench returned to Cambridge in October 1831 to study for holy orders. He was married on May 31, 1832; the following October he was ordained a deacon. No churches were available at that time, so once again Trench found himself drifting and waiting. In January 1833 he became curate to Hugh James Rose at Hadleigh in Suffolk, a post he held until September, when Rose left to become professor of divinity at the University of Dublin.

Here we meet one of those quirks of history that makes us want to ask, "What if . . . ?" While Trench was serving at Hadleigh, two important events took place that ultimately shook the Anglican church to its foundations. The first was John Keble's "assize sermon" preached at St. Mary's, Oxford, on July 14. That sermon marked the beginning of the Oxford Movement, although nobody knew it at the time. The second event grew out of the first: Rose, impressed by Keble's sermon on "national apostasy," invited a number of his clerical friends to Hadleigh to discuss ways to stir the church and bring about needed changes. Keble did not attend the conference, nor did his good friend John Henry Newman. How much Trench participated we do not know for certain; probably he was on the fringes of the meetings, being only a lowly curate.

But suppose he had been captivated by the challenge? Suppose he had been enlisted by the influential Richard Hurrell Froude, the man who perhaps more than any other influenced Newman, the man who eventually left the Anglican for the Roman church? Would Trench's skills have made any difference in the Oxford Movement? He was definitely not a fighter, but he was a scholar. He was not a strong preacher, but he was a capable writer. His sympathies did not lie with either the evangelical party or with Rome. He could never have abandoned the Anglican church because his roots went too deep into her traditions. But could he have influenced others to remain? We will never know.

Once again, Trench found himself without a place of ministry. He returned to live with his father until January 1834, when he accepted a curacy at St. Peter's, Colchester. But a health problem ended that ministry almost before it started. He traveled in Europe with his family, arriving back in England in June 1835. On July 5, he was ordained to the Anglican priesthood. In September he became the minister of St. Peter's, Curdridge, where he served for six delightful years. At last he could devote himself to study and service. In 1841, he published his great work on the parables.

Though books on the parables are legion, Trench's volume is outstanding. Be sure to purchase the edition that includes English translations of the quotations from the church fathers. It is unnerving to have the archbishop write, "The greatest insight into this truth is given by St. Augustine," and then follow with three paragraphs of Latin! Even Charles H. Spurgeon recommended Trench on the miracles and parables, although he admitted that Trench's doctrine was not always to his taste.

During his ministry at Curdridge, Trench became a close friend of Samuel Wilberforce, third son of the great William Wilberforce whose association with the evangelicals in the Church of England helped him in his victory over slavery. Samuel was an energetic leader whose personal charm won him the nickname "Soapy Sam." If opposites attract, then we should not be surprised at Trench's friendship with this future bishop of Oxford and Winchester. Wilberforce enjoyed ecclesiastical politics as much as Trench detested them. Wilberforce asked Trench to become his "examining chaplain" for ordination, a high honor indeed.

At the close of 1844, Trench moved to Itchenstoke, where he served for eleven years. There he prepared his great book on the miracles, another classic. He also got involved in Irish relief ministry. Since

Ireland was the land of his birth, he visited and tried to assist the multitudes suffering from the 1846 potato blight. This experience opened Trench's eyes to the real weaknesses and problems of the Irish Church.

Trench was appointed professor of divinity at King's College, London, in February 1846. At last he was in his element. The students not only profited from his lectures, but actually enjoyed them. The substance of his lectures on the vocabulary of the Greek New Testament appears in *Synonyms of the New Testament*. He believed that theology must be grounded on the study of words. "The *words* of the New Testament," he said, "are the *stoikeia* [elements, ABCs] of Christian theology." What a time Trench would have had with a complete set of the *Theological Dictionary of the New Testament* edited by Gerhard Kittel and Gerhard Friedrich!

On June 21, 1856, a statement appeared in the *Times* that Richard Trench had been appointed the new bishop of Gloucester and Bristol. The news hit everybody like a sonic boom, especially Professor Trench. He was even accused of planting the item so he would get the appointment. His friend Samuel Wilberforce interceded with Queen Victoria, and Trench was absolved; but the consequences were most unpleasant to the quiet scholar. He received nearly three hundred letters from pastors asking for places in his diocese!

The Lord had something better for the man who would not promote himself. On August 15, 1856, William Buckland died and the deanery of Westminster became vacant. On October 23 Trench was installed as dean of Westminster, the ideal place for the scholar/pastor. It was a difficult move for him and his family, for they were accustomed to the lovely English towns. Now they had to live in the busy, dirty city. At that time the abbey was surrounded by slums, described by one pastor as a "reeking and irreclaimable center of filth and misery."

Nobody expected the new dean to do anything more than enjoy "learned leisure" but Trench surprised them. He and other London clergy were distressed that great ecclesiastical centers like St. Paul's and Westminster Abbey were not being used to reach the masses.

Complicated church rules governed who could and could not preach in these historic pulpits. On December 3, 1857, Trench and his associates decided to open the abbey for Sunday evening services, an unprecedented idea at that time. No doubt the great success of Spurgeon's evening meetings helped them make their decision. On January 3, 1858, the first Sunday evening service was held. The weather was cold and icy, and the dean was certain nobody would attend. But a crowd gathered, Trench preached, and the service was somewhat of a success. The problem was that the service was not "popular" enough, the building was too cold, and the common people in attendance did not follow the liturgy too well. Trench persisted, however, and his experiment encouraged St. Paul's to follow his example.

Trench would have enjoyed remaining at Westminster, but the failing health of Richard Whately, archbishop of Dublin, meant that a successor would be needed. And who would be better than scholarly Dubliner Richard Trench? When his friend Wilberforce suggested the move, Trench wrote him:

> England is my world, the land of all my friends; the English Church seems to feel full of life and hope and vigor, of which I see little in the Irish. Then I know myself deficient in some of the most needful qualifications for the episcopate. I have few or no gifts of government, little or no power of rallying men round me and disciplining them into harmonious action.[2]

Trench himself had told a friend years before that no one could wish to be a bishop who was not a hero or a madman. But on January 1, 1864, he was consecrated archbishop of Dublin and was introduced to one of the most perplexing problems in English church history: the disestablishment of the Irish Church. The Episcopal church in Ireland was a Protestant island in a Roman Catholic sea. It was the church of the well-to-do English landowners, not of the common people. As a missionary church, it had failed. The poor citizens accused the Irish Church of bleeding the people. There were less than 700,000 adherents to the Irish Church, while 4,500,000 people claimed loyalty to Rome.

The scholarly Trench lacked the experience and ability to handle so complex an issue. He was not a diplomat; he lacked the political know-how to play one group against another. On July 26, 1869, the Disestablishment Bill was given royal assent and the battle was over. Trench had lost. He was then given the task of reconstructing a new church. This precipitated controversies that the learned archbishop was unable to handle. Bravely he stayed at his post, doing the best he could with a bad situation. On November 22, 1875, he suffered a disabling accident while going to London for a meeting of the New Testament Revision Committee. In the spring of 1883, he was laid low with bronchitis; by the fall of 1884, it was obvious he would have to resign. This he did on November 28; on March 28, 1886, he died, and was buried in Westminster Abbey on April 2.

What choice volumes of Greek word studies and Christian theology might this man have written had he not become involved in ecclesiastical politics? Is becoming an archbishop necessarily a promotion? Would not Trench have made a greater contribution to the church by remaining in "learned leisure" at Westminster? This same fate overtook J. B. Lightfoot when he was taken from the university and made bishop of Durham. Those of us who love the study of words (and we have good company in G. Campbell Morgan and John Henry Jowett) are tempted to wish that Bishop Wilberforce had minded his own business and not moved Richard Trench to Dublin.

10

Andrew Bonar

1810–1892

One of the richest experiences you can have is reading the diaries and journals of great men and women in Christian history. Among many that I enjoy, perhaps my favorite is *Andrew Bonar: Diary and Life* edited by his daughter, Marjory Bonar, and published by Banner of Truth Trust.

Most people know Andrew Bonar as the brother of hymn-writer Horatius Bonar and the close friend of Robert Murray McCheyne. He was also the editor of the best edition of Samuel Rutherford's *Letters*, and the author of both a devotional commentary on Leviticus and *Christ and His Church in the Book of Psalms*, which has been reprinted by Kregel Publications.

But when you read his journal, you will meet and learn to love a truly great man of God. He lived and labored at a critical time in the church in Scotland, and God used him in wonderful ways to uphold his truth and build his people.

Andrew Alexander Bonar was born on May 29, 1810, in Edinburgh, Scotland, the seventh son of James and Marjory Bonar. He was surrounded by spiritual influences, but not until he was twenty years old and in college did he have assurance of his salvation.

Later he became a divinity student, and during that time cultivated his friendship with McCheyne. He served as an assistant pastor and city missionary in Jedburgh and at St. George's in Edinburgh. In 1836, he candidated at St. Peter's Church, Dundee, but the congregation called McCheyne instead.

In 1838, Bonar accepted a call to the Presbyterian Church in Collace, where he was ordained and remained for eighteen fruitful years. When he arrived, there were probably only half a dozen true believers in the parish, but God sent revival to the area and many turned to Christ. While Bonar and McCheyne were on a special missionary deputation to the Holy Land in 1839, God used William Burns to bring a fresh wind of the Spirit to McCheyne's church in Dundee, and the blessing spread to other churches.

1843 was a difficult year for ministers and churches in Scotland, for in that year more than four hundred dedicated ministers left the Established Church and founded Free Church. Those who seceded protested the modernistic tendencies of the denomination and the interference of the civil courts in church affairs. At Collace, Bonar preached in a tent until the congregation, which had forfeited its property, could build a new place of worship.

In 1856, Bonar became pastor of a new church on Finnieston Street in a needy area of Glasgow; and there he remained until his death on December 30, 1892. Before long, what had begun as a small work had grown to a congregation of more than a thousand members, with a strong Sunday school program and an evangelistic outreach into the city. The work was difficult, but Bonar preached the Word and trusted God. When a friend asked one day how things were going, Bonar replied, "Oh, we are looking for great things!" When his friend admonished him not to expect too much, Bonar replied, "We can never hope for too much!"

A confirmed premillennialist, Bonar enjoyed preaching about the return of Jesus Christ. He had a remarkable ability to remember names and faces. One day he addressed by name a little girl on the street, and she ran home and announced, "Mother, Mother, he knows me!"

He could detect when a member was absent on Sunday and during the week would visit to see if there was a special problem or need. He also had a marvelous sense of humor. One child called him "the minister with the laughing face." One day he told an invalid he was visiting, "I have a new medicine for you: 'A merry heart doeth good like medicine.'" When a man told Bonar he had felt an angel touch him during an illness, Bonar said, "Have you a cat in the house? Don't you think it may have been the cat?"

He believed in pastoral work, particularly visiting in people's homes. "There is a blessing resting on visiting," he wrote to a pastor friend. "What else is fitted to make us know the state of our flocks? Were it not for their good but only for our own, is not this department of work most important? It is only thus we can know our people's spiritual state." He usually visited every afternoon from one o'clock to five, walking great distances to bring encouragement and help to his beloved people.

I think the greatest value of the *Diary and Life* is its record of Bonar's interior life. He was able to accomplish much with people in public because he spent time with God in private. There are scores of references in these pages to prayer, meditation, and self-examination. They also record times of discouragement and defeat, when Bonar felt he had failed the Lord and his people. God's choicest servants rarely evaluate their own ministries with accuracy and balance, and often Bonar was too hard on himself.

During the Kilsyth Revival of 1839–40, Bonar wrote to his brother Horace: "Pray for Collace. We have no more than a few drops as yet, and I believe I am to blame. I *work* more than I *pray*." Later he wrote in his journal: "I was living very grossly, namely, laboring night and day in visiting with very little prayerfulness. I did not see that prayer should be the main business of every day." Again, he wrote: "I see that prayerlessness is one of my great sins of omission. I am too short, ask too little, ask with too much want of forethought. Then, *too little meditation upon Scripture.*"

He discovered that even his books and his literary ministry could create problems in his spiritual life. "Tried this morning specially to pray against idols in the shape of my books and studies. These encroach upon my direct communion with God, and need to be watched." As he was writing *Christ and His Church in the Book of Psalms,* he noted in his diary: "I distinctly see now that Satan's chief way of prevailing against me is by throwing in my way a great deal of half literary work, half biblical." When he was preparing *Rutherford's Letters,* he wrote: "A piece of extra work this year has been an edition of *Rutherford's Letters,* which I fear has been a snare to me, inasmuch as it has sometimes shortened prayer, yet it has also helped me."

Bonar tried to keep each Saturday evening as a time of prayer and special preparation of his own soul for the ministry on the Lord's Day, a practice I strongly recommend to preachers today. But he discovered that he was especially vulnerable to Satan's attacks on Saturday evenings and Monday mornings. He often sought for "Saturday assurances" from God to encourage him for his Sunday ministry. He observed that Christ, after a busy day of ministry, arose early to pray (Mark 1:35); and he tried to follow that example on Monday mornings.

In spite of his success as a pastor, preacher, and writer, Bonar often saw himself as a failure in the pulpit. On December 5, 1857, he wrote in his diary: "Got such a sight of the impotence of my preaching that I felt as if I need never to attempt it more." One day he received special encouragement from Proverbs 23:16, "Yea, my reins shall rejoice, when thy lips speak right things." He wrote in his journal, "Christ listening to our sermons!"

Bonar realized that he could not go on forever, no matter how much his people loved him. There is a deeply touching entry in his diary for September 11, 1890, when he was eighty years old.

> I see distinctly that my Lord is teaching me to "glory in my infirmities" and to be willing to be set aside. My voice fails; some of my people, specially the younger part, going elsewhere; my class melts away. Some very mortifying cases of ingratitudes on the part of some; my influence with brethren manifestly declines—all this is saying, "He must increase, but I must decrease."

On October 14, a committee met with him to arrange to call a successor. "I read with them Numbers 27:15–18, and prayed with thanksgiving, and the business went on pleasantly," he wrote.

"Oh, I don't think anything about growing old," Bonar once told D. L. Moody's associate, Major D. W. Whittle. But those closest to him detected a gradual failing of his strength, even though he continued in ministry as much as possible; and after only two days of illness, he went home to glory on Friday, December 30, 1892.

Each time I read Bonar's *Diary and Life*, I find something new to ponder, or I am reminded of something I had already read and underlined but had forgotten. His personal character has always impressed me. He was not envious at the success of others, but rejoiced at God's blessing, even if he disagreed with the methods other men used. When many Calvinists were opposing Moody and Sankey, Bonar was praying for them and laboring with them. Moody invited him to minister at his Northfield Conference, and in 1881 Bonar sailed to America and ministered in several cities. Like F. B. Meyer, Henry Drummond, and many other ministers of the Word, Bonar was greatly helped by his friendship with Moody.

I have also been impressed with Bonar's emphasis on evangelism. He kept two texts (in the original Hebrew) in his study: "He that winneth souls is wise" (Prov. 11:30) and "For yet a little while, and He that shall come will come and will not tarry" (Hab. 2:3). When the church in Finnieston Street moved to a new location in 1878, "He that winneth souls is wise" was carved in Hebrew over the front door. Bonar had a special burden for the Jews, and he hoped that the text would not only attract them but also remind his own people of the importance of witnessing.

Although Bonar was criticized by some and ignored by others, he stuck to his premillennial interpretation of the Word and greatly advanced the study of prophecy in Great Britain. He viewed the Lord's return as a practical motivation for life and ministry. His views closed doors for him, but they also opened many hearts.

Bonar noted in his diary on July 5, 1847, "I have been much impressed with the sin of choosing my text without special direction from the Lord. This is like running without being sent, no message being given me." He also tried to relate each text to the needs of his people. "I feel as if I had not got my subject from the Lord," he wrote in 1858. "This whole matter had led me to search into my feelings toward my people, and I have discovered that I do not sufficiently think of them individually and pray for them . . . Lord, give me a larger heart and a holier to me."

In my own preaching ministry, I have quoted some of Andrew Bonar's "spiritual sayings," and I want to close with some of my favorites.

The best part of all Christian work is that part which only God sees.

If the Father has the kingdom ready for us, He will take care of us on the way.

Lot would not give up Christ, but he would not give up much *for* Christ.

Let us be as watchful after the victory as before the battle.

God likes to see His people shut up to this, that there is no hope but in prayer. Herein lies the Church's power against the world.

Love is the *motive* for working; joy is the *strength* for working.

We have got more from Paul's prison-house than from his visit to the third heaven.

He had a card in his study near the mantelpiece that read:

He who has truly prayed has completed the half of his study.

The sins of teachers are the teachers of sins.

Beware of the bad things of good men.[1]

Bonar was pleased when the University of Edinburgh granted him a Doctor of Divinity degree in 1873. But when he was made Moderator of the Free Church Assembly, he said, "Alas! How far down our Church has come when it asks such as me to take this office!"

"Many want salvation, but they do not want the Savior."

Finally, "You need not be afraid of too much grace. Great grace never makes a man proud. A little grace is very apt to make a man be puffed up."

I hope you will get acquainted with this delightful man of God—a wholesome example in ministry, and a saint who encourages us to live in the Holy of Holies with God.

11

Robert Murray McCheyne
1813–1843

I t is not great talents God blesses so much as great likenesses to Jesus. A holy minister is an awful weapon in the hand of God."

Those words were written on October 2, 1840, by Robert Murray McCheyne, pastor of St. Peter's Church in Dundee, Scotland. They are typical of McCheyne, for "likeness to Jesus" was the emphasis of his life and ministry. "I heard you preach last Sabbath evening," a stranger wrote him, "and it pleased God to bless that sermon to my soul. It was not so much what you said, as your manner of speaking that struck me. I saw in you a beauty in holiness that I never saw before."

I wonder if this "beauty of holiness" is not a missing ingredient in ministry today. We hear people boasting that their pastor is a good expositor (and there is nothing wrong with that), a good counselor, a man who is "fun to be with"; we rarely hear people say, "Our pastor is a holy man of God." The people in Dundee could say that of McCheyne.

Robert Murray McCheyne was born in Edinburgh, Scotland, on May 21, 1813. His family discovered early that he was a precocious child: at the age of four, while recovering from an illness, he learned the Greek alphabet and was able to write the letters on his slate. He entered Edinburgh University in November, 1827, still an unconverted youth. The death of his brother David in 1831 stirred him deeply, and as a result he trusted Christ. That year, McCheyne entered the Divinity Hall and dedicated himself to the ministry of the gospel. One of his fellow students, Andrew A. Bonar, became his close friend; and it is Bonar who, in 1844, published *The Memoirs and Remains of the Rev. Robert Murray McCheyne*, today recognized as a great Christian classic.

He was licensed by the Presbytery (along with Andrew Bonar) on July 1, 1835; the following November he began his ministry as an assistant in the church at Larbert, near Stirling. From the very outset of his ministry, he withdrew himself in total dependence upon the Lord. He fed himself daily on the Word of God, and each Lord's Day would share his spiritual nourishment with the congregation. "I see a man cannot be a faithful minister, until he preaches Christ for Christ's sake," he wrote in his journal, "until he gives up striving to attract people to himself, and seeks only to attract them to Christ." We wonder what McCheyne would think of all the so-called Christian celebrities we have today—and the people who run after them.

On August 14, 1836, McCheyne was asked to be a candidate at a new extension church that had opened in May in Dundee (Andrew Bonar was also a candidate). The population of Dundee had grown in recent years to more than fifty thousand; and there was a desperate need for a church in the northwest corner of the expanding city. It would not be an easy place for ministry, for there was a great deal of poverty and vice, and the minister would have over four thousand souls in his parish. "A city given to idolatry and hardness of heart," was the way the youthful preacher described Dundee. But then he added, "Perhaps the Lord will make this wilderness of chimney-tops to be green and beautiful as the garden of the Lord, a field which the Lord hath blessed!"

The church called McCheyne to be their pastor, and he was ordained and installed on November 24, 1836. He would minister at St. Peter's less than seven years; he preached his last sermon there March 12, 1843, and was called home on March 25. But in those few years, he made an impact on Scotland that is still felt, and that spiritual impact has continued over the years and has spread throughout the church. The reason that McCheyne's life and ministry continue to enrich us is because he was a true man of God.

To begin with, McCheyne was careful and consistent in his devotional life. It was his happy custom to spend time before breakfast reading the Scriptures (three chapters a day), singing hymns (he was an excellent musician), and praying. He followed the counsel of godly, seventeenth-century Anglican Jeremy Taylor: "If thou meanest to enlarge thy religion, do it rather by enlarging thine ordinary devotions than thy extraordinary." This is good counsel for today. Far too many Christians are scurrying around looking for special meetings, thinking that extraordinary experiences will make them better Christians. In my own ministry in pastors' conferences, I have discovered that too many ministers neglect their daily devotional time, or hurry through it, so they can get involved in "more important matters."

Another factor was McCheyne's sincere burden for souls. He wrote to his friend, Rev. W. C. Burns: "I feel there are two things it is impossible to desire with sufficient ardor—personal holiness, and the honor of Christ in the salvation of souls." Early in his ministry, in 1834, when he heard that a sinner had turned to Christ through hearing him preach, McCheyne wrote in his journal: "The precious tidings that a soul has been melted down by the grace of the Savior . . . Lord, I thank Thee that Thou has shown me this marvelous working, though I was but an adoring spectator rather than an instrument."

When McCheyne preached, it was out of a full heart of love for his people. He lamented in his journal: "In the morning was more engaged in preparing the head than the heart." When his friend Bonar told McCheyne that his text the previous Sunday had been, "The wicked shall be turned into hell," McCheyne asked, "Were you able to preach it with *tenderness*?" He used to pray, "Give me Thy gentle Spirit, that neither strives nor cries."

He prepared his messages carefully and was a diligent student. "Beaten oil," he used to say, "beaten oil for the lamps of the sanctuary" (referring to Exod. 27:20). He brought into the pulpit fresh manna that he gathered himself in his personal fellowship with the Lord. No borrowed sermons, no last minute concoctions. His sermons were considered long, but they were full of spiritual nutrition. He wrote to a friend, "I cannot say that my sermons are much shorter, though I have tried to shorten them." He received many invitations to preach and had a difficult time refusing. In one of his last letters, he wrote, "I preached twenty-seven times when I was away, in twenty-four different places."

McCheyne drew spiritual help from the great saints of the past. In his journal and letters, you find him mentioning such classics as *The Letters of Samuel Rutherford* (another saintly Scot), *The Memoirs of Henry Martyn*, *The Christian Ministry* by Charles Bridges, *The Life and Journal of David Brainerd*, Richard Baxter's *Call to the Unconverted*, and *The Works of Jonathan Edwards*. How much richer we would be if we would refuse the books of the hour and discover again the books of the ages.

Because of his saintly life and Spirit-anointed ministry, McCheyne was envied by some ministers and criticized by others, but he maintained a loving attitude toward all. In fact, he rejoiced at the blessings God gave to his brethren in the ministry. While McCheyne was on a missionary tour for the Church of Scotland in 1839, a revival broke out in his church under the ministry of Rev. William C. Burns. On hearing the good news, McCheyne wrote to Burns: "You remember it was the prayer of my heart when we parted, that you might be a thousandfold more blessed to the people than ever my ministry had been."

During a period of illness, he asked several ministers of different denominations to take his place, and for this he was publicly criticized. He published an open letter in the *Dundee Warder*, in which he stated that

> all who are true servants of the Lord Jesus Christ, sound in the faith, called to the ministry, and owned of God therein, should love one another, pray one for another, bid one another God-speed, own one another as fellow-soldiers, fellow-servants, and fellow-laborers in the vineyard; and, so far as God offereth opportunity, help one another in the work of the ministry.

He was a man with a large heart and a great love for the people of God.

McCheyne had never been a strong man, and he overtaxed himself in his work. Once he fainted in the pulpit, and often he had to lie still for hours to encourage his palpitating heart to quiet down. He became ill at a church meeting on March 13, 1843, and had to be put to bed and given constant medical attention. He became delirious on the twenty-first, but even then was repeatedly praying or quoting Scripture. On Saturday morning, March 25, while his doctor was standing by, McCheyne lifted his hand as if to give a benediction, and then stepped into eternity.

"Live so as to be missed!" was one of his favorite sayings. Between six and seven thousand people assembled for the funeral procession; business was almost at a standstill in Glasgow. He was buried next to St. Peter's Church, and his grave can be visited today. I recall standing there one quiet June evening, reading the inscription on the monument. Then we were ushered into the vestry where the church officer opened a closet and brought out McChenye's own Bible. I am not given to sentiment, but I must confess that I was deeply moved as I turned the pages of the Bible and read McCheyne's own annotations in the margins. It was a high and holy hour I cannot forget.

He was only thirty years old when he died, and he had ministered less than seven years at St. Peter's Church; yet his ministry and influence go on (it is interesting that two of his models in the ministry also died young: David Brainerd, at thirty; and Henry Martyn, at thirty-two). *The Memoirs and Remains of the Rev. Robert Murray McCheyne,* by his dear friend Andrew Bonar, is a Christian classic that should be in every believer's library. Get the complete Banner of Truth edition, not a condensed version, and do not speed-read the book; read it carefully and meditate on what you read. I have often turned to McCheyne in dry, disappointing hours and have never failed to find refreshment for my soul.

"To gain entire likeness to Christ," he wrote, "I ought to get a high esteem of the happiness of it. I am persuaded that God's happiness is inseparably linked in with His holiness."[1]

May our happiness be in his holiness and in a growing likeness to Jesus Christ.

12

F. W. Robertson
1816–1853

It is August 3, 1841. A young British preacher is visiting Geneva, hoping to restore both his faith and his broken health. He visits the celebrated Henri Caesar Malan, the Swiss evangelical leader whose fearless ministry has aroused the resentment of the established church. The young preacher opens his heart to the man for he too finds his position in the established church an uncomfortable one. As the two pastors discuss matters both theological and ministerial, the godly Malan looks at his visitor, shakes his head, and announces: "You will have a sad life and a sad ministry!"

The prophecy was fulfilled. The young man died at the age of thirty-seven, after only thirteen years of ministry; when he died, he considered himself a failure. Nevertheless, within a few years of his death, his printed sermons were making an impact on thinking Christians (and even unbelievers) that has not diminished to this day. He lived a sad, almost tragic life, and his ministry was filled with both physical and emotional pain, yet Frederick W. Robertson is known as "the preacher's preacher," and his failure has turned into success.

Robertson was born on February 3, 1816, in London. His father was a captain in the Royal Artillery, and Robertson spent his first five years at Leith Fort near Edinburgh. In 1821, Captain Robertson retired and moved the family to Yorkshire, where young Frederick grew up enjoying the outdoors and dreaming of a soldier's life. Both his father and grandfather had served gallantly in the army; his three younger brothers were to follow in their steps. But not Frederick. Though he prepared himself and applied for his commission, two years passed before he heard from the Crown. But before that, something interfered.

In March 1837, a neighbor introduced him to Mr. Davies, a devoted clergyman who asked Robertson what he planned to do with his life. When told that the young man planned to enter the army and was even then waiting for his commission, Davies asked, "Have you ever considered the church?" Robertson replied, "No, never! Not that! I am not fit for that!" After further conversation, Robertson asked Davies what he should do; the wise pastor said, "Do as your father likes, and pray to God to direct your father aright." In true military fashion, Robertson followed his counsel, and Captain Robertson decided that the place for his son was the church. On May 4, 1837, Robertson entered Oxford. Five days later his army commission arrived.

Robertson was disappointed in Oxford. The students, having little sense of duty or devotion, jested about sacred things; the Anglican church was seething with division and debate. John Henry Newman was preaching at Oxford at that time, and the famous Tractarian movement that ultimately led Newman back to Rome was getting underway. Robertson's studies were not too systematic, nor did he strive to win prizes. He did focus attention on the Bible, and each morning while shaving he tried to memorize certain portions. His biographer claimed that Robertson memorized *all* of the New Testament in English and much of it in Greek!

On leaving college he plunged into his ministerial career and on July 12, 1840, was ordained by the Bishop of Winchester. Interestingly enough, the text of the ordination sermon was "Endure hardness as a good soldier of Jesus Christ." That was exactly what Robertson would have to do for the next thirteen years, and at times he would be tempted to quit. His first sermon, given a week later, was on Isaiah 55:1: "Ho, every one that thirsteth!"

Apparently he and Mr. Nicholson, the rector, got along beautifully, for the young man had a mind to work. Nicholson was in poor health, and many of the pastoral responsibilities fell to his young assistant, who performed them with sympathy and success. Unfortunately Robertson developed the bad habit of "unwise self-dissection" during that year, and the constant examination of his spiritual condition did not make for spiritual health. He became overly sensitive to his faults and gradually overcritical of the faults of others. He lived too under a self-induced conviction that he was going to die soon, and this outlook tended to make him melancholy.

His morbid attitude only made his symptoms worse. The doctors recommended that he tour the Continent, and in July 1841 he set off for Geneva. It was there he met the Swiss preacher César Malan. It was also there that he met Helen Denys, daughter of a British nobleman; they were married after a brief acquaintance.

The Robertsons returned to England, and in 1842 he began his ministry at Christchurch, Cheltenham, working with Archibald Boyd, the rector. Boyd was what was known in those days as "a pulpit giant," and Robertson learned much about preaching and studying during his five years at Christchurch. Up to this point Robertson had been somewhat careless about sermon preparation, sometimes leaving it until Saturday! Now he saw that real preaching was born of painstaking work and agonizing prayer and study.

But he had his problems in Cheltenham. To begin with, Robertson was ministering to the wealthy, and his heart was with the poor. The city was "a resort for the lame and lazy and rich," and Robertson had no desire to be a popular preacher to a pleasure-seeking society. But his most difficult problem was with the evangelicals in Cheltenham. Robertson himself had been brought up in the evangelical tradition, but he was pained by the bitterness, narrowness, and downright meanness that seemed to characterize some of their leaders. Their publications seemed to thrive on name-calling, tests of orthodoxy, and the reaffirming of traditional truths in the same traditional language. When Robertson's preaching did not completely conform to their standards, they began to shoot at him. "I stand nearly alone," he wrote, "a theological Ishmael!" He was too conservative for the liberals and too liberal for the conservatives.

At this point, "the sudden ruin of a friendship . . . accelerated the inward crisis," and Robertson was plunged into a spiritual conflict that shook him to his very foundations. "It is an awful moment," he wrote, "when the soul begins to find that the props on which it has blindly rested so long are, many of them, rotten, and begins to suspect them all." It was his "dark night of the soul."[1]

He left his wife and children in England, took a leave of absence from the church, and headed once again to the Continent, to struggle alone with himself and his God. Even his dreams afflicted him. He dreamed that members of the church were gossiping about him and tearing down his work. He would awaken, go back to sleep, and then dream he was being reproached for work left undone. Neither change of scenery nor strenuous exercise up and down the mountains could cure his deep melancholy and the painful conviction that his ministry was a failure. He returned home, resigned from the church, served as interim at another church for two months, and then moved to Trinity Chapel, Brighton, where he was to carry on a brave and noble ministry for six brief years.

Brighton was a fashionable seaside resort of about seventy thousand people, one-fourth of them holiday vacationers. There were thirteen Anglican churches in the city, as well as nineteen independent churches, a Quaker meeting, a Jewish synagogue, and a Roman Catholic church. But the churches seemed to make little difference in the lives of the people, who were interested primarily in pleasure and money. Every weekend a new army of pleasure-seekers invaded the city from London, and the worldliness of Brighton became a burden on Robertson's heart.

He turned to the poor and to the workingmen of the city, and this upset the rich of the congregation. He refused to be labeled, and as a result he was libeled. His sermons were too pointed, and he dared to name the sins of the rich right in the presence of their servants!

Anonymous letters attacked him; some of these even found their way into the local newspapers. Because he dared to search into the truth of the Bible and let the Bible open up its own message, he was condemned by those who rested on a secondhand faith and never knew the "dark night of the soul" through which he had won his own convictions.

One of the main organs of criticism was *The Record*, published by the evangelical party of the church. When one of his London pastor friends wrote to *The Record* to defend him, Robertson wrote to thank him and said: "*The Record* has done me the honor to abuse me for some time past, for which I thank them gratefully. God forbid they should ever praise me! One number alone contained four unscrupulous lies about me, on no better evidence than that someone had told them, who had been told by somebody else." But Robertson was human, and these barbs often penetrated deeply into his heart. A tinge of bitterness crept into his personality, though he was always kind to people—including those who differed with him.

In 1852 the young men of the congregation presented a public testimonial to their pastor, which he gratefully accepted. However, he confessed in a letter to a friend, "In the midst of the homage of a crowd, I felt alone, and as if friendless."

He sensed that the end was near; the physical demands of his ministry were too much for him, let alone the strenuous demands he made on himself in sermon preparation. He suffered from splitting headaches. Often he would sit alone for hours, gritting his teeth and silently waging war against indescribable pain. At night he slept with his head against the rung of a chair. There was an abscess in his brain, and nobody could do anything about it. A group of his friends raised the money to provide an assistant for the church, but the vicar of Brighton rejected the man they chose because of a long-standing grudge between them!

Robertson's last sermon at Trinity concluded a series on 2 Corinthians; the text was, "Finally, brethren, farewell!" It proved to be prophetic. On August 12, 1853, he wrote his last letter; his closing words were: "His will be done! I write in torture." When his physician and his wife tried to move him to a more comfortable position, he said, "I cannot bear it; let me rest. I must die. Let God do His work." On August 15, 1853, he finished his course. Two thousand people attended his funeral, and all of Brighton was draped in mourning. Even some who had bitterly attacked him realized that he had taught them something important and, even more, that he had lived before them the message that he preached.

One is tempted to ask, "Why was such an effective preacher so constantly discouraged and overshadowed by a dark cloud of failure?" No doubt there were physical reasons: Robertson was not a robust man and the seeds of death were working in his body years before his friends knew they were there. A pastor's health may not be as important as his doctrine, but Paul does not separate the two in 1 Timothy 4:6–8. "I am impressed," said Phillips Brooks in his *Lectures on Preaching*, "with what seems to me the frivolous and insufficient way in which the health of the preacher is often treated." Bodily weakness need not be an obstacle to a successful ministry (witness McCheyne and Brainerd, for example), but certainly it is no advantage. It was when Elijah was weary and hungry that he entered the valley of despair and sat under the juniper tree.

A second factor in Robertson's attitude was, I believe, disappointment. He had always wanted to be a soldier, and when he was made a minister instead, he continued to live like a soldier. He read the "war news" of his day eagerly and often imagined himself leading a battalion to victory. He confessed to a friend that he could not witness military maneuvers without experiencing a choking sensation. He often wore a dragoon cloak, and the emphasis on *duty* in his preaching is obvious. He would have fled from Brighton the first year of his ministry, had not a soldier's sense of duty kept him there. I am not suggesting that he was not dedicated to the ministry, or that he ministered in a half-hearted way, but rather that his concept of the ministry was primarily *militant*, and in war you either win or lose. In ministry the victories are not always that definite; Robertson was never really able to evaluate honestly the good he was doing through his preaching.

Perhaps a chief cause of depression was his tendency to be a loner. He had few close friends or confidants, probably because he did not want to be crushed by another broken friendship as he had been in Cheltenham. Even his wife does not seem to have entered into his ministry the way a pastor's wife normally would. There are suggestions in his letters that he and his wife did not agree on church matters—and that on more than one occasion she was right!

Because he could not find a group that agreed with him and because he had too much humility to start one of his own, he identified himself with no group and ultimately ended up criticizing all of them! His ministerial loneliness robbed him of the balance he needed, both emotionally and spiritually. "I would rather live solitary on the most desolate crag," he wrote, "shivering, with all the warm wraps of falsehood stripped off . . . than sit comfortably on more inhabited spots, where others were warm in a faith which is true to them, but which is false to me." It seems to me that his alternatives are not honest: a man can have convictions and still have companions. Again, this is the soldier in Robertson: he was on the defensive, always protecting his citadel of truth and never suspecting that others were trying to defend it too. The pastor is a lonely enough man without making the situation worse!

What is Robertson's contribution to our preaching today? Perhaps his "six principles" still have something to say to us: (1) establish positive truth instead of only destroying error; (2) since truth is made up of two opposite propositions, look for a doctrine large enough to include both; (3) preach suggestively, not exhaustively; (4) start with Christ's humanity, then move to his deity (Brooks would say, "Find the place where truth touches life"); (5) truth works from the inward to the outward; and (6) try to find the basis of truth even in error. We may not totally agree with all these propositions, but we must confess they give us a great deal to think about.

Robertson's weakness was in the area of systematic theology. His Oxford training was definitely inadequate here, and even during his own personal studies he never did arrive at concrete statements of the great doctrines of the faith. Principal A. M. Fairbairn wrote:

"The very incompleteness of his work was the secret of his power. He said what many had been feeling, but he did not help the many to translate their feelings into a rational substitute for what he so vigorously swept away."[2] It is his vagueness that attracts people of different schools, but we must confess that this vagueness leaves the soul a bit dissatisfied.

Robertson was not, as is often claimed, the "father of the two-point sermon." He learned it from his beloved rector at Christchurch, Archibald Boyd. But it was Robertson who perfected the approach and made it popular. I feel I would tire of it week after week, as would my congregation, but it is worth studying and incorporating into our own kits of homiletical tools.

Before you rush out and purchase everything by and about F. W. Robertson, acquaint yourself with the man. I suggest you start with *The Preaching of F. W. Robertson* edited by Gilbert E. Doan Jr., a volume in the excellent Preacher's Paperback Library published by Fortress Press. Along with a brief biography and a fine study of his preaching are ten of Robertson's best sermons. Do not read these sermons quickly! Read them carefully, slowly, meditatively, beginning with "The Loneliness of Christ," which is perhaps Robertson's most autobiographical sermon.

If you find yourself excited by what you read, then secure *The Soul of Frederick W. Robertson* by James R. Blackwood. This is the best study of Robertson you will find; it is based on careful scholarship and a fine sympathy for the man. (The author is a son of the eminent Princeton professor of homiletics, Andrew W. Blackwood.) You may also want to read Lewis O. Brastow's study of Robertson in his *Representative Modern Preachers*.

If at this point you are still interested, then purchase Stopford A. Brooke's definitive *Life and Letters of Frederick W. Robertson*, available in several different editions. Brooke spent eight years writing this book. At times it is tedious, but for the most part it permits the preacher to speak for himself. The author's most subjective chapter is chapter 7 in the first volume, where some of his views need to be taken with a grain of salt. Of course, you will then want to add all of Robertson's sermons and addresses to your library, index them, and refer to them as you study. You will also want to read a sermon now and then just for your own edification.

In his monumental *A History of Preaching*, Edwin C. Dargan called Robertson "one of the most pathetic and powerful figures in all the history of English preaching."[3] Perhaps so, but could we not use in the church today a bit more of the "soldier spirit" that gives a man the courage to keep ministering in spite of the odds? Robertson once suggested that all clergy be "forced to serve in the army for five years previous to ordination, to make them men." We may not agree with this suggestion, but we do agree with Paul's admonition—and Robertson's ordination charge—to "endure hardness as a good soldier of Jesus Christ."

John Charles Ryle
1816–1900

Beware of divisions. One thing the children of the world can always understand, if they do not understand doctrine; that thing is angry quarrelling and controversy. Be at peace among yourselves."

So wrote Bishop John Charles Ryle in his farewell message to the ministers of the Liverpool Diocese on February 1, 1900, as he closed nearly twenty years of faithful ministry among them. Four months later, on June 10, he died, but he left behind a spiritual legacy that has enriched believers and strengthened the church.

The Church of England, to which Ryle belonged, was not a united people. For years there had been a high-church faction that promoted ritual and always seemed to be drifting nearer to Rome; a broad-church group that was tolerant of diverse religious emphasis but not too enthusiastic for the gospel; and then the low-church segment, known as the evangelicals. It was to this latter group that Bishop Ryle belonged.

The evangelicals in the Church of England grew out of the great revivals of Whitefield and Wesley. Converts who left the national church and united with independent groups were called Methodists. But those who remained in the Anglican Church and were true to their doctrinal convictions were called evangelicals, and they were a great and glorious host. Some of the greatest gospel-preaching ministers in English church history were a part of the evangelical movement—men like William Romaine, Henry Venn, Charles Simeon, William Grimshaw, John Fletcher, and John Newton, who wrote "Amazing Grace."

It was not easy to be an evangelical in the established church. Evangelicals would not be recognized by those in authority, and would probably not be promoted or offered the better churches. The majority of the clergy endured the presence of the evangelicals the way a fishing party endures gnats and mosquitoes—always hoping they will somehow go away. Evangelical clergy were not appointed to the boards of various church ministries or, for the most part, asked to preach at important church functions. But the evangelicals practiced their faith and made monumental contributions to both the church and the nation. It was the evangelicals who led the fight against slavery, child labor, poor factory conditions, and the abuse of the poor and the insane. Much of what we value in modern social legislation, and perhaps take for granted, grew out of the ministry of Wesley and Whitefield and their successors.

The evangelicals also founded a number of effective organizations to promote the spread of the gospel: the Church Missionary Society (1799), Religious Tract Society (1799), British and Foreign Bible Society (1804), and several more. They had a burden for Israel and started a mission board for witness to the Jews. In both home and foreign missions, they led the way, seeking to win the lost and build new churches. They shocked their more proper brethren by daring to preach out-of-doors, as Jesus and Paul did. They even held evangelistic services in unconsecrated buildings. For all of this, of course, they were criticized; but their only concern was to please their Master, so they kept right on.

John Charles Ryle was born May 10, 1816, in Macclesfield, Cheshire, the center of the great silk industry in Britain. The Ryle family had long been established there and were quite prosperous. Several of their men, including Ryle's father, had served as mayor.

There was a strong evangelical element in the family's faith, going all the way back to 1745, when John Wesley himself had preached in that region.

At age twelve Ryle entered prep school, leaving in 1827 to enter Eaton, from which he graduated in 1834. He then enrolled in Oxford, and in the year he graduated (1837) he was soundly converted. His sister and cousin had been converted earlier and had witnessed to him. A serious illness just before his final examinations also gave him time to reflect on his life and consider spiritual things.

He had attended one of the parish churches one Sunday afternoon, but neither the sermon nor the hymns made any impression on him. But when a man began to read the second Scripture lesson for the day, the Word gripped Ryle's heart. The passage was Ephesians 2, and when the reader got to verse 8, he read it with special emphasis: "For by grace are ye saved—through faith—and that not of yourselves—it is the gift of God." Young Ryle believed that Word, and God saved him.

In preparation for sharing his father's banking business, Ryle studied law in London, but after six months he had to return home because of ill health. However, he soon recovered and entered into business with enthusiasm. He was considered one of the most eligible bachelors in the district: young, popular, successful, and a devoted Christian. But he was afraid of women. His father offered him a house and a large sum of money if he would marry, but even these incentives did not move him.

In June 1841, the bank failed and the family lost everything. Ryle's father had followed some bad advice and had hired an untrustworthy manager; the combination of the two brought ruin. The family was left with Mrs. Ryle's dowry, some personal property, and their clothes. Mr. Ryle spent the next twenty years paying back every cent of his debt, with each member of the family assisting in every way possible. Even when John was rector at Helmingham, he wore threadbare clothes in order to save money and assist his father. He firmly believed that his father's spiritual falling away was the real cause for the failure of the bank.

Before the year 1841 was over, young John determined that God had called him to the ministry. He was ordained December 12 and preached his first sermon December 19. He began his ministry at Exbury and then was appointed to Winchester; these brief experiences helped prepare him for the longer ministries that were to follow. From 1844 to 1861, he served at Helmingham, where he had a rather difficult time with the lord of the manor, who tried to run both the town and the church. Ryle went through the valley during those years, burying his wife of less than two years in 1847 and his second wife in 1860.

From 1861 to 1880, Ryle ministered at Stradbroke, and during that time he met and married his third wife. These were happier years. For one thing, there was no rich landlord throwing his weight around and, for another, Ryle's people loved him and were eager to hear the Word preached. He led them in the physical restoration of the old church, making certain that the pulpit was given its proper place of prominence. He had the workmen carve on the pulpit "Woe is unto me if I preach not the gospel!" When the workmen had finished, he took a tool and underlined the word "not" with a deep groove.

In 1880, John Charles Ryle was appointed the first Bishop of Liverpool, a new diocese that had been carved out of the Chester diocese. How did it happen that an evangelical was appointed to this important position and given the opportunity to build an evangelical ministry from the ground up? From the human point of view, the appointment may have just been a piece of religious politics, but God certainly overruled it for the good of his church.

At the February 1880 election, Prime Minister Benjamin Disraeli suffered an overwhelming defeat at the hand of Gladstone. Disraeli was anxious that a staunch Protestant be appointed to the new post, and the leading churchmen of Liverpool were behind him. The fact that Liverpool was Gladstone's hometown made Disraeli's decision even more significant. Ryle was given a very little time to consider the offer because time was working against them; he immediately accepted, and three days before Gladstone took office all the formalities had been completed.

On May 4, Oxford University conferred the Doctor of Divinity degree on him, and on June 11 he was consecrated as bishop. It is doubtful that Ryle would ever have been considered for the post had he not proved himself to be a sane, spiritual evangelical who was willing to listen to those he disagreed with and ignore those who threw stones of accusation from the fringes of the camp. Ryle let it be known from the beginning where he stood on the great doctrines of the faith; he also made it clear that he was going to use his new position to promote harmony, not conflict, in the church.

One of Ryle's first tasks was to build a ministry in Liverpool, and this he did, gathering around him like-minded Christians who wanted to share the gospel and build churches. Instead of raising money to construct an ornate cathedral, Ryle used the funds available to extend the church. He built ninety places of worship and staffed them with 136 ministers. He established a ministry of "Bible women" to assist the resident clergy and to take the gospel to the poor. He organized ministries for children and even used secular buildings for religious services. He was too conservative for the liberals and too liberal for the conservatives, so he was attacked from both sides. But he valiantly carried on a positive ministry, never dishonoring the Savior or diluting the doctrines of the Reformed faith. Before long, church life in the Liverpool diocese began to take on a new spirit of excitement, and God began to bless.

Always a man with a great heart, Ryle saw nothing wrong in cooperating with the nonconformists, including D. L. Moody and Ira Sankey when they came to Liverpool in 1883. His friendly attitude toward the Methodists rankled some of the more exclusive Anglican clergy, but their criticisms did not disturb him.

On February 1, 1900, Bishop Ryle resigned from his charge. He had lived to see nearly one-fourth of the parishes in his diocese staffed by evangelicals. When he was buried in Liverpool, his old Bible was placed in his hand in the coffin. Two texts were quoted on his gravestone: Ephesians 2:8 and 2 Timothy 4:7, which states, "I have fought a good fight, I have finished my course, I have kept the faith."

Baker Books has reprinted a number of Bishop Ryle's books, including his monumental *Expository Thoughts on the Gospels*, a set that ought to be in every Bible student's library. *The Best of J. C. Ryle* is a good sampler for the reader not yet acquainted with this giant of the faith. His books *Holiness*, *The New Birth*, and *Call to Prayer* deal with essentials of the Christian life. *The True Christian* is a collection of Ryle's sermons on many subjects that relate to the Christian life.

Ryle was always a true son of the church, but he took a very definite evangelical interpretation of the Thirty-Nine Articles of the Church of England. He explains his position in *Knots United*, published by James Clarke.

Banner of Truth Trust has reprinted *Warnings to the Churches*, a series of addresses that focus primarily on the church and its ministry (several of these chapters also appear in *Knots United*). Ryle's biographical studies, *Five Christian Leaders* and *Five English Reformers*, are also available from Banner of Truth.

Ryle's successor, Bishop Chavasses, started the construction of the Liverpool Cathedral, with the laying of the foundation stone by King Edward VII in 1904. Queen Elizabeth II shared in the service of dedication when the building was completed on October 25, 1978. It is a beautiful sandstone building, and my wife and I visited it a few years ago. It was the south choir aisle I was especially interested in, for in that aisle is a monument to the glory of God and in honor of his servant, Bishop John Charles Ryle. However, his greatest monument is not man-made. It is in the *living* church, in the lives of men and women who even today are touched by his ministry.

"I am firmly persuaded," he wrote, "that there is no system so life-giving, so calculated to awaken the sleeping, lead on the inquiring, and build up the saints, as that system which is called the *evangelical* system of Christianity. Wherever it is faithfully preached, and efficiently carried out, and consistently adorned by the lives of its professors, it is the power of God. . . . We have the truth, and we need not be afraid to say so."

14

Fanny Crosby
1820–1915

"I believe myself still really in the prime of life!" wrote Frances Jane Crosby at the age of eighty-three. She lived twelve more years, and when she died on February 12, 1915, the news flashed around the world that America's beloved composer of gospel songs, Fanny Crosby, was home with her Lord and at last could see.

Donald P. Hustad, a recognized authority on hymnology, has called Fanny Crosby "the most prolific and significant writer of gospel songs in American history." She wrote more than eight thousand songs, most of which are now forgotten. But many continue to minister to God's people: "To God Be the Glory," "Blessed Assurance," "Praise Him! Praise Him!" "Redeemed," "Jesus, Keep Me Near the Cross," "Rescue the Perishing," "All the Way My Savior Leads Me," and others. The Hope Publishing Company has hundreds of Fanny Crosby's poems in their files just waiting to be set to music.

She was born in Putnam County, New York, on March 24, 1820. When Fanny was only six weeks old she developed a minor eye inflammation, and the doctor's careless treatment left her blind. "It seemed intended by the blessed Providence of God that I should be blind all my life," she wrote in her delightful autobiography *Fanny*

Crosby's Life Story, "and I thank Him for the dispensation." The doctor who destroyed her sight never forgave himself and moved from the area, but Fanny Crosby held no ill will toward him. "If I could meet him now," she wrote, "I would say 'Thank you, thank you'—over and over again—for making me blind."

In fact, she claimed that if she could have her sight restored, she would not attempt it. She felt that her blindness was God's gift to her so that she could write songs for his glory. "I could not have written thousands of hymns," she said, "if I had been hindered by the distractions of seeing all the interesting and beautiful objects that would have been presented to my notice."

She wrote her first poem when she was eight years old. Here it is.

> Oh, what a happy child I am,
>   Although I cannot see!
> I am resolved that in this world
>   Contented I will be.
>
> How many blessings I enjoy
>   That other people don't!
> So weep or sigh because I'm blind,
>   I cannot, or I won't!

Fanny was greatly influenced by her mother and grandmother (her father died when she was very young). When the family moved to Connecticut, a neighbor, Mrs. Hawley, read to her from the Bible and taught her Bible stories. It seems unbelievable, but by the time Fanny was ten years old, she could recite the first four books of the Old Testament and the four Gospels! She could also repeat "poems almost without number." She sometimes compared her mind to a writing desk, with little compartments filled with information readily available.

It was clear that Fanny would need formal education, so on March 3, 1835, her mother took her to the famous Institution for the Blind in New York City. She proved to be an excellent student in everything except mathematics. In rebellion against the subject, she wrote the following poem:

I loathe, abhor, it makes me sick,
To hear the word Arithmetic!

Before long, she became the resident poet for the school, and the superintendent was concerned that the growing praise might go to her head. So he called her into his office and gently warned her to beware of pride. He also urged her to use her gifts to the glory of God. "His words were bombshells," she later admitted, "but they did me an immense amount of good." But the real bombshell fell some months later when she was instructed not to write any poems for three months. It was a great trial to the young girl, because even though she did not write them down, the poems came into her mind almost unbidden.

Then a strange thing happened. A noted phrenologist came to visit the school and offered to "read the bumps" on the heads of students and faculty. He correctly identified the leading mathematical genius in the school, and when he came to Fanny Crosby, he said, "Why, here is a poet! Give her every advantage that she can have; let her hear the best books and converse with the best writers; and she will make her mark in the world." The next morning, the superintendent called Fanny to his office and said, "You may write all the poetry you want to."

In 1844, she published her first book of poems, and it contained the first hymn she ever wrote: "An Evening Hymn." A second volume of poems followed in 1851 and a third in 1858. It is interesting to note that in the 1851 volume she noted her declining health in the preface, yet she lived for sixty-four more years!

Fanny Crosby's family was a great spiritual influence in her life, and so was Hamilton Murray, one of the instructors at the school. But it was on November 20, 1850, that Fanny Crosby received the assurance of her salvation. She had been attending revival meetings at the Broadway Tabernacle Methodist Church in New York City, and had even gone to the altar twice. But it was during the singing of "Alas! And Did My Savior Bleed?" that God met her need. "My very soul was flooded with celestial light," she said. "For the first time

I realized that I had been trying to hold the world in one hand and the Lord in the other."

Fanny Crosby was married in 1858 to Alexander Van Alstyne, who had also been a student at the school for the blind and, like Fanny, had taught there. He was a gifted musician and a perfect partner to the poetess. He died on June 18, 1902.

During the 1850s and early sixties, Fanny Crosby wrote the lyrics to many popular secular songs, some of which were even used in minstrel shows. But the turning point of her life came on February 2, 1864, when she met William Bradbury, the famous hymnwriter and publisher. "For many years, I have been wanting you to write for me," he told her. "I wish you would begin right away!" She did begin, and the result was her first gospel song, "Our Bright Home Above." Little did anyone realize that God would use her to pen over eight thousand songs in the next fifty-one years.

How did Fanny Crosby write her lyrics? "I never undertake a hymn," she explained, "without first asking the good Lord to be my inspiration in the work that I am about to do." It helped her to hold a small book in her hand, something she often did when she lectured or gave concerts. She would pray and meditate until she was in the right mood, and sometimes she would quote several hymns to herself to prime the pump. Then the ideas would come, and she would write the song in her mind and commit it to memory. At times, she would have as many as forty different songs stored away in her mind. She would let each song lie still for a few days before dictating it to a friend, who would then send it off to the publisher.

Like many prolific writers, Fanny Crosby used various pseudonyms; in fact, she used nearly two hundred. Some of them are Julia Stirling, Frank Gould, Carrie M. Wilson, Lyman Cuyler, Victoria Stewart, Maud Marion, and Ella Dale.[1] D. L. Moody's associate, Major Daniel Whittle, wrote many hymns under the pseudonym "El Nathan," so this was not an uncommon practice.

We are shocked to learn that Fanny Crosby was paid an average of only two dollars for each of her poems, although in later years it was increased to ten dollars (of course, a dollar went further back in those days). But she certainly earned eternal rewards through her ministry of song, and we today are the richer for her faithfulness.

Fanny Crosby was just a few weeks away from her ninety-fifth birthday when she was called home, a hope she had often written about in her songs. For the first time, she could see and, best of all, she could see her Savior. Have you ever noticed how often she wrote about *seeing* in her lyrics? Watch for these references the next time you sing a Fanny Crosby song. Perhaps the best known of all is the chorus of "Saved by Grace."

> And I shall see Him face to face,
> And tell the story—Saved by grace.

Fanny Crosby's Life Story has been long out of print (I found my copy in an old barn in Rumney, New Hampshire), but you can secure two recent books to help you get better acquainted with this charming lady. *Fanny Crosby Speaks Again*, edited by Donald P. Hustad, is a collection of 120 previously unpublished poems by Fanny Crosby. The brief foreword and the pictures enhance the volume. It is published by Hope Publishing Company. The second volume is *Fanny Crosby* by Bernard Ruffin (Pilgrim Press), a careful biography of this composer whom the author calls a Protestant saint. *Her Heart Can See* by Edith L. Blumhofer is excellent. It is part of the "Library of Religious Biography" published by Eerdmans.

It was said of another blind hymnwriter, George Matheson, that God made him blind so he could see clearly in other ways and become a guide to others. This same tribute could be applied to Fanny Crosby, who triumphed over her handicap and used it to the glory of God.

15

Alexander Maclaren
1826–1910

Years ago, every Scottish father wanted a son in the ministry. David Maclaren was no exception. A gifted lay preacher and dedicated Christian businessman in Glasgow, Maclaren did all he could to encourage his son. One day he took him to see the Reverend Charles Stovel, a pastor friend.

"Do you think the lad would make a minister?" Maclaren asked.

The pastor thought for a while, then replied, "Well, perhaps he might."

It was a historic ecclesiastical understatement, for Alexander Maclaren became one of the greatest preachers of the nineteenth century—an era that gave us Charles H. Spurgeon, R. W. Dale, Joseph Parker, and Henry Liddon. His printed sermons are models of scholarly, yet practical, exposition. His monumental *Expositions of Holy Scripture* is an excellent homiletical tool that has continually proved its worth ever since the first volume on Genesis was published in 1904. "A man who reads one of Maclaren's sermons," said W. Robertson Nicoll, "must either take his outline—or take another text." One listener said, "This man is a prophet, and you must either listen and swallow, or flee." Parker said there was "no greater preacher than Alexander Maclaren in the English-speaking pulpit."

How did he do it? The answer is simple: through hard work, disciplined study, and concentration on the one important thing—preaching the Word. He turned down most speaking and social invitations. He stayed home, did his work, and built a great church. "I began my ministry," he told a group of young preachers, "with the determination of concentrating all my available strength on the work, the proper work of the Christian ministry, the pulpit. . . . I have tried to make my ministry a ministry of exposition of Scripture." Maclaren would weep if he saw how some pastors today rarely if ever preach; they prefer bringing in guest luminaries to disciplining themselves to study and preach the Word of God. Maclaren was known to devote sixty hours to the preparation of a single message.

He was born in Glasgow, Scotland, in 1826. His father was recognized as a capable expositor of the Word; even though his business often took him away from home for long periods of time, David Maclaren had a godly influence on his son. (By the way, the family name was originally spelled "McLaren," but during his student days Alexander changed it. "I do not like the Highland way of spelling the name," he wrote to his family. You will see both spellings in homiletical literature.) After wrestling with the doctrine of election, young Alexander finally yielded to Christ and in 1840 was baptized into the fellowship of the Hope Street Baptist Church. (Some books, including the biography by Carlile, incorrectly give the year as 1838.)

The family moved to London, and Maclaren enrolled in Stepney College in 1842. He immediately proved to be a leading student. He loved Hebrew and Greek and graduated with honors in both. All his life, Maclaren read two chapters a day in the original, one from the Old Testament and one from the New. He did his sermonic work directly from the Hebrew and Greek.

In 1845 he was sent to preach at a run-down church in Southampton; the people were so impressed they called him to be their pastor. After graduation the following year he began his ministry at Portland Chapel, a church that had suffered greatly under an incompetent pastor who had plunged them into debt and given the church a bad reputation in the community. The building needed repair, and the church was not even sure it could pay the new pastor's salary. "If the worst comes to worst," Maclaren wrote home, "I shall at all events not have to reflect that I have killed a flourishing plant, but only assisted at the funeral of a withered one. . . . The difficulties will keep me busy and prevent my relapsing into idleness."

Years later he told ministerial students:

> I thank God that I was stuck down in a quiet, little, obscure place to begin my ministry; for that is what spoils half of you young fellows. You get pitchforked into prominent positions at once, and then fritter yourselves away in all manner of little engagements that you call duties . . . instead of stopping at home and reading your Bibles, and getting near to God. I thank God for the early years of struggle and obscurity.[1]

It is worth noting that Joseph Parker, G. Campbell Morgan, and Charles H. Spurgeon all began their ministries in small places, and during those "hidden years" laid the foundations for their future works.

The work at Portland Chapel prospered. Debts were paid, the building repaired, and the district awakened to the young preacher. His hard work and godly life were paying spiritual dividends. In 1856 Maclaren married his cousin, Marion Maclaren; he claimed later that his ministry would have been impossible without her. Two years later he was called to preach at Union Chapel, Manchester. He accepted and there began an amazing forty-five-year term that gave him the name "Maclaren of Manchester."

He loved nature, and yet he was placed in the midst of an ugly manufacturing city. He was shy and retiring, yet surrounded by thousands of people. He was a student of the Word, and yet the cosmopolitan population that would attend his church would expect a "message for the times." The demands would be heavy, and yet he must find time to study, meditate, and pray.

History repeated itself: the church grew and had to move into a new edifice that seated nearly two thousand. Maclaren had changed his location, but not his disciplines. He still refused most invitations and concentrated on studying the Word and feeding his people. He was not a visiting pastor, and he repeatedly challenged the adage that "a home-going pastor makes a church-going people." He reminded ministerial students that the adage is true only if, when the people come to church, they hear something worth coming for.

Maclaren's natural shyness led many to think he was proud and aloof. He rarely gave interviews to the press. His first was to Arthur Porritt, the noted Christian journalist, who tells about it in his charming book *The Best I Remember*:

> Dr. Maclaren was rather an exasperating subject for an interviewer. He said the most interesting things, downright indiscreet things (which of course, make the best "copy"), but having said them he would purse his lips in a roguish way and say, "I'm thinking that that will not have to go into the interview; you'll leave it out, won't you?"[2]

One vacation he had his picture taken by a local photographer who did not know how famous his customer was. The photographer put the portrait in his window and was amazed at the number of people who wanted to purchase copies—but he had destroyed the negative! "That man might have told me he was famous," he complained, "but he didn't look like it!" Maclaren was simply obeying his own admonition: "To efface one's self is one of a preacher's first duties. The herald should be lost in his message."

It was probably fear of becoming a popular idol that motivated him to refuse an invitation many wish he had accepted—the opportunity to deliver the Yale lectures on preaching. He was begged to accept, but to this too he said no.

Surprisingly, Maclaren was haunted all his life by a sense of failure. Often he suffered "stage fright" before a service, but in the pulpit he was perfectly controlled. He sometimes spoke of each Sunday's demands as "a woe," and he was certain that his sermon was not good enough and that the meeting would be a failure. After accepting an invitation to preach at some special occasion, he would fret about it and wonder if there were any way to escape. After the meeting he would lament that he had done poorly. Sometimes he became depressed, but then he would say, "Well, I can't help it, I did my best, and there I leave it."

Maclaren was a perfectionist and an idealist. Hence he was never satisfied with his own work. Perhaps that is how the Lord keeps gifted people humble, and Maclaren was both. Maybe there is a warning here for preachers: let God evaluate your ministry, for often when we think we are doing our poorest, we are really doing our best. Woe to the man who becomes satisfied with his ministry!

To Maclaren, preparing messages was hard work. He often said he could never prepare sermons while wearing slippers: he always wore his outdoor boots. Studying was work, and he took it seriously. When you read his sermons, you can quickly tell that they were not "manufactured" between conferences and committee meetings. Maclaren was an expositor; he let the Bible do its own preaching. He studied a passage in the original language, meditated on it, sought its divine truth, and then "opened it up" in such a way that we wonder why we didn't see it before. No artificial divisions, no forced alliteration, nothing sensational; just divine truth presented so simply that any listener (or reader) could understand and apply it.

If you have not read Maclaren, start with *The Best of Alexander Maclaren*, edited by Gaius Glenn Atkins and published by Harper in 1949. Here are twenty of Maclaren's choice messages, a homiletical "sampler" that will whet your appetite for more. Then get the three-volume series *Sermons Preached in Manchester*. *Week-day Evening Addresses, The Secret of Power, A Year's Ministry, The Wearied Christ, Triumphant Certainties*, and *The God of the Amen* are other titles to watch for, and there are many more. His greatest literary achievement is the *Expositions of Holy Scripture*.

The standard biographies are: *Alexander Maclaren, D.D.: The Man and His Message* by John Charles Carlile; *Dr. McLaren of Manchester: A Sketch* by his cousin and sister-in-law, E. T. McLaren, who explains the spelling of the last name; and *The Life of Alexander Maclaren* by

David Williamson. There is also an article on him in *Princes of the Church* by W. Robertson Nicoll.

What was the "secret" of Maclaren's ministry? It could be summarized in two words: devotion and discipline. He was devoted to the Lord, and he walked with the Lord.

"Power for service is second," he told the Baptist World Congress in 1905. "Power for holiness and character is first." He said to a group of ministers, "The first, second, and third requisite for our work is personal godliness; without that, though I have the tongues of men and angels, I am harsh and discordant as sounding brass, monstrous and unmusical as a tinkling cymbal."

He fed on God's Word—not as a book for sermons, but as the source of his spiritual life and power. He meditated long hours and sought to understand the heart and mind of God. When he discovered a truth, he first applied it to himself and then sought the best way to share it with his people. But devotion without discipline can become shallow mysticism, and this pitfall Maclaren avoided. He scheduled his time and saw to it that none of it was wasted. He knew how to enjoy a vacation or an evening of relaxation, but even those times were opportunities for meditation and preparation. He did more by doing less. He knew how to say no. He did not feel obliged to attend every meeting, sit at every table, or grace every platform.

"This one thing I do" characterized his life as it ought to characterize our lives today. We may not have Maclaren's gifts, but certainly we can seek to follow his example.

16

J. B. Lightfoot
1828–1889

The English Revised Version of the New Testament was placed in the hands of the British people on May 17, 1881, culminating ten years of work by fifty-four outstanding scholars. Public response was predictable: this new version, with all its announced accuracy, could never replace the Authorized Version with its beauty and, above all, familiarity.

The Anglican clergy were confused: could they legally use the new version when only the old version was officially authorized by the church? The man in the street was critical and skeptical. After all, the translators had promised not to deviate too much from the King James Version, and yet they had made 36,000 changes. Perhaps the new version was more accurate, but the public preferred tradition to scholarship. Prime Minister William Gladstone stated the problem clearly: "You will sacrifice truth if you don't read it, and you will sacrifice the people if you do." But Charles H. Spurgeon put the finger on the real problem: "It is strong in Greek, weak in English."

Indeed the new version *was* "strong in Greek," and one reason was the presence on the New Testament Committee of the "Cambridge triumvirate"—B. F. Westcott, F. J. A. Hort, and J. B. Lightfoot—names that still stand for scholarship in New Testament studies. Of the three, Lightfoot was undoubtedly the best scholar. In fact, Owen Chadwick called Lightfoot "the greatest scholar in the Jerusalem Chamber."[1] In his memorial essay on Bishop Lightfoot, W. Robertson Nicoll called him "pre-eminently the scholar of the Church of England."[2]

If you have ever used Lightfoot's commentaries on Galatians, Philippians, and Colossians, or any of his studies on the church fathers, you probably agree with Nicoll's conclusion. But what you may not know is that Bishop Lightfoot was a godly man, a teacher of pastors, and a preacher with a burden for lost souls. "When goodness is joined to knowledge, it counts for much," wrote Nicoll, "and when these are crowned by spiritual power, paramount influence is the result. Lightfoot had all three."[3]

Joseph Barber Lightfoot was born in Liverpool on April 13, 1828. He was taught at King Edward's School, Birmingham, by the noted James Prince Lee, whose pupils seemed to capture every prize and move into places of influence, particularly in the church. Lee taught Lightfoot to love the Greek New Testament; and the teacher saw in the pupil tremendous potential for both Christian character and scholarship. "Give him the run of the town library!" Lee ordered.

At age nineteen, Lightfoot entered Trinity College, Cambridge, where he studied under Westcott. ("He was Westcott's best pupil," Hort later admitted.) He captured several honors and prizes and seemed destined for a teaching position. In 1854 he was ordained a deacon in the Church of England, and in 1858 he was ordained as a priest. The next year he became a tutor at Trinity College, and in 1861 was named Hulsean Professor of Divinity. So popular were his New Testament lectures that they had to be given in the college's great hall. Ten years later he was made canon of St. Paul's, sharing the ministry with the great Henry Liddon and Dean R. W. Church. He was named Lady Margaret Professor of Divinity in 1875, and it seemed that his ministry as scholar, writer, and teacher was established.

But in 1879 he was appointed bishop of Durham, and the scholar had to make the most critical decision of his life. In the last public message Bishop Lightfoot preached, on June 29, 1889, he confessed that he had spent a "long wakeful night" making the decision to leave Cambridge and a life of scholarship for Durham and a life of administration. He wrote to his friend Westcott:

> At length I have sent my answer "Yes." It seemed to me that to resist any longer would be to fight against God. My consolation and my hope for the future is that it has cost me the greatest moral effort, the greatest venture of faith which I ever made. Now that the answer is sent I intend to have no regrets about the past.

Westcott called the decision "a kind of martyrdom," and perhaps it was.

In the months that followed, Lightfoot received letters from all kinds of people urging him to continue his studies and writing in spite of his new ministry. In a memorial sermon to Lightfoot, given on November 24, 1929, George R. Eden said: "Few men can have passed through such an agony of choice as we know he suffered. . . . Yet the choice was made—upon his knees, 'wrestling with the Angel in prayer.'" It is interesting to note that R. W. Dale warned Westcott in 1883: "Forgive me for saying—do not let them make you a bishop. I do not know what Dr. Lightfoot may have done for Durham; for those of us who are outside he has done nothing since his elevation."

What did the great Greek scholar do for Durham and for the Church of England? His years as bishop are still called "the golden age of Durham."

Westcott preached the consecration sermon (April 25, 1879) and urged the new bishop to "choose between the important and the routine . . . and do the important." Lightfoot did so gladly, delegating routine matters to his associates and concentrating on the things only a bishop could do. Lightfoot was gifted with the mental, physical, and spiritual equipment a man needs to make a success of such a high office. He had a robust constitution and a love of hard work. An early riser, he put in two or three hours of study before breakfast, and he often remained at his desk when the rest of the staff had gone to bed. He had a remarkable memory and could tell a secretary where a quotation was in a given book, even its location on the page.

During a holiday in Norway, he was seen correcting proofs while riding in a cart on a rather precipitous road. He was a gifted linguist, fluent in French, German, Spanish, Italian, and Latin, as well as Greek; he was able to use Hebrew, Syriac, Arabic, Coptic, Ethiopic, and Armenian. He enjoyed telling the story about the professor who isolated several newborn babies to discover what language they would speak if not influenced by English. After a pause, Lightfoot would say, "The poor little children spoke pure Hebrew."

The new bishop was a worker and an innovator, much to the surprise and delight of the clergy under his jurisdiction. One of his first innovations was the "Brotherhood." Never married, Lightfoot each year "adopted" several young men who studied with him for a year before their ordination. It was an internship program on the highest level. But the bishop made it clear to applicants that the fellowship was "a brotherhood in Christ, not an exclusive association of clique or caste," and that their union was based on "participation in a common work and the loving devotion to a common Master." The bishop was their leader, teacher, example, and spiritual father. As one member of the Brotherhood put it, "We read, we worked, because Lightfoot was working and reading."

Men in the Brotherhood—"the sons of the house," as the bishop called them—were kept busy. They breakfasted with Lightfoot at 7:45, at 8:15 were in the chapel for morning prayers, and by 9:00 were either reading or listening to lectures. They ate lunch at 1:15, then scattered for practical ministry in the diocese. Each man was assigned a district where he worked with resident clergy. The men gathered during the week to share experiences and learn from one another, always under the watchful eye of the bishop. As the program developed, Bishop Lightfoot set aside St. Peter's Day (June 29) for an annual reunion of the "sons of the house." (Spurgeon followed a similar pattern with the men in his Pastors' College.)

The bishop viewed the Christian ministry highly, and he applied high standards to himself before he applied them to others. His essay

"The Christian Ministry" in his commentary on Philippians upset more than one Anglican, who saw it as a departure from Church of England tradition. His friend Canon Liddon requested him to withdraw the essay, but Lightfoot refused to do it. "The Christian minister, whatever else he is—and I shall not enter upon controversial questions—is, before all things, a pastor, a shepherd," said Lightfoot in his last public appearance in his diocese.

Bishop Lightfoot also blended scholarship and Christian devotion. I once listened to an impassioned sermon by a well-known preacher on the impossibility of being both "a soul-winner and a deep Bible student." The apostle Paul would have smiled at that sermon, as would Charles G. Finney, Jonathan Edwards, R. A. Torrey, Charles Spurgeon, and J. B. Lightfoot. All Greek students should write on the flyleaf of their Greek New Testament these words of Bishop Lightfoot: "After all is said and done, the only way to know the Greek Testament properly is by prayer."

Lightfoot's own walk with God was the secret power of his life, and his concern to obey God and help others find Christ motivated him. He reorganized his diocese so that pastors would be able to reach more people and build more new churches. A great admirer of John Wesley, Lightfoot organized lay evangelists who helped carry the message from district to district. He mobilized the women of the diocese and encouraged them to serve in "sisterhoods" or as deaconesses. Before long, Durham was vibrating with new power and excitement because a great Greek scholar had placed himself and his ambitions on the altar that he might serve God. What he said to the Brotherhood, he practiced himself: "You go where you are sent, you work till you drop."

Lightfoot is best remembered as a writer. His commentaries on Galatians, Philippians, Colossians, and Philemon ought to be in every pastor's library. These scholarly works are part of a series that he had projected with his friends Westcott and Hort. The series was not completed, but Westcott did publish excellent commentaries on the Gospel of John, Hebrews, and the Epistles of John. Lightfoot died before he could write his commentary on Ephesians to complete the quartet. Lightfoot also wrote four articles for *Smith's Dictionary of the Bible* (Acts, Romans, 1 Thessalonians, and 2 Thessalonians) and published the definitive edition of *The Apostolic Fathers*. The latter work demolished the position of the Tübingen school that centered around F. C. Baur, the German critic. More of a historian than a theologian, Lightfoot was at home with ancient documents and textual problems.

When an anonymous author attacked his friend Westcott in *Supernatural Religion*, Lightfoot took up his pen and wrote a series of articles for the *Contemporary Review* that pushed the bestselling book off the market. His facts were so devastating that the public rejected *Supernatural Religion*, and the book ended up glutting the used-book stores. Lightfoot's book *On a Fresh Revision of the English New Testament* is still available, as are several posthumous collections: *Ordination Addresses*, *Leaders in the Northern Church*, *Cambridge Sermons*, *Sermons Preached on Special Occasions*, *Sermons Preached in St. Paul's*, and *Historical Essays*.

Lightfoot had requested that no official biography be written; however, a memoir, *Bishop Lightfoot*, was published anonymously in 1894. Hort wrote the excellent article on Lightfoot in *The Dictionary of National Biography*; in fact, it was the last thing Hort wrote before his death. *Lightfoot of Durham: Memories and Appreciations* was edited by George R. Eden and F. C. Macdonald, and published in 1933.

Westcott did not heed Dale's warning. Not only did he become a bishop, but he succeeded Lightfoot at Durham. And his successor was one of Lightfoot's students, Handley C. G. Moule, also a Greek scholar and writer of commentaries. Durham was privileged to have men who combined academic excellence with spiritual fervor, resulting in a balanced ministry.

The day after Bishop Lightfoot died, one of the leading British newspapers, the *Times*, said: "He was at once one of the greatest Theological scholars and an eminent Bishop. It is scarcely possible to estimate adequately as yet the influence of his life and work." In preparing his "sons" for ordination, Bishop Lightfoot used to say:

"Forget me, forget the [ordination] service of tomorrow, forget the human questioner. Transport yourselves in thought from the initial to the final inquiry. The great day of inquisition, the supreme moment of revelation, is come. The chief Shepherd, the universal bishop of souls is the questioner. . . . The 'Wilt thou' of the ordination day is exchanged for the 'Hast thou' of the judgment day." This is good counsel for all of us, but especially for those who serve as ministers and who want to hear our Master say, "Well done."

17

R. W. Dale
1829–1895

Whenever John Angell James stepped into the pulpit of the Carr's Lane Congregational Church in Birmingham, England, he silently prayed that God would give him a successor who would carry on the great work of the church. Carr's Lane was one of the most influential churches in Great Britain, and James had been its pastor for over fifty years. He had a right to be concerned about his successor! How God provided that man is a remarkable story.

James wrote a religious bestseller called *The Anxious Inquirer After Salvation*, which sold some 200,000 copies within the first five years of publication. A copy of this book fell into the hands of an assistant schoolteacher in the little village of Andover in Hampshire, and the reading of that book led to the young man's conversion. Robert William Dale was fourteen years old at the time. Ten years later, in 1853, he was installed as co-pastor of the famous Carr's Lane Church; in 1859, when James died, Dale became the sole pastor. He devoted thirty-six years to that one church. When Dale died in 1895, the church called the famous John Henry Jowett to succeed him, and he remained there until 1911. It was during Jowett's ministry at Carr's

Lane that A. T. Pierson made the statement that "Carr's Lane is the finest church in the world."

The transition from James to Dale was not easy, either for the church or for the young successor. James was Calvinistic in his leanings, although he preached the Word of God and not a doctrinal system. "I do not seem to find much about Calvinism in the Bible!" he once told a friend who asked him why he was not preaching more Calvinistic sermons. When Dale began questioning unconditional election, total depravity, and limited atonement, some of the saints were horrified. Were it not for the fact that James privately intervened and told his unhappy leaders to be patient with their associate, Dale probably would have been dismissed. In fact, early in his ministry as co-pastor, Dale felt he was definitely out of place at Carr's Lane. An opportunity opened in a church in Manchester, and some of Dale's friends urged him to accept the call; loyal to his senior pastor, Dale laid the matter before James and asked him to make the decision. Without hesitation, James replied, "Stay!" And Dale stayed! Subsequent events would indicate that the decision was a wise one.

R. W. Dale was a perplexing combination of preacher, theologian, politician, and denominational leader. Most pastors are happy to encourage their members to get involved in matters of government while they themselves concentrate on spiritual matters. But Dale's convictions drove him right into the middle of some of England's most explosive political issues. Dale saw no difference between God's working in the church and his working in government. To him there was no separation between the secular and the sacred. God was just as concerned about the government of Birmingham as he was the government of Carr's Lane Church. For this reason, nearly one-third of the 750-page biography written by his son is devoted to matters of British politics. Those of us who have never been initiated into the mysteries of home rule, parliament, and the British educational system will probably read these pages dutifully but not very profitably.

It was as a theologian and a preacher of doctrine that Dale excelled. "I hear you are preaching doctrinal sermons to the congregation at

Carr's Lane," an experienced preacher said to Dale one day when they met on the street. "They will not stand it." Dale replied, "They will *have* to stand it." And they did. From these doctrinal sermons came some of the books that helped make Dale a famous man: *The Atonement, Christian Doctrine, The Living Christ and the Four Gospels,* and *Christ and the Future Life.* His books on the Ten Commandments, Ephesians, and James are familiar to most well-read pastors.

There is an interesting story in connection with his book *The Living Christ and the Four Gospels.* Dale was preparing an Easter sermon when the truth of Christ's physical resurrection burst upon him with compelling power. "Christ is alive!" he said aloud; "He is alive—alive!" He began to walk about the room saying to himself, "Christ is living! Christ is living!" Not only that following Easter Sunday, but for months afterward he exulted in the theme of the resurrected Christ. He even began the practice of having a resurrection hymn sung each Sunday morning, just to remind the people that they were worshiping a living Christ.

Dale wore his hair cut short, but had a full beard and moustache. Some of the older people in his church were scandalized when the moustache appeared, and several even wrote letters to the newspapers in protest! They felt it gave him "an air of levity and worldliness." There is no record that anybody was upset over his smoking. "Food and drink he could forego without a pang," wrote his son, "but cut off from tobacco, he was little better than a lost soul."

A dark thread of depression ran through Dale's life, and often he spoke of "the strange, morbid gloominess" that he had to battle, sometimes for weeks at a time. These periods of depression may have had their physical causes, but it is likely that Dale's own personal struggles with doctrine and duty were partly responsible. Once he wrote, "I do not envy those who walk through life with no questionings, no mental struggles." These seasons of depression would come without warning and often leave as suddenly as they came.

One day Dale was in a depressed mood, walking down a Birmingham street, when a poor lady passed him and said, "God bless you, Dr. Dale!" He asked her name, but she refused to give it.

"Never mind my name," she said, "but if you could only know how you have made me feel hundreds of times, and what a happy home you have given me—God bless you!"

As she hurried away she seemed to take the dark cloud with her. Dale said, "The mist broke, the sunlight came, I breathed the free air of the mountains of God." (Church members take note: sincere appreciation is good medicine for faithful pastors.)

Shortly after he became the sole pastor of Carr's Lane, Dale began to have sincere doubts about the traditional Christian doctrines of man's immortality and eternal punishment. When he attempted to preach on judgment, he found the experience "costly." Fifteen years later, in 1874, he publicly committed himself to the doctrine of annihilation—the idea that only those possessing eternal life in Christ would live forever.

When Moody and Sankey came to Birmingham in 1875 for their first revival meeting, Dale threw himself into the effort with enthusiasm. Years later, Dale told G. Campbell Morgan that D. L. Moody was the only preacher whom he felt had a right to preach about hell. "I never heard Moody refer to hell without tears in his voice." Many of the clergy in Birmingham were opposed to the Moody meetings, some because of his simple gospel message and others because of his "American methods." More than one preacher published rather severe criticisms, including Archibald Campbell Tait, the archbishop of Canterbury. Dale rose to Moody's defense and published a pamphlet called *The Day of Salvation: A Reply to the Letter of the Archbishop of Canterbury on Mr. Moody and Mr. Sankey*. No doubt Dale and Moody had their own disagreements, but this did not keep them from being friends and laboring together to win souls. Dale reported that he received about two hundred new members from the meetings, and he concluded years later that about seventy-five percent of them "stood well."

Now for an interesting sequel to these events: nine years later Moody returned to Birmingham, and again Dale cooperated with the meetings. But Dale thought he detected a change in the evangelist and in the converts. Moody's emphasis in 1875 had been the free grace of God, but now his emphasis seemed to be repentance "as though it were a doing of penance." Dale wrote that Moody was "just as earnest, as vigorous, as impressive as before. People were deeply moved. Hundreds went into the inquiry room every night. But the results, as far as I can learn, have been inconsiderable.... I have seen none of the shining faces that used to come to me after his former visit." Dale did the Christian thing and wrote to Moody, sharing his convictions; the evangelist replied that Dale's letter had "set him a-thinking." Whether it was Moody's preaching or Dale's doctrinal vantage-point that had changed, we do not know.

Whether or not Dale's theology is agreeable, it must be admitted that it was a living reality to him and not a dead abstraction. What he believed, he sought to live—no matter the cost. If his beliefs led him to the lecture platform to oppose the state church, or into the political arena to fight for better education, he willingly obeyed.

In 1877 Dale was invited to give the Yale lectures on preaching, and there is every indication that he was quite a success. His series is published under the prosaic title *Nine Lectures on Preaching*. It is not an exciting book, but it is a helpful one. When he returned home, Dale tried to persuade Charles H. Spurgeon and Alexander Maclaren to accept the invitation to lecture at Yale, but both refused. Spurgeon's reply to the invitation was "I sit on my own gate and whistle my own tunes and am quite content."

Dale was a man who loved the city, and the city of Birmingham in his day was hardly the Garden of Eden. Dale could have pastored a comfortable church in a quiet town, but he chose to minister in the city. This, he felt, was God's calling. While on a European holiday in 1863 he wrote to his wife: "The Lake of Lucerne . . . is before me—the noblest scenery, as some think, in all Europe; but I declare that there is nothing in this magnificent view which makes me feel half the thrill I have sometimes felt when I have looked down on the smoky streets of Birmingham from the railway, as I have returned to my work among you after a holiday. The thought of having to do, more or less directly, with all that mass of human thought and action, which is covered with the ceaseless smoke which hangs over us—the thought that you and I together may, with God's help, save multitudes—sends the blood through one's veins with the exultation and glow which the most magnificent aspects of the material universe cannot create." In this day when our great cities desperately need a steady evangelical witness, this kind of excitement is heartening. May his tribe increase!

In June 1893, G. Campbell Morgan began his ministry at the Westminster Road Congregational Church in Birmingham, England; a month later he visited Dr. and Mrs. Dale in their home. Since he was not a graduate of a recognized college or seminary, Morgan was concerned about his "inadequate qualifications" as a pastor in the great city of Birmingham. He shared his concern with Dale, and Dale solved the problem immediately. "Never say that you are untrained! God has many ways of training men. I pray that you will have much joy in His service."

Two years later on March 13, 1895, Dr. R. W. Dale died, bringing to a close thirty-six years of ministry at Carr's Lane. An unfinished sermon lay on his study desk. The last sentence read: "—that, after our mortal years are spent, there is a larger, fuller, richer life in—." The sentence was broken, but the life was completed.

The biography of Dale written by his son, Sir A. W. W. Dale, was published in 1898 by Hodder and Stoughton in London. Be prepared to wade through 750 pages of material, some of which—particularly the sections dealing with British politics—is painfully dull. But Principal A. M. Fairbairn's appendix on "Dale as a Theologian" is probably the best analysis of Dale's doctrinal position you will find anywhere. I especially like the sentence, "He ceased to be a Calvinist without becoming an Arminian."

Regardless of his theological classification, R. W. Dale is a man worth knowing, especially in this day when there is a tendency for us to divorce theology from ethics and from the practical ministries of the church. As Fairbairn put it, "It is not simply the heart, it is the whole man that makes the theologian."[1] Perhaps we need this kind of wholeness today.

18

Joseph Parker
1830–1902

If some homiletically inclined archangel were to permit me to select another time and place in which to live, I immediately would ask to be transported to Great Britain during the reign of Queen Victoria. What a paradise for preachers! On any given Lord's Day you could hear Charles H. Spurgeon at the Metropolitan Tabernacle or, at the other end of the spectrum, Canon Henry Liddon at St. Paul's. Pick the right year and D. L. Moody might be in London or any one of a dozen other cities in Great Britain; F. B. Meyer would be leading people into a closer walk with Christ; William Booth would be thundering against the sins of the city; and Alexander Maclaren in Manchester, R. W. Dale in Birmingham, and Alexander Whyte in Edinburgh each would be opening the Word to crowded congregations. But if I were in London on a Lord's Day and had already heard Spurgeon preach, I would hasten to the City Temple and there sit at the feet of Joseph Parker, whose congregations were second in size only to those of Spurgeon. That saintly friend of great preachers, W. Robertson Nicoll, said of Parker, "I have never heard him preach without saying, 'I want to be a better man.'" The popular evangelist John McNeill called Parker "Matthew Henry up to date—the Gladstone of the pulpit." Without benefit of formal training, this son of a Northumbrian stonemason ministered the Word of God in power for more than fifty years, and his ministry continues today in the books that he has left us.

Joseph Parker was born on April 9, 1830, at Hexham-on-Tyne, Northumberland, and spent the first twenty-two years of his life in that town. While just a lad, he was led to faith in Christ by his father and his Sunday school teacher while the three of them were walking home from church one summer Sunday night. He soon began to teach a Sunday school class and to study the Bible diligently. In fact, he used to get up at 6:00 each morning in order to have time for reading, and he met with a local minister who tutored him in Greek. One June afternoon in 1848, he preached his first sermon. He stood at the sawpit on the village green and (as he described it) "broke like a sudden thunderstorm on that rural calm with the text: 'It shall be more tolerable for Tyre and Sidon at the judgment, than for you' (Luke 10:14)." The assembled saints had already heard two speakers, but Parker was sure God wanted him to preach; so he borrowed a New Testament from the second speaker, opened his mouth, and preached! "In accompanying my friends to the place of meeting," he wrote that same year, "the idea of preaching did not occur to my mind. I went out a hearer; I came back a preacher."[1]

In 1851 he married Ann Nesbitt, and the next year he went to London as an assistant to John Campbell at Whitefield's Tabernacle. Campbell recognized Parker's gifts just as readily as he did his limitations and determined to assist the young man in his desire to preach the gospel. Nearly half a century later, Joseph Parker would lay the cornerstone for the new Whitefield's Tabernacle, and he would be known as one of the preaching giants of his day.

He remained at the tabernacle until November 8, 1853, when he became the pastor of the Banbury Congregational Church in Oxfordshire. The place was run down, but before long it was throbbing with activity and a new and larger sanctuary had to be built. During his five years at Banbury, Parker took courses at the University College in London and also managed to publish four books that met with moderate success. He also had seven invitations to other churches, none of which he accepted. "All the Banbury days were happy so far as they could be made happy by friendship and love and sympathy," he wrote in *A Preacher's Life*. "A very happy life is the life of a country pastor."

But he was not to remain a country pastor. In July 1858, he accepted a call to the Cavendish Street Congregational Church in Manchester. "I was never more coldly received in my life," he said, describing the first Sunday he preached as a guest minister. He preached two Sundays and then was asked to preach a third Sunday inasmuch as the next man, Samuel Martin of Westminister Chapel, had been forced to cancel. It was a wealthy church, and the coldness of the people in "their Gothic sepulcher" irritated Parker. "Every man seemed to be looking at me over the top of a money-bag!" But the Lord conquered, and Parker accepted the call. That same year Alexander Maclaren came to the Union Baptist Chapel in Manchester, and the two men were to become close friends. In 1862, Parker was granted an honorary doctor of divinity degree by the University of Chicago. He published four more books during his eleven years in Manchester and shared in the wider work of the Congregational Union.

"It never entered my mind that I could leave Manchester," he wrote. "What could any man desire more than some two thousand regular hearers, one of the finest buildings in Nonconformity, and one of the greatest cities in the country!" But on October 22, 1867, a deputation from the Poultry Chapel in London met with Parker and asked him to come and rescue their work. The church had an illustrious past. It had been founded in 1640 by that eminent divine Thomas Goodwin, meeting first in Anchor-Lane, Thames Street. It moved four times in the next two centuries, finally settling at Poultry in Cheapside. But the area was changing, and the ministry had to find both a new location and a new lease on life.

The church issued a formal call to Parker on November 7, 1867, and on March 11, 1868, he declined the call. But they renewed the call on June 25, and Parker gave it serious consideration. The Poultry Chapel had been without a pastor for fifteen months, and the situation was desperate. Parker was very happy with his Manchester ministry and had no earthly reason to make a change. But there was a divine reason: the Head of the church wanted him to minister in London. On September 19, 1869, Joseph Parker began thirty-three phenomenal years as pastor of the City Temple. He preached for three years in the old Poultry Chapel, then sold it and built a new auditorium at the Holborn Viaduct in the City of London (London consists of twenty-eight boroughs, plus the City of London where the Lord Mayor and his council function). On May 19, 1874, the new City Temple was opened with Lindsay Alexander of Edinburgh bringing the message from John 1:16. From that pulpit Parker preached three times a week: twice on Sundays and at noon every Thursday. His Sunday congregations filled the auditorium, which seated three thousand; he would address a thousand or more at the noonday service.

What kind of a man was Joseph Parker? His close friend W. Robertson Nicoll warns us: "To estimate aright a personality so great, so complex, and so many-sided as that of Dr. Parker, is a task so difficult that I shrink from attempting it."[2] He then proceeds to give us the finest study on Parker that you will find anywhere!

Some called Parker an egotist. The famous theologian P. T. Forsythe remarked, "At one time I thought Dr. Parker was a good man touched with egotism; I have come to believe that he is an egotist touched with goodness." In his chapter on Parker in *The Best I Remember*, Arthur Porritt commented: "The judgment was harsh; but Dr. Parker always drew the lightning. Men either believed in him implicitly or voted him a poseur and a charlatan."[3]

To begin with, his was a strong personality. He was a law unto himself, and nobody inside or outside his church dared to annul that law. After the stewards took the collection, they handed it over to him. He managed all the financial affairs of the church—and gave an accounting to nobody. When they were designing his new church, the architects asked him what style of building he wanted, and he replied: "Any style! But build me such a church that when Queen Victoria drives into the city she will say, 'Why, what place is that?'—and she will be told, 'That is where Joseph Parker preaches!'"

An egotist? Perhaps not. A dramatist? In every fiber of his being! J. D. Jones put it this way in his delightful autobiography, *Three Score Years and Ten*: "He was boisterous, sometimes perhaps bombastic, but he had drama, he had passion, he had genius, he had great flashes of inspiration which made other preachers seem dull in comparison. When Parker died our greatest preacher passed. We never shall see his like again."[4]

His physical appearance immediately attracted attention. "His massive figure, and his leonine head, with its shaggy locks, would have attracted attention anywhere," Alexander Gammie wrote in *Preachers I Have Heard*. "The gleaming eyes, the sweeping gestures, the constantly changing inflection of his wonderful voice, at one moment like a roar of thunder and the next soft as a whisper, held any audience spellbound. And there was always the element of the unexpected in what he said and how he said it."[5]

Yet beneath Parker's rough exterior and dramatic pose was a feeling of inferiority that tortured him. He was not academically trained; he was a shy man who really had few close friends; he had a constant fear that the weather would rob him of his huge congregations; he feared criticism; he lived in perpetual fear that he would say or do something wrong. He did not believe that people really loved him or appreciated his ministry, and he had to be told over and over again that his congregation's affections for him were real and lasting.

He lived for his wife, his preaching, and his writing; nothing else really mattered. Perhaps Parker himself has given us the best picture of the man. When a smaller congregation invited him to become their pastor, he replied: "An eagle does not roost in a sparrow's nest!" That is what he was—an ecclesiastical eagle, living in solitude in the heights, surveying God's revelation, and descending to deliver his oracles. But is there anything wrong with eagles?

In 1889, A. C. Dixon was in London for the International Sunday School Convention, and he visited the notable churches. He sent this impression back home:

Joseph Parker, at the City Temple, is said by some to be the personification of pomposity. He did not so impress us. He has a stately manner, but his thoughts are stately. Both of the sermons we heard were thoroughly evangelical, and Christ was held forth with a pathos and a power that melted many hearts. We thanked God for Joseph Parker. The one criticism that we could make is that he puts too much condensed thought into one sermon. It made my head ache to follow him for one hour.[6]

That criticism is not heard much today!

Joseph Parker was first and foremost a preacher, and he held the highest possible views of preaching. One Sunday evening, September 28, 1884, Parker announced to his congregation that he was planning to preach straight through the Bible and have the sermons stenographically recorded and then published in a twenty-five volume set to be called *The People's Bible* (not *The Speaker's Bible*, as stated in *20 Centuries of Great Preaching*;[7] *The Speaker's Bible* was edited by James and Edward Hastings). For the next seven years, three times a week, he preached in this manner, with his publishers regularly issuing new volumes of the sermons. In May 1895, Parker wrote the final paragraphs for volume 25, completing what he considered to be his lifework. This set ought to be in the library of every serious preacher of the Word. It has been reprinted by Baker Books under the title *Preaching Through the Bible*.

This is a remarkable series of sermons. His stenographer—and one of his biographers—Albert Dawson tells us that Parker did not like to read what he had preached, so it was left to his secretary to read the proofs. The prayers and sermons in *The People's Bible* are exactly what Parker spoke from his pulpit. "The language is the language of the moment," he wrote in that final volume.[8] "Every man can best follow his own method. I have followed mine." You will find as much spiritual food in Parker's prayers as in his sermons, so be sure to read them. In fact, reading a prayer daily, or at the beginning of each Lord's Day, might be a profitable exercise for the pastor.

How was he able to accomplish so much? He tells us in a chapter entitled "Retrospective" in *Studies in Texts*: "I have lived for my work. That is all. If I had talked all the week, I could not have preached on Sunday. That is all. If I had attended committee meetings, immersed myself in politics and undertaken the general care of the Empire, my strength would have been consumed. That is all. Mystery there is none. I have made my preaching work my delight, the very festival of my soul. That is all. Young brother, go thou and do likewise, and God bless thee!"[9] Parker was in his study every morning at 7:30. He would read the newspapers and answer correspondence and then devote himself to his studies or to writing. He would then take a long walk, usually on Hampstead Heath, during which he meditated on his texts, often talking to himself. He would put a few notes on paper and preach from that outline. Early in his ministry he had written his sermons in full, but he later abandoned that practice. "When I stand up to preach," he confessed, "I hardly ever know the sentence I am going to utter. The subject itself I endeavor to know well."

His concern for young pastors led him to establish The Institute of Homiletics, which met Monday mornings at the City Temple, with Parker presiding. Some of his Institute addresses, and evaluations of sermons, are found in the helpful set *Studies in Texts*, originally published in six volumes but reissued by Baker Books in three volumes. While not as valuable as *The People's Bible*, the set is still a treasury of homiletical gems that the hardworking preacher can mine for himself. Most of Parker's other books (he wrote at least forty) have passed from the scene; but no matter. The valuable books he left behind will establish him as one of history's greatest preachers.

As he grew older, Parker was concerned about the future of the City Temple. After all, "what can the man do that cometh after the king?" (Eccles. 2:12). It seems that Parker himself was confused: he told J. H. Jowett that he wanted him to be his successor, and apparently the City Temple officers agreed with this; but Parker also laid hands on R. J. Campbell, the popular pastor of Union Church in Brighton. Parker knew Campbell and felt the young man would carry on the kind of ministry to which Parker had given his life. But Parker was wrong.

Parker died on November 28, 1902, and Campbell was called. For the first two years Campbell's ministry was exciting and successful; but then Campbell began preaching his "new theology," and the bullets began to fly. (One theologian compared Campbell's "new theology" to a bad photograph—under-developed and over-exposed!) Along with his liberal views of the Bible, Campbell had socialistic convictions that did not impress his congregation, and ultimately he had to leave the church. In 1916 he was ordained in the Church of England, an act that would have stunned Parker. For when Parker had stood in the pulpit reading his wife's burial certificate, he burst into tears when he got to the part about her being buried in "unconsecrated ground." Parker had said during his ministry, "Should a time ever come when any message other than the pure gospel of Christ should go forth from this pulpit, let 'Ichabod' be written across the portals!" During Campbell's ministry, some brave soul did actually paint "Ichabod" in living color against the grey stone facade of the church!

"In my judgment," wrote Parker seven years before he died, "the only preaching that can do profound and lasting good must be biblical. . . . Any pulpit that founds itself on personal invention, cleverness, ingenuity, audacity or affected originality will most surely cover itself with humiliation and pass into merited oblivion." In his autobiography, *A Preacher's Life*, he wrote, "I believe in the permanence of the institution of preaching." For this reason, today's preachers would do well to read Joseph Parker and get acquainted with preaching that not only meets the needs of the times, but stands above the times because it is founded on the Word of God.

19

J. Hudson Taylor
1832–1905

A Presbyterian moderator in a Melbourne, Australia, church used all his eloquence to introduce the visiting missionary speaker, finally presenting him to the congregation as "our illustrious guest." He was not prepared for James Hudson Taylor's first sentence: "Dear friends, I am the little servant of an illustrious Master."

Nearly twenty years before, Hudson Taylor had written in an editorial: "All God's giants have been weak men, who did great things for God because they reckoned on His being with them." As he looked at himself, Hudson Taylor saw nothing but weakness; but as generations of Christians have studied Taylor's life, they have become acquainted with a man who dared to believe the Word of God and, by faith, carried the gospel to inland China—and saw God work wonders! "Want of trust is at the root of almost all our sins and all our weaknesses," he wrote in that same editorial, "and how shall we escape it but by looking to Him and observing His faithfulness. The man who holds God's faithfulness will not be foolhardy or reckless, but he will be ready for every emergency."

How Hudson Taylor became a man of faith is a story that every Christian—and every Christian worker in particular—ought to know well, because in that story is the kind of spiritual encouragement that we need in these difficult days.

Begin by reading *Hudson Taylor's Spiritual Secret*, written by his son and daughter-in-law, Howard and Mary Taylor. It is available in several paperback editions, although a cloth edition may still be available from the Overseas Missionary Fellowship, formerly known as the China Inland Mission. You may want to read the book twice—it is not long or difficult—and then secure the one-volume biography of Taylor by the same authors. The China Inland Mission published a beautiful centennial edition in 1965, but it is difficult to secure now. Fortunately, Moody Press has reprinted it in paperback with the title *God's Man in China*. This one-volume biography is a careful abridgement of a definitive two-volume work—*Hudson Taylor in Early Years* and *Hudson Taylor and the China Inland Mission*. If I were teaching a pastoral theology course in a seminary, I would require my students to read these two books to discover how God builds a man and then uses that man to build a work. It is unfortunate that this set is now out of print. The abridgement gives us all the important material we need, but the larger work includes sidelights and details that delight any reader interested in living history.

James Hudson Taylor was born on May 21, 1832, in Barnsley, Yorkshire, England. Taylor's parents were godly people who had dedicated their firstborn to the Lord, for their heart's desire was that their son serve Christ. Even while still a child of four or five, Hudson Taylor showed a concern for the "heathen" in foreign lands. "When I am a man," he would tell visitors in the home, "I mean to be a missionary and go to China." His father was a chemist (American translation: druggist) by trade and was very active as a Methodist preacher in his district. Often the local pastors would gather at the Taylor table to discuss their work, and young Hudson would listen with keen interest. "I used to love to hear them talk," he recalled years later. "Theology, sermons, politics, the Lord's work at home and abroad, all were discussed with so much earnestness and intelligence. It made a great impression upon us as children."

He had just turned seventeen when he was converted, and a short time later he felt a call to Christian service. He had experienced most of the trials and temptations of youth, and the tugging of the Holy Spirit on his heart; but for some reason he had resisted the call of God. The story of his conversion has often been told, but it is one that gets more wonderful with each telling. His mother had left him home alone while she visited a friend nearly a hundred miles away. Impressed by the Spirit to pray for her son, she left the table, went to her room, locked the door, and prayed for hours until she sensed in her heart that young Hudson had trusted Christ. Back at home, Hudson had found a tract in his father's library and was reading it primarily for the interesting stories that it might contain. While he was reading, he was struck by the phrase "the finished work of Christ." Immediately the words of Scripture leaped into his mind: "It is finished!" He said to himself, "If the whole work was finished and the whole debt paid, what is there left for me to do?" He fell to his knees and yielded himself to Christ; and when his mother returned home two weeks later, she told him she already knew!

Most people forget that Taylor was trained in medicine, and it was during his student days that he learned to trust God for every need. He realized that he could not leave England for some foreign land if he had not learned to prove God at home. How he trusted God for finances, not only for himself but also for others; how he was miraculously spared after being infected in the dissecting room; and how he grew in his exercise of faith are all told in the biographies, and what exciting chapters they are! You feel as if you are revisiting the book of Acts.

At this point Taylor's life takes on special interest for the Christian worker, for it is easy to see that Taylor permitted God to prepare him for the work he was calling him to do. It is for this reason that his biographers have devoted an entire volume of over five hundred pages to these first twenty-eight years of his life, his years of preparation. They say in the introduction to *Hudson Taylor in Early Years*:

At first sight it might appear to some that to devote not less than half of the biography of one who did a great deal of public work, to a description of his preparation for that work, evidences some lack of the sense of due proportion. The authors were fully alive to this aspect of the subject; but as they studied and pondered over the materials at their disposal, it was impressed upon them, with growing force, that the experience and the career of Mr. Taylor furnished a notable illustration of the truth that when God raises up a man for special service He first works in that man the principles which later on are, through his labors and influence, to be the means of widespread blessing to the Church and to the world.[1]

We need this emphasis today. We have too many "celebrities" and not enough servants—"nine-day wonders" that may flash across the scene for a time and then disappear. Before God works *through* us, he works *in* us, because the work that we do is the outgrowth of the life that we live. Jesus spent thirty years preparing for three years of ministry! The statement may have become a cliché, but it is still true that "God prepares us for what he is preparing for us."

On September 19, 1853, Hudson Taylor sailed for China as a representative of the Chinese Evangelization Society; even on the ship he had opportunity to witness for Christ and to trust God for miracles. At one stage of the voyage the ship lost its wind and began to drift toward a dangerous reef. Taylor and three other Christians on board prayed earnestly for God's help, and after a brief time of prayer, Taylor was convinced in his heart that God had answered. He went on deck and suggested to the first officer ("a godless man") that he let down the mainsail and make ready for the wind. The man cursed and refused to act. At that point the corner of the topmost sail began to tremble, and Taylor urged the man to move quickly. Before long, a strong wind began to blow and the ship was on its way!

From the very outset of his ministry in China, Hudson Taylor preferred to work independently. He had no particular denominational connections, yet was friendly with all who professed to know Christ. (His own convictions were Baptist.) He did medical work but was not a doctor; he did pastoral work but was not ordained.

His life of discipline and sacrifice distinguished him among the missionaries. This does not mean that he rejected those who worked in the traditional ways. It was just that he preferred an independent ministry that left him free to follow God's leading without consulting the plans of men. It was this kind of devotion to Christ that led him to resign from the Chinese Evangelization Society in June 1857. Eight years later, on June 27, 1865, he officially founded the China Inland Mission.

On January 20, 1858, Hudson Taylor married Maria J. Dyer in China, and their romance is a love story that no fiction writer could concoct! For a detailed account read *Hudson Taylor and Maria* by John Pollock. Pollock claimed that the official biography errs in the order of events relating to Hudson's courting of Miss Dyer, suggesting that the missionary's memory failed him when he told his daughter-in-law the story years later.[2]

But the real bombshell in the Pollock book is his claim that in 1869, during the darkest hours of the mission, Hudson Taylor was so discouraged that he was tempted to end his own life! "Maria stood between Hudson and suicide," stated Pollock.[3] I once asked a veteran CIM missionary about this, and he claimed it was probably a misunderstanding. Pollock's source, he added, is "an unpublished note in the Taylor papers." Even if Hudson Taylor *did* express this kind of despair, two things are true: greater men than he have done the same (Moses and Elijah, for example); and he expressed it only *before* he experienced "the exchanged life." In fact, it was the valley experience of the Yanchow riots that prepared the way for his life-changing meeting with Christ.

There is no need for me to retell the story; you have it in *Hudson Taylor's Spiritual Secret*. On Saturday, September 4, 1869, Taylor read in a letter from missionary John McCarthy about the new freedom that had come into McCarthy's life. "Not a striving to have faith," McCarthy wrote, "but a looking off to the Faithful One seems all we need; a resting in the Loved One entirely, for time and for eternity." "As I read," said Taylor, "I saw it all. I looked to Jesus, and when I saw— oh, how joy flowed!" The "theology of the deeper life" is disturbing to some people, and for this reason they avoid it; but for Hudson Taylor "the exchanged life" was as simple and as real as salvation itself. His associates noticed the difference: he had a new power in ministry and a new poise in facing the problems of the mission. "He cast everything on God in a new way, and gave more time to prayer," wrote one co-laborer. "Instead of working late at night, be began to go to bed earlier, rising at 5:00 to give time to Bible study and prayer." I cannot urge you enough to read the whole story for yourself and then take it to heart.

One of the byproducts of reading Taylor's life is the introduction you receive to so many well-known Christians who, in one way or another, played a part in his life and ministry. For instance, D. L. Moody was on the platform when, in 1872, Taylor gave the opening address at the "Mildmay" conference for the deeper life.

The Student Volunteer Movement that grew out of Moody's Northfield ministry attracted Taylor tremendously. When he came to America in 1888, Taylor spoke at Northfield and Moody had to arrange extra meetings to allow the students to get the most out of Taylor's ministry. Of course the story of "the Cambridge seven" had reached North America, and it is possible that the dedication of these young men was one of the seeds that helped to bring the Student Volunteer Movement into fruition. There is little question that Moody's ministry in England assisted the progress of foreign missions in a tremendous way, and the China Inland Mission profited from this.

Moody and Taylor, of course, would disagree on the matter of financing the Lord's work. Both of them believed in prayer and trusting God, but Taylor refrained from asking anybody for support. "When our work becomes a begging work, it dies," said Taylor. Moody, on the other hand, was bold in asking Christians for financial support and raised huge sums for Christian enterprises both in the United States and Great Britain. While he greatly admired men like Hudson Taylor and George Müller, Moody felt that his own ministries operated by faith just as much as did theirs. He also felt that, sincere as they were, their emphasis on "making no appeals" was in itself an appeal. Thank God for the variety of men He uses, and thank God for men who can disagree without being disagreeable!

You also will meet other evangelical notables as you read the life of Hudson Taylor: F. B. Meyer (who was deeply moved by the Cambridge seven); H. Grattan Guinness, the British evangelist and Bible teacher (his daughter Mary Geraldine married Hudson Taylor's son, Howard, and helped him write the biography); Howard Kelly; W. J. Erdman; and many others. I was interested to discover that the founder of the Scandinavian Alliance Mission, Fredrik Franson, was greatly influenced by both Moody and Taylor. Taylor's pamphlet *To Every Creature* stirred this Swedish evangelist to form the Swedish Alliance Mission.

Taylor's principles of ministry may not be agreeable to everybody, but they are certainly worth considering. He is the originator, as far as I know, of the oft-quoted statement "God's work done in God's way will never lack God's supplies."[4] "And what does going into debt really mean?" he asked. "It means that God has not supplied your need. . . . If we can only wait *right up to the time*, God cannot lie, God cannot forget: He is *pledged* to supply all our need."[5] It was also a principle of his to promote *missions* and not simply the work of his mission alone. "We do not need to say much about the CIM," he wrote. "Let people see God working, let God be glorified, let believers be made holier, happier, brought nearer to Him and they will not need to be asked to help."[6] In this day when too many men and their ministries are glorified and when some Christian enterprises have been fiscally irresponsible, perhaps Hudson Taylor's counsel is appropriate. His word about trials is also needed: "We might be lifted up, perhaps, or lose spiritual life and power, if success were unaccompanied by discipline."[7]

After you have become acquainted with James Hudson Taylor through the books written *about* him, start reading the books written *by* him. The Moody Colportage series used to carry *Union and Communion*, Taylor's devotional commentary on the Song of Solomon (written while he was courting Maria!) and *A Retrospect*, his personal recollections. In 1931, the China Inland Mission published *Hudson Taylor's Legacy*, a series of devotional messages taken from

Taylor's various articles and editorials originally published in the mission's magazine. This book was edited by Marshall Broomhall, whose ancestors were a part of the CIM ministry from the beginning. The book is especially valuable in that it presents, in his own words, Taylor's basic philosophy of missions and ministry. These three books are worth adding to your library.

One of Taylor's close associates, J. W. Stevenson, wrote of him, "Oh, his was a life that stood looking into!" I suggest you do more than "look into" his life. I suggest you get to know Hudson Taylor intimately; for when you do, if you are open at all to God's truth, the Holy Spirit will do something fresh and lasting in your heart. For the Christian seeking faith in troubled times, for the servant thirsting for fresh power, for the worker longing to know how to build for God, the life of James Hudson Taylor can point the way to Christ—the final answer to every need.

Taylor died on June 3, 1905, during his last visit to China, and he was buried in that land whose people he loved so dearly. But thanks to the printed page, "he being dead yet speaketh."

20

Charles H. Spurgeon
1834–1892

Perhaps one of the highest compliments anyone could pay a preacher would be to say that he preaches like Spurgeon. It would be nigh impossible to locate many people today who actually heard Charles H. Spurgeon preach (he died on January 31, 1892), but the compliment is valid just the same.

Spurgeon was a wonder in his own day, and he is still a wonder today. When the sermons of other men are covered with dust, Spurgeon's will still be read—and preached! But Spurgeon the man also needs to be discovered by each new generation of preachers, and perhaps rediscovered by some of us who first met him years ago. "Sell all that you have . . . and buy Spurgeon!" wrote Helmut Thielicke in his *Encounter with Spurgeon*, and with this counsel we heartily agree.

Charles Haddon Spurgeon was a many-sided individual. You find his name appearing in almost every book that touches upon the religious scene in Victorian England. Just think of the years spanned by his ministry. In the year he was called to New Park Street Chapel, the Crimean War began. The year he opened the great Metropolitan Tabernacle, the United States Civil War began.

While he was ministering, Karl Marx wrote his *The Communist Manifesto* and Charles Darwin his *Origin of Species*. He was contemporary with Phillips Brooks, Alexander Whyte, D. L. Moody, F. B. Meyer, Alexander Maclaren, R. W. Dale (whose theology he criticized), and Joseph Parker. To get acquainted with Spurgeon is to become familiar with one of the greatest eras of preaching in the history of the church.

I suggest you begin with *C. H. Spurgeon* by W. Y. Fullerton. Published in 1920, this book has the value of having been written by one who was close to the great preacher. In fact, from 1879 to 1893 Fullerton served as one of Spurgeon's assistants at the tabernacle, and often preached when he was away. For several years Fullerton edited Spurgeon's sermons for publication each week and became so imbued with the great preacher's style that it is almost impossible to detect where Spurgeon leaves off and his assistant begins! While Fullerton naturally wrote with great admiration for Spurgeon, this did not prevent Fullerton from gently disagreeing with his hero. It is a delightful, informative, and even an inspiring book; it bears reading and rereading. His final paragraph is a masterpiece: "To me he is master and friend. I have neither known nor heard of any other, in my time, so many-sided, so commanding, so simple, so humble, so selfless, so entirely Christ's man. Proudly I stand at the salute!"

Now that you have the broad landscape of Spurgeon before you, you can obtain his autobiography, published by Banner of Truth in two volumes entitled *Spurgeon*. The original autobiography was published serially between 1897 and 1900 and was compiled from his letters and records by his wife and private secretary. These four volumes are not easy to secure, so we are grateful for this new two-volume edition. It is not identical to the original autobiography in that some extraneous material has been omitted—primarily sermon outlines, newspaper quotations, and unimportant letters. But in two respects the new edition is superior: the editors have rearranged some sections to give greater continuity, and have added helpful footnotes. The beautiful thing about these two large volumes of more than one thousand pages is this: you can read a chapter at a sitting and, before you know it, complete the book! They are perfect to keep on your bedside table or near your favorite easy chair. Spurgeon wrote just as he preached—in clear Anglo-Saxon English—and his latest editors have not tried to improve upon his style.

It may shock you to discover that Spurgeon was not only a preacher; he was a fighter! He boldly preached the truth as he saw it in Scripture, and if his sermons hurt some individual or groups, he did not apologize. "Some things are true and some things are false—I regard that as an axiom," he said in one of his famous lectures to his students. "But there are many persons who evidently do not believe it. . . . We have a fixed faith to preach, my brethren, and we are sent forth with a definite message from God." However, he warned his young students, "Don't go about the world with your fist doubled up for fighting, carrying a theological revolver in the leg of your trousers." He practiced what he preached, but when his preaching did lead to controversy, he was not one to retreat. The best study of this aspect of Spurgeon's ministry is *The Forgotten Spurgeon*, written by Iain Murray. In nine carefully documented chapters, the author takes us through Spurgeon's battles over baptismal regeneration, Arminianism, and liberalism in the Baptist Union.

Spurgeon preached no diluted gospel, and when he heard other men preach that way, he heard a call to arms. His first declaration of war came shortly after he began publishing his weekly sermons in 1855. His Calvinistic theology upset some of the brethren: he was not Calvinistic enough for one group and he was too Calvinistic for another. The controversy raged in the pages of religious publications, with some writers even questioning Spurgeon's conversion! "I am not very easily put down," Spurgeon wrote to a friend. "I go right on and care for no man on God's earth."

The second controversy grew out of the sermon against baptismal regeneration, which was preached at the tabernacle on June 5, 1864.[1] His text was Mark 16:15–16. Spurgeon was sure that the message would completely destroy the ministry of his printed sermons, but just the opposite occurred. His publishers sold over a quarter of a million copies! Fullerton stated that a "blizzard of pamphlets and sermons" swept down upon the churches as a result of this one message and that Spurgeon seemed to enjoy it!

"I hear you are in hot water," a friend said to him.

"Oh, no," Spurgeon replied. "It is the other fellows who are in hot water. I am the stoker, the man who makes the water boil."

Of course Spurgeon was aiming at something much larger than the doctrine of baptismal regeneration. He was concerned about the growing influence of Romanism in England, and he was bold to say so. This was the Puritan in Spurgeon, fighting for biblical truth and making any sacrifice necessary to defend the doctrines of God's grace.

Spurgeon's third controversy was perhaps the most painful for him because it touched the fellowship of the brethren in the Baptist Union. In 1887 he published, in his *Sword and Trowel* magazine, several articles dealing with the growing heresy in Baptist churches. The first two articles were called "The Down-Grade," and this led to the popular identification of the battle as the "down-grade controversy." "It now becomes a serious question," Spurgeon wrote, "how far those who abide by the faith once delivered to the saints should fraternize with those who have turned aside to another gospel. Christian love has its claims, and divisions are to be shunned as grievous evils; but how far are we justified in being in confederacy with those who are departing from the truth?" On October 28, 1887 (Fullerton said October 8, but this is an error), Spurgeon withdrew from the Baptist Union.[2] "Fellowship with known and vital error is participation in sin," he wrote in the November *Sword and Trowel*. His decision was final and it was public; now the Baptist Union had to act. What they did and how they did it is beautifully recorded in Murray's book, and it stands (in my opinion) as a sorry indictment of a group of men who should have known better. Fullerton believed that Spurgeon himself should have come to the Baptist Union assembly, but since he had already resigned, this would have been impossible.

Alexander Maclaren was one of four pastors assigned to meet with Spurgeon, but he kept himself completely out of the matter. We wonder why. After Spurgeon's death, the Baptist Union put in the entrance to its headquarters an imposing statue of Spurgeon!

But let's turn from these disappointing events and consider some other facets of this man's amazing life and ministry. It is well known that Spurgeon smoked, although it must be admitted that many famous British preachers smoked. (I have been told by one who ought to know that Campbell Morgan smoked as many as eight cigars a day! And R. W. Dale said that he could get along without food more easily than without his tobacco.) Once Spurgeon was gently reprimanded for his smoking by a Methodist preacher. "If I ever find myself smoking to excess, I promise I shall quit entirely," Spurgeon said.

"What would you call smoking to excess?" the man asked.

"Why, smoking two cigars at the same time!" was the answer.

In *Echoes and Memories*, Bramwell Booth's interesting book of reminiscences, this son of the founder of the Salvation Army mentioned Spurgeon's habit of smoking. Scheduled to preach at a Salvation Army meeting, Spurgeon arrived "in a fine carriage, smoking a cigar. His remark that he smoked to the honor and glory of God is one of those oft-quoted sayings which have done infinite harm to the world, putting into the mouth of many a youth not only a poisonous weed but a flippant and irreligious apology."[3]

Strange to say, while Spurgeon saw no harm in tobacco, he did oppose the theater. In fact, it was this (among other things) that precipitated his famous "open-letter" controversy with the famous Joseph Parker, eloquent pastor of the City Temple in London. Parker's congregation was second in size only to Spurgeon's, but his ecclesiastical circle was much wider and much more diversified. Spurgeon had been preaching in London for fifteen years when Parker came to Poultry Chapel (which later became the famous City Temple), and the men were on good terms. They exchanged pulpits and on occasion preached in support of various Christian enterprises in the city. On February 23, 1887, Parker invited Spurgeon to address an interdenominational gathering in defense of "the old evangelical faith." The next day Spurgeon wrote a letter of refusal, kindly pointing out that Parker's own ministry did not consistently defend the faith. The fuse had been lit. Parker immediately wanted to know if there was "aught against thy brother" and, if so, why Spurgeon had not told him sooner. Spurgeon replied, among other things: "The evangelical faith in which you and Mr. Beecher agree is not the faith which I hold; and the view of religion which takes you to the theater is so far off from mine that I cannot commune with you therein." Parker's reply was on a postcard: "Best thanks, and best regards—J. P."[4]

The matter was forgotten until April 25, 1890, when Parker published an open letter to Spurgeon in the influential *British Weekly*, edited by W. Robertson Nicoll. Spurgeon's Pastors' College Conference was in session that week, making Parker's attack that much more devastating. Nicoll himself was a great admirer and defender of Spurgeon, and it is difficult to understand why he published the letter. It said in part:

> Let me advise you to widen the circle of which you are the center. You are surrounded by offerers of incense. They flatter your weakness, they laugh at your jokes, they feed you with compliments. My dear Spurgeon, you are too big a man for this. Take in more fresh air . . . scatter your ecclesiastical harem. I do not say destroy your circle: I simply say enlarge it.

Spurgeon ignored the letter and advised his staff and pastor friends to do the same. Parker should have known that Spurgeon's power lay in concentration, not diffusion. He functioned best within his own household of faith, although he was generous to evangelicals in other denominations. "I am quite sure that the best way to promote union is to promote truth," he said in a sermon. "It will not do for us to be all united together by yielding to one another's mistakes." There are men like Parker, Campbell Morgan, and D. L. Moody, who seem to belong to all believers, regardless of denominational affiliation; but there are also men like Spurgeon, Maclaren, and Truett, who helped the evangelical cause best by concentrating on their own denominational ministry. We need both kinds of preachers, and one should not be quick to condemn the other.

You will want to read *Spurgeon: Heir of the Puritans* by Ernest W. Bacon, one of the best biographies; and also *A History of Spurgeon's Tabernacle* by Eric W. Hayden, who pastored the tabernacle for five years beginning in November 1956. The book is published in this country by Pilgrim Publications in Pasadena, Texas, and I urge you to secure it. It contains a wealth of information about the ministry of the tabernacle following Spurgeon's death, and the bibliographies of titles by and about Spurgeon are excellent.

But, above all else, read Spurgeon himself! Get a *complete* edition of his *Lectures to My Students* and read it carefully. Granted, some of the material is antiquated, but much is relevant to our ministry. "The Minister's Fainting Fits" and "The Need of Decision for the Truth" ought to be required reading for all ministerial students.

I enjoy reading *An All-Round Ministry*, a collection of Spurgeon's presidential addresses to the students and alumni of the Pastors' College. I say "enjoy reading," but I must confess that these messages have more than once driven me to my knees in confession and prayer. Perhaps they will do the same for you.

Spurgeon was a lover of good books, with a library of some twelve thousand volumes. His views on books are found in the delightful volume *Commenting and Commentaries*, first published in 1876 and reprinted by Banner of Truth in 1969 (the new edition includes a complete index of Spurgeon's sermons). If nothing else, simply enjoy reading his comments, many of which he must have written with a broad smile on his face. Naturally he favors the Puritans; but he had some kind words for writers of other schools—except the dispensationalists.

Of C.H.M.'s *Genesis* he wrote, "Precious and edifying reflections marred by peculiarities." Of *Exodus*, "Not free from Plymouth errors, yet remarkably suggestive." He warned that *Leviticus* "should be read cautiously." By the time he got to *Numbers*, he used both barrels: "Like the other notes of C.H.M., they need filtering. Good as they are, their *Darbyism* gives them an unpleasant and unhealthy savour." His comments about Darby's books are not flattering: "Too mystical for ordinary minds," he wrote about *Practical Reflections on the Psalms*. "If the author would write in plain English his readers would probably discover that there is nothing very valuable in his remarks." Of that other great Brethren writer, William Kelly, Spurgeon wrote: "Mr. Kelly's authoritative style has no weight with us. We do not call these lectures expounding, but confounding." Four decades later, C. I. Scofield would preach often in Spurgeon's pulpit during the pastorate of A. C. Dixon, who, by the way, had resigned from Moody Church to go to London.

One could go on and on about Spurgeon, citing facts and recalling anecdotes; but this is something you need to experience yourself. Plunge right into his sermons, his autobiography, and his other writings, and revel in the grace of God that was so real to this mighty preacher. Like all of us, Spurgeon had his faults and weaknesses, but he magnified God's grace and glorified God's son. We cannot all be Spurgeons, but we can all be faithful, as he was, in preaching the gospel of Jesus Christ.

21

Phillips Brooks
1835–1893

The year 1877 was a memorable one for Phillips Brooks, well-known rector of Trinity Episcopal Church in Boston. On February 9, a new church edifice was consecrated, five years after the old structure had burned down ("She burned majestically," Brooks wrote to a friend; "she died in dignity"). During the Lenten season Brooks participated in D. L. Moody's meetings in Boston at the six-thousand-seat tabernacle. One night, when Brooks led in prayer, Moody introduced him as "Phillip Brook" and shocked the proper Bostonians. On another occasion Brooks filled in for the evangelist and delivered a stirring sermon from Acts 26:17. But the event of 1877 that excited Brooks most was the privilege of delivering the annual Yale lectures on preaching. His was the sixth in the series, but he was the fourth lecturer since Henry Ward Beecher had given the first three series. Phillips Brooks was forty-two years old and at the height of his ministry, exercising a powerful influence not only in America but also in Europe. Published as *Lectures on Preaching*, this series ranks with the finest homiletical literature ever produced by any preacher of any denomination. Subsequent Yale lecturers have quoted Brooks and Beecher more than any other men, and since Beecher had three opportunities to deliver the lectures, this puts Brooks at the head of the list.

Brooks had been preaching for twenty years when he delivered the lectures. He was born on December 13, 1835, "the consummate flower of nine generations of cultured Puritan stock." (That was the opinion of Lewis O. Brastow, professor of practical theology at Yale at the turn of the century. His book, *Representative Modern Preachers*, is worth studying.) After graduating from the Boston Latin School at the age of sixteen, Brooks entered Harvard and graduated in 1855, thirteenth in a class of sixty-six. He returned to the Latin School to teach and, as long as he taught younger children, did quite well. But when he was given older pupils, he began to have discipline problems and the headmaster "released" him. This was a blow to the young man, and for nearly nine months he suffered, living under a cloud of defeat and discouragement. ("I have never known any man who fails in teaching to succeed in anything else," the headmaster had told him!)

He then talked with the president of Harvard and the pastor of his family's church, and both of them suggested he enter the ministry. Interestingly enough, the pastor, Dr. Vinton, told Brooks that conversion was a prerequisite to confirmation and the ministry—and Brooks confessed that he did not know what conversion was. The end result was entrance into the Episcopal Theological Seminary in Alexandria, Virginia, and three years of study. The faculty at that time was weak, so Brooks invested much of his time in wide reading. After graduation in 1859, he began his ministry at the Church of the Advent in Philadelphia, remaining there almost three years. From 1861 to 1867 he pastored the Church of the Holy Trinity in that same city, and then in 1869 began his phenomenal ministry at historic Trinity Church in Boston. He remained there for twenty-two years, resigning in 1891 when he was elected bishop. His untimely death on January 23, 1893, caught Boston by surprise and silenced a powerful voice.

Brooks never married; he was married to his pulpit. He was a big man—six feet, four inches tall—and at one time weighed nearly three hundred pounds. (The Harvard students who served as pall-bearers at his funeral practiced by carrying a heavy casket with three hundred pounds of metal in it. In spite of this, one of the young men fell into the grave when the casket was lowered!) He walked rapidly, ate rapidly, and loved to drive fast horses. He was fond of antique furniture, books (especially biographies), travel (his church sent him to Europe and once he sailed as far as Japan), sweets, and iced drinks. His cup of coffee began as a cup of sugar, then the coffee was poured in! In spite of his mother's pleas, Brooks continued to smoke; his ideal vacation was made up of "plenty of books and time and tobacco."

During his ministry Brooks published five volumes of sermons, and five more were published in the years following his death. They are often seen in used-book stores and, if the prices are not too high, they should be purchased. I suggest, however, that you first read the thirty-one sermons collected by William Scarlett, published in 1949 by E. P. Dutton under the title *Phillips Brooks: Selected Sermons.* This volume contains the best of Brooks's preaching, including his two famous sermons "The Candle of the Lord" and "The Fire and the Calf." If while reading these sermons you take a liking to Brooks, you can obtain the other volumes. Please do not expect expository sermons or messages vibrant with obvious evangelical doctrine and evangelistic warmth! Brooks considered himself evangelical and perhaps in some ways he was, but even in his own day his theology was suspect. The day he was consecrated bishop of Massachusetts, the procession into the church was delayed to allow two bishops to read a letter of protest! Of the fifty-two dioceses in the state, fifteen voted against him. Some of the furor was over his baptism: he had been baptized by a Unitarian and had refused to submit to the Episcopal rite. The brutal attacks in the religious press often kept him awake at night.

Basically, Brooks was a Christian humanist. He emphasized Christ's incarnation, not his death and atonement for sin. He felt that all men are children of God and that, once told this good news, their lives will change. He preached that all men are naturally religious and only need God's grace to reach their fulfillment in God. Yet, strange to say, the most moving of his Yale lectures is the last one, "The Value of the Human Soul." "If we could see how precious the human soul is as Christ saw it, our ministry would approach the effectiveness of Christ's," he stated. He then described the effects of "a concern for souls" on a man's ministry. He closed by saying: "May the souls of men always be more precious to you as you come always nearer to Christ and see them more perfectly as He does. I can ask no better blessing on your ministry than that."

His ministry attracted and helped people from all levels of society, and even some ardent evangelicals appreciated his work. On December 3, 1879, a pastor in Garrettsville, Ohio, wrote Brooks: "I would like here to acknowledge the debt I owe you for inspiration in my individual religious experience and in my public work. . . . Give us other works still." That pastor was R. A. Torrey, who later became president of Moody Bible Institute. One reason for this wide attraction, I think, is that Brooks did not deal with specifics. He preached on timeless themes and loved to use abstract words like *truth*, *goodness*, *humanity*, and (his favorite) *sympathy*. In fact he himself admitted to a pastor friend: "When I am interesting I am vague; when I am definite I am dull." The pastor who expounds the Scriptures or who explains a text finds it necessary to be specific—but this does not mean he has to be dull!

Phillips Brooks is an interesting man who (in spite of his bachelorhood) led an interesting life. If you wish to learn more about him, read the official biography by Alexander V. G. Allen. Avoid the original two-volume edition of 1900 and get the one-volume abridgement published in 1907. The book is as big as the man—nearly seven hundred pages of biography and extracts from his many letters. If you do not feel up to that much reading, locate *Focus on Infinity* by Raymond W. Albright, published in 1961. This book is as scholarly as Allen's massive work, and it has the added advantage of the perspective of time. (For some reason, each book has an interesting typographical error. Allen wrote about "D. S. Moody" and Albright about "Charles W. Spurgeon.")

Now for Brooks's *Lectures on Preaching*, a book every preacher ought to read once a year for five years, and then once every other year for the rest of his life. What makes these lectures so valuable is that they deal with basic principles, not with transient methods. The preacher who is looking for shortcuts will not find them here.

In the first lecture Brooks defined *preaching* as the communication of divine truth through human personality. The divine truth never changes, but the human personality does. This explains why two preachers can take the same text and develop two different sermons, or why the same preacher can preach often from the same Scripture passage and always discover something fresh. "The truth must come really through the person," said Brooks, "not merely over his lips, not merely into his understanding and out through his pen. It must come through his character, his affections, his whole intellectual and moral being."[1] This means, of course, that the preparation for the ministry "is nothing less than the making of the man." The preacher of truth must be a man open to truth—*all* truth, no matter where it is found, because truth can come only from God. In his lectures on "The Influence of Jesus," Brooks described "the man of truth" as "a man into all whose life the truth has been pressed till he is full of it, till he has been given to it, and it has been given to him, he being always the complete being whose unity is in that total of moral, intellectual and spiritual life which makes what we call character."[2] This leaves out in the cold the "busy preacher" who dives into his books for an outline or illustration, or, worse yet, who depends on "preachers' helps" for his messages week by week. It is not enough to write a sermon, said Brooks; we must have *a message*, "a message which we cannot transmit until it has entered into our own experience, and we can give our own testimony of its spiritual power."

The second lecture discusses "The Preacher Himself" and answers the question, "What sort of man may be a minister?" God uses different kinds of men because each man's experience helps to interpret the truths of the Bible. But let each man be open to truth. Brooks abhorred narrow-minded bigotry that prevents a man confronting truth from many sources. He also emphasized the importance of contact with humanity. "No man preaches well," he stated, "who has not a strong and deep appreciation of humanity." He advised us to "find the human side of every truth, the point at which every speculation touches humanity." He had some wise warnings in this lecture against some "dangers in the ministry."

"The Preacher in His Work" is the theme of the third lecture. "The powers of the pastor's success are truth and sympathy together. 'Speaking the truth in love' is the golden text." He emphasized the balance between *preaching* and *pastoring*, an emphasis sorely needed today. "The preacher needs to be pastor that he may preach to real men. The pastor must be preacher that he may keep the dignity of his work alive. The preacher who is not a pastor grows remote. The pastor who is not a preacher grows petty." He called for manliness in the ministry and deplored "the absence of the heroic element" in the churches.

Lectures four and five are on "The Idea of the Sermon" and "The Making of the Sermon," and they show how Brooks applied his philosophy of preaching to the practical problems of the work. "We hear a good deal about preaching over people's heads," he commented. "There is such a thing. But generally it is not the character of the ammunition, but the fault of the aim, that makes the missing shot." While Brooks did not have too good a word for expository preaching, he did say a great deal about the making of a message that will help even the most experienced preacher. I especially appreciate his reminder that no sermon should be considered alone. We are ministering to people week after week, and one message fortifies another. The harvest is not the end of the meeting; it is the end of the age.

"The Congregation" is the theme of the sixth lecture; as you might expect, Brooks discussed the different kinds of hearers that attend church. He saw four: the "pillars of the church," the skeptical, the habitual, and the sincere seekers after truth. I like the "three rules" that he gave early in the lecture: "First, have as few congregations as you can. Second, know your congregation as thoroughly as you can. Third, know your congregation so largely and deeply that in knowing it you shall know humanity."

If you are tired of hearing the words *relevant* and *contemporary*, then the seventh lecture, "The Ministry of Our Age," will do you good. Listen to Brooks:

> The man who belongs to the world but not to his time grows abstract and vague, and lays no strong grasp upon men's lives and the present causes of their actions. The man who belongs to his time but not to the world grows thin and superficial. . . . Truth and timeliness together make the full preacher.

The era he was discussing was in many ways different from our era, but in many ways it was similar, simply because human nature is the same. He discussed several classes of people that exist in every age—the critics, the people who accept everything science says, the frightened—and he showed how the gospel meets their needs. As he ended this seventh lecture, Brooks said: "I must not close without begging you not to be ashamed or afraid of the age you live in, and least of all to talk of it in a tone of weak despair." It seems that every age has always been the worst and that every preacher has looked back and longed for "the good old days!"

I have already commented on the eighth lecture, "The Value of the Human Soul." It is this concept that empowers the ministry. "Without this power, preaching is almost sure to become either a struggle of ambition or a burden of routine. With it, preaching is an ever fresh delight." He then explained the effects in a man's ministry of this supreme motivation: the doctrines of the faith become more meaningful, there is joy in seeing lives changed, there is a permanence to our ministry, and the preacher himself grows in courage and grace. "Go and try to save a soul and you will see how well it is worth saving, how capable it is of the most complete salvation. Not by pondering upon it, nor by talking of it, but by serving it you learn its preciousness."

After you have read *Lectures on Preaching*—Baker Books published a paperback edition—look for a copy of Phillips Brooks's *Essays and Addresses*, edited by his brother John. There is much that is good in this collection, but the most valuable piece is a lecture he delivered at the Yale Divinity School on February 28, 1878, one year after he gave the Yale lectures. The address is entitled "The Teaching of Religion," and it ought to be included in all future editions of Brooks's *Lectures on Preaching*. In it Brooks comes to grips with the question: how can we communicate spiritual truth to men today? If his *Lectures on Preaching* is dinner, then this address is the dessert! This address gave Brooks the opportunity to clarify and expand several of the important ideas in his original lectures, and for this reason it is important to the preacher who has benefited from that great series.

Permit me to close with a few quotations from Brooks that may help to whet your appetite:

> If your ministry is to be good for anything, it must be *your* ministry, and not a feeble echo of another man's.

> Let a man be a true preacher, really uttering the truth through his own personality, and it is strange how men will gather to listen to him.

> Fasten yourself to the center of your ministry, not to some point on its circumference.

> This surely is a good rule: whenever you see a fault in any other man, or any other church, look for it in yourself and in your own church.

> Let us rejoice with one another that in a world where there are a great many good and happy things for men to do, God has given us the best and happiest, and made us preachers of His Truth.[3]

Amen and Amen!

Frances Ridley Havergal
1836–1879

Frances Ridley Havergal was to Great Britain what Fanny Crosby was to the United States, and the two women had a great deal in common. Both had to put up with physical limitations: Crosby was blind, and Havergal endured what the Victorians called "delicate health," including a great deal of pain, all her life. Each of them was converted early in life and then had a deeper life experience in later years. Both were gifted singers and instrumentalists as well as gifted writers, and both had phenomenal memories.

Though they never met on earth, the two Franceses corresponded and loved one another across the miles. Havergal sent Fanny Crosby a long poem, "An English Tribute to Fanny Crosby," which ends:

> Dear blind sister over the sea.
> An English heart goes forth to thee!
> We are linked by a cable of faith and song,
> Flashing bright sympathy swift along;
> One in the east and one in the west,
> Singing for Him whom our souls love best;
> "Singing for Jesus," telling His love,
> All the way to our home above,

Where the severing sea, with its restless tide,
Never shall hinder, and never divide.
Sister, what will our meeting be,
When our hearts shall sing and our eyes shall see!

While Fanny Crosby excelled in writing the gospel songs, Frances Ridley Havergal's songs were more of a devotional nature, calling believers to a deeper dedication to Christ. Her most famous dedication hymn is "Take My Life and Let It Be," which she wrote on February 4, 1874, after a thrilling night of praise and prayer because of a very special victory the Lord had given her.

But we are also familiar with "Lord, Speak to Me that I May Speak," "Like a River Glorious," "Who Is on the Lord's Side?" and "I Gave My Life for Thee."

Frances Ridley Havergal was born December 14, 1836, in Astley, Worcestershire, England, where her father, William Henry Havergal, was vicar of the Astley Anglican church. She inherited her musical ability from her father, who was quite well known as a writer and publisher of church music. She learned to read by the time she was three, and when she was four, she was reading the Bible.

She discovered her talent for writing verse when she was seven and kept a notebook of what most people would call childish rhymes. But those rhymes prepared the way for her prolific writing ministry in later years. Her mother often said to her, "Fanny dear, pray to God to prepare you for all that He is preparing for you." Frances even wrote long letters in rhyme to her brother Frank and to some of her young friends. One of her little poems proved to be prophetic.

Sunday is a pleasant day,
    When we to church do go;
For there we sing and read and pray,
    And hear the sermon too.
And if we love to pray and read
    While we are in our youth,
The Lord will help us in our need
    And keep us in His truth.

Her mother died when Frances was only eleven years old. On that day, July 5, 1848, Frances wrote in her notebook:

Eye hath not seen, nor ear heard,
  Neither can man's heart conceive,
The blessed things God hath prepared
  For those who love Him and believe.

God had been working in her heart, and she desperately wanted to know for sure that she was converted and going to heaven. The struggle lasted more than three years. A sermon she heard on divine judgment "haunted" her, and each time she witnessed the Lord's Supper she was deeply moved. But it was while she was away at school in 1851 that she found the peace of salvation. God used the witness of a newly converted friend and the counsel of Miss Caroline Cook, who later became her stepmother, to bring her assurances of eternal life.

Frances spent a year in Germany and there received professional confirmation that she did indeed have musical and poetic gifts of the highest quality. A remarkable student, she was competent not only in music and writing, but also in languages: she knew Greek, Hebrew, Latin, German, French, and Italian. According to her sister Maria, Frances had memorized all of the Gospels and Epistles, as well as Isaiah (her favorite book), the Psalms, the Minor Prophets, and Revelation!

In 1858 she returned to Germany with her father, who was seeking further treatment for his afflicted eyes; it was then that she wrote "I Gave My Life for Thee." Visiting a pastor's home, she saw a picture of the crucifixion on the wall, and under it the motto, "I did this for thee. What hast thou done for me?" Quickly she took a pencil and wrote the words that are so familiar to Christians everywhere; but she was dissatisfied with them, so she threw the paper in the fire. *The paper immediately came out unharmed!* She kept the poem and later showed it to her father, who not only encouraged her to keep it but also wrote a tune for it. However, the tune we usually use today was written by Philip P. Bliss.

As Frances matured, she found herself being used by God in writing, teaching the Bible, visiting the poor and afflicted, and corresponding with people who felt led to share their problems with her. She taught a children's Sunday school class at whatever church her father was pastoring, and she kept a permanent register of her students' names so that she might pray for them. I wonder what would happen to our children and young people if each teacher who had ministered to them continued to pray for them?

In 1865, Frances was very ill, at a time when many opportunities were open to her. "I am held back from much I wanted to do in every way, and have had to lay poetizing aside," she wrote in 1866. "And yet such open doors seem set before me. Perhaps this check is sent that I may consecrate what I do more entirely. . . . I suppose that God's crosses are often made of most unexpected and strange material."[1]

In 1869, her first book, *Ministry of Song*, was published. A decade earlier her doctor had told her that she must choose between writing and living, because her health would not permit her to do both. "Did you ever hear of anyone being very much used for Christ who did not have some special waiting time, some complete upset of all his or her plans?" she wrote. When *Ministry of Song* was published, Frances testified that she saw "the evident wisdom of having been kept nine years waiting in the shade."

There were other tests besides her recurring illnesses and almost constant weakness. In 1874, her American publisher went bankrupt in an economic crash; since she had an exclusive contract with him, this put an end to her American publishing until the business could get back on its feet again. This meant, of course, a loss of income as well.

"Two months ago, this would have been a real trial to me," she wrote to a friend, "for I had built a good deal on my American prospects; now, 'Thy will be done' is not a sigh but only *a song!* . . . I have not a fear, or a doubt, or a care, or a shadow upon the sunshine of my heart."

The secret of her victory was found in an experience she had on December 2, 1873, just two months before she received news of the crash. A friend had mailed her a copy of a little booklet entitled *All for Jesus*. It kindled in her heart a deep desire for greater consecration and wider usefulness, and she began to pray to that end. God answered her prayers. She wrote: "Yes, it was on Advent Sunday, December 2nd, 1873, I first saw clearly the blessedness of true consecration. I saw it as a flash of electric light. . . . There must be full surrender before there can be full blessedness." She discovered the meaning of 1 John 1:7 and the importance of trusting Christ *to keep her* as well as to save her. She totally rejected all ideas of "sinless perfection," but claimed the clear biblical teaching of constant victory. "Not a coming to be cleansed in the fountain only," she explained, "but a *remaining* in the fountain, so that it may and can go on cleansing." Her knowledge of Greek told her that the verb in 1 John 1:9 is present—"keeps on cleansing." The next time you sing "Like a River Glorious," keep in mind that it is Frances Ridley Havergal's testimony to the reality of the victorious Christian life.

Frances never sat down with the determination to write a poem or a song. "Writing is *praying* with me," she said, "for I never seem to write even a verse by myself, and feel like a little child writing; you know a child would look up at every sentence and say, 'And what shall I say next?' That is just what I do." It was her conviction that God had a message for her to share and that he would direct her in the writing of it. If nothing came to her, she accepted the silence and went on to other things. "The Master has not put a chest of poetic gold into my possession and said, 'Now use it as you like!'" she wrote to a friend. "But He keeps the gold, and gives it to me piece by piece just when He will and as much as He will, and no more." Sometimes that gold included chords and melodies as well, for Frances was an accomplished musician.

In 1876, Frances went through another fiery trial: the offices of her British publisher burned down, and with it went the complete manuscript and plates of *Songs of Grace and Glory*, which she had recently completed. She had not kept a copy of much of this material, so she had to begin all over again, not only with the words but also the music. "I have thanked Him for it," she wrote to her sisters, "more than I have prayed about it. It is just what He did with me last year, it is another *turned lesson*." God gave her sufficient health and strength to do the work again.

Her daily quiet time with the Lord was kept with loving discipline, and she always devoted extra time to serious Bible study. (One wishes that some of our contemporary composers would spend more time in their Bibles and put more solid theology into their songs.) Hymn writing was not a business with Frances; it was a ministry. Even her singing and playing in public were not considered performances but opportunities for her to glorify Christ and share him with others. She had a very sane and scriptural view of true consecration.

"Consecration is not so much a step as a course," she wrote in her devotional classic *Kept for the Master's Use*, "not so much an act as a position to which a course of action inseparably belongs. . . . Does this mean that we are always to be doing some definitely religious work, as it is called? No, but all that we do is to be always definitely done for Him."[2] There was a time in her life when she decided she would not sing or play secular songs, although she did not criticize those who did so. She could have become a famous concert artist had she pursued such a career, but to her, it was not consistent with her Christian witness. She made this decision several months before she wrote:

> Take my lips, and let me sing,
> Always, only, for my King.

During 1873, on a visit to Switzerland, she was almost killed in a climbing accident; and in 1874 she suffered for eight months with typhoid fever. But she continued to write, as the Lord enabled her, and she carried on a wide correspondence. In one six-month period, she received over six hundred letters.

Her last year of ministry on earth was 1879. She kept a "Journal of Mercies," and some of the entries are interesting when you consider her weakened condition. "Able to come downstairs for the first time," she wrote on New Year's Day. On January 14, she wrote,

"Being withheld from resuming work, and sense of God's wise hand in it." "Strength for extra pulls" was the entry for February 5, and on February 23 she wrote, "Freedom from pain."

During those difficult days, she also kept a prayer list with daily needs and special requests for each day. She also made a list of "work for 1879, if the Lord wills." On that list was her desire to prepare for the press *Kept for the Master's Use*, and God granted her that desire. She finished revising the proofs shortly before her death on June 3, 1879. At the time, she was living at Caswall Bay in Wales, near Swansea; but the family took her body back to Astley where she was buried on June 9 beside other family members in the beloved churchyard of her childhood days.

The next year, her sister Maria published *Memorials of Frances Ridley Havergal* (London: James Nisbet), a book that is now long out of print. Baker Books has reprinted *Kept for the Master's Use* and *Royal Bounty*, two of her finest devotional books. Both books reveal her love for Scripture and her ability to understand and teach it. She was far more than a musician and poetess. She was a unique woman with a penetrating ministry that was fashioned in the furnace of suffering.

When her doctor said to her, "Goodbye, I shall not see you again," Frances asked, "Then do you really think I am going?" He replied, "Yes."

"Today?" she asked, and he said, "Probably."

Her response was, "Beautiful—too good to be true!" But that would be the response of any believer who had honestly said:

> Take my life, and let it be,
> Consecrated, Lord, to Thee!

23

Alexander Whyte
1836–1921

When some future artist paints a series depicting great scenes in church history, I hope he includes a moving scene from an October day in Edinburgh, 1873. The great preacher and principal of New College, Robert S. Candlish, was dying. He summoned two men to his bedside: Robert Rainy and Alexander Whyte. Whyte told the story:

> I had no sooner entered the room than the dying man put out his hand to me and said: "Good-bye. I had hoped to be spared to help you a little longer"—he was always my helper, the humble soul [Whyte was Candlish's assistant at Free St. George's Church]— "but it is not to be. Good-bye." And then he motioned to Dr. Rainy to kneel at his bedside. He threw his withered arms around Rainy's neck and kissed him and said: "I leave the congregation to Whyte and I leave the New College and the Assembly to you." It was a scene never to be forgotten. And it was a dedication and a sanctification to have seen it and shared in it.[1]

And so the mantle fell on Whyte, still in his thirties, to fill the pulpit of Edinburgh's leading church and one of Scotland's most important places of ministry. And he filled it—for over forty years, Alexander Whyte preached solid, biblical messages that magnified the grace of God. "Never think of giving up preaching!" he wrote a Methodist pastor who had sought his counsel. "The angels around the throne envy you your great work!" Whyte's pulpit was his throne, and though he has laid down his scepter, his power is still felt wherever men read his sermons.

Whyte was born out of wedlock into great poverty on January 13, 1836, in Kirriemuir. His father, John Whyte, offered to marry his mother, Janet Thompson, but she refused. Whyte left town soon after Alexander was born, established a business in the United States, and became a useful citizen. He fought in the Civil War at the first battle of Bull Run, was captured, and spent many days in a Confederate prison camp. He later visited Scotland, met his son—then a student—and apparently established a warm relationship with him. John died in 1871. In the last letter to his son he had written: "Pray that all my former sins are forgiven and that I shall hereafter trust in Him, the Savior of the world."

Janet Thompson had raised her son in material poverty but spiritual plenty. Even at a young age Whyte had two passions: books and preaching. One day, when he was supposed to be caring for a neighbor's cows, he was dreaming about his future plans and allowed the cows to invade a cornfield. The neighbor came running out, shouting, "I don't know what you're going to do or how in the whole world you'll ever earn an honest living!"

The lad replied, "What would you think if one day I was to wag my head in a pulpit?"

Another day he was trying to help his mother harvest in the fields, and she exclaimed: "Get out of my road, laddie! You may be good at your books, but you'll never make a shearer!"

He *was* good at his books, and his Sunday school teacher, James Kennedy, and two pastors, Daniel Cormick and David White, encouraged him. (How soon we forget the men who helped make other men great!) When Whyte was seven years old, Robert Murray McCheyne visited Kirriemuir and gave the boy a tract.

In his early teens Whyte was apprenticed to a shoemaker, but he assured his mother that his final goal was the pulpit. Once when she was particularly discouraged, he said, "Don't cry, Mother; don't be afraid, for I will go and serve out my time—but mind you, I am going to be a minister!" During those difficult early years, Whyte learned to use his time and to discipline his will, achievements that helped make him a success later on.

From 1858 to 1866 Whyte was a student, first in Aberdeen and then in Edinburgh. The going was tough, but the boy was tougher. He sacrificed to purchase books, and he listened to the great preachers of that day. The call of the pulpit became stronger and stronger. During those student years he made several friendships that lasted his whole life. Upon graduation from New College, Edinburgh, he became an assistant at Free St. John's in Glasgow, and here he was ordained on December 27, 1856. He remained there until 1860 when he was called to Free St. George's in Edinburgh to work with the famous Robert S. Candlish (if you have not read Candlish's remarkable exposition of 1 John, by all means do so—prayerfully). This was the beginning of forty-seven remarkable years of ministry in one church, first as assistant and then as pastor.

Above everything else, Whyte was a preacher. Preaching, to him, meant work. "I would have all lazy students drummed out of the college," he said, "and all lazy ministers out of the Assembly. I would have laziness held to be the one unpardonable sin in all our students and in all our ministers." A voracious reader and a diligent student, Whyte did not neglect his pastoral ministry or his family. In 1898, when Whyte was called to be moderator of the Assembly, he exhorted the pastors to concentrate on humility, prayer, and work. "We have plenty of time for all our work did we husband our time and hoard it up aright," he told them. "We cannot look seriously in one another's faces and say it is want of time. It is want of intention. It is want of determination. It is want of method. It is want of motive. It is want of conscience. It is want of heart. It is want of anything and everything but time."[2]

The sales manager of a successful Christian publishing house tells me that pastors are not buying books. "Most of the books sold in

Christian bookstores are sold to and read by women," he said. If our pastors are not using their valuable time for study, what are they using it for? Perhaps Whyte had the answer: "We shroud our indolence under the pretext of a difficulty. The truth is, it is lack of real love for our work."

Alexander Whyte loved books, and he read them to his dying day. The Puritans in general and Thomas Goodwin in particular were his main diet. But he also thrived on the mystics and the princes of the Scottish church, such as Samuel Rutherford. Whyte constantly ordered books for himself and his friends in the ministry. However, he cautioned young pastors against becoming book-buyers instead of book-readers. "Don't hunger for books," he wrote a minister friend. "Get a few of the very best, such as you already have, and read them and your own heart continually." Whyte often contrasted two kinds of reading—"reading on a sofa and reading with a pencil in hand." He urged students to keep notebooks and to make entries in an interleaved Bible for future reference. "No day without its line" was his motto. He wrote to Hubert Simpson: "for more than forty years, I think I can say, never a week, scarcely a day, has passed, that I have not entered some note or notes into my Bible: and, then, I never read a book without taking notes for preservation one way or another."

In his preaching, Whyte magnified the vileness of sin and the graciousness of Christ. His sermons were (for lack of a better word) surgical. Alexander Gammie reported Whyte's criticism, expressed in a conversation with a friend, of Henry Drummond: "The trouble with Hen-a-ry is that he doesna' ken [know] onything aboot sin." Whyte certainly knew a thing or two about sin, and he was not afraid to preach what he knew. This was the Puritan in him, and he felt his sermon was not a success if he did not sting the conscience and expose the heart. Let me hasten to add that the preacher was more conscious of his own sins than those of others. In his study of sanctification, *The Pure in Heart*, William Sangster told of an evangelist who came to Edinburgh and criticized the ministers. A friend told Whyte, "The evangelist said last night that Dr. Hood

Wilson was not a converted man." Whyte jumped from his chair. "The rascal!" he cried. "Dr. Wilson not a converted man!" Then the friend reported that the evangelist also said that Whyte was not converted. At that, Whyte stopped short, sat down, put his face in his hands, and was silent for a long time. Then he said to the visitor, "Leave me, friend, leave me! I must examine my heart!"

Another story illustrates the effect of Whyte's surgical sermons on his hearers. Two Highland miners, visiting Edinburgh, worshiped at St. George's. Whyte's sermon that Sunday was one of his typically dramatic exposures of sin, and the two men left the church in deep silence. After a few blocks, one said: "Sandy, yon man must have been a *deevil* when he was a laddie!"

An incident in Whyte's childhood illustrates his theology of conviction. Whyte caught his arm in a threshing machine and everyone thought he would lose it—except a neighbor who was skilled in such matters in a homey way. She would not let them take the boy to the hospital for surgery. The pain became severe, and Whyte's mother summoned the neighbor again. She looked over the situation and said: "I like the pain. I like the pain." She was right. The arm healed. The pain had been the first step toward recovery. When people complained that Whyte's sermons were too critical, he could well reply, "I like the pain—I like the pain."

Whyte was not only a great preacher and student but also a great pastor. In his *Bunyan Characters* he stated boldly:

> For I am as sure as I am of anything connected with a minister's life, that a minister's own soul will prosper largely in the measure that the souls of his people prosper through his pastoral work. No preaching, even if it were as good preaching as the apostle's itself, can be left to make up for the neglect of pastoral visitation.[3]

Even in the dismal winter days, people would see Whyte walking the streets of Edinburgh to visit his people. His visits were not long, but they always brought a blessing. He was pastor not only to his people but also to a host of pastors who looked to him for encouragement and counsel.

Alexander Whyte was a great appreciator, almost to a fault. When George Morrison went to Edinburgh to be Whyte's assistant, a friend cautioned him, "Remember, all of Whyte's geese are swans!" Whyte loved nothing more than encouraging someone with a word of appreciation. He constantly sent postcards to friends thanking them for some article they had published or congratulating them for some achievement. Morrison had the same habit; he must have learned it from Whyte. Today, when so much ink is spilled criticizing God's servants, some of us need to start majoring more in encouragement. "Give, and it shall be given unto you."

Whyte was so much of an encourager he forgot that Christians cannot accept every doctrine men preach, though the men may be fine people. As you read G. F. Barbour's magnificent biography of his uncle, you discover that Whyte was very ecumenical. He was a great admirer of Cardinal Newman (though he certainly disagreed with his theology) and even published an "appreciation" of him, to which he added selections from the cardinal's writings.

When Abdul Baha Abbas, leader of the Bahai movement, came to Edinburgh, Whyte received him warmly into his home and invited friends to come hear him. An action like that could be misinterpreted and could encourage a non-Christian movement.

Martyn Lloyd-Jones has told of a letter written by Whyte in which the great preacher praised a book that was very liberal, saying "I wish I had written a book like this myself." We can well understand Whyte's desire to encourage, but surely he had to realize that his endorsement might lead somebody astray.

He defended Robertson Smith before the Assembly when it was likely that Smith's views of inspiration would only undermine the faith. "Fathers and brethren," Whyte cried, "the world of mind does not stand still! And the theological mind will stand still at its peril." True, but the theological mind must still depend on the inspired Word of God for truth and direction. Once we lose that anchor, we drift.

W. Robertson Nicoll stated Whyte's weakness perfectly: "He could not endure controversies with individuals." He would go to almost any length to build bridges, even if he had to build them on sinking sand.

But he was a great preacher and a great soul-winner, in spite of his charitable excesses. When D. L. Moody came to Edinburgh in 1874, Whyte shared in the meetings with great enthusiasm. He often spoke at meetings on behalf of Moody's work and was especially interested in the evangelist's work with the YMCA. When Chapman and Alexander came to Edinburgh in 1914, again Whyte threw himself into the work. A friend asked him how he could spare the time and strength (he was then seventy-eight years old), and Whyte replied, "I simply can't stay away."

Do not put off reading Whyte's sermons. His *Bible Characters* is a must for every preacher's library. How he can make Bible people live! *In Remembrance of Me* contains sermons given during communion seasons at St. George's. Of particular interest are Whyte's final messages: the last sermon he preached at St. George's, and the last sermon he prepared but was unable to preach. *Lord, Teach Us to Pray* is probably the finest single book of sermons on prayer by any evangelical preacher. *With Mercy and Judgment* contains some great preaching, as does *The Nature of Angels*. Baker Books has published *The Treasury of Alexander Whyte*, edited by Ralph Turnbull. In it is John Kelman's "Memorial Address" on Alexander Whyte, which is certainly worth having. *The Spiritual Life* is Whyte's study of Thomas Goodwin, the Puritan preacher whose works were never out of Whyte's hands. Whyte urged young preachers to find one author who excited and helped them and to master his works. *The Walk, Conversation, and Character of Jesus Christ Our Lord* is a remarkable series of sermons on the life of Christ, flashing the kind of homiletical imagination for which Whyte was famous. He maintained that if a message is to have life and power, "it must be fused by the glow of personal experience and lit up by the flash of imagination."[4]

Alexander Whyte would not want any of us to imitate his style or approach to preaching—except for his study and hard work. When one of his assistants attempted to imitate his style, Whyte simply said, "Deliver your own message." That settled the matter. But I am sure all of us can benefit from Whyte's contribution to sermonic literature by pondering his messages, making them a part of our own spiritual experience and then translating their truths into daily living and helpful preaching. No man could preach one of Whyte's sermons as his own and get away with it. And no man can read one of his sermons and easily get away from it.

"A congregation is awaiting you," Whyte said to some theological students one day, "to be made by you, after you are made by God." Here is a great preacher's philosophy of pastoral work: God makes a man; the man makes a ministry; the ministry makes a church. It worked in Edinburgh, and it will work today where you and I are ministering in the power of the Spirit.

Barbour's biography, *The Life of Alexander Whyte*, is one of the greatest biographies of an evangelical preacher ever written. It is a massive book of nearly seven hundred pages; and since it was published less than three years after Whyte's death, the author had to work diligently to release it so quickly. The best thing about the book is its emphasis on Whyte's inner life rather than on his activities and achievements alone. But I must warn you that the first three chapters are slow reading—to make it through them you must believe in the perseverance of the saints! After that the book becomes delightfully easy and entertaining—and edifying. I wish every seminary student were required to read chapters 16 through 18 to learn how this man studied, prepared sermons, and pastored his church.

While reading this biography, I was impressed with the amazing variety and number of friends who were woven into the fabric of Whyte's life. The book's index runs to seventeen pages, and most of it is devoted to the names of people Whyte knew and worked with as a pastor, preacher, denominational leader, author, and friend.

One of these names is Dr. Joseph Bell, who, as you may know, was the original Sherlock Holmes. Dr. Bell was Whyte's friend and physician for nearly forty years. He was also a beloved elder at Free St. George's. Dr. Bell taught at the University of Edinburgh, and one of his students was a young man named Doyle. In fact, it was Doyle who often ushered in the patients during Dr. Bell's lectures, and the good doctor would proceed to reveal all manner of facts about them without asking them a single question! In his delightful book *The Life of Sir Arthur Conan Doyle*, John Dickson Carr described the amazing Dr. Bell as "very lean, with dexterous hands and a shock of dark hair standing up on his head like the bristles of a brush."[5]

Bell's uncanny faculty for observation enabled him to discern a man's occupation by observing his hands or the peculiar characteristics of his clothes. Diagnosing cases seemed like child's play to him. "The trained eye," he explained it. "A simple matter!" A few years after graduation Doyle used his old professor as the model for the world's most famous detective. "If he needed a model for his detective," wrote Carr, "he need look no further than a lean figure in Edinburgh, with long white dexterous hands and a humorous eye, whose deductions startled patients."[6] Thus, Sherlock Holmes was born. Even Whyte's biographer mentioned that Bell's "acuteness of observation was so striking that he was commonly believed to have suggested to Sir Arthur Conan Doyle, when a medical student in Edinburgh, the character of Sherlock Holmes."[7]

But the gifted doctor and the celebrated preacher did not always agree. Whyte was usually ready to throw his influence behind any cause that, to him, seemed right, and he also had a weakness for seeing good in projects that others considered dangerous. In 1887 when "the Irish question" was at its stormy height, Whyte found himself endorsing a controversial Irish leader named Dillon by inviting the man to speak to a private group of Presbyterian leaders at Whyte's home. Three weeks later, the pastor received a strong remonstrance signed by thirteen prominent members of the church, including eight elders; one of those elders was Dr. Joseph Bell. Whyte's physician agreed with his colleagues that their pastor was in danger of losing his influence in the pulpit by associating with those who, to the public, represented party politics. The letter cut Whyte deeply, particularly because it was signed by so many who were his friends. But Dr. Bell won his point. Whyte's oldest son, Fred, explained: "He

[Whyte] showed no hesitation in his choice. His calling as a Minister had first claim on him then as always."[8]

In 1892, the church session accepted their pastor's request for an assistant. Dr. Bell had stood with his pastor and urged the officers to secure help as soon as possible. Whyte had been working tirelessly, and the pressures of the ministry were going to break him. For some unknown reason, the much-needed assistant was not called at that time, but we can be sure that Dr. Bell did not allow the matter to rest. Two years later, Dr. Hugh Black was called to Whyte's side.

But hard work took its toll. When he was seventy-three, Whyte accepted the principalship of New College in Edinburgh—in addition to his pastoral duties! The result was a breakdown in health at the end of 1909, a sudden heart attack that gave his doctor cause for concern. Dr. Bell managed to get his illustrious patient through the winter, but a second heart attack followed a year later. Bell had often encouraged Dr. and Mrs. Whyte to take long holidays; once he had sent them to Italy for a much-needed rest. Perhaps it was Bell who inspired Whyte's "advice for a successful ministry": talk to no one after services, and always take long holidays! Alexander Whyte was a great preacher, but let us pause to give thanks to Dr. Joseph Bell, a faithful elder and friend, and a wonderful physician. Perhaps it was Bell's ministry that helped make Whyte the kind of man he was.

So much for doctors and detectives. As you peruse the list of names in the index to *The Life of Alexander Whyte*, you also find D. L. Moody mentioned. I was encouraged to learn that it was Reverend John Kelman of Leith, among others, who had first invited Mr. Moody to preach in Edinburgh. Kelman's son, John, would become an assistant to Whyte in 1907, and in 1919 would succeed John Henry Jowett at New York's Fifth Avenue Presbyterian Church. Whyte's illustrious predecessor at Free St. George's, R. S. Candlish, died shortly before the Moody-Sankey meetings started, but he had predicted for Edinburgh "a great blessing which should not be despised though it come strangely." It was in Edinburgh that Sankey composed "The Ninety and Nine."

Whyte threw himself into the revival campaign, and as a result saw an exceptionally large communicant's class the next year. He also saw his Tuesday night prayer meeting move from the church hall into the sanctuary itself. It would be interesting to discover the spiritual contributions Moody made to the life of that historic church.

I wonder what Alexander Whyte's attitude was toward fellow Presbyterian preacher John Kennedy of Dingwall. Kennedy was an opponent of the Moody-Sankey meetings and did not hesitate to express his opposition publicly. He was "rigidly conservative," said one biographer. He rejected hymns as "human inventions" and permitted only the singing of psalms in his services. He also opposed church organs. (He was not the only Scot who was horrified at Sankey's little organ—his "chest full of whistles." One dear lady in Edinburgh ran out of the meeting, shouting, "Let me oot! Let me oot! What would John Knox think of the like of ye?" She took refuge in the overflow meeting across the street, and when Sankey showed up there to sing, she repeated the same performance!) Known as the "Spurgeon of the Highlands," Kennedy was particularly opposed to Moody's theology, especially the use of the inquiry room. He wrote a strong pamphlet against the evangelist, something Whyte would not have done.

One of Alexander Whyte's best friends died over two hundred years before Whyte was born. I speak of Lancelot Andrewes, whose *Private Devotions* was one of Whyte's favorite books. In fact, Whyte named one of his sons Lancelot in honor of the Anglican divine who had lived from 1555 to 1626 (during the tense reign of King James I). It is unfortunate that Andrewes is almost forgotten today. The famous poet T. S. Eliot tried to stir up interest in Andrewes by publishing in 1926 his essay *For Lancelot Andrewes*, but he failed.

Andrewes was a scholar. Even when a student, he used his annual holiday to learn a new language; it was said that he mastered fifteen languages. In 1586 he was made a chaplain to Queen Elizabeth, and in 1601 dean of Westminster. He assisted in the coronation of King James on July 25, 1603, and was present in January 1604 at the Hampton Court Conference, at which the request was made for a new translation of the Bible. Andrewes was one of "fifty-four learned

174

men" appointed to help translate the new Bible, serving as chairman of the group responsible for Genesis through 2 Kings. (If you wish to read a delightful account of the work of translating the King James Version, secure *The Learned Men* by Gustavus Swift Paine.[9] It may surprise you to discover the strange assortment of men that produced this masterpiece of English literature!)

But it was not Lancelot Andrewes the translator that captivated Alexander Whyte; it was Lancelot Andrewes the man of prayer. You will want to secure Whyte's *Lancelot Andrewes and His "Private Devotions,"* one of the series of *Appreciation* volumes written by Whyte, because that is the best introduction to Andrewes. The learned bishop was not a great preacher, although many of his sermons are still available in old volumes. His *Sermons of the Nativity* are available in *The Ancient and Modern Library of Theological Literature*, but you will find no exciting messages in these pages. Andrewes preached these seventeen sermons before King James; it was a standard procedure on Christmas Day that the bishop so address the court.

Andrewes was known even in his day as a great man of prayer, spending hours daily in his devotional exercises. Out of this came the book that so captured Whyte: *Private Devotions*. Andrewes did not write these devotions for publication. He gave his copy to his friend William Laud in 1626 (the year of Andrewes's death), and in 1675 Oxford Press published the first English translation (the original devotions had been written in Greek, Hebrew, and Latin). There have been several translations since then, but the book has never, to my knowledge, had wide distribution. After reading Whyte's *Appreciation*, you may want to secure a copy of *Private Devotions*. The best edition is the one edited by F. E. Brightman, originally published in 1903 but reprinted by Meridian Books in 1961. A second edition, edited by Thomas S. Kepler, was issued by World Publishing Company in 1956.

Andrewes's *Devotions* are not brief sermons or "helpful thoughts" based on Scripture. They are expressions of praise, penitence, faith, and intercession taken directly from the Bible and the church fathers.

He included prayers for each day of the week, based, for example, on the week of creation described in Genesis 1. He had devotional exercises from Scripture for both the morning and evening. "There is nothing in the whole range of devotional literature to be set beside Andrewes's incomparable *Devotions*," wrote Whyte. I am sure that what captured Whyte's interest was Andrewes's emphasis on sin and repentance (Whyte was himself a master of surgical preaching on sin and confession), but perhaps we could use this emphasis today.

Not every believer will be set on fire by Andrewes; if you are not, do not despair. But if you are, you will have acquired a source of spiritual help that will never fail you, because it is grounded in the Word of God. It will take you time to master the bishop's approach. It will take concentration—spiritual concentration—to keep from merely reciting prayers in a routine fashion. But once you have leaped these obstacles, you will discover a new power and satisfaction in your personal devotional exercises. Using the *Private Devotions* will never make you another Alexander Whyte, but it can help to make you a better saint of God.

We have come a long way, from Sherlock Holmes to the sainted Bishop Andrewes, and Alexander Whyte has been our guide all the while. I encourage you to read Barbour's magnificent biography of his uncle. Who knows what interesting people you may meet in its pages, and Whyte himself will be the most interesting one of all!

Whyte died on January 6, 1921, and a few days later Nicoll wrote in the *British Weekly*: "What a gift he was to his Church, to his nation! How wide were the irradiations of faith and love and hope and repentance that came from his intense and prayerful life!"

24

Dwight L. Moody
1837–1899

Dwight Lyman Moody was perhaps the most remarkable Christian layman America ever produced.

Yes, I said "layman," because D. L. Moody was never ordained, nor did he ever have any formal training for the ministry. He preferred to be called "Mr. Moody," and he readily admitted his educational limitations. In fact, whenever a group of preachers met with him, Moody usually asked them pointed questions about the Bible and the interpretation of difficult passages. "I have never been through a college or a theological seminary," he once said to a gathering of London pastors, "and I have invited you here to get all the valuable teaching I can out of you to use in my work!"

And he readily admitted when his interpretations were wrong and his sermons had to be changed!

One time Moody invited Dr. Henry Weston of Crozier Seminary to be one of the speakers at his Northfield Conference. (Dr. Weston was one of the original editors of the *Scofield Reference Bible*.) As Weston stepped to the pulpit, Moody picked up one of the platform chairs, stepped off the platform, and sat right in front of the pulpit, literally at the preacher's feet.

Dr. Weston began to expound the Word, and suddenly Moody exclaimed, "There goes one of my sermons!" Weston stopped and asked the evangelist what he had meant by that statement. Moody explained that Weston's exposition had shown him that his own sermon on that text had been built on a misinterpretation and was now useless.

Weston continued to preach, and Moody said it again, "There goes another!" Weston smiled and kept right on speaking, because in his seminary classes the students had used Moody's sermons to challenge their professor's interpretations—and now the situation was reversed!

As I review the life of D. L. Moody, I am again amazed to discover how many important servants of God were influenced by this energetic Yankee's life and ministry. Ira Sankey, Moody's soloist, would probably have died an unknown Internal Revenue collector had Moody not recruited him. The saintly F. B. Meyer, proper British pastor, had his life transformed through meeting and working with Moody. The godly American pastor, S. D. Gordon—whose series of *Quiet Talk* books is still popular—was converted in Moody's campaign in Philadelphia (1875–76). Moody laid hands on intellectual Reuben Archer Torrey and God made a soul-winning evangelist out of him. Spurgeon's gifted assistant, W. Y. Fullerton, gladly admitted that he "discovered his life's business"—the winning of the lost— at Moody's Belfast meetings in 1874. And the great expositor Dr. G. Campbell Morgan was "discovered" by Moody and brought to America before Morgan's gifts were really appreciated in Britain. (In all fairness, we must admit that Moody himself was "discovered" in Britain before he became popular in America.)

Dr. A. T. Pierson estimated conservatively that Moody brought the gospel to 100 million people during his lifetime—without radio, television, or even a public address system! And it is remarkable to discover some of the people who sat in his congregations—a lad named Harry Ironside, for one. When Moody held his Los Angeles campaign in 1888, twelve-year-old Ironside was sitting in Hazzard's Pavilion, listening intently. Little did either of them realize that, for eighteen years (1930–48), Ironside would pastor Moody Church in Chicago.

When Moody was preaching in Denver, a young lad wanted to hear the evangelist but could not get into the building. "I'll get you in!" said a heavyset man at the back door. "Just hold on to my coat-tail." The man was D. L. Moody, and the boy was Paul Rader, who grew up to become one of America's greatest preachers and also a pastor of Moody Church (1915–21).

In the late 1800s, when Moody was preaching in western New York, a boy named Harry Emerson Fosdick was in the congregation— more than once! Apparently the gospel message did not impress the lad, for he grew up to become America's leading liberal preacher and an opponent of the fundamentals of the faith.

How could this relatively unlearned shoe salesman become such a forceful and effective evangelist and teacher? Moody's success lay in his tremendous burden for the lost and a willingness to do whatever God asked of him. The life and ministry of this humble man of God is an example to us of what the Lord can do in the life of an ordinary person who is totally yielded to him.

Dwight L. Moody was born in Northfield, Massachusetts, on February 5, 1837. When he was four months old, young Victoria was crowned Queen of England, and Moody lived through almost all of the Victorian era. He died December 22, 1899, and Victoria died January 22, 1901.

The Moody family was poor, and the situation became even worse when their father died in 1841, leaving their mother with seven children. Twins were born to her just a month after her husband died. The creditors swooped down on her, taking even the fuel from the woodpile. One especially cruel neighbor tried to foreclose on the mortgage. (Forty years later, Moody bought the man out!)

When Moody was seventeen years old, he went to Boston to work in his uncle's shoe store. Sam Holton made his nephew promise that he would attend Sunday school and church, which young Dwight dutifully did. Fortunately, he had a teacher who was burdened for the lost. On April 25, 1855, Edward Kimball visited Moody at the store and led him to faith in Jesus Christ. (Seventeen years later, Moody would lead Kimball's son to the Savior.)

"I was in a new world," said Moody as he recalled the experience. "The next morning the sun shone brighter and the birds sang sweeter . . . it was the most delicious joy that I'd ever known."[1]

A month later, Moody applied for membership in the Mt. Vernon Church, but he was rejected because he simply could not answer the questions put to him by the committee. One officer told him, "Young man, you can serve the Lord better by keeping still!" It took Moody a year to join the church; he was finally admitted on May 4, 1856.

Four months later he was in Chicago, selling shoes for the Wiswall Company on Lake Street. Moody was nineteen years old, a hard worker and a growing Christian; and, like Joseph in Egypt, he prospered because the Lord was with him.

Moody joined the Plymouth Congregational Church where Dr. J. E. Roy was pastor. He rented five pews and filled them with young men Sunday after Sunday. One day he walked into a little mission on North Wells Street and told the superintendent that he wanted to teach a Sunday school class. Apologetically, the superintendent confessed that he had almost as many teachers as students, so Moody decided to recruit his own class. The next Sunday he showed up with eighteen ragged pupils, thus doubling the size of the school.

"That was the happiest Sunday I have ever known," Moody later stated. "I had found out what my mission was."

During the summer of 1858, he taught his growing class on the shores of Lake Michigan. When winter set in, he moved them into an old, abandoned saloon on Market Street. By 1859 there were one thousand pupils in Moody's Sunday school, and the creative ministry of their leader had won for him the title "Crazy Moody." In fact, when Moody returned to Northfield for a visit in January 1860, his uncle Zeb Allen said he was crazy! To compensate for this kind of opposition, however, something very special happened on November 25, 1860—Abraham Lincoln visited Moody's school and commended his work.

In June of that year Moody learned a lesson that helped transform his life and direct him into his future ministry. One of his faithful teachers was dying of tuberculosis and was greatly burdened for his pupils. Before he went to heaven, he wanted to be sure all of them were converted. The man was too weak to visit them alone, so Moody went along. For ten days, the two men visited home after home; and at the end of that time, they saw each of the children won to the Lord. When the teacher left for his widowed mother's home to die, the entire class was at the railroad station, singing songs about heaven.

This experience made a lasting impression on Moody. From it he got "the strongest impulse for trying to bring souls to Christ." Being successful in business meant less and less to him. The only business that counted was God's business—winning the lost to Jesus Christ.

During the Civil War, Moody ministered effectively to the soldiers. In fact, this was his training ground for later ministry. He gradually overcame his shyness in public speaking and learned how to deal personally with people in great need. Moody built a chapel at Camp Douglas (where the Illinois Institute of Technology now stands) and saw that the gospel was preached to the men. He made nine visits to the front. He was on hand at Pittsburg Landing, Shiloh, and Murfreesboro, and was one of the first to enter Richmond.

Moody prospered as a shoe salesman and had saved $7,000—quite a sum in that day! He decided it was time he thought about marriage. He had noticed a lovely Christian girl teaching in the Sunday school. Her name was Emma Revell, and her father had been a British shipbuilder who had come to America to make a new beginning. Dwight and Emma were engaged in 1860, and on August 28, 1862, they were married. If the name *Revell* sounds familiar to you, it is because Emma's brother, Fleming H. Revell, founded the Christian publishing firm that bore his name. In fact, he went into publishing primarily to make Moody's songbooks and sermons available at a popular price to a wider audience. D. L. Moody was probably the originator of the Christian paperback.

As Moody's Sunday school prospered, he faced a problem. Most of his converts did not feel at home in the established churches of the city. They wanted to be with Mr. Moody. Always the innovator and the pioneer, Moody built the Illinois Street Independent Church and laid hands on a fellow named Wheeler to be the pastor. Of course, nobody doubted who the leader of the church was.

Moody was now in the Lord's business full-time. He allowed himself to be appointed to the Illinois State Sunday School Union Board. Always the activist, Moody never did shine while serving on committees; however, his presence certainly kept everybody else on their toes. In 1866 he was elected president of the YMCA in Chicago, a position he held until 1870. In that day, the "Y" was an evangelical ministry, seeking to reach the young people in the city. It was a perfect base of ministry for a man like Moody.

Despite his early successes, D. L. Moody still had some important lessons to learn about the Bible and about evangelism. At that moment God was preparing the man who would teach Moody these lessons. And the truths that would revolutionize Moody's ministry were to come—not from the great theologians and preachers of the day—but from an ex-prizefighter in Great Britain.

"I do not expect to visit this country again." Dwight L. Moody made that statement shortly after arriving in England in March 1867. He had been seasick during the voyage from America and was also a bit discouraged with the "dull and formal" church life in England. In short, he was homesick.

But Mr. Moody was wrong in his evaluation. During his ministry he would visit Britain seven times, and his fourth visit would last more than two years and result in thousands coming to Christ. In fact, it was Britain that really discovered Moody and Sankey and made their names household words before the men were famous in America.

During that first visit, Moody had practically no public ministry. He went to the Metropolitan Tabernacle and heard Charles Spurgeon preach. Although an usher tried to keep Moody out of the Tabernacle because he didn't have a ticket, the quick-talking shoe salesman argued his way in. Spurgeon was one of his spiritual heroes, and Moody was not about to visit London without hearing him. Moody was greatly moved by the message from "an untrained man" like himself.

In the weeks that followed, Moody also met John Nelson Darby (founder of the Plymouth Brethren movement) and George Müller (pioneer of the famous "faith ministry" with orphans).

Moody gave a brief address at the anniversary breakfast of the Aldersgate YMCA in London. He was introduced as "our American cousin, the Reverend Mr. Moody from Chicago."

"The vice-chairman has made two mistakes," Moody said in reply. "To begin with, I'm not 'the Reverend Mr. Moody' at all. I'm plain Dwight L. Moody, a Sabbath school worker. And then I'm not your 'American cousin.' By the grace of God, I'm your brother, who is interested with you in our Father's work for his children."

In the speech that followed, Moody "unstarched" the British brethren, won many friends, offended a few saints, and started a fresh wind blowing. The noon prayer meetings at the YMCA took on new power and blessing, thanks to the influence of Moody. This brief contact with some of Britain's religious leaders would bring rich dividends in Moody's later ministry, particularly the 1873–75 campaign.

But in retrospect, the most important man he met on that trip was the ex-prizefighter Harry Moorehouse. Converted out of a life of great sin, Moorehouse had become a bold evangelist for the Lord. He and Moody had a great deal in common, but Moody was to learn from Moorehouse two important lessons.

"If you are ever in Chicago, plan to preach at my church," Moody casually told Moorehouse, and then Moody forgot the matter completely. But Moorehouse did not forget. No sooner had Moody returned to Chicago than he received a letter from Moorehouse, informing his new friend that he had arrived in New York and would be coming to Chicago to preach! Moody had to be out of the city, so he told the church officers to let the young man preach.

When Moody returned home, he asked Emma how the British preacher had done, and she gave her husband an enthusiastic report.

"He proves everything he says from the Bible," she said, "and he has preached both nights from the same text—John 3:16." Always ready to learn new truths and pick up new ideas, Moody went to the meeting and was amazed to see his own people carrying Bibles and using them during the message. Moorehouse began at John 3:16 and took the people from Genesis to Revelation as he talked about the love of God and the divine plan of redemption.

Privately, Moorehouse gently rebuked Moody. "Learn to preach God's words instead of your own. He will make you a great power for good." Then Moorehouse showed Moody how to use the Bible and trace the great themes of Scripture. It was like a second conversion for Moody. He purchased a *Cruden's Concordance* and began to get up two or three hours before breakfast so that he might read and study the Bible. Years later, at the 1887 Northfield Conference, Moody said: "Take up the Bible, with a concordance. I believe Alexander Cruden did more to open up the Bible than he could ever have dreamed."

But Moorehouse did more than teach Moody how to study the Bible. He taught him to love sinners to the Savior. Night after night, as the ex-prizefighter preached on John 3:16, he emphasized the love of God for lost men and women. As Moody listened, his eyes were opened and his heart was melted. "I never knew . . . that God loved us so much! This heart of mine began to thaw out; I could not hold back the tears."

From 1867 to the fall of 1871, Moody kept busy in Sunday school work and the program of the YMCA. He became a popular speaker at state Sunday school conventions and was even elected to various offices in the associations, including that of president of the Illinois State Sunday School Association.

In 1870 Moody made a second trip to Britain. That same year, at the "Y" convention in Indianapolis, he heard Ira Sankey sing and decided he was just the man he needed for his own ministry. "Where are you from?" Moody asked. "What is your business? Are you married?" Sankey answered Moody's questions, wondering what he was driving at.

It took Moody six months to convince Sankey that ɛ
was his calling; but the man finally yielded, and the team ɩ
and Sankey" was born.

One story about Sankey must be repeated. While serving in the
Union army, Sankey was on guard duty one night and felt inspired
to sing a hymn. What he did not know was that he was in the sights
of a Confederate rifleman who, when he heard the song, lowered his
rifle and did not shoot. If ever a man had been "compassed about
with songs of deliverance" (see Ps. 32:7), it was Ira Sankey.

It appeared that everything was now in place, and Moody could
move ahead in Sunday school work, the YMCA ministry, and the
winning of souls. But something was still missing in Moody's life
and ministry, and he had to experience some further crises before he
would become the man God wanted him to be. If ever there was a
busy man serving the Lord, it was Dwight L. Moody. But deep within,
Moody knew that something was missing from his ministry.

Enter at this point two somewhat eccentric women, Aunt Sarah
Cooke and Mrs. Hawxhurst, both of whom were identified with
"the holiness movement" of greater Chicago and northern Indiana.
Cooke belonged to the Free Methodist Church but fellowshiped
widely with God's people and called herself simply "the handmaiden
of the Lord."

"Mr. Moody was an earnest, whole-souled worker," Sarah Cooke
wrote in her memoirs, *Wayside Sketches*, "but ever to me there
seemed such a lack in his words. It seemed more the human, the
natural energy and force of character of the man, than anything
spiritual."[2]

Cooke and Hawxhurst often discussed Moody and his ministry
and then decided to talk to the man himself. They told him that they
were praying for him that he might receive the power of the Spirit.
At first Moody was surprised at their concern and suggested that
they pray for the lost. Then he became convicted and began to pray
with the ladies every Friday afternoon.

"At every meeting," Sarah Cooke reported, "he would get more
earnest, in agony of desire for this fullness of the Spirit."

But before the "fire" of God's power came upon him, Moody experienced another kind of fire, for on October 8, 1871, the great Chicago fire broke out. From Belden Avenue on the north to 12th Street on the south, and as far west as Halsted Street, the fire destroyed more than 17,000 buildings and property worth nearly $200 million.

Moody was preaching that night at Farwell Hall on the theme "What Will You Do with Jesus?" He admitted later that what he did that night was foolish—he ended the message by asking the people to take a week to decide and then come back to report their decision. But even while Sankey was singing the closing song (ironically it was "Today the Savior Calls"), the noise of fire engines and warning bells drowned out the meeting. Moody dismissed the crowd and set about doing what he could to rescue his family and a few possessions.

The Moody family found refuge with Horatio Spafford, the author of the hymn "It Is Well with My Soul." Later Moody said that the fire had taken from him "everything but my reputation and my Bible." When a well-meaning friend said, "Moody, I hear you lost everything!" Moody opened his Bible to Revelation 21:7 and said, "Well, you understood wrong. I have a good deal more than I lost!" Then he read the verse: "He that overcometh shall inherit all things; and I will be his God."

With his family cared for, Moody left for the East Coast to preach, rest, and raise money to replace his church building. It was while ministering in Theodore Cuyler's church in Brooklyn that Moody had his life-changing experience and the power of the Spirit came upon him. He was walking down Wall Street in New York City, mulling over the impotence of his preaching and the failure of his fund-raising program, when the Spirit of God filled him.

"Oh, what a day!" he later reported. "I cannot describe it; I seldom refer to it; it is almost too sacred an experience to name. . . . I can only say that God revealed Himself to me, and I had such an experience of His love that I had to ask Him to stay His hand."

It is unfortunate that some groups have tried to use Moody's experience to promote their own special views of the baptism of the Spirit and speaking in tongues. There is no evidence that D. L. Moody ever spoke in tongues, and during his many campaigns in Great Britain, he and Sankey always avoided the people who promoted tongues and prophesying. If somebody in a meeting began to speak out or swoon, Moody would either call for a hymn or close the meeting.

One of the leading specialists on the theology of D. L. Moody is my friend Dr. Stanley Gundry, whose definitive book *Love Them In: The Proclamation Theology of D. L. Moody* should be in every pastor's library. Originally published by Moody Press, the book was reprinted by Baker Books.

Dr. Gundry says:

> One must proceed cautiously when examining Moody's statements on this matter (the filling of the Spirit), for it is all too easy to impose upon Moody's statements a meaning that he did not intend.... Moody himself seldom went into the details of his 1871 experience, or at least existing sermons seldom give the details. But on those rare occasions when he did, he described it as a filling, a baptism or an anointing that came upon him when he was in a cold state. His selfish ambitions in preaching had been surrendered, and he then received power by which to do his work for Christ.[3]

Moody returned to the rather dismal "revival" meeting at Cuyler's church, and the fire began to burn. More than one hundred people professed faith in Christ, and the blessings spread to other congregations. Moody was preaching the same messages, but his preaching contained a new tenderness, and the power of God was evident in the meetings.

Something also happened to Moody, the fund-raiser. Instead of depending on his own experience as a salesman, Moody began to trust God for guidance as he approached people with his needs. He was still aggressive, but in a new way. Before long he had the needed funds to replace the church building. On December 24, 1871, he dedicated the new tabernacle with more than 1,000 children and their parents assisting him.

Perhaps this is a good place to mention the history of the church that Mr. Moody founded in 1864. It was originally called the Illinois

Street Independent Church, with Mr. Wheeler as the pastor. Of course, everybody knew that Mr. Moody was their leader, but he was not an ordained minister. From 1866 to 1869 J. H. Harwood pastored the church, but there was no regular pastor from 1869 to 1871. Moody had many friends who enjoyed assisting in the work, so there was always somebody in the pulpit. Often Moody did the preaching himself.

After the fire, the new structure was called the North Side Tabernacle, and in 1876 the church relocated to Chicago Avenue and La-Salle Street and became the Chicago Avenue Church. The esteemed pastors were William J. Erdman (1876–78), Charles M. Morton (1878, 1879), George C. Needham (1879–81), Charles F. Goss (1885–90), and Charles A. Blanchard (1891–93). From 1894 to 1906, Reuben Archer Torrey pastored the church, which was renamed Moody Church in 1901. Mr. Moody would never have put his name on the church, but it seemed to be an appropriate way to honor his memory after his death.

Beginning in 1889, the newly founded Chicago Evangelistic Society (later Moody Bible Institute) used the church's facilities, and Dr. R. A. Torrey served as both pastor and superintendent of the school. When Torrey left in 1906 to start the Church of the Open Door in Los Angeles, Dr. A. C. Dixon became pastor (1906–11). One of America's greatest preachers, Paul Rader, became pastor in 1915, and the church moved a mile north on LaSalle Street to North Avenue, where a 5,000-seat tabernacle was built. Rader preached to thousands of people night after night, and multitudes were saved.

Rader resigned in 1921, and P. W. Philpott accepted the pulpit, remaining until 1929. During his ministry the congregation tore down the old tabernacle and, in 1925, dedicated the present building that is officially named the Moody Memorial Church. For eighteen fruitful years (1930–48), Dr. H. A. Ironside ministered the Word to large congregations, and on every Sunday except two he saw public decisions for Christ.

S. Franklin Logsden followed Dr. Ironside as pastor. Logsden was succeeded by Dr. Alan Redpath from England. From 1966 to 1971,

Dr. George Sweeting was pastor. I had the privilege of succeeding Dr. Sweeting, serving from 1971 to 1978. The present pastor is Dr. Erwin Lutzer, a former instructor at Moody Bible Institute.

Whenever former Moody pastors or Moody church "alumni" get together, there are often spirited discussions about what Mr. Moody would have done had he lived longer. Would he have approved the construction of a 4,000-seat cathedral-type church building? Would he perhaps have scattered the congregation to various locations in Chicago, to build fifty or one hundred soul-winning churches? Paul Rader wanted to build a "skyscraper" with an auditorium for 2,500 people and classrooms and offices for the church; and then he planned to rent the rest of the structure out to help pay the bills!

Unless Mr. Moody tells us in heaven, we will never know what he would have done; therefore, it is useless to speculate. We do know that both Moody Church and Moody Bible Institute, with its many ministries, have been used by God over the years to bless countless people around the world.

Moody made another trip to Britain in 1872, during which he was introduced to "dispensational truth" and met evangelist Henry Varley. It was Varley who said to Moody (and this seems to be the accurate version): "Moody, the world has yet to see what God can do with and for and through and in a man who is fully and wholly consecrated to Him." Varley did not remember making the statement, but Moody never forgot it.

One of the ministers asked Moody to preach at a church in Arundel Square, London, and that service turned into a two-week meeting during which four hundred people professed faith in Christ. Part of the secret behind the harvest was the praying of Marianne Adlard, a bedridden girl who had read about Moody in a newspaper and had been praying daily that he would come to her church and preach. God answered her prayers, and Moody caught a new vision of what God could do through him in Britain.

In fact, it was a crisis experience for him. As a result, he determined to concentrate on evangelism and give himself completely to the winning of lost souls. The result was the great campaign of 1873–75.

"I go where I can do the most good. That is what I am after. It is souls I want—it is souls I want!"

Moody spoke those words to some British friends in 1873. He had recently arrived in Britain, responding to an invitation from three leading English Christians—Henry Bewley, Cuthbert Bainbridge and William Pennefather. To his dismay, he discovered that Bainbridge and Pennefather were both dead and that Bewley was not expecting him.

But Moody was not the kind of man who quit easily. He had in his pocket a letter from George Bennet, who was secretary of the YMCA at York, so he wired Bennet that he was coming. The man was shocked by the news and informed Moody that it would take weeks for them to get ready for a meeting. Bennet's arguments meant nothing to Moody, who promptly went to York and started preaching the Word, with Sankey singing his way into the hearts of the people.

The British congregations were suspicious and for a time kept their distance. "One has an organ and performs on that," went the report. "The other tells stories." And everybody waited to see what the "catch" was and how these uninvited American guests would make a profit out of the meetings. Attendance was not large, and the spirit of the meetings was nothing exciting.

Then God touched a pastor's heart, and the whole atmosphere began to change. The young pastor of the Priory Street Baptist Chapel was brought under deep conviction at the noon prayer meeting. He had been "beating the air" in his ministry, and when Moody had preached on the Holy Spirit, the pastor realized his need and how God could meet it. That man was F. B. Meyer, whose ministry of the Word would be greatly used around the world and whose many books minister to hearts even today.

Meyer even permitted Moody to use his church building for extra services, and by now the tide was beginning to flow in. A large crowd came to hear Moody at the Corn Exchange, and one of the leading religious newspapers in England began to report the meetings. F. B. Meyer was so blessed with his new vision of evangelism and ministry that his enthusiasm offended some of his officers, and he was asked to leave the church. "This is not a gospel shop!" the irate officers told him. God opened the way for him to establish a new church in Leicester, "Melbourne Hall," which still maintains a faithful witness.

After the ministry at York, Moody and Sankey moved to Sunderland and then Newcastle. Their friend Harry Moorehouse joined them and shared in the meetings. It was at Newcastle that *Sacred Songs and Solos* was first issued, published on September 16 by Marshall, Morgan, and Scott. Known as the "Sankey Hymnbook," this volume was just what Moody needed in his meetings, as most of the church hymnals did not contain gospel songs with an evangelistic emphasis.

Since that time, more than ten million copies of *Sacred Songs and Solos* have been sold. When the initial royalties started to come in, Moody offered them to his British friends for whatever ministries they chose; but they refused the money. So Moody sent the money back to Chicago where it was used to complete the Chicago Avenue Church building.

The tide continued to come in, so the team decided to invade traditional, evangelical Scotland; on November 23, they opened a campaign in Edinburgh. It was not an encouraging beginning. For one thing, Moody was ill with tonsillitis; for another, Sankey's organ was in need of repairs. But they started the meetings, and God began to bless.

Let me interrupt this report with an interesting sidelight. On October 19, just a few weeks before Moody and Sankey arrived, the leading "spiritual giant" of Scotland, Dr. R. S. Candlish, died. Before he died, he predicted that there would come to Scotland "a great blessing which should not be despised, though it come strangely." Moody and Sankey were the "strange" bearers of that blessing.

Here's a humorous sidelight on the Edinburgh meetings. Sankey finally got his organ repaired (the Scots called it "a chest of whistles") and sang the gospel in the meetings. At one point, it was necessary to hold two meetings across the street from each other in order to accommodate the crowds. Sankey would sing in one church while Moody preached in the other, and then they would exchange places.

As Sankey began to sing and play his organ in the one meeting, a faithful Presbyterian lady jumped up and ran from the meeting, shouting, "Let me oot! Let me oot! What would John Knox think of the like of ye?" She was offended, of course, by Sankey's use of a musical instrument in a church. She then went across the street to the other meeting, and when Sankey appeared to sing there, she jumped up and ran out again, still shouting, "Let me oot! Let me oot! What would John Knox think of the like of ye?"

It is worth noting that Sankey sang "The Ninety and Nine" for the first time in the Edinburgh campaign. The words were written by a frail Scottish lady, Elizabeth C. Clephane, who lived near Edinburgh. Sankey had found the poem in a newspaper he had purchased at the train depot and, impressed with the message, had put the clipping in his pocket. After preaching on the Good Shepherd, Moody turned to Sankey and asked him to sing an appropriate song. Asking God for help, Sankey put the words on his organ, struck A-flat, and composed the tune as he went along. Moody then gave his invitation, and many "lost sheep" entered the inquiry room to find the Shepherd.

On February 8 the campaign moved to Glasgow, but all was not well. One of Scotland's most famous preachers, the Reverend John Kennedy ("The Spurgeon of the Highlands"), opposed Mr. Moody's ministry. The fact that some 3,000 persons had been received into the Edinburgh churches as a result of Moody's work did not impress Kennedy. He published a pamphlet "proving" that it was not scriptural for Moody to use "human hymns" instead of the Psalms, to play the organ in a church, or to invite sinners into inquiry rooms.

Not all of the leading clergy were opposed to the campaign, however, among them the saintly Andrew Bonar, noted pastor and special friend of Robert Murray McCheyne. "The tide of real revival in Edinburgh has been stirring up all of us," he wrote in his journal on January 1, 1874. On February 10, he wrote: "This city has been at last visited; Moody and Sankey, sent by the Lord." Bonar and many other pastors prayed earnestly that God would break through the religious complacency of the churches and that many sinners would come to the Savior.

God answered their prayers as the tide kept deepening. On February 24, some 101 men professed faith in Christ in one meeting! When the campaign closed on April 19, the record showed that there had been more than 6,000 professions of faith and that 7,000 persons had united with local churches. Bonar wrote in his journal that he had a communicant's class of fifty-two, all of them clear as to their salvation experience, and that fifty-four people came to the Lord's Table for the first time.

Moody and Sankey spent the summer months in the Scottish Highlands, ministering from town to town, and then in September moved to Ireland. In spite of some inclement weather and the prejudice of some Roman Catholic people, the meetings were a great success. Buildings were packed, and people responded to Moody's simple presentation of the gospel.

After five weeks in Belfast, the men moved their witness to Dublin where only one-fourth of the population was Protestant. The crowds came, however, even though the archbishop had issued an edict forbidding his people to attend. Even ridicule did not affect the ministry, as the following story proves.

A couple of clowns performing at a Dublin circus tried to ridicule the evangelists with this routine:

"I'm rather Moody tonight. How do you feel?"

"I feel rather Sankeymonious."

The audience began to hiss the so-called comedians and then began to sing "Hold the Fort."

For the most part, the Roman Catholic publications were sympathetic to the meetings. One editor wrote: "The deadly danger of the age comes upon us from the direction of Huxley and Darwin and Tyndall, rather than from Moody and Sankey." Moody's positive message carried the day, and the *British Weekly* called the meetings "a Pentecost."

The Irish campaign closed on November 29, and Moody then preached in Manchester during December, in Birmingham in January, and in Liverpool in February. The crowds came and people were converted, although not as many as Moody had hoped. On March 9 he tackled London with its three million people. Once again his biggest problem was with the clergy, so Moody held an informal session to answer their questions.

"How are you paid?" one minister asked.

"I have money enough for myself right in my pocket," said Moody, "and do not ask for a cent." (The fact was that Moody had single-handedly raised thousands of dollars for the construction of YMCA buildings and missions in Britain.)

"I am a ritualist," said another minister. "Will you send me all my proper and rightful converts?"

Moody replied, "I am not here to divide up the profits but to get as many as I can to give their hearts to Jesus Christ."

It seems that every Christian evangelist, from Peter to Martin Luther to John Wesley to Moody to those of our present day, has had his greatest problems with the ministers who should have been out winning the lost themselves.

An entire book could be written about the miracles of the London campaign. Wealthy sportsman Edward Studd came to Christ through Moody's ministry, and eight years later his son C. T. Studd trusted Christ when Moody preached at Cambridge. Fifteen thousand men attended a special "men only" meeting and many of them found Christ. It was estimated that 2.5 million people heard Moody and Sankey during the campaign and that the men conducted 285 different public meetings. The total budget ran $140,000!

On August 4, 1875, Moody left for home, arriving in the United States ten days later. It had been a triumphant campaign for Christ. He had won the battle for Britain.

Before we leave Moody and Sankey, let's try to answer the question that many people asked then and still ask today: what was the secret of their success, not only in their British campaign but also in their ministry in general? When you read the reports and evaluations written in Moody's day, you start to get a composite answer that seems to be valid.

To begin with, Moody himself was a Spirit-filled man who was burdened for souls. He had no interest in making money. He was not intimidated by "important people," nor was he afraid to try something new. In fact, Moody stands as one of the great innovators in Christian ministry. If one approach did not work, being a good businessman, he tried another.

The meetings were undergirded with prayer. The noon prayer meeting was the most important meeting of the day to Moody. If it became dull or dead, he livened it up and got the people praying. "I'd rather be able to pray than to be a great preacher," he once said. "Jesus Christ never taught his disciples how to preach, but only how to pray."

Third, he worked in and through the church and encouraged ministers to forget their minor differences and work together to win the lost. This was not easy in Britain where the state church and the independents sometimes engaged in mutual suspicion and attack. "Satan separates," said Moody. "God unites. Love binds us together."

Moody used the Bible and kept the Bible before the people. During the two years of the British campaign, publishers could hardly keep up with the demand for Bibles. "I have observed that Mr. Moody speaks to inquirers with an open Bible in his hands," wrote one reporter. Moody did not argue theology; he simply quoted the Bible and let God speak for himself.

Several leaders mentioned the order and atmosphere of the meetings as a factor in Moody's success. There was a spirit of worship, and ushers were trained to deal immediately with disturbances. When applause broke out in one meeting, it was instantly silenced; and often Moody would call for times of silent prayer and worship.

Everybody knew that Ira Sankey's music was a key factor in the blessing of God on the meetings. Even the dour Scots finally yielded to the wooing of the portable organ and songs of the American singer. One reporter wrote: "He spoils the Egyptians of their finest music and consecrates it to the service of the tabernacle." Both Moody and

Sankey were courageous enough to use new hymns and gospel songs in spite of the opposition of the traditionalists.

The campaign seemed a failure at the start, but God worked in a remarkable way and gave Britain perhaps the greatest spiritual movement since the days of George Whitefield and John Wesley. And he did it through two ordinary men who would not quit but who trusted God to bless his Word.

God can still do that today in our land or in any land. Henry Varley's words are still true: "The world has yet to see what God can do with and for and through and in a man who is fully and wholly consecrated to Him."

George Matheson
1842–1906

Most people know two things about George Matheson: he was blind, and he wrote "O Love That Will Not Let Me Go." Some people still believe the myth that he wrote the hymn after his sweetheart broke their engagement because he was going blind. Matheson began to go blind at age eighteen months, and he was never engaged. "I have never been in love," he once told his friend M'Kenzie Bell.

Matheson told about the experience of composing the hymn: "It came to me spontaneously, without conscious effort; and I have never been able to gain once more the same fervor in verse." He admitted a crisis had been involved, but he did not say what it was:

> My hymn was composed in the manse of Innellan on the evening of 6th June 1882. I was at that time alone. It was the day of my sister's marriage, and the rest of the family were staying overnight in Glasgow. Something had happened to me, which was known only to myself, and which caused me the most severe mental suffering. The hymn was the fruit of that suffering. It was the quickest bit of work I ever did in my life. I had the impression rather of having it dictated to me

by some inward voice than of working it out myself. I am quite sure
that the whole work was completed in five minutes.[1]

I believe Matheson made far greater contributions to the cause
of Christ than his hymn, as beautiful as that is. His courage and accomplishment are a tremendous inspiration to anyone in the ministry
who has to fight a handicap.

George Matheson was born in Glasgow on March 27, 1842.
His eyesight began to fail, but he managed to complete his basic
schooling wearing very strong glasses. By the time he was eighteen, however, he had to have assistance. His two sisters were his
greatest helpers, even learning foreign languages to tutor him. At
the University of Glasgow he devoted five years to earning his MA
and another four years to an MDiv. He won honors, particularly in
debate and public speaking, and he was popular. At one point he
wanted to train for a legal career, but the call of Christ prevailed.
On June 13, 1866, he was licensed by the presbytery; six months
later he was named assistant to John Ross MacDuff at Sandyford
Church. MacDuff was a devotional preacher whose books sold in
the millions. Influenced by MacDuff, Matheson also became a very
successful devotional writer.

Early in 1868, Matheson was recommended to the church of Innellan in one of Glasgow's resort areas. When Glasgow citizens re-
laxed in Innellan during summer months, they wanted to hear good
sermons. Matheson's blindness gave rise to some strong opposition
in the church, and they called him by a very narrow majority. Before long, however, the new pastor won the hearts of the people.
They ordained him on April 8, 1868, and he remained with them
for eighteen years. Not only was he faithful in his preaching, but
he also spent time with his people. Like most Scottish pastors, he
invested his mornings in the study and his afternoons in visitation
and counseling. Imagine what it would be like for a blind man to pastor a church. Matheson did have the capable assistance of his sister
and the officers of the church. But only he could gather the material
for his messages, plan the Sunday services, and lead the church in

worship. He memorized not only his message, but also the hymns and the Scripture readings. And he never missed a word!

Early in his Innellan ministry, Matheson experienced an eclipse of faith that would even have defeated a person without handicaps. "With a great thrill of horror," he told a friend, "I found myself an absolute atheist! After being ordained at Innellan, I believed nothing; neither God nor immortality." He shared his problem with his officers and even offered to resign. They wisely counseled him to wait; he was young, and all young ministers (they said) had times of doubt. He waited and won the battle. Without abandoning his traditional faith, he saw deeper meaning in it and felt he could still preach it without losing his integrity.

In 1879 he was granted a DD by Edinburgh University. He also became one of Innellan's greatest attractions. When he resigned the church in 1886 to go to St. Bernard's, Edinburgh, he temporarily threatened the economic stability of the resort!

His call to St. Bernard's Church is an interesting story in itself. One stormy winter's Sunday, Matheson preached to only a handful of worshipers. He went home rather discouraged because he felt his message had been especially good. A stranger in the Innellan congregation, however, never forgot either the sermon or the preacher. More than seven years later, when St. Bernard's needed a pastor, this man recommended Matheson. Each occasion of ministry deserves our best. The results may be slow in coming, but they will come.

Matheson was installed as pastor of St. Bernard's Church on May 12, 1886. He remained with the church for thirteen years. In 1896 he offered his resignation, but it was rejected. He preached his farewell sermon on November 17, 1899, and then retired to write and occasionally to preach. He preached his last sermon on February 14, 1904, at Morningside Church, Edinburgh, a pulpit made famous in recent years by James S. Stewart. While on his annual holiday, George Matheson took sick; he died on November 28, 1906.

His friends claimed that Matheson's blindness was actually his making. It compelled him to "walk by faith" and live in the highest levels of spiritual meditation. He was not deceived or distracted by the surface things of life. He had the ability to penetrate deeper even though he could not see. A Presbyterian council heard him preach once and responded: "The Council all feel that God has closed your eyes only to open other eyes, which have made you one of the guides of men."

Beside being a courageous man and an outstanding preacher, Matheson was an exacting scholar and capable writer. His first book was *Aids to the Study of German Theology* (1874). Preachers with normal vision would hesitate to tackle a subject like that. Three years later he published a two-volume work, *Growth of the Spirit of Christianity*, attempting to apply Hegelian philosophy to church history. In 1881 he published *Natural Elements of Revealed Theology*, the Baird lectures for that year. But we most remember Matheson as a devotional writer of amazing perception and poetic ability. *My Aspirations* (1883) was his first devotional book. He also wrote *Moments on the Mount, Words by the Wayside, Leaves for Quiet Hours, Rests by the River, Sidelights from Patmos*, and many others. Any preacher who has ever delivered a series of biographical sermons would appreciate *The Representative Men of the Bible* (two volumes), *The Representative Men of the New Testament*, and *The Representative Women of the Bible*. His *Studies of the Portrait of Christ* (two volumes) and *Spiritual Development of St. Paul* are valuable contributions to these areas of Bible study.

So much "devotional writing" today is shallow and sentimental and not at all spiritual. A Bible verse, a paragraph of approved platitudes, an exhortation, and a prayer make up the average "meditation." The people who manufacture these things need to listen to Matheson's convictions about devotional writing:

> Devotion must be the child of reflection; it may rise on wings, but they must be the wings of thought. . . . It should aim at the marriage of qualities which are commonly supposed to be antagonistic—the insight of the thinker and the fervor of the worshiper. . . . Religious sentiment, if it is worth anything, must be preceded by religious perception.[2]

Matheson blended the intellectual power of the theologian and the spiritual perception and devotion of the mystic. In the preface to *Times of Retirement*, he wrote: "It is often said that devotion is a thing of the heart. I do not think it is either mainly or merely so. I hold that all devotion is based upon intellectual conviction." No wonder his writing is like that "sea of glass, mingled with fire." His devotional writings are characterized by depth and variety. He laid hold of a great spiritual truth, saw new and exciting possibilities in it, and then applied it in a way that was practical without being preachy. He combined fact and feeling. Each selection generally has two parts: the spiritual thought for the mind and a prayer directed to the heart. George H. Morrison once defined "sentiment" as "feeling without responsibility." Matheson would have agreed, because he avoided the mawkish or maudlin. He never used religious words to manufacture artificial feeling.

Perhaps the secret of his balanced devotional experience was sincere prayer. One of his faithful parishioners wrote: "Dr. Matheson's first prayer [in the worship service] was often the finest part of the service. And what a prayer it was! . . . How many of our preachers draw tears from the eyes of the worshipers as they pray?" Another worshiper said: "In that prayer we have been to the mount of worship, and we could go away content even if we heard no more. It was wonderful the way in which that blind preacher talked with God and uttered the aspirations of the people." Matheson himself admitted: "Prayer never causes me an effort. When I pray, I know I am addressing the Deity, but when I preach, the Devil may be among the congregation."

In his early days of ministry, Matheson attempted to reconcile evangelical doctrine with the new German theology and the views of evolution. For some he succeeded; but at the same time he failed to minister to the needs of the masses. In his later years he wrote for the common people, and God gave him a wide and useful ministry. That ministry continues in his many books.

Matheson did not try to generate false fire. He warmed one's heart as the Savior had those of the Emmaus disciples; Matheson opened up the Scriptures and revealed Jesus Christ. He fed himself on the truths of the Word in long hours of meditation and then shared those truths with others. He made truth luminous. He made it exciting. We would do well to rediscover Matheson in this day of much superficial devotional preaching and writing. Some publisher could do us a great service by reprinting his best books, or perhaps an anthology of his best selections. The preacher would be wise to read Matheson and seek to attain that beautiful blending of doctrinal precision and devotional passion. George Matheson was blind, yet through his books he helps us see better.

26

C. I. Scofield
1843–1921

Strictly speaking, the Authorized (or King James) version of the Bible was never "authorized." King James favored the project for both personal and political reasons. But as the spiritual head of the Church of England, he did not *order* the use of the new translation. For years, the new translation received severe criticism—similar to the criticism leveled at today's translations. Even Lancelot Andrewes, one of the most learned of the King James Version translators, preferred to use the Geneva Bible.

Perhaps the Geneva Bible most irritated King James and convinced him that a new version was needed. The marginal notes in the Geneva Bible were critical of monarchies and national churches. The fact that the Calvinists in Geneva had helped produce the Geneva Bible was an added incentive for a new version in the language of the people. At any rate, one of the rules given to the King James translators was: "No marginal notes to be affixed," except notes relating to Hebrew or Greek.

Today the situation is reversed: we honor the King James version and resist its critics, and we prefer it with as many notes as possible. Annotated editions of the King James Bible continue to be published, and the public buys them. Like makes of cars or brands of toothpaste, each edition has its promoters and detractors, almost to the point of making one's choice of study Bible a test of orthodoxy or spiritual fellowship. The young Bible student looking for a study Bible has so many choices that he may not know how to make a sane selection. Perhaps the best known is the *Scofield Reference Bible*, edited by C. I. Scofield and published in 1909 by Oxford University Press. A corrected edition appeared in 1917, and in 1967 *The New Scofield Reference Bible* was published. More than a million and a half copies of this new edition have been sold. (I understand that there is a group dedicated to preserving the *original* edition! Apparently they feel the editors of the 1967 edition deviated too much from Scofield's interpretations.)

Cyrus Ingerson Scofield was born on August 19, 1843, in frontier Lenawee County, Michigan. While he was still a lad, his family moved to Wilson County, Tennessee, where he lived until he was seventeen. When he should have been enrolled in college, he enlisted in the Confederate Army and served with distinction for four years. He received the Cross of Honor for bravery at Antietam. After the war he relocated to St. Louis with his oldest sister, who had married into a wealthy family. Unwilling to permit his brother-in-law to pay for his education, Scofield went to work as a land clerk, examining titles. In two years his promotion to chief clerk provided sufficient money to study law. He passed his bar examinations at age twenty-six and was elected to the Kansas legislature. An efficient lawyer and politician, he was appointed by President Grant as U.S. Attorney for Kansas. He served for two years and then returned to St. Louis to practice law.

Another attorney, Thomas S. McPheeters, a dedicated Christian, was one of Scofield's close friends. Scofield was battling alcoholism. McPheeters came to Scofield's office in September 1879 and said: "For a long time I have been wanting to ask you a question that I have been afraid to ask, but that I am going to ask now. Why are you not a Christian?" He then took out his pocket New Testament and reasoned with the lawyer. Scofield wanted more time to consider the matter, but McPheeters would not give in. The Holy Spirit won the case: the two men prayed together, and C. I. Scofield gave his heart to Jesus Christ. Instantly the chains were broken, never to be forged again. Scofield wrote in later years: "The passion for drink was taken away! Divine power did it, wholly of grace. To Christ be all the glory!"

Like Dwight L. Moody, with whom he would be associated, Scofield became active in the YMCA. He also grew under the ministry of James H. Brookes, whom he called "the greatest Bible student I have ever known." Scofield developed a hunger to know the Word of God. One day he visited C. E. Paxson, a Christian friend, and found him drawing lines in a new Bible. "Man, you're spoiling that fine new Bible!" Scofield protested. But Paxson showed him he was connecting Acts 8:5 and 8:8 to demonstrate that Philip's preaching of Christ brought great joy to the city. Scofield's logical mind instantly caught the importance of the lines that were "ruining" Paxson's Bible, and from that hour he marked cross-references in his Bible. Scofield's experience in Paxson's office was his first step toward editing the most famous study Bible in English.

Scofield abandoned law in 1882 to pastor a new Congregational church in Dallas. There were twelve members, eleven of them women. Within two years a new building had to be constructed to accommodate two hundred members. Scofield's Bible-teaching ministry was blessed by God both at home and in the various conferences where he spoke, including the famous ones at Niagara and Northfield.

In 1895, Scofield became Moody's pastor at the East Northfield Congregational Church, where he ministered for seven years. He also served as president of the Northfield Bible Training School. He returned in 1902 to the First Congregational Church in Dallas, but the most important event of that year took place in New York City. While there to minister, Scofield visited Alwyn Ball, a Christian businessman who had encouraged his ministry. Ball asked what projects he was working on now that he had finished writing a correspondence course. Scofield replied that he had been thinking for years of preparing a reference Bible, to help serious students study the Word more systematically. Ball immediately approved the project, and the two of them took it as confirmation of the Lord.

Scofield tried pastoring the church while preparing the reference Bible, but after a year of frustration, he resigned. Much of his work from 1902 to 1909 was done in Montreaux, Switzerland. On several occasions Scofield was too ill to work, but his wife would continue with the project until he could rejoin her. We who read the *Scofield Reference Bible* today can appreciate the enormous amount of editorial work and proofreading. Of course Scofield consulted other Bible teachers (whose names appear on the title page), but the final writing and editing were his own.

On two occasions the work was almost destroyed. After he shipped the material from Europe to America, the boxes were lost. He and his wife prayed fervently until they located the priceless shipment among the baggage of immigrants who had come over on the same ship. While completing the final manuscript, the Scofields lived in a tent in New Hampshire, and the tent caught fire. Had the wind shifted, the manuscript in a nearby shed would have been destroyed.

Scofield did his work well. Even those who do not follow the dispensational approach to Scripture can benefit from the chain-reference system, the definitions, and the doctrinal summaries. The men who gave us the revised edition helped strengthen some points and solve some problem areas of interpretation.

The success of the Scofield Bible has encouraged other editors and publishers to enter the field. One of the latest—and best—is the *Ryrie Study Bible*, published in various editions by Moody Press and edited by Charles C. Ryrie, former professor of systematic theology at Dallas Theological Seminary. Ryrie's credentials as a Bible scholar and teacher certainly need no defense; even those who do not follow the Scofield-dispensational approach to the Bible admit that Ryrie is well-equipped for such an ambitious task.

This is not a "reference Bible" as such, although it does have a good system of cross-references. Rather it is an annotated Bible, with hundreds of marginal notes that explain and apply the text. While much of this information is available in standard Bible helps, it is good to have it alongside the text. These annotations cover more ground than those of Scofield, including historical data, archaeological information, cultural background, and doctrinal definitions and explanations. There is such a great wealth of information in these annotations that even the seasoned student will find them useful.

Ryrie introduces and outlines each book of the Bible. Some of the outlines are analytical (e.g., Matt., John, Acts, and 1 Thess.), while others are interpretive (e.g., 2 Tim. and 1 Peter). I prefer interpretive outlines that "open up" the book. But all the outlines are good, though some are a bit long. I am glad Ryrie did not caption the outlines, "*The* Outline of . . ." As G. Campbell Morgan said, "There is no such thing as *the* outline of a Bible book. I prefer to say *an* outline." No outline is inspired or final.

The editor is to be congratulated for breaking away from some time-honored dispensational "doctrines," such as a pre-Adamic race and a "gap" between the first and second verses of Genesis. He also makes it clear that Cain's sin was his unbelief, not his bloodless sacrifice. I have not yet read every note, but the ones I have read are helpful and practical. The experienced student who finds some of the annotations rather obvious (Luke 7:24–25, for example) must remember that this Bible will be used by believers who are at much earlier stages in their spiritual growth and Bible knowledge.

The *Ryrie Study Bible* is available in two texts: the Authorized Version and the New American Standard Bible. I commend Ryrie for preparing notes for both texts; it must have been a monumental task. He has also provided at the back of the Bible a number of extra helps: a harmony of the Gospels, a summary of Bible doctrine, various articles about the Bible and its origin, a topical index, an index to the annotations, maps, and other helps. There is also a concordance.

We have come a long way since King James ordered the omission of interpretive notes, and I am glad we have. As long as we keep in mind that the text, not the notes, is inspired, and that even the wisest men make mistakes, we will profit from the dedicated scholarship that produces such tools. There is no excuse except laziness for the

Christian who lacks a working knowledge of the Bible. Which study Bible is best? The one that helps you the most. Let every man be fully persuaded in his own mind. The important thing is to study God's Word consistently, using whatever helps are available, and then put it into practice.

27

F. B. Meyer
1847–1929

When Jack Johnson defeated James Jeffries for the 1911 world heavyweight championship, negotiations were begun to pit Johnson against the British champion, Bombardier Wells. But a well-known British Baptist preacher stepped into the ring and opposed the contest. So effectively did he protest from pulpit and platform, as well as in the press, that the fight was called off. The sporting public was enraged. F. B. Meyer hardly seemed the type to get involved in controversy. A harmless mystic with a saintly face, he was popular throughout the English-speaking world as a devotional preacher. Even today his devotional books and biblical biographies are on almost every pastor's shelves.

But Frederick Brotherton Meyer was a *militant* mystic. He was, as Carl Sandburg described Abraham Lincoln, "velvet steel." His gentleness was not weakness, but power under control. Once he determined that something was wrong, he fought it—even if he had to fight alone. Attacked in one church because of his strong evangelistic ministry, he resigned and built a church of his own. Hindered in his program of rehabilitating ex-convicts, he organized his own business and put the men on his payroll. There was no stopping F. B. Meyer.

Nothing in Meyer's birth hinted that a spiritual soldier had come on the scene. In fact, he was born with the coveted silver spoon in his mouth. As they said in that Victorian era, the family had "good connections." He was born on April 8, 1847, at Lavender Terrace, Wandsworth Road, London (even the address seems to glitter). Home life in Brighton was happy and comfortable, but also spiritual. His mother taught the children the Bible, and his father set the example as a dedicated Christian businessman. On Sunday mornings they attended the Bloomsbury Chapel, and in the evenings they held family services at home.

When Meyer was fifteen, business reverses forced the family to leave their lovely home in Brighton and return to London. His father tried to settle all the accounts honestly, which left little for the family. Meyer's silver spoon was gone, but not his sterling Christian character. In later years Meyer gave thanks for the experience because it helped him discover the things that mattered most. In his itinerant ministry he was always sensitive about large offerings and honoraria. More than once he returned love offerings he thought were too large.

From his earliest years, Meyer felt called to the ministry. He had even preached during family devotions. When he was sixteen he told his father his decision to enter the ministry, and both went to see William Brock, pastor of Bloomsbury Chapel. The great preacher asked young Meyer to preach a trial sermon for him—hardly easy for a teenager. But he passed the test.

At this critical point Brock counseled Meyer to spend at least two years working in a London business office before entering college. So Meyer joined the tea firm of Allan Murray, working there for two years. He saw city life firsthand. He learned to keep accurate records, make sensible decisions, plan his day well, and use his time efficiently. Later he counseled theological students to get business experience. "By all means let them graduate in the college of city life," he would say, "and study attentively the great books of human nature. It is impossible to preach to young men unless you *know* young men, and possess some knowledge of their peril and temptation." Not surprisingly, Meyer's Saturday afternoon meetings for young men were successful. In all his churches he attracted men from every level of life. The seed sown during those two years in the tea business bore fruit.

Meyer graduated from Regent's Park College in 1869. While a student, he ministered for about a year at Duke Street Baptist Chapel, Richmond, Surrey, a church made famous in recent years by the ministries of Alan Redpath and Stephen Olford. Upon graduation he was appointed assistant to Charles M. Birrell at the Pembroke Baptist Chapel, Liverpool. A godly scholar, Birrell unconsciously overpowered his young assistant, who imitated him almost to the point of idolatry. "In preparing my sermons and addresses," wrote Meyer, "I naturally followed the lines of the senior minister. This was a mistake, for Birrell's habit was to write out and memorize. Such a method was totally unsuitable for me."

Meyer was married in 1871. The next year he and his wife moved to York, where he pastored Priory Street Baptist Chapel. This move proved to be the turning point in his life and ministry, for two years later Dwight L. Moody and Ira Sankey ministered at Meyer's chapel. Moody had a gift for "finding" men—and Meyer was one of his greatest discoveries.

The other side of the coin is this: humanly speaking, the Moody-Sankey ministry in Britain received a boost from Meyer. The meetings at the York Independent Chapel had not begun too successfully, and the noon prayer meeting at the Cooney Street "Y" were limping along. At one of the prayer meetings Meyer heard Moody preach on the Holy Spirit. So convicted was the young pastor that he spent the next two days wrestling with God. He returned to the prayer meeting on Saturday and testified that God had met him and given victory. For two years he had preached without any special blessing. "I was just beating the air," he confessed. But now he had experienced a new touch from God. In spite of ministerial opposition, Meyer courageously opened his chapel to Moody and Sankey. For the first time in Meyer's ministry there, he saw the place filled. People were converted; the inquiry rooms were busy. Meyer learned some of his greatest spiritual lessons from Moody.

Moody taught this "proper" Baptist minister to be himself and not imitate others. "What an inspiration when this great and noble soul first broke into my life!" wrote Meyer. "I was a young pastor then . . . and bound rather rigidly by the chains of conventionalism. Such had been my training, and such might have been my career. But here was a new ideal! Mr. Moody was absolutely unconventional and natural."

Moody also taught Meyer the value of winning souls by every legitimate means. Those few days in York with Moody lit a fire in Meyer's soul. He once told Moody, "I have not preached one sermon, since God gave me that anointing, that there have not been conversions."

But Moody taught Meyer a third lesson: ministry is much larger than one church or denomination. In one of his autobiographical books, *The Bells of Is*, Meyer wrote: "I caught a glimpse of a wider, larger life, in which mere denominationalism could have no place, and in which there was but one standard by which to measure men, namely their devotion to, and knowledge of, the Son of God."[1] Meyer's church became the base of his ministry, not its sphere.

Meyer accepted a call from the Victoria Road Baptist Church, Leicester, in 1874. This was a typical "wealthy and influential church," and the young pastor gave himself sacrificially to his ministry. Had he still been a "proper pastor," the church would have been happy. But his concern for the lost and his willingness to pioneer new trails irked the comfortable officers. The tension climaxed when a wealthy deacon burst in one Sunday evening and told the pastor: "We cannot have this sort of thing here. This is not a gospel shop!" A few years before, Meyer would have apologized and resumed business as usual. But he had been with Moody and had experienced the blessing of serving God in the Spirit, letting the wind blow where it would. Meyer promptly resigned the church and planned to leave Leicester. No doubt fault lay on both sides: Meyer's enthusiasm had not yet caught fire in the congregation, and the comfortable officers felt threatened by his zeal.

When word got out that Meyer had resigned from Victoria Road, several other churches immediately issued him calls. Meyer wrote a letter of acceptance to the Glossop Road Church, Sheffield. On his way to mail the letter, he providentially met Arthur Rust (brother-in-law of W. Y. Fullerton, the evangelist who would later assist Charles H. Spurgeon). Meyer told Rust about the letter he was mailing, and Rust told Meyer about a group of earnest Christians in Leicester who wanted him to form a new church; fifteen young merchants would guarantee his salary. Meyer agreed, and the eventual result was the church at Melbourne Hall. At first the group met in one of the museum halls. (One lady arrived early each Lord's Day to cover the statues and pictures!) In five months they were strong enough to organize into a church. On July 2, 1881, they held their first service in their own building, Melbourne Hall. The building was a combination local church, rescue mission, social center, Sunday school, and Bible institute.

At Melbourne Hall, Meyer practiced another lesson learned from Moody: organize your work and enlist the help of new converts. Before long, Meyer was ministering to a congregation of two thousand. They in turn were ministering to thousands outside the church. The congregation did not pay their pastor to do the work; they worked *with him* and relieved him of routine matters. They were willing for him to "leave the ninety-and-nine" and search for that one lost sheep.

The ministry at Melbourne Hall can be described by one word: *miracles*. Meyer carried on a great work among prisoners, a work that resulted from a young girl's request of him: "My father is going to be released from jail tomorrow morning, and I'm afraid he will get into bad company. Could you meet him at the gate and try to keep him from his bad companions?" The successful pastor of a new church certainly did not need one more task. But how could he say no? He promised to be at the gate the next morning. When he arrived, he discovered that the prisoner had been transferred to another jail. Instead of hurrying home, Meyer waited across the street and watched the newly released prisoners. Almost to a man they headed for a nearby public house. "Is this what goes on here most mornings?" he asked some men lounging in the street.

"Yes, sir, mostly," they replied.

"But if a man comes out at yonder jail door and goes into the door of the public house," Meyer protested, "he appears to me to come out of the jail by the *front* door and go into it again by the *back* one! For I reckon that the public house is the back door to the jail."

"Well, what's a chap to do?" the men argued. "There's nowhere else for him to go."

Without replying, Meyer walked across the street to the jail and asked to see the governor, Miles Walker. Walker received him courteously, listened to his plea, and agreed to cooperate in every way. "All I want to do," Meyer explained, "is meet these men and take them to a nearby coffee-house for some decent food and a word of encouragement."

Little did Meyer know that this ministry would result in some of his greatest burdens, as well as his greatest blessings. In his delightful *The Bells of Is*, Meyer admitted that his second thoughts about the new ministry made him miserable.

> I fear that I more than once repented of the promise I had given the Governor, and wished that I have never undertaken the cause of the discharged jail-birds. . . . Altogether, between my fear of what the discharged prisoners would do to me, and what my own people and towns-folk would think of me, I had an uncomfortable time of it. . . . I had not then learned what it is to be the slave of Jesus Christ—a condition of mind in which one becomes blessedly oblivious to what men may say or do, so long as the light of His approval shines warm and fresh upon the heart.[2]

That first morning the entire group of men agreed to go to breakfast with him. During his years at Melbourne Hall, Meyer gave breakfast to nearly five thousand men. Many were converted; some, in spite of the hard work of both pastor and people, fell back into their old ways. The ministry continued even after Meyer left. Since many of the men could not find work, Meyer organized a window-washing brigade. Then he got into the wood-cutting business. He established a savings bank for the men, and even founded Provident House to give them a place to live while getting back on their feet. The citizens of Leicester were never sure what the creative pastor of Melbourne Hall would think of next. They saw signs announcing "F. B. Meyer— Firewood Merchant" and "F. B. Meyer—Window-Washing."

Meyer even bought a man a glass of ale to get him to stop drinking. "My friend, what do you say to signing the pledge this morning?" Meyer asked the former prisoner. "You know as well as I do that you have been falling under the power of drink." The man hesitated, then explained he had vowed to drink a pint of ale when he got out of jail. He wanted to keep his vow. Meyer explained that the vow was a bad one, but the man insisted on a pint of ale. "If you have that pint of ale," Meyer asked, "will you give me your solemn word and honor that you will sign the pledge immediately?" The man agreed, so Meyer went to the nearest public house to purchase the ale. The man greedily took a large swallow, then two more. "This is the miserablest pint of ale that I ever drank!" he exclaimed, putting down the mug. "Where is the card, sir? I may as well sign it as drink any more." He gave up alcohol and later was converted.

Meyer became pastor of Regent's Park Chapel in London early in 1888. The church was at low ebb when he arrived, but before long it was flooded with activity. Though this was one of London's select congregations, Meyer was not happy serving a denominational church and limiting his sphere of ministry. He longed to reach the lost.

After four years Meyer resigned and started fifteen years of ministry at Christ Church, Westminster Bridge Road, London, which had been founded in 1873 by Rowland Hill. Nominally Anglican in its association, congregational in government, and operated on nondenominational lines, it was ideal for a man like Meyer. "I never was an ardent denominationalist," Meyer confessed. But he did ask the trustees of Christ Church, which required no one form of baptism for membership, to install a baptistry.

Attendance averaged about one hundred when Meyer began, but within two years the 2,300-seat auditorium was filled. He organized fellowships for women, children, youth, and men. The Men's Brotherhood became a great power in Christ Church. "No leader of men should ever ask another to do what he is not prepared to do himself," Meyer affirmed. "On the other hand, never do work yourself that you can get another to do. To set one soul at work is to open stores of blessedness."

Meyer expressed his view of the local church:

> It is urgently needful that the Christian people of our charge should come to understand that they are not a company of invalids, to be wheeled about, or fed by hand, cosseted, nursed, and comforted, the minister being head-physician and nurse—but a garrison in an enemy's country, every soul of which should have some post of duty, at which he should be prepared to make any sacrifice rather than quit it.[3]

Anyone pastoring a city church ought to read Meyer's book *Reveries and Realities*, in which he gave some practical principles for a successful city ministry.

Meyer resigned Christ Church in 1907 for a two-year world tour, then returned to Regent's Park Chapel. He resigned that work in 1915 and went back to Christ Church for five years. His remaining years were spent in an itinerant ministry. During his lifetime he made twelve trips to the United States and visited many other countries as well.

Meyer always claimed that he was "an ordinary man" and that God could do as much through anyone who has yielded to him. Perhaps so, but Meyer was unique. His close friend Fullerton listed seven factors that contributed to Meyer's success: (1) Puritan heredity and training; (2) the spiritual influence of Birrell, Meyer's senior minister in Liverpool; (3) an enthusiasm for the whole church without "artificial and narrow boundaries"; (4) a willingness to be himself and not copy others; (5) a practical mysticism, "that sense of the Unseen"; (6) a democratic sympathy that enabled him to touch people in every level of life; and (7) a fervent spiritual idealism, "devotion to great aims."[4]

He may have been a mystic, but Meyer worked hard and never wasted time. His ability to concentrate on one task at a time enabled him to work his way through a long agenda without being distracted. Constantly on the go, he learned to use his hours of railway travel productively. "If he had a long journey before him," one friend wrote, "he would settle himself in his corner of the railway carriage with a sigh of relief, open his dispatch case (which was fitted up as a sort of stationery cabinet), and set to work in supreme contentment on some abstruse article, quite oblivious of his surroundings." He could also go to sleep almost at will and awaken himself at just the right time. "The Lord always wakes me up just when I ask Him," Meyer once told a friend. To prove his point, he said he would take a nap for twenty minutes. He awoke on time, fresh and ready for the evening's meeting.

In some respects Meyer had so much to do he had to keep going. Once he was browsing through W. Robertson Nicoll's huge library, complaining because he did not have enough leisure to examine the books as he should. "Now you know, Meyer," Nicoll replied, "you would not be here an hour before you would be asking for *Bradshaw's Railway Guide!*"

Meyer said he had spent "many a holy hour . . . while rushing through the country at express speed" and had "felt the railway carriage to be the house of God and the gate of heaven."

F. B. Meyer is known primarily as a devotional preacher and writer. Besides his two autobiographical volumes, he wrote ten books on great men of the Old Testament and three on those of the New Testament.[5] He wrote expositions on such books as Exodus, Isaiah, John, Hebrews, and 1 Peter, and on such passages as the Sermon on the Mount. His more than twenty books of devotional messages still challenge believers who hunger for a deeper life. *Light on Life's Duties* and *Back to Bethel* have always been favorites of mine, perhaps because they were put into my hands shortly after my conversion. *Our Daily Homily* is a priceless collection of expositions drawn from every chapter in the Bible, useful as both a daily devotional guide and a "pump primer" for the preacher.

Meyer majored in Bible exposition. He explained his approach in *Expository Preaching*. His early mentor, Birrell, pointed him in that direction. "That was quite a good sermon you gave this evening," Birrell told Meyer as they walked home after the service, "but it was a topical sermon, and if you are going to make topical sermons your model, you will presently come to the end of your topics, and where will you be then? I advise you to do as I have done for the last thirty years—become an expositor of Scripture. You will always retain your freshness and will build up a strong and healthy church." Meyer's method was not unlike that of G. Campbell Morgan: he read a Bible book repeatedly until he grasped its central message, then divided the book into sections and related them to that central truth. In each section he located what he called a "pivot text."

"Meyer preaches," said Spurgeon, "as a man who has seen God face to face." A printed sermon by Meyer transformed the ministry of J. Wilbur Chapman, who confessed, "I owe more to this man [Meyer] than to anyone in the world."

Meyer preached his last sermon on February 10, 1929, in Wesley Chapel, City Road, London. Three days later he entered a nursing home where, in spite of loving care, his health failed rapidly. "Read me something from the Bible," he whispered the day before he died, "something brave and triumphant!" He died on March 28.

The next time you read one of Meyer's more than fifty books, remember him as much more than a devotional writer. He was an evangelist with a burden for the city; a pastor who loved the whole church; a crusader who hated social evils; a spiritual man who guided many believers into a closer fellowship with Christ; an ambassador whose calling carried him far beyond his own local church and denomination. Joseph Parker put it perfectly: "He never leaves me without the impression that I have been face to face with a man of God."

W. Robertson Nicoll
1851–1923

He read an average of two books a day and edited a weekly journal, three monthly magazines, and a steady stream of scholarly books which included *The Expositor's Bible* (fifty volumes) and *The Expositor's Greek New Testament.* He was undoubtedly the most prolific and respected religious journalist in the English-speaking world from 1886 to his death in 1923. Not only was he the "unofficial literary agent" for such men as Marcus Dods, George Adam Smith, A. B. Bruce, and Alexander Maclaren (he persuaded Maclaren to publish his expositions), but he managed to write over forty books of his own, and compile, edit, or supervise the publication of over 250 more titles. Yet when he was knighted in 1909, William Robertson Nicoll wrote: "I had never contemplated a literary career. I had expected to go on as a minister, doing literary work in leisure times, but my fate was sealed for me."

His fate was "sealed" by ill health. Born at Lumsden, Aberdeenshire, on October 10, 1851, a son of the manse, Nicoll never was a "sturdy laddie." His father was a bookworm who preferred to pastor a small flock of about a hundred people and spend the rest of his time in his library. In spite of a meager income, the Reverend Harry Nicoll acquired a library of seventeen thousand volumes, probably the largest library belonging to any pastor in Scotland. In his charming little book *My Father*, Robertson Nicoll described this library and how his father used it.

Robertson's mother died when he was only eight years old. They called it "consumption" in those days, and it usually lingered with the family. Nicoll's weak lungs were to plague him for the rest of his life, ultimately (and providentially) taking him from behind the pulpit into the editor's chair. He often preached, but he could never have preached full time.

He graduated from Aberdeen University in 1870 and from the Free Church Divinity Hall in 1874. He was licensed to preach in 1872. From 1874 to 1877 he ministered at the Free Church in Dufftown, and from 1877 to 1885 at the Free Church in Kelso. Those were interesting years in Scotland: D. L. Moody was ministering there with great power, the Free Church was being torn asunder by Robertson Smith and his higher critical views, and new theological ideas were drifting over from the Continent.

Nicoll began his literary career while a student at the Divinity Hall. There were three weekly newspapers in Aberdeen at that time, and Nicoll was on the staff of the *Journal*, contributing reviews and literary notes and writing a weekly column, "Things in General." Reading and writing: these would be the hinges on which his long and influential life would turn. The long winter months in Scotland would make him a "prisoner" in his own house. "One had the absolution of the snow for any failure to discharge pastoral duties," he said. "I always look back with pleasure to my three months each winter there, when I was a prisoner alone with my cat and my books."

A year after he was inducted at Kelso, he married and settled down to the life of a pastor and a literary man. In 1884 he was made editor of *The Expositor*, a monthly theological journal published by Hodder and Stoughton and edited from its inception in 1875 by the famous Hebraist Samuel Cox (his volume *An Expositor's Note-Book* is worth adding to your library). Life was smiling upon the gifted young pastor, and then seeming tragedy struck. In 1885 Nicoll's younger brother died of tuberculosis, and while on a holiday in Norway, Nicoll himself was infected with typhoid and became dangerously ill. No sooner did he start to regain his health when pleurisy set in, and for a time it looked as though Nicoll would succumb to the same disease that had taken his mother, sister, and younger brother. The best doctors in Edinburgh agreed that he would have to resign the church, give up preaching for two or three years, and concentrate on regaining his health.

Nicoll and his wife went to the south of England, near Torquay. He continued his editing and admitted that he did not miss preaching— "I feel so unequal to it." What did he miss? "I feel rather lonely and depressed here away from my books." In 1886 the Nicolls moved to the Upper Norwood section of London and became neighbors to Charles Haddon Spurgeon. All his life, Nicoll admired and defended Spurgeon. This relationship began in 1874 when Nicoll was the "summer pastor" of a little church at Rayne, about twenty-five miles from Aberdeen. He discovered a complete set of Spurgeon's sermons and read it through! Soon after Spurgeon's death, Nicoll wrote a strong letter to Marcus Dods and reproached him for some unkind things he had written about the great preacher. "Your paragraph about Spurgeon really vexed me," he wrote, "and it is the only thing you have ever said, or written, or done, that did vex me or that I thought not worthy of your magnanimity." Then Nicoll confessed: "Every Sunday night I spend at least an hour reading him, and there is no devotional writing pleases me so well."

The key date in Nicoll's life is November 5, 1886, for it was on this date that the first issue of the *British Weekly* appeared, published by Hodder and Stoughton. It was intended to be a "high-class weekly journal for the advocacy of social and religious progress," and it lived up to its purpose. Nicoll was so sure the journal would succeed that he agreed to work for nothing until the profits started coming in; it was not long before the paper began to flourish and take its place as the leading Nonconformist journal in Britain. Nicoll also had the genius for discovering and developing new writers. The bylines in the *British Weekly* read like a *Who's Who* of literature: Marcus Dods, a regular contributor from the very beginning; James M. Barrie; R. W. Dale; Joseph Parker; Henry Drummond; and a host of other "worthies."

Not content with a weekly journal to edit (his deadlines must have been frightening!), on October 1, 1891, Nicoll launched a monthly literary magazine called *The Bookman*. The entire first edition of ten thousand copies sold within a few days, and it was followed by two additional printings! Two years later he started another monthly magazine, *The Woman at Home*. He was now editing the *British Weekly* and three monthly publications: *The Expositor*, *The Bookman*, and *The Woman at Home*.

However, it is not as a magazine editor that Robertson Nicoll touches the lives of Bible students and pastors today. It is as the author and editor of theological books, some of which are classics. It was the year after the *British Weekly* was born that Nicoll began to publish *The Expositor's Bible*, a work that is now somewhat outdated but still valuable to the serious student. The series was released in fifty volumes between 1888 and 1905. I believe that Alexander Maclaren's *Colossians* was the first volume released, and George Adam Smith's commentary on the minor prophets the last.

Evidently Nicoll was as hard on his writers as he was on himself, and some of them protested. His good friend Marcus Dods wrote, "Pharaoh might have taken lessons from you!" And Maclaren wrote, "I hope that *you* are not having any holiday this autumn! It would be some alleviation to think of you as stewing in Paternoster Row." But the editor had his problems too. When he received the manuscript for George Adam Smith's *Isaiah* (for *The Expositor's Bible*), Nicoll wrote Marcus Dods: "I am wrestling with George Adam Smith's *Isaiah*: he has chopped up the prophet terribly."

Oddly enough, Nicoll did much of his work while in bed! His close friend and biographer, T. H. Darlow, wrote: "It was weird to watch him as he lay there, amid a medley of newspapers and books and pipes and cigarette ashes, and to know that his brain was busy absorbing knowledge and incubating ideas all the time." He kept a fire in his study almost all the year and claimed that fresh air was an invention of the devil! He had almost no interest in music or art and, unlike the traditional Scotsman, was not excited by sports. Why waste on games, time that could be invested profitably in books? His books and his cats and his publications were his life.

Like most extensive sets written by many writers, *The Expositor's Bible* is quite uneven in quality. Kellogg on Leviticus is a classic, as are Maclaren's three volumes on the Psalms and his exposition of Colossians. Unless you are wealthy and have a lot of empty shelves, do not purchase the fifty volumes separately. The entire set is available in a six-volume edition with large, double-column pages. I believe that this edition was originally published by Eerdmans. It may be out of print, but used sets are often available. *The Expositor's Greek New Testament* (also reprinted by Eerdmans) is still in print and is still considered a standard work for the careful student of the Greek New Testament, although some students prefer Dean Henry Alford's *Greek Testament*, published by Moody Press.

One of my favorite sets, edited by Nicoll, is one that is usually forgotten or is dismissed as unimportant. It is *The Sermon Bible*, originally published in twelve volumes and containing nearly five thousand outlines and précis of sermons actually delivered by famous preachers in the last half of the nineteenth century. It was republished by Baker Books as *The Sermon-Outline Bible* and comprises the first six volumes of a fourteen-volume series called *The Preacher's Homiletic Library*. I highly recommend this set, particularly to the pastor who is not too tired (or lazy) to dig again the homiletical wells of the past. (The other eight volumes of the set are *Homiletic Studies in the Gospels* by Harold F. J. Ellingsen, a rich mine of sermonic suggestion, and *Proclaiming the New Testament*, a book-by-book, chapter-by-chapter homiletic survey of the New Testament, edited by Ralph Turnbull.) This set gives the student the best of the old and the best of the new.

It may be that you have no interest in old sermons. If so, then *The Sermon-Outline Bible* will bore you. But before you consign it to the antique shop, let me suggest that you consider some of the men represented in these volumes: Joseph Parker, Henry Alford, Alexander

Maclaren, Marcus Dods, Phillips Brooks, Adolph Saphir, R. W. Dale, Henry Ward Beecher, John Henry Newman, William Taylor, James Stalker, and J. J. Stuart Perowne, to name a few. Many of these men have written learned commentaries that are still available, but their sermons are difficult to come by. I do not know of any one set that offers so much historic material in such a convenient form.

But better still, the set also contains sermons by relatively unknown preachers whose works are even less accessible today. For example, there are a number of sermons from Henry Melville, whom Spurgeon called "the Demosthenes of London." Coming from Spurgeon, that is quite a tribute! Henry Scott Holland is also represented in these pages. In his day (1847–1918) he was recognized as one of the leaders in applying Christian faith to the needs of the common man. I was amazed to also find dozens of sermons from Samuel Martin, who pastored Westminster Chapel, London, from 1841 to 1878. Under his leadership the present church building was erected. (Interestingly enough, Samuel Martin was an architect before entering the ministry; yet the design of the Westminster Chapel does not seem to reflect it. When Jowett pastored there, he said he felt as if he were preaching in the Charing Cross railway station. Martyn Lloyd-Jones has stated that the building helped to hasten the death of more than one pastor who preached there week after week.) Martin's sermons are probably available nowhere else today. Also represented in *The Sermon-Outline Bible* are Samuel Cox, Nicoll's predecessor at *The Expositor*; John Ker, who was George Morrison's favorite preacher; Horatius Bonar; Handley C. G. Moule; J. Oswald Dykes; and F. D. Maurice, who greatly influenced Phillips Brooks. These are not sermons that you will preach—their style and approach are not contemporary—but they are sermons you should read and study.

One of my favorite Nicoll books is *Princes of the Church*, a collection of thirty-four biographical essays on "notable figures in the Christian world." Spurgeon is here ("He has fallen like a tower, and his removal means for many a change in the whole landscape of life"), but so are Henry Drummond, Robertson Smith, R. W. Dale, the great Roman Catholic preacher Cardinal Vaughan, George Matheson,

Silvester Horne, Andrew Bonar, and Bishop Westcott. His essay on "The Centenary of Frederick Robertson" is one of the most perceptive I have ever read on this fascinating preacher from Brighton.

Nicoll's library contained twenty-five thousand volumes, including five thousand biographies! "I have for years read every biography I could lay my hands on, and not one has failed to teach me something," he wrote. His own biography, *William Robertson Nicoll: Life and Letters*, was written by T. H. Darlow and published in this country by the George H. Doran Company in 1925. Nicoll's long-time associate at the *British Weekly*, Jane T. Stoddart, wrote a brief biography, *W. Robertson Nicoll, LL.D., Editor and Preacher*. In a very real sense, Nicoll was the father of modern religious journalism, but he was also a strong churchman and preacher. He died on May 4, 1923, and among his last words were "I believe everything that I have written about immortality!"

If you are a lover of good books and good men—and every pastor should be—then get acquainted with W. Robertson Nicoll and the rich literary heritage he has left us.

29

Henry Drummond
1851–1897

N ever have I known a man who, in my opinion, lived nearer the Master, or sought to do His will more fully." So wrote Dwight L. Moody in the May 1897 issue of the *Record of Christian Work*. He was writing about Henry Drummond, who died on March 11, 1897, at age forty-five. Drummond was one of Moody's friends, and Moody called Drummond "one of the most lovable men I have ever known." Moody wrote to James Stalker: "No man has ever been with me for any length of time that I did not see something that was unlike Christ, and I often see it in myself, but not in Henry Drummond. All the time we were together he was a Christ-like man and often a rebuke to me."

And yet Drummond was an evolutionist and an advocate of higher criticism. His approach to evangelism was different from that of Moody in that he rarely preached about the cross or referred to the atonement. "As to his theology," wrote W. Robertson Nicoll, "no theologian would admit that it was satisfactory or coherent. Of the atonement, for example, he made nothing; not that he rejected it, but that he had no place for it, and received it as a mystery."[1]

Drummond's ministry was more than once a source of trouble to Moody, and yet the great evangelist remained true to his friend. In July 1893, when Drummond came to Northfield to speak, a deputation of concerned ministers asked Moody to remove Drummond from the conference program. Some questioned the soundness of Drummond's theology; he did not defend verbal inspiration and even questioned some of the miracles. Others opposed his evolutionary teachings and his cigar smoking. Moody asked for a day to think the matter over. He met the deputation after breakfast the next morning and informed them that he had "laid the matter before the Lord, and the Lord had shown him that Drummond was a better man than himself; so he was to go on." Apparently this frank reply did not solve the problem, for Drummond reported: "At Northfield I felt a good deal out of it, and many fell upon me and rent me. . . . It was not a happy time."

That same year Drummond refused to help Moody in the Chicago World's Fair campaign, a decision that cut Moody deeply. "Well, Mr. Moody, you know why he refused," George Adam Smith told Moody while visiting Northfield in the summer of 1899. "It was because he was afraid to compromise you further with the men with whom you were working."

"I know it," Moody replied. "He did it out of pure love, but that he should have had to do it cut me."

Perhaps this explains why, in spite of their differences, Moody and Drummond were dear friends: both of them preached "God is love," and practiced that love.

Henry Drummond was born into a devout evangelical family in Stirling, Scotland, on August 17, 1851. At age fifteen he entered the University of Edinburgh, graduating in 1870. He then entered New College, Edinburgh, but he did not get his degree until 1876; the reason for this delay is the most important part of the story. On November 23, 1873, Moody and Ira Sankey opened the "Great Mission" in the Edinburgh Music Hall, an event that was to change Drummond's life. Nobody is quite sure how Drummond became involved in the campaign. More than one student had gone to hear

Moody "on a lark," only to be arrested by God and put to work by the evangelist. Drummond was keenly interested in personal work, and personal work was what Moody emphasized. In fact, just a few weeks before the meetings opened, Drummond had read a perceptive paper on "Spiritual Diagnosis" before the Theological Society, advocating the very thing Moody was practicing in his inquiry room. So Drummond began as a counselor in the inquiry room, and Moody was quick to detect his gifts.

When the mission moved to Glasgow and was so singularly blessed by God, Moody sent to Edinburgh for reinforcements and Drummond rallied to the cause. Before long he was not only dealing with inquirers but also speaking to large meetings of new converts, and God was using his messages. He was Moody's "Timothy," and the bond between the two men grew stronger as the months passed.

"I got a treat last night," Drummond wrote to his mother from Liverpool on February 15, 1875. "Moody sat up alone with me till near one o'clock telling me the story of his life. He told me the whole thing. A reporter might have made a fortune out of it." In 1894 Drummond wrote a personal tribute to his friend, titled simply *D. L. Moody*, and it is a valuable contribution to Moody lore. After Moody's death, George Adam Smith added "A Personal Tribute" to Drummond's tribute, and the two were published together in 1900.

After the mission ended, Drummond returned to New College and graduated in 1876. Moody wanted Drummond to go with him to America, but Drummond remained in Scotland. How he made this decision is the first of four providential events that could be considered coincidences, were it not for the impact they made on his life and ministry.

In the early days of the Moody mission, Drummond became fast friends with Robert W. Barbour, son of wealthy cotton merchant George F. Barbour. Often Drummond would visit his friend at the family home, Bonskeid House. During one of these visits Drummond stumbled over a stone and wrenched his knee, resulting in confinement for nearly two weeks. During that time he discussed Moody's invitation with Mrs. Barbour, who wisely counseled him to finish school and let God give him a ministry of his own. This counsel he followed; but during that final school year he continued his evangelistic ministry by holding meetings on Sunday evenings in the Gaiety Theater, not far from school. Some of the students who assisted him in these services were James Stalker, John Watson (later known as Ian Maclaren), Charles William Gordon (later known as Ralph Connor the Sky Pilot), and George Adam Smith.

After graduation, Drummond became an assistant at the Barclay Free Church. In 1877 he began lecturing in natural science at the Free Church College in Glasgow. During the second year he became pastor of a mission in Possilpark, a suburb of Glasgow. The mission was under the jurisdiction of the Renfield Free Church, whose pastor, Marcus Dods, was to have tremendous influence over Drummond for the rest of his life.

At this point we must pause to examine the spiritual and academic situation that prevailed in the Free Church in the last quarter of the nineteenth century. There were two forces beating away at the citadel: biblical criticism and evolution. In 1878 W. Robertson Smith, professor of Old Testament at the Free Church College in Aberdeen, was charged with heresy because of an article he had written for the *Encyclopaedia Britannica*. The church was divided over the issue, and even the godly Alexander Whyte defended Smith's orthodoxy and his right to academic freedom. In 1881 Smith was finally suspended; Drummond wrote that Smith had been "lynched." Charles Darwin had published his *Origin of Species* in 1859, and evolution was the "going thing" by the time Drummond began studying science in Edinburgh. Higher criticism was basically an application of evolutionary theory to the documents of the Bible. First and foremost, Drummond was a scientist. Though ordained, he preferred to be called *Professor* Drummond rather than *Reverend* Drummond. One hundred years later we have a clearer view of both evolution and higher criticism, so we must be somewhat sympathetic with men like Drummond, who faced the impact of these issues in ways that we do not today.

Now for the second "coincidence" in Drummond's life. During his regular ministry as a pastor, Drummond had delivered a number of sermons that sought to express spiritual truth in terms of modern scientific beliefs. He felt there was no conflict between science and Christianity if each was properly understood. He saw the Christian life in terms of evolution, something his friend Moody certainly did not do. Nicoll explained Drummond's ministry in this way:

> He saw that the age was essentially scientific. He saw that there appeared to be between science and religion a spanless and fathomless abyss. He saw that the materialists were swiftly poisoning the nation. . . . He threw himself with all his strength into the work of effecting a reconciliation, and though we do not propose in this place to discuss the value of his work, it may certainly be said at the very least that it helped to change the situation, and to bring into many minds, scientific and religious, more than a ray of hope.[2]

One day Drummond "happened" to meet H. M. Hodder on Paternoster Row, London, and the publisher asked about some of Drummond's papers that had been rejected by two or three other houses. Drummond promised to send the manuscript to the firm of Hodder and Stoughton, and the result was the publication of *Natural Law in the Spiritual World*, a book that took both the scientific and religious worlds by storm. But when the book came off the press in June 1883, Drummond was steaming toward East Central Africa to investigate the area's natural resources for a trading firm in Scotland. Not until he received his mail somewhere near Tanganyika did Drummond discover his book was a bestseller and he was famous. By the time he died in 1897, well over 100,000 copies had been sold, and the book had been reviewed in practically every major journal.

In 1884, Drummond was promoted to professor of natural sciences. In his inaugural address, titled "The Contribution of Science to Christianity," he reaffirmed his belief in evolution as God's method of both creation and revelation. Drummond's new position, plus the success of *Natural Law in the Spiritual World*, made him somewhat of a folk hero among the students, and he used this popularity as a means of reaching them for Christ.

On Sunday evening, January 25, 1885, Drummond gave the first of his "addresses" in the Oddfellows Hall, Edinburgh; for nine years these meetings continued, reaching students by the hundreds. The meetings were supervised by a "secret committee" composed of Alexander Whyte, A. R. Simpson, A. H. Barbour (brother to Robert), and Dods. (Whyte's interest in Drummond stemmed from the fact that Mrs. Whyte was Jane Elizabeth Barbour, sister to Henry's dear friend, Robert. Whyte's nephew, G. F. Barbour, wrote Whyte's biography.)

It is worth noting that Moody as well as Drummond had tremendous appeal to students, but for different reasons. Both were utterly transparent and sincere, but Moody appealed to the authority of Scripture while Drummond spoke to the intellect and reasoned with students. Drummond felt that the Christian faith had to be presented in the language and categories of a scientific age—the "new evangelism" he called it. Moody presented the Christ of the cross; Drummond emphasized Christ's perfect life.

That Drummond believed in the efficacy of the atonement is beyond question; his scientific attitude, however, prevented him from trying to explain it. Even Sankey, Moody's song leader, had his doubts about the professor; in 1892 Sankey wrote Drummond and asked why he did not emphasize the cross. Drummond's explanation was that he was called to preach "the forgotten truths," not those that are being repeated by others again and again.

In 1887 Drummond came to Northfield. While in this country, he visited many Eastern colleges and universities. Everywhere he went the students turned out in droves and, from every indication, tremendous spiritual results followed. William Lyon Phelps said of Drummond's visit to Yale, "I have never seen so deep an impression made on students, by any speaker on any subject."

But 1887 is important for another reason: Drummond delivered his famous address on 1 Corinthians 13, and Moody insisted that he publish it. *The Greatest Thing in the World* is still in print today.

The third "coincidence" in Drummond's life occurred in 1890, when he was ministering in Australia. It was decided that Drummond should visit mission stations in the New Hebrides, and for the first time Drummond came face to face with the gospel's confrontation with raw heathenism. He was so impressed that he delivered a powerful paper at the college that November on "The Problem of Foreign Missions." This paper influenced a number of mission leaders and was indirectly responsible for the great Edinburgh missionary conference of 1910.

Drummond was always interested in children and young people, though he never married. A Glasgow businessman and Drummond, while walking down the street one day, saw a merchant throw a stack of round strawberry cartons into the gutter. Instantly a group of boys swooped down upon the cartons and put them on their heads for caps. Then they lined up in military formation and "marched" away. "There's an idea for you," Drummond told his friend; and out of that "coincidence" grew the Boys' Brigade program that God still uses to win boys to Christ.

After two years of suffering, Drummond died on March 11, 1897. He was laid to rest next to his father in Stirling.

If you want to become better acquainted with Drummond, begin with *Henry Drummond: An Anthology*, edited by James W. Kennedy. The brief biographical chapter will give you the basic facts about Drummond's life and ministry, and the selections from his writings will give you insight into his thinking. I know of no single volume that better explains Drummond to space-age Christians. The official biography was written by George Adam Smith: *The Life of Henry Drummond* (1899). Smith included several extracts from Drummond's addresses to students, but Kennedy's selections are, I think, better. Not long after his death, Drummond's *"The Ideal Life" and Other Unpublished Addresses* was published. Two memorial sketches preface the fifteen popular addresses, one by Nicoll and the other by John Watson, Drummond's lifelong friend. Drummond's address "Ill Temper" is one of the best sermons on the elder brother in Luke 15 that I have ever read.

After Moody's death in 1899, some cited his friendship with Henry Drummond as proof that Moody was theologically liberal. Even his son, Paul Moody, wrote an article for *Christian Century* suggesting that the evangelist had been liberal, but this was immediately refuted by no less an expert on the subject than R. A. Torrey. He wrote from Los Angeles on August 20, 1923:

> It is true that Mr. Moody loved Henry Drummond as he loved very few other people. . . . But Mr. Moody did not sympathize at all with some of the views into which Prof. Henry Drummond was led. . . . Though Mr. Moody loved him still, and loved him to the end, he would not use him, and greatly regretted the position which Prof. Henry Drummond had taken up.[3]

At one of the memorial services for Moody, J. M. Buckley said: "Mr. Moody had his prejudices, for I once heard him declare that he would own fellowship with everybody that believed himself to be a sinner and trusted in Christ; but, said he, 'God being my helper, I will never own fellowship with a man who denies the deity of my God and Savior Jesus Christ, or sneers at His atonement.'" Moody and Drummond had their differences, but each was used to bring Jesus Christ to lost sinners. Had Drummond ever cast one slur on the person or work of Jesus Christ, Moody would have defended his Lord and denounced his friend. Moody loved his friend, but he loved his Savior more.

30

R. A. Torrey
1856–1928

Young man, you had better get to work for the Lord!"
D. L. Moody, during his New Haven campaign of 1878, addressed that statement to a Yale Divinity School senior who had asked him about winning souls to Christ. That student was Reuben Archer Torrey and, to Torrey's credit, he stayed around long enough to learn how to win the lost to Christ. Moody gave the students some verses to use in soul-winning and then said, "Now, gentlemen, go at it!"

At the meetings, Torrey saw a young lady he had met at a dance prior to his own conversion and decided to try out his evangelistic skill on her. It took two hours of answering questions and referring to Scripture, but she finally yielded to the Lord and became the first convert of the man who would eventually win thousands to Christ in his worldwide ministry.

R. A. Torrey was born the son of a well-to-do banker in Hoboken, New Jersey, on January 28, 1856. The family was associated with the Congregational Church, but only his mother was a true believer. It was her prayer that her son would become a minister of the gospel, but Reuben decided he wanted to be a lawyer. However, deep within, he had the haunting feeling that God had indeed called him to be a preacher—yet he was not even a professed Christian.

One night he had a vivid dream that his mother was dead. Suddenly, she appeared in his room in the form of an angel and begged him to give himself to the ministry. In the dream he promised her that he would do so, but in his waking hours, the prospects of going to Yale University excited him so much that the impact of the dream faded from his mind.

He entered Yale in 1871 and soon found himself caught up in what his mother would have called worldly living: gambling at cards, drinking, dancing, and smoking. Chapel was compulsory but not very exciting spiritually, and even though Reuben attended church faithfully on Sundays, read his Bible daily, and kept up the image of being a Christian, he knew he was far from the kingdom.

At the end of his sophomore year he faced the crisis. His worldly life did not satisfy him, he was not really "making it" on campus (his choice fraternity did not elect him), and he was still haunted by the feeling that God had called him to preach. One night he became so despondent and desperate that he decided to commit suicide. He reached for his razor, but God arrested him, and, instead, Torrey fell to his knees and prayed: "God, if you will take away this awful burden, I will preach!" God lifted the burden, God's peace filled his heart, and he fell sound asleep and woke up the next morning knowing that he was in God's hands.

What brought about the change? Torrey explained: "My mother, 427 miles away, was praying and praying that I would become a minister of the gospel. And though I had gotten over sermons and arguments and churches and everything else, I could not get over my mother's prayers."[1]

He entered Yale Divinity School in 1875. In 1877, both of his parents died within three weeks of each other. Unfortunately, the Torrey estate had all but disappeared during the panic of '73, so Reuben was not made a wealthy man by his father's death. "I'm glad I did not inherit a fortune," he said later. "It would have ruined me."

While he was at Divinity School, Torrey first met D. L. Moody and learned from him how to win souls. Torrey graduated in 1878, and on November 9 of that year became pastor of the Congregational Church in Garrettsville, Ohio, population 969. He was still rather ignorant of the Bible, but he devoted his morning hours to concentrated study. Gifted by the Lord with a brilliant mind, Torrey learned rapidly and tried to practice and share what he learned. The church prospered, and he even found himself a bride and was married on October 22, 1879.

Torrey might have remained in pastoral ministry were it not for Howard Bell, a wealthy Yale classmate, who urged him to study in Germany and even offered to pay the expenses. Torrey refused his generous gift but did accept a loan, and in the fall of 1882 he sailed for Europe with his wife and little daughter. He divided his time between the universities in Leipzig and Erlangen, studying under such famous scholars as Franz Delitzsch and Theodore Zahn. That year of concentrated study further convinced him that the "old faith" was true and that the message of the gospel was the only hope for a lost world.

When he returned to the United States, he had two invitations for ministry: a wealthy church in Brooklyn, and a small group of believers in Minneapolis who wanted to begin a new ministry. Torrey decided for Minneapolis. There he threw himself into personal evangelism, preaching, and teaching. He organized the People's Church (Congregational) and rejoiced in the blessings God gave.

In 1906, Torrey led a sixteen-year-old lad to Christ, and that lad, Oswald J. Smith, would one day organize the People's Church in Toronto.

During his years of ministry and study in Minneapolis, Torrey reached some definite conclusions about doctrinal matters. Trained as a lawyer, he knew that all the evidence he needed was in the Bible, and he was willing to accept all that the Bible taught. For one thing, he became a convinced premillennialist, and all his life he preached the blessed hope of the Lord's return. He also became an immersionist, but he never made baptism a test of fellowship. His study of Scripture also convinced him of the doctrine of eternal punishment.

Two doctrinal matters that, in later years, gave him some trouble with other conservative believers were divine healing and the baptism of the Spirit. While Torrey did not believe in healers, with all of their religious promotion, he did believe in "the prayer of faith" (James 5:14–15) and personally experienced healing from God. He often prayed for others, and they were healed.

In all his ministry, Torrey emphasized the importance of the power of the Holy Spirit. At one point he determined not to preach again until he had been "endued with power from on high" (see Luke 24:49), so he shut himself up for a week and prayed. God answered his prayer, and others could tell that God's hand was powerfully upon him. Like Moody, Torrey did not quibble over terminology, something that he probably would change if he were on the scene today. He seemed to equate "the baptism of the Spirit" with "the fullness of the Spirit."

When a friend told D. L. Moody about Torrey's ministry in Minneapolis, the evangelist said, "You make my mouth water for him!" Moody usually got what he wanted; so on September 26, 1889, R. A. Torrey began his ministry as superintendent of the Chicago Evangelization Society, later to be known as the Moody Bible Institute. Torrey developed the curriculum and made sure it emphasized consecration, zeal for souls, a knowledge of the Bible, and a willingness to sacrifice. In a very real sense, Torrey was the architect who made the design for every Bible institute that has been founded since his time.

From 1894 to 1906, Torrey also served as pastor of the Chicago Avenue Church, which later became the Moody Memorial Church. The building seated 2,200 people, and it was usually packed at each service, with people having to sit in overflow rooms. More than two thousand members were received into the church during Torrey's ministry, and multitudes were converted. So effective was his ministry that invitations came to him from across the nation and even from other countries.

During a revival prayer meeting at the church, Torrey was strangely led to pray that God would send him around the world and give him thousands of souls in response to the preaching of the gospel. Shortly after this, two Christians from Australia invited him to hold a campaign in Melbourne. As God provided adequate leadership for both the church and the school, Torrey felt led to accept the invitation.

On December 23, 1901, he left on the world tour, ministering in Japan, China, Australia, New Zealand, India, and Great Britain. The well-known evangelistic singer Charles Alexander joined him in Australia, and Torrey and Alexander were to become as famous a team as Moody and Sankey. The records indicate that more than one hundred thousand persons made decisions for Christ during this worldwide campaign, from 1902 to 1905. R. A. Torrey, like D. L. Moody before him, returned to the United States to find himself a famous man.

In 1906, Torrey resigned the pastorate of the church, and two years later resigned from the school. On February 8, 1908, he helped found the Bible Institute of Los Angeles (BIOLA) and served as its dean from 1912 to 1924. On September 3, 1915, he became founding pastor of the Church of the Open Door in Los Angeles, starting with eighty-six charter members. He also assisted in establishing the Testimony Publishing Company, funded by the Stewart brothers of Union Oil fame. This new company published *The Fundamentals*, a series of inexpensive books that defended the faith.

Those were busy years for Torrey as he was writing, preaching, directing a school, and pastoring a church, while preaching at key conferences across the nation. In 1908 he organized the Montrose Bible Conference in Montrose, Pennsylvania, and this soon became a meeting place for hungry Christians eager to study the Bible. By 1924 he felt that he needed to slow down, so he resigned from all his ministries and "retired" to Asheville, North Carolina. He then teamed up with Homer Hammontree and went out on the evangelistic circuit again.

He held his last campaign at the First Presbyterian Church in Orlando, Florida, from November 28 to December 11, 1927. He began to experience throat trouble and had to cancel all his meetings. He spent the summer at his beloved Montrose, unable to participate in any personal ministry. At the close of the season, he returned to Asheville, and there he died on October 26, 1928. The funeral was at Montrose, and he was buried on beautiful Sunset Knoll.

Some years ago I heard an eloquent preacher tell several thousand Christians that they had to make the choice between serving God as "deep Bible teachers" or as soul-winners. If Reuben Archer Torrey had been in that meeting, he would have protested. He himself was a man with a keen mind, a profound ability to teach the Word, and a sincere burden for the lost. His studies in Germany gave him the weapons to fight German higher criticism and theological liberalism. He had wrestled with theological problems and found the answers in the infallible Word of God.

Torrey was a *balanced* man; in fact, he was a man who seemed to have everything. He was a powerful evangelist and also a concerned pastor. He was an educator and yet a stirring teacher. His books are still being published and are exerting a lasting influence in the lives of new generations of Christians. His most recent biographer, Roger Martin, calls R. A. Torrey "the apostle of certainty." He stood like a giant at the time when winds of doctrine were blowing against the church and causing people to stumble and fall. In Reuben Archer Torrey, God proved once again that education and evangelism, depth and soul-winning, need not destroy one another. If a man submits to the Word and is filled with the Spirit, he can have an enlightened mind and a burning heart—and he can reach people for Christ.

How to Work for Christ and *What the Bible Teaches* are perhaps Torrey's most treasured books, and they are still available. You will also want to read his books on prayer and the Holy Spirit. *How To Succeed in the Christian Life* is excellent for new believers. *R. A. Torrey: Apostle of Certainty*, by Roger Martin, is published by Sword of the Lord Publishers and is worth reading.

During his British campaign, Torrey said to a vast audience:

> I would rather win souls than be the greatest king or emperor on earth; I would rather win souls than be the greatest general that ever commanded an army. . . . My one ambition in life is to win as many as possible. Oh, it is the only thing worth doing, to save souls; and men and women, we can all do it.[2]

D. L. Moody started it all when he said, "Young man, you had better get to work for the Lord!"

Perhaps the Lord is saying the same thing to *you*.

31

Thomas Spurgeon
1856–1917

The first time I saw my future husband, he occupied the pulpit of New Park Street Chapel on the memorable Sunday when he preached his first sermons there." So wrote Mrs. Charles H. Spurgeon of that "memorable Sunday," December 18, 1853.

It was not easy to be the fiancée of London's most popular preacher. So engrossed was Charles Spurgeon in his ministry that he often shook hands with Susannah at church meetings without recognizing her! When they were alone, he would correct proofs of his sermons while his beloved sat by quietly. "It was good discipline for the pastor's intended wife," she wrote in later years. Spurgeon baptized Susannah on February 1, 1855, and she became a member of New Park Street. A year later, on January 8, they were married. After a ten-day honeymoon in Paris, they returned to London and to what would be one of the greatest ministries in the history of the church.

Susannah presented her husband with twin sons on September 20, 1856. The firstborn was named Charles, the other Thomas. The boys attended local schools and also had a private tutor. It was discovered early that Thomas had a gift for drawing. Both boys became Christians early and often distributed copies of their father's sermons. On

September 20, 1874, their father preached from the text "I and the children" (Gen. 33:5); the following evening he baptized his sons.

Their famous father sometimes hinted that he would rejoice if one of his sons succeeded him at the Metropolitan Tabernacle. In a sermon titled "Now: A Sermon for Young Men and Women," Spurgeon said:

> It may not be my honor to be succeeded in this pulpit by one of my sons, greatly as I would rejoice if it might be so; but at least I hope they will be here in this church to serve their father's God, and to be regarded with affection by you for the sake of him who spent his life in your midst.

At first it did not appear that either son would enter the ministry. The boys preached when opportunity arose, and they helped found the Northcote Road Baptist Church. But Charles entered a mercantile career, and Thomas was apprenticed to a wood-engraver named William Holledge. Both young men served the Lord zealously, but neither devoted their full time to the Christian ministry.

Tom's health was poor, so he went on a sea voyage to Australia. Tom Holledge, William's son, went along. Their three-masted schooner left on June 15, 1877, and arrived in Melbourne on August 28. During the voyage Spurgeon preached often to the passengers and crew. His father had given Thomas a letter of introduction in which he said, "He can preach a bit." Thomas had intended to set up an engraving business in Melbourne, but the name *Spurgeon* opened doors of ministry that he could not ignore. "Young Spurgeon does not possess the fire and dash of his father," one newspaper reported, "but he has much originality, humor, and force." Wherever he preached, he drew great crowds. Some came to criticize and compare, but many went away convicted. Young Thomas was not C.H.S., but he was still God's servant and a capable preacher.

About this time Thomas was falsely accused of conduct unbecoming to a minister. "Whether it was the tongue of slander in the old land, or some misinformation or mistake, I do not know," he once said. "But there came to my dear father's ears a story which did not reflect credit upon his absent son. It came in such a form that he was almost bound to believe it." (We wonder if C.H.S. remembered the slander that had been spread about him in early years.) "I left the matter with God," said Thomas, "and He espoused my cause." In a few days his father cabled: "Disregard my letter; was misinformed."

In September 1878, Thomas received word that his mother was ill. Immediately he sailed for home. When he arrived, he found her much improved, but his father was suffering. On Sunday, November 10, Thomas Spurgeon had to preach for C.H.S. at the great tabernacle. His brother Charles also came to his aid during his father's illness.

Thomas enrolled in the Pastors' College, but his poor health forced him to miss so many classes that he decided to return to Australia. This decision deeply hurt his father, who had long hoped his son would share his ministry and eventually take his place. Spurgeon's dear friend and associate, W. Y. Fullerton, wrote: "Only twice in his life C. H. Spurgeon spent a whole night in prayer. . . . One of these nights of intense supplication was for a personal need. . . . The other was when the hopes he had built on his son Tom being by his side were shattered."[1] Tom settled in New Zealand, and for the first year he supplied the pulpit of the Hanover Street Church in Dunedin. Family history repeated itself, for in that church he met Lila Rutherford, who on February 10, 1888, became Mrs. Thomas Spurgeon. In January 1882 Thomas became pastor of the Baptist church in Aukland. The work prospered; they built a new auditorium (a tabernacle, of course!) and many found Christ. The pastor returned to Great Britain for five months in 1884 to raise funds for his work. On December 14, 1884, he sailed for New Zealand, bidding goodbye to his father, who told him he could not bear the pain of another parting.

There were to be no further partings. On June 7, 1891, C.H.S. preached his last sermon at the tabernacle; and on January 31, 1892, he was "called home." The death of "the governor" (as his officers called him) ushered in the "tabernacle tempest" that was watched with great interest by Christians all over the English-speaking world. The question was: Who will keep the tabernacle going? Spurgeon's brother James, who had assisted in the tabernacle ministry, was asked to serve as acting pastor. A. T. Pierson had been preaching at the tabernacle during Spurgeon's last illness, but since he was a Presbyterian, he could not be a candidate for the pulpit. Pierson stayed with the work for a year, but then he had to return to the States. The officers asked Thomas Spurgeon to come to preach for three months; and on June 10, 1892, he arrived in London with his wife and son. He closed his ministry on October 9, and then Dwight L. Moody arrived for a series of meetings at the tabernacle.

Pierson returned following Moody's ministry and discovered a deep division in the congregation. The "tabernacle tempest" was dividing families and breaking lifelong friendships. On March 28, 1893, some two thousand members met and asked the officers to call Thomas Spurgeon home for a year's ministry, after which the church would decide what to do next. Thomas accepted the call. He also remembered something Moody had said to him during his previous ministry at the tabernacle: "You are yet to come back to this place, and I am going to pray God here and now that it may be so!" He began his ministry in London on July 30, 1893. Before the year was over, the church knew that Thomas Spurgeon was the man for the pulpit. On March 21, 1894, the church called him as pastor, and he remained until 1908.

One of the most tragic events in the ministry of Thomas's father had occurred when young Charles was preaching to a huge crowd at the Surrey Gardens Music Hall. Troublemakers in the audience began to cry "Fire! Fire!" and the result was catastrophe. Seven people were killed, twenty-eight hospitalized. It seemed that Spurgeon's ministry was doomed. God overruled, however, and vindicated his servant. A trying time in Thomas's ministry also involved fire.

On April 20, 1899, the great Metropolitan Tabernacle burned to the ground, leaving Spurgeon with a congregation and no place to house it. The fire was caused by an overheated flue in the adjacent Pastors' College. At the Pastors' Conference the day before, the Scripture reading, Hebrews 12, had ended with "Our God is a consuming fire." Thomas Spurgeon preached on the theme "No Strange Fire." The slogan for the annual conference was "Does the fire burn brightly on the alter?" And oddly enough, *Old Moore's Almanack* had predicted, "About the middle of the month [April] the destruction of a famous building by fire may be expected." Spurgeon had built a tabernacle in New Zealand; now he would rebuild one in London. When he was standing by the ruins shortly after the fire, a stranger approached him and slipped some money into his hand. "This is to build it up again, sir!" he said. God would multiply those five shillings into thousands of dollars; and on September 19, 1900, the new tabernacle was opened. Ira Sankey sang at the dedication services, and F. B. Meyer and John Henry Jowett assisted Spurgeon in the preaching.

Thomas Spurgeon resigned as pastor of the tabernacle on February 8, 1908, and the church reluctantly accepted his resignation. They held a great farewell service for him on June 22. For the next nine years he preached often, assisted in raising funds for the orphan homes his father had founded, and worked hard to maintain his health. He celebrated his diamond jubilee on September 20, 1916, and received well-deserved honors from an appreciative Christian public. He died on October 20, 1917, and was buried near his father's tomb in Norwood Cemetery. A. C. Dixon, the new pastor of the tabernacle, read the Scripture; Dinsdale Young prayed; the children from the orphanage sang; and F. J. Feltham preached. At C.H.S.'s burial service, a dove had flown from the direction of the tabernacle towards the tomb, glided over the sorrowing crowd, seemed almost to hover, and then flown away. For Thomas Spurgeon there was no dove, but there certainly was peace.

Early in his ministry, Thomas wrote to his father: "If I can have but a portion of my father's mantle, I might be well content." Did his illustrious heritage cripple him? I think not. He knew and accepted himself. He did not try to be his father, although he certainly learned from his father. No doubt many people came to hear him because he was a Spurgeon; but after they heard, they came back. They detected an authentic note. Thomas Spurgeon was a voice for God, not an echo of his father. The gifts God had given him would have made him a successful minister of the gospel even without the name *Spurgeon*.

Certainly Thomas Spurgeon is to be honored and remembered for daring to be himself. He never permitted his father to determine God's will for his ministry. When Thomas returned to London for a year's ministry at the tabernacle, he wisely left his wife and son in New Zealand, lest their presence be interpreted as overconfidence on his part. He had great gifts as an evangelist. His itinerant ministry in Australia and New Zealand was greatly blessed by God. Like his father, he had a keen sense of humor and often had to struggle to control it. To say that Thomas Spurgeon was not as gifted or as marvelously used by God as his father is to say nothing. How many preachers even begin to measure up to the stature of Charles Haddon Spurgeon? In uniting a great congregation, maintaining a wide and varied ministry, and rebuilding a great and historic structure, Thomas Spurgeon performed, under God, one of the greatest ministries of modern times. He will always be overshadowed by his father, but nevertheless will receive his own "Well done!" when all Christians stand before the Lord.

32

Samuel Chadwick
1860–1932

Samuel Chadwick is not as well known as he deserves to be, and I propose to remedy that situation as best I can. I am amazed to discover that Chadwick is not named in either *The Wycliffe Biographical Dictionary of the Church* or the monumental *New International Dictionary of the Christian Church*, although the former finds room for the poet Chaucer, and the latter gives space to the English devotional writer Richard Challoner. I suspect that as an evangelist, educator, and editor, Samuel Chadwick did more to win the lost and to build the church than all the poets and devotional writers of his day.

He was born September 16, 1860, in a modest home in Burnsley, Lancashire, England. Burnsley was a mill town, and Chadwick said that "there was not a blade of grass, a tree, or a flower" in the area where he lived. "It would be difficult to imagine anything more drab, prosaic, and uninteresting than our street!"

At the age of eight he went to work in the cotton mills, and thus developed the discipline of early rising, a practice he continued throughout his life. In later years he thanked God that he grew up among the laboring people, so that he might understand their needs and minister to them. At an early age he became interested in political meetings, mainly because he enjoyed listening to the speakers. He used to read aloud the speeches of Gladstone and Disraeli as reported in the newspapers. Unconsciously, he was preparing to become one of England's greatest preachers.

When he was ten years old, Chadwick was converted to Christ through the ministry of Samuel Coley, a guest speaker at the Sunday school anniversary meeting. From the very beginning of his spiritual life, Chadwick emphasized prayer. "I went apart three times a day," he wrote, "and prayed in the Spirit all the time between. The habit of three times a day was not easy. The dinner hour was short, the family was large, and the house small, but I managed!"

In 1875, when he was fifteen years old, Chadwick felt a call to ministry, a decision he pondered and prayed about for a whole year. His resources were limited, his health was not good, and he had received little education. His family was poor and would not be able to send him to school. But he was determined to serve Christ; so after working twelve hours a day in the mill, he devoted five more hours to personal study at home.

The Methodist superintendent in the Burnsley Circuit, Josiah Mee, discovered Chadwick's desire to serve Christ and encouraged him to preach. Almost every Sunday he would walk to various preaching stations in the Methodist Circuit and share the Word of God. He enjoyed preaching, but for some reason he did not see any fruit from his ministry. It would be seven years before the Lord would reveal to him the secret of spiritual fruitfulness. In 1881, Chadwick was appointed lay evangelist at nearby Stacksteads, a district saturated with open sin and opposition to the gospel. Proud of his preaching ability and his file of sermons, the young evangelist went to work—but the forces of Satan were too much for him. He desperately needed power. He banded together with a small group of burdened people and covenanted with them to pray daily for revival.

As Chadwick prayed, God dealt with him, particularly in the area of his pride. At three o'clock one Sunday morning, the young Methodist preacher burned all his sermon outlines and made a complete surrender to the Lord. That was the beginning of revival. At the early prayer meeting, he led his first soul to Jesus Christ. Before that Lord's Day had ended, Chadwick led seven people to the Savior.

Sensitive to the Spirit's leading, Chadwick wisely suspended all the regular services of the church and called the congregation to prayer. Tuesday evening two women in the church, known to be enemies, patched up their differences and knelt together in prayer at the communion rail. Others joined them, and the Spirit began to move among the people. There was no excessive display of emotion, but everyone knew that God was in their midst.

The turning point came when the town drunkard, Robert Hamer, showed up at the meeting. He was known as "Bury Bob," and there was hardly a sin or crime that he had not been involved in one way or another. People had seen him eat glass, fight rats with his teeth, break furniture, swallow knives, and fight policemen. That night, he asked for a Band of Hope pledge card, signed his X, and vowed he would never drink again. The following Sunday Bury Bob was converted, and his life and home were so transformed that it led to the salvation of many others.

What the congregation did not know was that behind the scenes their youthful pastor had been praying that God would stir things up by converting some notorious sinner. Chadwick had been studying John 11 and 12, and had noticed that the resurrection of Lazarus had led to the conversion of many people. "That's the solution!" he said to himself. "We need a Lazarus!" God answered his prayers; Bury Bob was his Lazarus, raised from the dead and given new life in Jesus Christ. From that time on, in every church he pastored and every evangelistic crusade he conducted, Samuel Chadwick asked God to give him a Lazarus.

"If God is at work week by week raising men from the dead," he said, "there will always be people coming to see how it is done. You cannot find an empty church that has *conversion* for its leading feature. Do you want to know how to fill empty chapels? Here is the answer: Get your Lazarus."

From 1883 to 1886, Chadwick was a student at Disbury College, where he read every book he could secure and listened to the lectures as though his instructors were inspired apostles. It was his one opportunity for formal training, and he wanted to give his best to his Lord. His concern for lost souls and his unsophisticated ways bothered a few of the students and staff, but fortunately, his education did not put out the fire that God had ignited in his heart. "Passion does not compensate for ignorance," he used to say in later years. He was indeed a balanced man.

He ministered as an assistant pastor in Edinburgh for one year following graduation, and then as minister at the Clydebank Mission in Glasgow for three years. At Clydebank, he had a new building but no congregation; so he set out to win people to Christ and build his own church. He visited in homes, preached on street corners, fought the brewers and gamblers, and quickly assembled a band of men and women who loved the Lord and their young pastor.

One classic story must be repeated from those Glasgow days. The brewers had applied for five new licenses to put up pubs in strategic places, and Chadwick went to court to oppose them. The attorney for the brewers did his best to ridicule the young pastor, ending his speech with, "I should like to ask this young-looking shepherd, what hast thou done with the few sheep in the wilderness?"

Chadwick jumped to his feet and replied, "Don't you trouble about my sheep! I'm after the wolf today!"

In 1890, the Methodists officially ordained Samuel Chadwick and sent him to Wesley Chapel, Leeds, where he ministered for three years. He then went to London for a year, but in 1894 he was back in Leeds, this time at the prestigious (but spiritually dead) Oxford Place Chapel. For the rest of his life, he would be known as Chadwick of Leeds. He ministered there for thirteen years, and again saw miracles of grace in the lives of sinners as he preached the gospel of Jesus Christ.

"I sat at the table at my first Band Meeting," he reported, "and listened to their doleful tales of difficulty and despair, laughing at their fears. I knew no way of conducting a mission except that of getting people saved." Within the first six months God gave him not one Lazarus but half a dozen.

There was a strong agnostic movement in Britain at that time, with Secularist Societies springing up in almost every city. One Sunday evening, the entire Secularist Society of Leeds filled the gallery of the church, hoping to disrupt the ministry. But that night, their leader was converted. And within the next few weeks, every single officer in the group was won to Christ.

After thirteen fruitful years in Leeds, Chadwick accepted a call to teach at Cliff College, the Methodist school in Sheffield, Yorkshire. He promised them five years, but even while he was teaching he was busy holding evangelistic meetings and helping to establish missions in South Yorkshire. In 1913, Chadwick was made principal of Cliff College, and embarked on a program of training young people for ministry. For nearly twenty years he taught students how to pray, depend on the Spirit, preach the gospel, and seek to win lost souls to Christ.

Chadwick was unique, and space does not permit retelling all the stories that came out of his life and ministry, but here are a few instances. There was a student who asked him for permission to smoke his pipe, even though it was against the rules. "I have been a smoker for twenty years," he argued, "and I am just dying for a smoke!"

"Are you really dying for a smoke?" Chadwick asked.

"I am, sir," the student replied.

"Then," said Chadwick, "sit down in that chair and die!"

Before long, the student was on his knees beside the principal, and God answered prayer. The boy was delivered from the habit.

Then there was the time when a ministerial candidate was almost ejected because he was short of stature. Chadwick stood to his feet and protested. "The only fault the Committee had to find with this candidate," he said, "is that his legs are short; and I want to know how long this Conference has been measuring men at the end!"

When some of the "intellectual" young pastors tried to bring a "new gospel" into the Methodist movement, Chadwick opposed them. "Go down to the South Yorkshire coalfields and try your new gospel," he cried out at the conference, "and see what it will do. Until you have got a gospel that works—shut up! This is not an age for twiddling your thumbs!"

Chadwick used to hold large anniversary services at Cliff College, and he always prayed for generous offerings to help the college. After one morning service, a guest gave him a large check and said, "I have been blessed this morning!" Chadwick took the check, lifted his eyes to heaven and prayed aloud, "Lord, bless him again tonight!"

Chadwick made several visits to the United States and ministered at such important centers as D. L. Moody's Northfield and Winona Lake Bible Conference. God used him to stir Christians to have a concern for the lost and a desire for holy living. For many years he was editor of *Joyful News*, the official publication of the Joyful News Mission, which eventually merged with the Wesleyan Home Mission Committee. His articles on prayer were published in book form in 1931 as *The Path of Prayer*. It is still one of the best books on the subject and has been reprinted by the Christian Literature Crusade.

The Way to Pentecost is another of Chadwick's books that has had a wide ministry. It was published by Hodder and Stoughton in London and is distributed in the United States by the Christian Literature Crusade. You need not agree with every detail of the author's theology to benefit from the insights and impact of this book. I especially appreciate his sane approach to the delicate subject of spiritual gifts. In his own inimitable way, Chadwick writes, "The Gift of Tongues comes last on the list, and is first in controversy!"

Before I leave Samuel Chadwick, I want to point out that he was a very close friend of Dr. G. Campbell Morgan. It is worth noting that Morgan also, in his early ministry, wrestled with pride of preaching and burned his sermon outlines. Like Chadwick, Morgan rose from obscurity to become one of England's greatest preachers and Bible teachers. In 1904, when Morgan was considering the call to Westminster Chapel, London, he had a long talk with his friend Chad before he made his decision. Chadwick wrote to Morgan when the Morgan family moved to America in 1919:

I cannot tell all your friendship has meant to me. I am flattered when people bracket my name with yours, and though I know the distance at which I follow, it pleases me that they think of us together. The privilege of your friendship I reckon among God's best gifts and my chiefest joy.

Chadwick served as president of the Methodist Conference in 1918 and the president of the Free Church Council in 1922. In 1927 and again in 1930 he underwent serious surgery that left him quite weak, but he carried on as best he could in the strength of the Lord.

He died on Sunday, October 16, 1932, at the age of seventy-two, but before his Homegoing, he called his colleagues to his bedside and gave them a farewell message:

Stand together for the Word of God. . . . Stand in a spirit of unity, of faith, of doctrine, according to the fourth chapter of Ephesians. . . . I have stood true to the last. I have had no doubts. I have been sure of the Living God. He knows my limitations, but I have loved Him and trusted in his mercy. My ministry has been the message of the Cross.

A Methodist through and through, Samuel Chadwick belonged to the whole evangelical world because he preached the fundamentals of the faith and sought to bring sinners to the Savior. "The qualities of powerful personality," he said, "are courage, power, sympathy, and sanity." He possessed all of them, and yielded to the Spirit, giving himself to the greatest work in the world—the winning of lost souls to Jesus Christ.

Charles E. Jefferson
1860–1937

A shepherd cannot shine," wrote Charles E. Jefferson in his book *The Minister as Shepherd*. "He cannot cut a figure. His work must be done in obscurity. . . . His work calls for continuous self-effacement. It is a form of service which eats up a man's life. It makes a man old before his time. Every good shepherd lays down his life for the sheep."[1] All of us know that *pastor* is the Latin word for "shepherd." The pastor of the local church is supposed to be a shepherd; but, alas, too often he is not. He may be a good preacher—and preaching is definitely important to pastoral work—and he may be a good organizer, but if he is not maintaining a personal interest in the flock, he is not fulfilling his divine calling. "It is the weaklings and not the giants, who neglect their people," Jefferson wrote. "It is the Pagan and not the Christian who shines in public and leaves undone the private duties which belong to him as an ordained steward of the Son of God."[2]

The Minister as Shepherd has been reprinted by the Christian Literature Crusade in the *Living Books for All* series, and I heartily recommend it to you. It is one of four valuable books by Jefferson directed especially to the pastor, the other three being *The Minister as Prophet*, *Quiet Hints to Growing Preachers*, and his Yale lectures,

The Building of the Church. These titles will have to be found in the used-book stores. His Yale lectures were published in a Baker Books edition in 1969. I urge the addition of these four volumes to every library, and I suggest they be read and reread; Jefferson's philosophy of the ministry is desperately needed today.

Charles E. Jefferson was born in 1860 and died in 1937. He started out not as a pastor, but as a superintendent of schools in Worthington, Ohio. He also taught at Ohio Wesleyan and Ohio State. In 1884 he entered the Boston University Law School, and it was while he was in Boston that the challenge of the gospel ministry took hold of his heart. As he visited various churches, he became thoroughly disgusted with the preaching that he heard. Then he heard Phillips Brooks at Trinity Church, and everything changed. He enrolled in the theological course at Boston University and graduated in 1887. After brief pastorates in New Hampshire and Massachusetts, he accepted a call to the 34th Street Tabernacle in Manhattan, where he was to labor for almost forty years. The tabernacle had a noble history; William M. Taylor was pastor there for twenty years (1871–92). If you do not have Taylor's sermons on Christ's miracles and parables, by all means get them! And while you are looking, secure his great biographical series on Moses, Joseph, Ruth, Esther, David, Paul, and other Bible greats. What preaching!

When Jefferson accepted the call, he knew God was placing him into a difficult situation. After seven years the church relocated and built a new edifice at the corner of Broadway and 56th Street, changing its name to the Broadway Tabernacle Congregational Church. At that time, Broadway was known as "the great white way," and it was to this kind of a constituency that Jefferson ministered for almost forty years. Though the church was in one of the most difficult parts of the city, he managed to fill the building week after week and to minister, with great power and blessing, to a "needy parade." He witnessed the exodus of more than one church from the downtown area, yet he remained. What an example for us to follow!

He had a pastor's heart, and the combination of preacher-pastor was what made him an effective minister in that difficult downtown location. He believed in the local church, in *building* the church to the glory of God, and not simply *using* it as a tool to build his own career. "It is sad to see a man turning away from the ministry because he does not understand the church," Jefferson wrote in his Yale lectures, "but it is tragic to see one entering the ministry with a wrong attitude to the church. Young ministers sometimes look upon the church as a necessary evil, an inherited encumbrance, a sort of device by which preachers are handicapped in their movements and held back from largest usefulness. . . . They want to do things on a broad scale. To deal with so small and insignificant a body as a church seems parochial and belittling."[3] This is why he titled his lectures *The Building of the Church*, taking the "architectural idea" in the New Testament and applying it to the preaching of the Word and the pastoring of the people. "The crowning and crucial work of a minister is not conversion, but church building."[4]

His first lecture deals with "the church building concept in the New Testament." What does this have to do with preaching? "The sermon," said Jefferson, "comes not out of the preacher alone, but out of the church. . . . He is nourished by his environment—the family of Christ."[5] What a tremendous concept for the growing pastor to grasp! "The church is a growing organism and the preacher must know the stages of its development before he can feed it."[6] "A physician always looks at his patient before he goes to the medicine chest. A wise preacher begins, not with his books, but with his church."[7]

Recently a seminary president complained to me that some of his school's finest graduates "were not making it" in their churches. "Do you know what one of our boys did?" he asked. "He hadn't been in his first church three months before he started to revise the consti- tution! He didn't stay long." It is too bad that graduate had not read *The Building of the Church*, especially this passage:

> Here again the preacher must begin by establishing right relations between himself and his church. . . . If a man has a contemptuous view of his church he is well-nigh certain to be afraid of it. But love casts out fear. If a man loves his church and proves his love by his life, he can say to it anything which is proper for a Christian teacher to say to

his pupils, anything which is fitting for a Christian man to say to his friends. The preachers who get into trouble by talking plainly to their people are as a rule preachers who do not love their churches.[8]

Of course the ministry of building demands time, and Jefferson pleaded for the longer pastorate. "He [the pastor] is a master-builder, and his task is not simply collecting material, but shaping it into a structure which shall become a shrine of the Eternal. . . . The highest place belongs to the man who, year after year, in the same parish, instructs men in the high and difficult art of living together, and trains them by long and patient processes in the work of bringing spiritual forces to bear upon the moral problems of the community."[9] "No matter how long he stays, there will be more work to do than there was in sight at the beginning. Men who engage in the building of the church know that the work is never done."[10] And yet some pastors are looking for new churches after two years of ministry!

In the remaining seven lectures, Jefferson applied the building concept to various aspects of the ministry in the local church: building the brotherhood ("To create an ampler and a warmer fellowship inside the church of Jesus is the first work for which preachers are ordained"); building the individual ("Many a man is preaching to a dwindling congregation because his sermons have lost the personal note. He chills by his vague generalities, or enrages by his wholesale denunciations");[11] building moods and tempers ("A congregation possesses a disposition as pronounced and characteristic as that of any of its members");[12] building thrones ("The preacher who would make his church a power must begin by trusting common people");[13] building the worldwide church ("Every preacher should do his work in the radiance of the vision of the church universal");[14] building the plan ("It is not a waste of time to give hours and days to the work of pondering and maturing schedules for future operations");[15] and finally, building the builder ("The secret of an extended pastorate is a growing man").[16] *The Building of the Church* is easily one of the finest books to come out of the Yale lecture series, and its message is greatly needed today.

Jefferson's other three books are not quite so massive and detailed. *The Minister as Shepherd* contains five lectures that Jefferson gave in 1912, but they are amazingly contemporary. He began with "The Shepherd Idea in Scripture and History," proving that the shepherd has a key place in the plan of God. "When church leaders began to lose the vision of the Good Shepherd, they at the same time began to drift away from the New Testament ideal of ministerial service."[17] He then covered the shepherd's work, opportunity, temptations, and rewards, and he did so in a manner that convinces you that he himself possessed a shepherd's heart. He pointed out that the Eastern shepherd was a watchman, a guard, a guide, a savior, a provider, and a man who personally loved his sheep. I appreciate the way he explained the relationship between preaching and shepherding, and it is here that the influence of Phillips Brooks is most clearly seen. "The pastoral instinct is nowhere more sorely needed than in the work of preaching," he wrote. "No part of a minister's work is more strictly, genuinely pastoral than the work of preaching."[18]

In *The Minister as Prophet* Jefferson dealt particularly with preaching and the importance of proclaiming the truth of God. I am tempted to quote several passages, but I will settle for this one: "A little man with narrow view can cause a world of trouble." I like his emphasis on patience in preaching and the importance he places on building the preacher as much as building the sermon. "I prepare my sermons by preparing myself," he told Edgar De Witt Jones. "Self-preparation is the most difficult work a preacher has to do. . . . A preacher who is spiritually anemic, or intellectually impoverished, or morally depleted, will wish often for a juniper tree."[19]

The fourth book, *Quiet Hints to Growing Preachers*, is somewhat of a pastoral fireside chat, twenty-six chapters on important ministerial matters that somehow have been omitted from the textbooks.

Many a man in the ministry fails, not because he is bad, but because he has a genius for blundering.[20]

If a man expects to move men by his preaching he must first do a deal of living, and the sooner he begins to live the better.[21]

No man can long be interesting in the pulpit who does not think. No man can think wisely who does not study.[22]

Probably no other single sin works such havoc in the Christian church as the impatience of her ministers.[23]

Popularity is the most fearful of all tests.[24]

This is the kind of book the pastor can keep on his desk and read a chapter of a day—all chapters are brief—and remind himself of the things that too easily are forgotten.

Jefferson wrote not only for pastors but also for the church at large, including a number of books of sermons. His own preaching was doctrinal in emphasis but not theological in content. He used short, crisp sentences and sought to express the truth in the simplest manner. His *Cardinal Ideas of Isaiah* (1925) and *Cardinal Ideas of Jeremiah* (1928) are helpful to the pastor preaching on those books and prophets.

When I read Jefferson's ideas about preaching, I discovered that he used several comparisons to make his point. In one place he compared the sermon to something cooking! "One never knows what is going to happen when he puts a truth to soak in the juices of the mind."[25] In another place he compared sermons to bullets. "How far they go does not depend upon the text or upon the structure of the sermon, but upon the texture of the manhood of the preacher."[26] But his favorite comparison was that of a sermon to a flower. "My sermons grow. They unfold. I never 'get up' a sermon. . . . A sermon of the right sort gets itself up. If I supply the soil and the seed and the sun and the rain, the sermon will come up of itself. My soul is a flower-garden. My business is raising sermons."[27]

I suppose the most helpful thing Charles E. Jefferson does for me is to remind me of the importance of the local church and the work the pastor must do if the church is to grow and glorify God. The pastor is a shepherd, a prophet, a builder. Jefferson himself was all three. Any man who can make a success of a city church in a difficult place is worth reading, and Jefferson is such a man. Get to know him soon!

34

W. H. Griffith Thomas
1861–1924

When William Henry Griffith Thomas died in Duluth, Minnesota, on June 2, 1924, the religious press in both America and England paid tribute. In the *Sunday School Times* for June 21, W. Graham Scroggie wrote:

> By the passing of Dr. Thomas the Christian Church has lost a scholar and teacher. . . . I can with utmost confidence say that the reading of Dr. Thomas's books creates in one a deeper love of and desire for God as is revealed in His Word, and that is more than can be said of much which the Christian press of today is turning out.

(Scroggie should have seen some of the books that are being published now!) R. A. Torrey wrote in the July 5 issue of the same publication:

> The first thing that impressed me about Dr. Thomas was his sound, wide, thorough, sane, well-balanced scholarship. His interpretations of Scripture were always scholarly and dependable. . . . Along with his scholarship and his clearness of vision there went a very unusual ability to state profound truth with a clearness and a simplicity to which very few attain.

James M. Gray, president of Moody Bible Institute at the time, wrote in the June 28 issue:

Many will speak of Dr. Thomas as an author, editor, preacher, and expositor; but I should like to say a word about him as a contender for "the faith which was once for all delivered unto the saints." He had a great advantage there in his broad knowledge and his early experience as an evangelical leader in the Anglican church before he came to this country.

Griffith Thomas had no advantages in childhood or early manhood. From the beginning, circumstances seemed to be against him. Yet in the furnace of affliction and on the battlefield of life, God made him a great man. His mother had been widowed before he was born on January 2, 1861, in Oswestry, Shropshire. He spent his early years with his grandfather William Griffith. His mother married again, but family financial pressure forced young Will to leave school when only fourteen. In later years he was recognized throughout the English-speaking world as a brilliant educator, teacher, and writer; yet his own education was obtained with the greatest difficulty and sacrifice.

When he was sixteen, he was asked to teach a Sunday school class at Holy Trinity Church in Oswestry. Not yet a professed believer, he thought he was volunteering for the choir! For four months he did his best, but he found it impossible to teach something he had never experienced. God used the witness of two young men in the church to bring him to salvation on March 23, 1878. "When I awoke the next morning," he related, "my soul was simply overflowing with joy, and since then I have never doubted that it was on that Saturday night I was born again, converted to God."

He moved to London in 1879 and worked in his uncle's office. From 10:30 p.m. to 2:30 a.m. he devoted himself to serious study, a discipline that made him into a scholar. He always admonished his students to devote themselves to reading and thinking no matter what price had to be paid. His vicar, the Reverend B. Oswald Sharp, offered him a lay curacy in 1882. This enabled him to attend morning lectures at King's College in London while fulfilling his pastoral responsibilities during the afternoons and evenings. He earned his AKC (Associate of King's College) degree and was ordained in 1885. At that service the bishop of London, Frederick Temple, admonished him never to neglect his Greek New Testament for a single day. (We wonder how seriously a young minister today would take that admonition.) "G. T." kept his promise to Bishop Temple by reading a chapter each day the rest of his life.

After three and a half years as curate of the church in London, Griffith Thomas accepted a curacy at St. Aldate's Church, Oxford. While there, he earned his BD in 1895 at the university, again as the result of disciplined study and the wise investment of early and late hours. When I visited the Bodleian Library in Oxford, I thought of Griffith Thomas studying there, hiding in a special corner known only to the rector, the beloved Canon Christopher. The canon, a kind, spiritual man and a great soul-winner, was failing in health and becoming deaf. Consequently much of the parish work fell to Griffith Thomas, who entered into it with as much zest as he did his Greek studies. He preached often, led the Sunday school, managed the various parish organizations, and did a thorough job of visitation. He was a scholar, but never in the slightest degree a recluse. Both young and old loved him, and he had a particular love for them.

About this time, the larger fellowship of the Anglican church began to notice him. I have in my file a copy of the *Record* for Friday, January 17, 1896, which includes a full report of the Islington Clerical Meeting held the preceding Tuesday. The vicar of Islington, Dr. Barlow, had invited the young curate to read a paper on the doctrine of the church, the first young assistant thus to be honored. "Mr. Thomas treated his subject popularly," the *Record* reported, "and he received the cordial recognition and praise of the entire Meeting." The great scholar Handley C. G. Moule, later the bishop of Durham, was also on the program; young Griffith Thomas was in good company.

Later that year Griffith Thomas accepted a call to St. Paul's, Portman Square, now devoted almost entirely to small hotels and business offices. St. Paul's Church today is located a few blocks from its original site.

Scholar that he was, Griffith Thomas did not make the mistake of trying to build his ministry on bookish sermons. He depended on prayer as well as careful preparation. The church conducted six prayer meetings each week! There were a multitude of organizations within the church. They even had an orchestra society and a cycling club. (Griffith Thomas, a cycling enthusiast, was such a big man that his bicycle had to be specially made.) The main meetings of the church emphasized the study of the Word. Most of Griffith Thomas's later expository books grew out of these early Bible classes. To learn his philosophy of Bible study, read *Methods of Bible Study*, published originally in 1902 and recently reprinted. For his views on preaching and pastoral work, read *The Work of the Ministry* (reprinted as *Ministerial Life and Work*).

In October 1905, Griffith Thomas was named principal of Wycliffe Hall, Oxford, the center of ministerial training for evangelical Anglicans. During his five years there he was the pastor, teacher, and friend of more than eighty students. He also conducted a weekly Greek New Testament reading at the university on Sunday afternoons. Attending one of these meetings were undergraduates T. E. Lawrence (Lawrence of Arabia) and his two brothers. During the years at Oxford, Griffith Thomas earned his doctoral degree (DDOxon). His dissertation was titled "A Sacrament of Our Redemption." Also during those years he began to minister at the British Keswick Convention. He was also busy writing, editing, and taking a leading part in church affairs that affected evangelicals.

He and his family moved to Toronto in 1910, where he joined the faculty of Wycliffe College, having been persuaded that a wider ministry would be his in Canada. Originally he had been invited to serve as professor of systematic theology, but when he arrived, he discovered that one of the local graduates had been given the position instead! A lesser man would have resigned and returned to England. But Griffith Thomas believed so strongly that God had called him to Canada that he remained and taught Old Testament literature and exegesis for nine years. The students were the losers, in that no one in the Anglican church at that time could surpass Griffith Thomas in teaching biblical theology. It was largely by this means, however, that he became known in both North America and many other parts of the world. When approached to return to an English parish, he replied, "But now a continent is my parish!"

In 1919, the family moved to Philadelphia, and Griffith Thomas carried on an extensive conference and writing ministry. He joined with Lewis Sperry Chafer and Alex B. Winchester in founding Dallas Theological Seminary. He was to have served as a visiting lecturer and later as a faculty member, but his untimely death in 1924 intervened. Today his library continues its ministry to the hundreds of students at the school, however, and his memory is also kept green through the annual W. H. Griffith Thomas Memorial Lectures.

Today we know W. H. Griffith Thomas primarily from the printed page. Add every one of his books to your library. Begin with his great commentaries on Genesis and Romans. Unfortunately, some of his best books have gone out of print, including *The Apostle John*, *The Apostle Peter*, and *Christianity Is Christ*. Still available are his masterly Stone lectures, presented at Princeton Theological Seminary in 1913, on *The Holy Spirit of God*, and his commentary on the Epistle to the Hebrews, *"Let Us Go On."* You do not have to be Anglican to appreciate *The Principles of Theology* and *The Catholic Faith*, both published in London by Vine Books (formerly Church Book Room Press), which plans to issue new editions of as many of his books as possible. *The Prayers of St. Paul* is a devotional gem, as is *Grace and Power*. He published twenty-six booklets and twenty-four larger works, a tremendous accomplishment for a man who began his career with severe educational limitations.

Griffith Thomas's daughter, Winifred G. T. Gillespie, has also edited and issued posthumously several volumes of her father's unpublished material: *Outline Studies in the Gospel of Matthew*, *Outline Studies in the Gospel of Luke*, *Outline Studies in the Acts of the Apostles*, *Through the Pentateuch Chapter by Chapter*, and *Studies in Colossians and*

Philemon. She has also worked on notes he used at Toronto in his course on Old Testament introduction.

Griffith Thomas's advice to young preachers was: "Think yourself empty, read yourself full, write yourself clear, pray yourself keen—then enter the pulpit and let yourself go!" He practiced this counsel himself, becoming a first-rank evangelical scholar and preacher, always keenly alert to encroachments of both modernism and ritualism. Academic achievement did not come without sacrifice—but then, it rarely does. He dedicated and applied himself, and the Lord did the rest. His books are exposition at its best: sound exegesis, pastoral concern, clear outlining, practical application, and relevance to the needs of the day. He did not attempt to be sensational; he wanted only to be biblical. Griffith Thomas was a rare blend of spirituality and scholarship, a true "pastor-teacher."

"We cannot make up for failure in our devotional life by redoubling energy in service," he wrote. "As water never rises above its level, so what we do never rises above what we are. . . . We shall never take people one hair's breadth beyond our own spiritual attainment. We may point to higher things, we may 'allure to brighter worlds,' but . . . we shall only take them as far as we ourselves have gone." In other words, the pastor must be both a man of God and a student. If he is careless in either his praying or his studying, he cannot enjoy God's blessing. One of his students at Wycliffe Hall, G. R. Harding Wood, wrote in the December 29, 1960, issue of *Life of Faith*: "One was conscious that all his work, especially his teaching, was steeped in prayer; and it was the same in the more intimate talks about personal problems. . . . He truly walked with God, and made that spiritual exercise something to be coveted and practiced." Can a man be both saint and scholar, a man of books and a man of *the* Book? W. H. Griffith Thomas is convincing proof that one can—if one is willing to pay the price.

35

A. C. Gaebelein and B. H. Carroll
1861–1945; 1843–1914

You could not find two more opposite men than Arno Clemens Gaebelein and Benajah Harvey Carroll. Gaebelein's ministry was, for the most part, an interdenominational one; Carroll was a devoted Southern Baptist and a strong denominational leader. Gaebelein held a dispensational view of Scripture; Carroll did not. Gaebelein was an itinerant Bible teacher; Carroll devoted most of his life to his church and to the seminary he helped to found. Why, then, bring these men together? For two reasons: both were self-made scholars with enviable reputations as teachers of the Word, and both have left behind sets of books dealing with the entire Bible. In Gaebelein's *The Annotated Bible* and Carroll's *An Interpretation of the English Bible* are two different approaches to Scripture from men who were devoted servants of the Lord and able ministers of his Word.

Gaebelein was a remarkable man. Born in Germany in 1861 (the year Carroll joined the Texas Rangers), he was converted to Christ at the age of twelve, and at the age of eighteen dedicated himself for Christian service. This dedication occurred on October 31 (the anniversary of Martin Luther's ninety-five theses), only a few months after he had arrived in America. "I had been reading my New Testament," Gaebelein wrote in his autobiography, *Half a Century*, "when suddenly a strong impulse came upon me to seek His presence and to tell Him that work for Him should be my life's work."

He identified with the German Methodists in Lawrence, Massachusetts, where he was living, and soon he found himself teaching classes and distributing tracts. A friend offered to send him to seminary, but Louis Wallon, the presiding elder of that district, advised against it. Gaebelein's training in Germany, which included Latin and Greek, actually put him ahead of some seminary graduates; and he was a tireless student on his own. Wallon loaned him theological books and encouraged him to study at home. Gaebelein was not critical of formal education, however; in later years he was to help found the Evangelical Theological College (out of which grew Dallas Theological Seminary), and he delivered annual lectures at the school.

In 1881, he moved to New York City to assist Wallon in a German church. It was there that he was introduced to the premillennial position, but at first he rejected it. Later he became pastor of a German congregation in Baltimore, and there he began his study of Semitic languages. It was his habit to be at his studies at 4:00 each morning. He ministered in various German churches, and his knowledge of Hebrew and his love for the Jews gradually brought him into prominence as a missionary to the thousands of Jews pouring into New York City at that time. He had been converted to the premillennial position, and his addresses on prophecy attracted great crowds of both Jews and Gentiles. This ministry finally led to the establishing of the Hope of Israel Mission and a monthly publication in Hebrew for the Jewish people. A year later, in 1894, Gaebelein founded *Our Hope* magazine, one of the finest and most influential of the many publications of that era. He edited it for fifty-one years until his death in 1945; it then merged with another publication and, unfortunately, ceased to exist. We could use today another Bible study monthly like *Our Hope*.

To read the life of A. C. Gaebelein is to come in contact with some of the great Bible teachers of that exciting era. The Niagara Bible Conference and other great conferences were in full swing during those years, and great crowds of believers gathered to study the Word in key centers across the country. In the pages of *Half a Century*, you meet James H. Brookes, C. I. Scofield, F. C. Jennings (whose commentary on Isaiah is a classic), Lewis Sperry Chafer, George C. Needham, and a host of other gifted men who tirelessly traveled from city to city to teach the Scriptures. There were giants in the earth in those days.

However great these men might have been, the one man in this autobiography who deserves our appreciation is Samuel Goldstein, a Hebrew Christian who belonged to Gaebelein's congregation in Hoboken, New Jersey. One day Goldstein came into his pastor's library and was surprised to see so many volumes in Hebrew and other Semitic languages. "It is a shame that you do not make greater use of your knowledge," said Goldstein. "You should go and preach the gospel to the Jews. I believe the Lord made you take up these studies because He wants you to go to my brethren, the Jews." That was the beginning of a remarkable ministry in New York City. Hundreds of Jewish people crowded into halls to hear Gaebelein expound their Old Testament Scriptures, and many found Christ as their Savior. For five years (1894–99) Gaebelein superintended the Hope of Israel Mission, wrote books and tracts, edited two magazines, and sought to win both Jews and Gentiles to Christ. In 1889, because of denominational problems, he severed his relationship with the German Methodist Conference and embarked on the itinerant ministry that was to make him a tremendous blessing to thousands of people in the United States, Canada, and Europe. But as great as his public ministry was, it is the treasure of his written ministry that we want to consider.

His first book was *Studies in Zechariah*, and there is an interesting story connected with it. Gaebelein sent a free copy of the book to every rabbi in the New York City area and never received any acknowledgment from any of them. Some time later, however, a young Hebrew Christian began to attend one of Gaebelein's meetings regularly, and it turned out he had been secretary to a well-known rabbi. The rabbi had thrown *Studies in Zechariah* into the wastebasket, but the secretary had rescued it, read it, and trusted Christ! If Gaebelein's commentaries on John, Acts, and the Psalms are not in your library, by all means secure them. *The Jewish Question*, on Romans 11, is a classic study of this critical chapter. *The Prophet Daniel* was highly praised by Sir Robert Anderson.

The Annotated Bible was begun in 1912 and completed ten years later. It originally appeared in nine volumes, but may be purchased today in a beautiful four-volume set. This work includes an outline of each chapter in the Bible, an introduction to each book, and a discussion of the teachings of the Word. It is not a commentary; it is one man's "interpretation" of the total revelation of Scripture, a unified "overview" of the Word of God.

Since Gaebelein was one of the original consulting editors of *The Scofield Reference Bible*, you can expect these studies to reflect a premillennial, dispensational approach to Scripture. In fact, *The Annotated Bible* is really an expansion of the basic teachings found in the *Scofield Bible*, with very practical applications throughout. However, a student need not agree with the author to benefit from his insights into the Word of God. There is a devotional warmth to Gaebelein's writings that goes beyond any one system of interpretation.

People often asked Gaebelein how he was able to travel and speak so much, edit a magazine, and write so many books. His answer was always the same: "I never wasted time!" When asked why he did not play golf, he replied: "Not because it is wrong, but because I can use my time in a better way." He was a devoted student, a systematic worker, and a dedicated man; and we today are the happy heirs of the treasures God enabled him to mine from the Word of God.

B. H. Carroll was another tireless worker and self-made scholar. He was born on December 27, 1843, in Carroll County, Mississippi, the seventh child in the family of Benajah and Mary Eliza Carroll. When he was seven years old, the family moved to Arkansas, and then in 1858 they relocated in Texas. It was in Texas that Carroll was to have his great ministry. It was B. H. Carroll who helped to "discover" George W. Truett and establish him in a ministry that is recognized today as one of the greatest in American church history (Andrew Blackwood called Truett "the mightiest pastoral evangelist since Charles H. Spurgeon"). It was B. H. Carroll who founded Southwestern Baptist Seminary and whose denominational leadership is remembered by Southern Baptists.

Strange as it seems, Carroll was a dedicated infidel until his conversion in 1865. From the first day he learned to read, Carroll had been a devoted student, reading whatever good books were available in that frontier region. He had an amazing memory and could recall at will material he had read years before, even to the point of giving the page locations! Eventually he was able to read three hundred pages a day without neglecting his regular responsibilities, and he even claimed to be able to read two lines at a time (actually, he was a forerunner of "speed-readers"; he read word groups instead of individual words, and he scanned pages). Even as an unbeliever, he read the Bible through several times, and few men dared to debate with him. He had a great mind and was a gifted orator. He also had a great, strong body; he stood six feet, four inches tall, and weighed two hundred pounds. His long beard, in later years, reached to his waist and gave him the semblance of an old prophet. One day, while boarding a train, he was asked by a stranger, "Where is your brother?"

"Which brother do you mean?" Carroll asked, since he had several brothers. "My brother Jimmie?"

"No!" said the stranger. "I mean your brother Aaron!"

Carroll enlisted in the Texas Rangers in 1861. Instead of carrying food in his saddlebags, he carried books! The next year, wanting something more exciting, he enlisted in the Texas Infantry and fought in the Civil War. He was seriously wounded at the Battle of Mansfield (Louisiana) and finally had to be sent home.

He was still a fanatical infidel and had even written a book on the subject; he had vowed never to enter a church again. But in 1865 he was persuaded to attend an old-fashioned camp meeting. The preacher challenged the people to make a "practical, experimental test" of Christianity and to give Jesus Christ a fair trial. When he asked for those to come forward who were willing to make the test, Carroll went. His action amazed and delighted his Christian friends, but he was careful to explain that he was not converted yet; he was simply acknowledging that he would give the Christian faith a fair hearing. While riding home, he got down on his knees in the woods and fought the battle out—and Jesus Christ won. Carroll's life was transformed, and his great gifts were dedicated to Christ. In November 1866 he was ordained to preach, and four years later he was called to the First Baptist Church of Waco, Texas, where he carried on an exciting ministry for twenty-eight years. He was dean of the department of Bible at Baylor until he founded the new seminary and was named its first president.

An Interpretation of the English Bible grew out of Carroll's own teaching and preaching ministry. His lectures and sermons were stenographically recorded, and some were written out by Carroll himself. After his death, his assistant at the seminary, J. W. Crowder, was given the responsibility of editing and compiling Carroll's studies, and it is largely because of his persistence and faith that we have this magnificent set of books today. It was originally published in thirteen volumes in 1916 by Fleming H. Revell, but that edition did not cover the entire Bible. In 1942 Broadman decided to bring out the set and commissioned Crowder to compile Carroll's material on the portions of Scripture not discussed in the first edition. This second edition went to seventeen volumes. It must be noted that J. B. Cranfill assisted in editing some of the volumes in that set. The completed edition was published in 1948. Baker Books reprinted an edition in six large volumes, a set that ought to be in every pastor's library.

For one man to produce this much material is a feat in itself; and when you consider that Carroll was limited in his formal schooling, the feat becomes even more amazing.

His mind was not a sponge, absorbing the ideas of others, but rather a fertile soil into which every fact and truth dropped, germinated and bore fruit. He was not an assimilator of the information and illustrations of others, but rather a tireless investigator searching out for himself and arranging his material in his own forceful manner.

So said George W. McDaniel in a memorial address at Houston on May 16, 1915. He added this word about *An Interpretation of the English Bible*: "As a commentary it is unique. Mark you, I don't rank it first; it is not himself at his best. For the average preacher, however, that commentary is a thesaurus of theology and a gold mine of homiletics." I have examined some of Carroll's other books, and quite frankly I believe that some of his *best* work is in this monumental set.

It is not actually a commentary; it is an "interpretation" on a broad scale. Sometimes Carroll pauses to preach a sermon; he may linger for pages on one verse, or he may skip over entire sections. I am glad the editors have not deleted his "asides," because they are sometimes the most interesting parts of a chapter! When Carroll reminisces about hearing some forgotten Baptist preacher, or when he lifts an experience out of his own exciting life, you find yourself suddenly paying close attention. This man was a giant of the faith, a great preacher, and a man who influenced men in a positive way toward faith in Jesus Christ. He is a man you ought to know.

Some students differ with Carroll's doctrine of the church or his views on prophecy, but these differences should not rob them of the values of this set of biblical studies (I usually learn more from those I disagree with than from those I agree with!). If a young pastor started reading this set faithfully and read only fifty pages a week, he would complete the set in about two years, and would have a knowledge of the Word of God from which he would profit for the rest of his ministry. If you only "consult" these books, you may be disappointed; but if you read them seriously, you will be enriched.

On March 7, 1933, Crowder, who edited all of Carroll's books, discussed Carroll's literary contribution in an address at Southwestern Baptist Seminary. I mention this because in this address Crowder made an interesting statement about D. L. Moody and the Moody Bible Institute. After rebuking another school in Chicago for departing from the faith, Crowder praised the institute for

> holding rigidly to the purposes of its founding, having through the years supplemented, magnified, and multiplied the literary productions and spirit of its founder. This has proved to be a great bulwark to the Moody Bible Institute. . . . The tests of scholarship are its final issues, its fruits. It may be a tree of life or a tree of death. Scholarship, or no scholarship, the productions of B. H. Carroll, like the productions of Dwight L. Moody, are a tree of life.

After warning the seminary family that their school, like others, could become modernistic, he suggested that Carroll's writings become the foundation, the fortification, against such doctrinal disintegration, even as Moody's writings had fortified the institute.

Carroll died on November 11, 1914, and the next day George W. Truett delivered the funeral message. "The pulpit was his throne," said Truett, "and he occupied it like a king." The king is gone, but some of the treasures of his reign are still with us. I encourage you to mine them; they will enrich your life and ministry.

36

G. Campbell Morgan
1863–1945

Dwight L. Moody had a knack for finding men and helping them channel their gifts into the work of soul-winning and building the church. One of his greatest "finds" was George Campbell Morgan—pastor, evangelist, Bible teacher extraordinary—the man who long before his death on May 16, 1945, was known throughout the English-speaking world as the "prince of expositors." Jill Morgan's life of her father-in-law, *A Man of the Word: Life of G. Campbell Morgan*, ought to be read by every Christian who is serious about teaching and preaching the Word of God. I try to read it again each year; it always sends me away with a new zest for studying the Bible and sharing it with others.

Morgan's beginnings were as inauspicious as possible. He was born on December 9, 1863, in the little village of Tetbury, England. His father was an independent Baptist minister with Brethren leanings, and he believed in courageous preaching and living by faith. Somewhat frail as a child, Morgan received his early education at home. He had always "played at preaching" as a child, setting up his sister's dolls and preaching to them; it was not a surprise when, at the age of thirteen, he asked to preach in a public meeting. He gave his first sermon in the Monmouth Methodist Chapel on August 27, 1876, and his theme was "salvation." Nobody in that little assembly that day realized that Campbell Morgan would be one of God's choicest instruments for spreading his Word in the years to come.

The family situation made it necessary for Morgan to find employment early, and he chose to become a teacher, a profession for which he was admirably gifted. But he took every opportunity to preach the Word, and God blessed his ministry. In the beginning he was quite aware of his gifts and was prone to display them. But one night a friend walked home from the meeting with him and gently pointed out his error; from that night on, Morgan preached to express the truth, not to impress the people.

Like many young men at that time, he went through an eclipse of his faith. In desperation, he locked all his books in a cupboard, secured a new Bible, and began to read it. "If it *be* the Word of God, and if I come to it with an unprejudiced and open mind, it will bring assurance to my soul of itself," he said. He canceled all his preaching engagements and devoted himself to the Bible. The result? "That Bible found me!" From that day on, Morgan never indulged in defending the Bible; he permitted the Bible to defend itself.

In 1886, Morgan was well known in his area as a Bible teacher, and he even conducted a follow-up mission for the hundreds who had been reached through Gipsy Smith's campaign in Hull. In his heart he felt a call to the ministry, but he knew he was unschooled. His first inclination was to join the Salvation Army, but both Gipsy Smith and Catherine Booth advised him to "go on with the work you are doing." Morgan appeared at the Lichfield Road Church in Birmingham on May 2, 1888, to preach a "trial sermon" in consideration for entering the Methodist ministry. He had been accustomed to addressing many hundreds of people in his meetings—the Hull meetings drew two thousand—and on that day, in a church auditorium that seated over one thousand people, he faced an audience of only seventy-five. He failed miserably and was rejected from the Methodist ministry. He wired his father: "Rejected!" His father wired back: "Rejected on earth—accepted in heaven."

On August 20, 1888, Morgan married Annie Morgan, better known as "Nancy." He hesitated to propose to her because all he could offer was the life of an itinerant evangelist, but she knew that God's hand was upon him. "If I cannot start with you at the bottom of the ladder," she wrote, "I should be ashamed to meet you at the top." After a year of the itinerant ministry, the Morgans settled down in the little town of Stone in Staffordshire, where he became pastor of the Congregational church; and on September 22, 1890, he was ordained.

As it did the writer of Hebrews, "time would fail me" to relate the life and travels of this amazing teacher of the Word. One of his best friends, Samuel Chadwick, said that Morgan was a "nomad," and no doubt he was right. Except for twelve years at the famous Westminster Chapel in London, Morgan's ministry was made up of short pastorates punctuated by brief periods of itinerating.

He left the Stone church to go to nearby Rugeley in June 1891, staying there two years. In June 1893 he went to the Westminster Road Congregational Church in Birmingham, where he stayed until December 1896. He was recommended to this church, by the way, by J. Gregory Mantle, the Methodist preacher who had helped to "reject" him eight years before! From 1897 to 1901, Morgan pastored the New Court Church in North London; and from there he moved to the United States to direct the Northfield extension ministry for Will Moody.

Morgan ministered in the States until November 1903, when he sailed back to Britain and was contacted by the officers of Westminster Chapel, one of Congregationalism's greatest churches, at that time in desperate shape. In September 1904 he began what was to be his longest pastorate. He finally terminated it in 1917 and became interim pastor, for one year, of the Highbury Quadrant Church in London. Then he returned to the States for nearly seven years of ministry, living first at Winona Lake, Indiana, and then moving to Athens, Georgia. He tried five months as pastor of the Covenant-First Presbyterian Church in Cincinnati, but it just did not work out and he resigned. For one year he was on the faculty of Biola College in Los Angeles, resigning because he felt a fellow teacher had been wrongly judged by the board. For three years he pastored the Tabernacle Presbyterian Church in Philadelphia, resigning in 1933 to allow his son Howard to become pastor (all of Morgan's four sons became preachers).

Next Morgan did a remarkable thing: he returned to Westminster Chapel in London to become pastor again. He had pastored the church during World War I, and now he would pastor it again during World War II. From 1938 on, D. Martyn Lloyd-Jones was his associate in the work; and when Morgan resigned in August 1943, Lloyd-Jones became pastor and continued to lead that great church by means of the devoted exposition of the Word of God. Morgan died on May 16, 1945.

I have read Morgan's life many times; I have read his books, his sermons, and his expositions. And I still ask myself, "How do you explain a man like this?" He did not have the privilege of studying in a Bible school or seminary, yet he wrote books that are used in these schools (and by preachers around the world). He sat on the faculties of three schools and for three years was the president of a college. He never resorted to cheap tricks or oratory to get a crowd, yet wherever he went, people had to be turned away. Both as a pastor and as an itinerant Bible teacher, he was relatively isolated from the common people; yet his messages show his deep understanding of the needs of the common man. How do we explain him?

One answer, I think, is the providence of God. Morgan himself said something at a 1937 Moody Centenary service in Westminster Chapel that, though he applied it to D. L. Moody, could just as easily be applied to Morgan. "In the history of the Church, times and a man have always seemed to come together . . . and . . . God generally finds the man where men are not looking for him." Morgan's successor, Lloyd-Jones, pointed out that Morgan came on the scene in Britain just after the great Moody-Sankey meetings, when thousands of new converts needed to be taught the Word of God. Morgan met that need. In his early days Morgan was a successful evangelist, but gradually the gift of teaching the Word came to the forefront. He exercised it widely and with wonderful results.

God had to prepare his man for his work, and he did that during Morgan's early pastorates, when he was "buried" and alone. He himself has admitted that "all the spadework" for his Bible studies was done during his two years at Rugeley, when the winters were long and cold and he was confined to his study. Instead of wasting his time because his church was small, Morgan invested it in the concentrated study of the Word, and God prepared him for a wonderful ministry as a result.

High on the list of events that helped to widen Morgan's ministry was his association with D. L. Moody. The evangelist had never heard Morgan preach, but he invited him to speak at Northfield and at the institute in Chicago in 1896. Morgan was to cross the Atlantic fifty-four times during his lifetime. He returned to Northfield in 1897 and again in 1899, the year that Moody died. "He is one of the most remarkable men who ever came to Northfield," said Moody. "I believe him to be filled utterly with the Spirit of God." After the evangelist's death, Will Moody sailed to England to ask Morgan to come and assist in the Northfield ministry, and Morgan accepted. "It's a plain case of burglary!" declared Joseph Parker when he heard that Morgan was moving to the States, and most of Britain's religious leaders agreed. But what else was Morgan to do? "I have long felt that God was preparing me for a ministry to the churches, rather than to one particular church," Morgan explained. "Now the door stands open for such a work. It has not opened in my own country where I had hoped and thought it would." In a sense, America "discovered" Morgan before Britain really understood what she had. When Morgan returned to Britain three years later, he was given a king's welcome. The prophet was no longer without honor in his own country.

I think the real secret of Morgan's ministry (apart from his spiritual devotion) is found in one word—*work*:

Let me state in the briefest manner possible what I want to impress upon the mind of those who are contemplating Bible teaching, by

declaring that the Bible never yields itself to indolence. Of all literature none demands more diligent application than that of the Divine
Library.[1]

When asked the secret of his success as an interpreter of the Word,
he would say, "Work—hard work—and again, work!" He himself was
in his study at 6:00 in the morning, and he never permitted anyone
to interrupt him before lunch. Some of us pastors may not be able
to avoid some interruptions, but certainly we can make better use of
our time. Morgan would read a book of the Bible forty or fifty times
before attempting to preach on it or write about it. Jill Morgan correctly titled her biography of her father-in-law *A Man of the Word*.

Along with *The Study and Teaching of the English Bible*, you will
want to secure two other books: *Preaching*, by Morgan; and *The Expository Method of G. Campbell Morgan*, by Don M. Wagner. These
three books are a good analysis of "the Morgan method." Of course
they are no substitute for reading Morgan's expository works, which
every preacher and teacher ought to do. You may also want to add
This Was His Faith, a collection of excerpts from Morgan's letters,
edited by Jill Morgan. You will be surprised to discover in this book
what Morgan believed about the condition of the heathen, Calvinism,
speaking in tongues, falling from grace, and a host of other topics.

During his ministry Morgan was criticized in two areas: money
and theology.

"You are an extravagant man!" someone said to Morgan one
day.

He replied, "I am not an extravagant man, but I am an expensive
man."

When other British preachers were trying to balance their budgets,
Morgan was enjoying a "motor-car"—and being criticized for it.
He received large honoraria for his ministry and, without question,
earned every bit of it. In all fairness to Morgan, it should be stated
that he did not make any of the arrangements for his meetings, nor
did he make any demands. Arrangements were usually done by his
associate, Arthur Marsh, or by some other Christian leader. So to

criticize Morgan would be completely wrong. Furthermore, he was lavishly generous toward others, even to the point of adopting entire families until they were able to make it on their own. No doubt Morgan's use of finances was more American than British.

As far as theology is concerned, Morgan was too liberal for the conservatives and too conservative for the liberals. He considered himself a preacher of the fundamentals of the faith, and certainly anyone who studies his books (especially *The Crises of the Christ*) will have to agree that he did. But he would not identify himself with any "theological camp" or carry the flag for any religious leader. He was his own man, and nothing would make him violate his conscience. He resigned from the Biola faculty because he thought his friend J. M. MacInnis was wronged. He even dedicated one of his books to MacInnis, describing him as "true as steel to the evangelical faith." He wrote:

> I have long felt that, whereas I stand foursquare on the evangelical faith, I have no patience with those people whose supposed fundamentalism consists in watching for heresy and indulging in wicked self-satisfaction because they have an idea that they alone 'hold the truth'—hateful expression! Whereas in many ways I agree with their theological position I abominate their spirit.

Especially during his latter years of ministry in the States, Morgan was attacked in the religious press. During a meeting in New York City, Morgan spoke openly in the pulpit about the cruel lies men had spread about him; and it so upset him that he actually fainted.

More than one writer has criticized Morgan for his "nomad ministry." Ernest H. Jeffs in *Princes of the Modern Pulpit* stated that Morgan might have been a better preacher had he stayed in one place and taken time to pastor a church. "A preacher who lives in a whirl of change and travel and ever-changing audiences loses touch to some extent with the daily problems of the ordinary man," Jeffs wrote.[2] No doubt this is true, but I cringe to think of what the world would have lost had Morgan wasted his time on committee meetings, denominational gatherings, and (as he said once) "arguing over who would have the key to the back door." He had a gift; he developed and exercised it; and the Christian world is the richer for it. True, he did not make pastoral visits, but this does not mean that his messages were divorced from the needs of the people. If this is true, why did thousands come to hear him? Had Morgan adopted the lifestyle of the typical pastor, we would have been robbed of a rich treasure.

There is one interesting thing about Morgan's preaching that I have never seen discussed anywhere—his seeming avoidance of the doctrinal epistles. He was basically a preacher of the four Gospels, but he never expounded, verse by verse, the great doctrinal epistles—Romans, Ephesians, and Hebrews. "He left them for me," Lloyd-Jones told me one day, "and I'm glad he did!" I think one reason Morgan avoided these letters is that he was basically a devotional preacher, not a doctrinal preacher. This does not mean he avoided doctrine, but only that he did not emphasize it (Lloyd-Jones is a doctrinal preacher *par excellence!*). Morgan's ministry was to *all* the churches, and doctrinal controversies found no place in his system.

Perhaps we need a man like Morgan today, one who will minister the Word with clarity and power and make the Bible "come alive," one who will ride above the ripples and waves of denominational competition and theological controversy, one who is true to the doctrines of the faith but who also is able to share the Word in love with Christians of many denominational affiliations. Certainly H. A. Ironside was such a man, as was A. C. Gaebelein. But even they were identified with certain "branches" of evangelical faith and to some degree limited in their ministries. G. Campbell Morgan seemed to belong to all the churches and to Christians everywhere, not because he compromised, but because he majored on the great essentials of the faith and did not get detoured by the accidentals. He paid a price for this, to be sure, but we are the richer because of the price he paid.

Whenever you find a book by Morgan, buy it and study it. Read his life story and get acquainted with this unique teacher of the Word. You do not have to agree with him to learn from him; he would be the first one to say that. "My work is wholly constructive," he wrote in 1923, "and I believe that that is the only kind that is really of value."[3] We need more of this constructive ministry today.

John Henry Jowett
1864 - 1923

If someone should erect a Sunday school teachers' hall of fame, he must enshrine J. W. T. Dewhirst of Halifax, Yorkshire. Dewhirst said to one of his pupils, "I had always hoped that you would go into the ministry." The pupil did, and he became "the greatest preacher in the English-speaking world." His name was John Henry Jowett.

Born on August 25, 1864, into a middle-class Christian home, Jowett planned to be a lawyer and perhaps enter politics. But two people strongly influenced him to enter the ministry: his mother and his pastor, Enoch Mellor. "At my mother's knee," he often said, "I gained my sweetest inspirations."

Mellor had come to the Square Road Congregational Church, Halifax, in 1847. The membership grew so large that they had to erect a new building. From 1861 to 1867 Mellor ministered in Glasgow. But in 1867 he returned to Halifax and served another fourteen years. During that second term, young Jowett came under his godly influence. The lad never met the pastor personally, but he nevertheless idolized him and listened attentively to his preaching. In later years Jowett modeled his own preaching after that of his boyhood pastor. "He was the finest platform orator it was ever my fortune to hear," he admitted. "Square Church was to me a very fountain of life, and I owe to its spiritual training more than I can ever express."

Jowett concentrated on his education from 1882 to 1889. He attended Airedale College, of which A. M. Fairbairn was principal, and also Edinburgh University. At that time the city of Edinburgh was enjoying the ministries of some of the great preachers—Alexander Whyte, George Matheson, and Henry Drummond, to name but a few. What a place for study and for preaching!

Jowett's first church was St. James's Congregational at Newcastle-on-Tyne. He began his ministry in October 1889 and was ordained on November 19. The building seated more than a thousand. The young preacher responded to this challenge with faith and courage. During his six-year ministry there, he always preached to large crowds. In fact Jowett drew crowds throughout his lifetime. The great R. W. Dale died on March 13, 1895, leaving vacant the influential pulpit of Carr's Lane Church, Birmingham. The church officers turned immediately to John Henry Jowett, and on October 6, 1895, he began his ministry there. Many had predicted that Carr's Lane would die with Dale, but their predictions proved false. Not only did Jowett help save the church, but the church helped save Jowett.

The young pastor, overwhelmed by his new responsibilities, read everything Dale had written. Dale, a massive intellect, preached Bible doctrine with clarity and passion. His books are still worth reading: *The Atonement, The Living Christ and the Four Gospels, Christian Doctrine*, and *The Jewish Temple and the Church*, to name several. As Jowett assimilated these books, he confronted the great themes and texts of the Bible. In his first sermon as pastor of Carr's Lane Church, Jowett said: "This pulpit has never been belittled by the petty treatment of small and vulgar themes." He determined to preach the great truths of the Word (what he liked to call "the fat texts"). This determination motivated his ministry for the rest of his life. "The grace of God" became his central theme.

His church officers made it easy for their new pastor to preach well. They relieved him of the many details of church administration that can rob a pastor of precious hours needed for study and meditation. They were rewarded, for the church prospered in every way. A. T. Pierson once called Carr's Lane Church "the greatest church in the world." During his ministry at Carr's Lane, Jowett was elected chairman of the Congregational Union and president of the National Council of Evangelical Free Churches. He was quite young, but he wore the honors with distinction. He received as many as thirty invitations a day to preach. But Jowett kept his life in balance and focused on building the church.

It was inevitable that calls would come from other churches. Late in 1909, Jowett received a call from the prestigious Fifth Avenue Presbyterian Church in New York City. He graciously refused, but they issued a second call in June 1910. Again he said no, but when the call was repeated at the end of the year, he felt led to accept, saying, "The scale of decision . . . turned by a hair."

On April 2, 1911, Jowett opened his ministry in New York City. The American press made a great deal out of his arrival, headlining him as "the greatest preacher in the world!" Retiring by nature, Jowett despised anything that smacked of promotion; he never quite adjusted to the "American system of ballyhoo." His preaching attracted great crowds, not only "up-and-outers" (for which Fifth Avenue was famous), but also common people who heard the gospel gladly. New York City was desperately in need of solid biblical preaching. "What a time this is for the preacher," he wrote in a letter to a friend. "Congregations tense, strained, burdened, wanting some glimpse of spiritual things amid this riot of material things, and yearning for a glimpse of the things which abide in all the fierce rush of things which are transient."

The advent of the war created new problems for the Jowetts, who longed to be in England but knew they had been called to New York. One good byproduct of Jowett's sojourn was the opportunity to give the Yale lectures on preaching in April 1912. If you had to name the six best volumes in this valuable series, surely you would include Jowett's *The Preacher: His Life and Work*.

The lecturer himself did not enjoy the experience. "I am here for ten days delivering the Yale lectures on preaching," he wrote to a friend. "The lectures have been a nightmare to me, and I am glad I am getting rid of them this week!" The theme of his seven lectures is summarized in one of Jowett's favorite sayings: "Preaching that costs nothing accomplishes nothing." "If they will only learn one thing," he wrote in a letter, "that preaching is not easy and that it costs blood, and if they will only learn another thing—that no one can attend to the deep wants of a church if he is running all over the country, I shall have discharged a very real service." I try to reread Jowett's lectures annually, if only to catch his passion for preaching. Some books on preaching and pastoral work almost make you want to turn in your ordination certificate—this is not one of them. "I love my calling," he said on the first page. "I have a glowing delight in its service. . . . I have had but one passion, and I have lived for it—the absorbingly arduous yet glorious work of proclaiming the grace and love of our Lord and Savior Jesus Christ."[1]

This book gives good counsel not only on sermon preparation, but also on the making of the minister himself and the conducting of public worship. Jowett was known as much for his public prayers as for his sermons. That friend and student of great preaching, W. Robertson Nicoll, after visiting Carr's Lane when Jowett was minister there, wrote: "The great simplicity, reality, sympathy, and tenderness of the prayers moved one strangely." Jowett's public worship, including the prayers, grew out of his private devotional life. "We cannot be strong leaders of intercession unless we have a deep and growing acquaintance with the secret ways of the soul," Jowett told the Yale students. He never considered the exercises before the sermon as "mere preliminaries." The hymns, the prayers, and even the offering were all part of worship and needed to be prepared with spiritual discernment. "If men are unmoved by our prayers," he said, "they are not likely to be profoundly stirred by our preaching."

He gave equal emphasis to the public reading of the Word of God. "It is a mighty experience when a lesson is so read that it becomes the sermon," he stated, "and the living Word grips without an exposition!" It was said of G. Campbell Morgan that you learned more from his *reading* of the Word than from anyone else's *preaching* of the Word. Jowett was almost as skilled as Morgan in this area.

If Jowett worshiped in some of our churches today, he would behold careless "preliminaries" hastily thrown together; he would hear prayers that sound tragically the same week after week; he would listen to the inspired Word of God being read without much feeling or understanding. He would miss that vital element he called "the strong gracious presence of reverence and order." He would be appalled by seeing preachers threatened by "the peril of ostentatious display." He warned his Yale listeners: "We never reach the innermost room in any man's soul by the expediencies of the showman or the buffoon. The way of irreverence will never lead to the Holy Place."

While ministering in New York, Jowett received calls to return to England. He was invited to succeed Whyte in Edinburgh and J. D. Jones in Bournemouth. Both calls he rejected. But on February 26, 1917, he received a call to succeed Morgan at Westminster Chapel, London; this call he accepted. He asked the church to wait one year while he fulfilled his commitments in America. On April 14, 1918, he said farewell to his church. On May 19 he preached his first sermon as pastor of Westminster Chapel. The next years should have been the most fruitful in his ministry, but Jowett was dying and did not realize it. Preaching in Westminster Chapel was taxing. More than one previous minister, including Morgan, had lost his health while preaching in the building. (D. Martyn Lloyd-Jones always claimed that the building had "killed" Samuel Martin, the pastor who had built it.) Jowett had anemia, and his strength slowly ebbed. On December 17, 1922, he preached his last sermon in the chapel; a year later, on December 19, he was "called home."

I urge you to secure every Jowett book you can find, not only his Yale lectures, but also his sermons. Begin with the volume in the *Great Pulpit Masters* series. This collection of twenty-seven sermons, which will introduce you to Jowett's ministry, has been reprinted in recent years, as have *The Eagle Life* (Old Testament devotional studies), *Life in the Heights* (devotional studies in the Epistles), and *Springs in the Desert* (devotional messages from the Psalms). Other books by Jowett are *The Passion for Souls* (Christian discipleship), *The Silver Lining, Things That Matter Most, Apostolic Optimism,* and *God—Our Contemporary.* I enjoy his devotional book *My Daily Meditation.* While you are at it, get a copy of Arthur Porritt's biography, *John Henry Jowett.* The foreword was written by Randall Davidson, archbishop of Canterbury. (Jowett once preached at an ecumenical service in Durham Cathedral and incurred the wrath of several Anglican divines; the archbishop was not one of them.)

The thing I appreciate most about Jowett is the dedication to preaching that he demonstrated. He constantly battled the subtle thieves that would steal his time. He arose early in the morning and devoted himself to study and prayer. He toiled over his messages. His hobby was words (he read the dictionary for a pastime), and he used them as an artist uses colors. He was a master of the perfect expression. He never used "almost the right word"; it was always exactly the right word. Perhaps his craftsmanship occasionally overshadowed his passion, so that the sermon was a sea of glass *not* "mingled with fire." But before we criticize him, let us be sure that we use words as accurately as he did.

Jowett was a devotional preacher. His major theme was the grace of God. His purpose was to win the lost and encourage the saved. He followed Joseph Parker's rule: "Preach to broken hearts." But his ministry was not sentimental. It was solidly doctrinal and centered in the cross. Jones, who knew Jowett well, called him "the greatest preacher of his generation." Jowett would blush to hear such a statement. But he was a great preacher, a homiletical craftsman with a compassionate heart.

38

J. D. Jones
1865–1942

He could have been F. B. Meyer's successor at Christ Church in Westminster, or John Henry Jowett's successor when Jowett went to Fifth Avenue Presbyterian in New York City. In fact, Fifth Avenue Presbyterian approached him after Jowett had first turned them down. He was offered the principalship of Lancashire College and was even encouraged to run for office by members of Parliament. But none of these things moved him, and J. D. Jones remained for thirty-nine years as the beloved pastor of Richmond Hill Congregational Church in Bournemouth, retiring on June 6, 1937.

John Daniel Jones was almost "Lincoln Jones." When he was born in the little Welsh town of Ruthin on April 13, 1865, his father wanted to call him Lincoln in honor of the American president whom he greatly admired (interestingly enough, Lincoln was assassinated the next day). But one of the grandmothers was opposed to "such fancy names in the family," and so Joseph David Jones called his third son John Daniel and saved Lincoln for his fourth son, born two years later. However, Grandmother may have been right, because the name Lincoln created some complications in later years when J. D. was pastoring Newland Congregational Church *in* Lincoln. People were constantly confusing "Lincoln Jones" with "Jones of Lincoln." But when J. D. Jones began his long ministry at Richmond Hill on June 5, 1898, people forgot about Lincoln and knew him simply as "Jones of Bournemouth."

Jones did his undergraduate work at Owens College, which he entered in 1882, and his graduate work at Lancashire College, receiving his degree in 1889. It was unusual for a new theological graduate to go directly into the pulpit of an important church, but that is just what happened. On January 2, 1889, before Jones completed his work, the Newland Church in Lincoln called him to be their pastor. In July of that same year, he was married. In his delightful autobiography, *Three Score Years and Ten*, Jones said this about his experiences as a young pastor in a leading church:

> Of course I blundered. At the very first Church meeting after my settlement my Church Secretary brought in a resolution to embody a certain liturgical element in our worship, and I backed him up. My Church—Puritan by tradition—would have none of it. It was a bit of a rebuff for a young minister. I remember visiting an old lady named Cropper shortly after and she said to me: "Don't take it too hard, laddie. We're a lot of stiffnecked 'uns down here."[1]

He remained almost ten years at Lincoln and then accepted the call to Richmond Hill in Bournemouth. The church sanctuary held over a thousand people and was ideally situated in the city. His predecessor was a fiery Welshman named Ossian Davies, whose intense personality had attracted great crowds; and Jones wondered if his own quiet preaching would really do the job. It did. The people came and kept coming, and for thirty-nine years benefited from his simple presentation of the Word of God. Bournemouth was a popular resort and retirement city, and many well-to-do people came to hear him preach, but J. D. Jones never tried to build a "rich man's church." The common people heard him gladly.

Peter Marshall once said that the first essential for success in the ministry is to be born in Scotland. But others would prefer Wales, that land of eloquent preachers and seers. Jones was a Welshman, and according to Ernest H. Jeffs "he spoke as if words were notes of music."[2] Oddly enough, he read his sermons from a manuscript, but his listeners could scarcely detect it. What they did detect was *witness*: here was a preacher whose life was controlled by the message he delivered. Jones himself once defined preaching as "a man—a real man—speaking real things out of a real experience." Even a manuscript could not stand between Jones and his hearers, for they always got the message.

He was a biblical preacher, but he was not an expositor of the same type as Alexander Maclaren or the gifted Welshman D. Martyn Lloyd-Jones. In the biography *J. D. Jones of Bournemouth*, Arthur Porritt remarked: "All his sermons were on a very high level. He was always on a plateau, but—as a friendly critic figuratively said—there were no mountains and no valleys—just a uniform level of excellence."[3] He was not one to "preach to the times" and announce sensational topics about current events. There are men who can do this well, but if a man *cannot*, he had better know it! Jones liked to refer to a story about Archbishop Leighton. Criticized for not "preaching to the times," the archbishop said, "While so many are preaching to the times, may not one poor brother preach for eternity?"

Jones's was a positive ministry, and a ministry of encouragement and comfort. He did not preach "easy Christianity"; he identified with his people in their needs and tried to make their pilgrim journey a bit more triumphant. In a remarkable sermon on "softness," with 1 Corinthians 6:9 as his text, Jones challenged his hearers to a courageous Christian faith. "All the calls of the gospel are calls to hardship, to sacrifice, to battle," he stated. "Christ would have no man follow him under the delusion that he was going to have an easy time of it." To him the word *comfort* carried the original Latin meaning, "with strength," and he sought to comfort his people by showing them the strength that is in Christ. Jones knew what it was to go through the valley himself. In July 1917, while he was preaching at Torquay, his wife became seriously ill and passed away before he had time to reach home. Six years later, his only son died in the Gold Coast of Africa, where he had been serving in the administration of a plantation. In September 1933 Jones remarried and had the joy of traveling and ministering with his wife and his daughter.

His very popular volume *If a Man Die* was published the same year his first wife died, and this was followed in 1919 by *The Lord of Life and Death*, a volume of sermons based on John 11. This book was reissued by Baker Books and should be on your shelf, particularly if you plan to preach from John 11. (Be sure to secure as well *Idylls of Bethany* by W. M. Clow and *Mary of Bethany* by Marcus L. Loane.) While on the subject of books, let me suggest that you secure *Richmond Hill Sermons*, *The Way into the Kingdom* (on the beatitudes), *The Model Prayer*, *The Glorious Company of the Apostles*, and *The Greatest of These* (on 1 Cor. 13). I wish some publisher would reprint Jones's commentary on the Gospel of Mark, which was originally written for the *Devotional Commentary*. When he first went to Bournemouth, Jones conducted a Tuesday morning ministry during the winter months, and his first series was on the Gospel of Mark. His commentary is homiletical rather than explanatory or doctrinal, but I still think it is one of the best.

J. D. Jones was a great denominational leader, although he tried not to let his outside ministry interfere with his pastoral duties. Congregational churches in his day were somewhat isolated from each other, and many of them were in deep financial straits. He accepted and defended the principle of local independence, but he was mature enough to see its dangers. He felt that among the free churches in general there was "a good deal of foolish rivalry, of needless competition and of consequent waste." Jeffs remarked, "Congregationalism was a good system for the strong man and the strong church. The price of the principle had to be paid by the weaker men and the little churches." But Jones did not use his position at Richmond Hill to build himself a kingdom: he used it to help others. He spearheaded programs that brought over two million dollars into the denominational coffers to increase the salaries of rural preachers and to provide for decent allotments at retirement. He and his people helped to establish thirty other churches, and he was always available to assist and encourage pastors in difficult places.

He was a great traveler, and often he was a representative to the Congregational International Council. He first visited the United States in 1899, and on Sunday, September 10, he heard D. L. Moody preach at the Plymouth Congregational Church in Brooklyn, where Henry Ward Beecher had ministered for almost forty years. Jones wrote that Moody looked "for all the world like a prosperous, countrified farmer." The evangelist spoke on the atonement and took the congregation literally from Genesis to Revelation, as only Moody could do. "He got down to the quick of things," wrote Jones, "and we felt the power of his speech." After the service, Jones and the other delegates met Moody in the vestry and enjoyed a pleasant talk about everything from Sunday newspapers to higher criticism! Moody told them that he felt that the bicycle, because of its popularity, was the greatest enemy of the Sabbath.

"I am glad, as I look back," wrote Jones, "that I had the chance of thus hearing and meeting D. L. Moody. I am glad I got a grip of his hand. Moody seemed to me a man of sterling common sense." Apparently Moody heard Jones speak at the Boston conference, because he invited him to speak at Northfield. Not until 1913 was Jones able to get to Northfield, and by that time Moody was dead and his son Will Moody was managing the schools and the conference. "I think Will Moody was dwarfed by the fact that he was D. L. Moody's son," Jones wrote in his autobiography. "Without doubt D. L. Moody was a very great man. W. R. Moody was not that . . . but he was an able man. . . . He had great organizing and administrative abilities." Jones told how Will Moody kept "a firm hand upon all the Conference speakers. After an address by an English speaker who had let off a lot of 'hot air' but had not managed to say much that was worth saying, Will Moody said to me: 'We'll have no more of that. We have plenty of men on this side who can pour out that kind of stuff. I shall tell him he need not trouble to stay.'" Jones added, "It took me all my time to persuade Moody to let him finish."

It is worth noting that, while Jones had a keen interest in British politics, he did not get as carried away with it as did R. W. Dale. During the 1906 election, Jones campaigned for several candidates of the Liberal Party, and every one of them lost in spite of the fact that the Liberals swept the country! When asked to run for office, Jones replied with the words of Nehemiah 6:3—"I am doing a great work, so that I cannot come down."

No doubt one of the secrets of his success was his concentration. Being a pastor was to him the highest calling possible, and it deserved the best that he had. When he rejected the principalship of Lancashire College, Jones received the following message from his friend W. Robertson Nicoll: "I have always held that the pastorate is the highest office open to a minister." The man who believes in the dignity of the pastorate and who has this sense of calling will accomplish far more in his ministry than the man who flits from ministry to ministry, always looking for some better opportunity.

Another strength of J. D. Jones was his faith in the preaching of the Word. No man could stay in one church nearly forty years if he were depending on his own resources. "When J. D. Jones took a text," wrote one religious editor, "it was the text that mattered, not the preacher's commentary upon it. The preacher's commentary had but one aim—to recall its hearers to the richness and wonder of the truth which the text enshrined. He never searched for excitingly unusual texts, nor did he strive to find startlingly unusual interpretations of his texts." The pastor who stops growing usually starts going. There is no substitute for a deepening knowledge of the Word of God.

A third factor in his ministry was his love for his people. His constant desire was to encourage them along the way. When you read *The Lord of Life and Death*, you will discover that these messages were written not from an ivory tower but from that difficult place "where cross the crowded ways of life." Because he knew and loved his people, he was able to make the Word meaningful to them from week to week.

We must not minimize the character of the man himself. When giving the "charge to the minister" at an ordination, Jones said:

The one indispensable condition of our usefulness and success in the work of the ministry is that we should be good men—men of pure and holy life—men of God. . . . We may be good ministers without being either learned or eloquent, but we cannot be good ministers without being good men. . . . The effect of our words on the Sabbath will really depend on our lives during the week, for it is always the man behind the speech which wields the power.

Finally, Jones realized that there was something more than the ministry of his own local church. He knew that he was a part of something much bigger than Richmond Hill, or even the Congregational Union. Without sacrificing his own convictions, he sought to build and encourage God's work everywhere. When the Episcopal and Free Church leaders met in their "conversations on reunion," Jones, giving the opening statement, made it quite clear that the Free Churches were not going to abandon their heritage. "There are certain principles—ecclesiastical and religious—which we hold dear. There are certain truths which—as we believe—have been committed to our trust. . . . We do not want our history and traditions to become a snare, but neither can we be expected lightly to flout and discard them." The largeness of his vision no doubt contributed to the greatness of his ministry.

Dr. and Mrs. Jones retired to Wales in 1937, although Dr. Jones was still quite active in his preaching ministry. His health remained good until August 1941, when anemia began to sap his strength. D. Martyn Lloyd-Jones visited him at Mrs. Jones's request, to share the word that he could not get better, and Jones accepted the news with his usual poise and courage. On Sunday, April 19, 1942, he was called home. On his tombstone in the Bournemouth cemetery it says: "John Daniel Jones, Preacher of the gospel. 'Simply to Thy cross I cling.'"

39

George H. Morrison
1866–1928

Whenever pastors get together and discuss their favorite preachers, they are sure to repeat such names as Charles H. Spurgeon, G. Campbell Morgan, Alexander Whyte, and J. H. Jowett, to name but a few. Rarely—only rarely—will you hear a pastor ask, "Have any of you read the sermons of George H. Morrison?" And the reply is usually, "George Morrison? Never heard of him! Who is he?"

No alert pastor in Great Britain during the first quarter of the twentieth century would have asked that question! "Morrison of Wellington" was easily the most popular preacher in Scotland. And he was not only a popular preacher, but also an effective pastor. His personal records reveal that he made over one thousand visits in an average year! When he died, he left a rich legacy of books of his messages that spoke meaningfully to hearts fifty years ago and still speak to hearts today.

Tragically, most of Morrison's writings are to be found only in secondhand bookstores. One that should be reprinted is *The Wings of the Morning*, one of his matchless volumes. Like most of Morrison's books, this is a collection of Sunday evening sermons. Morrison, like most Scottish pastors of his day, preached weighty expository sermons in the morning services, but his evening preaching was refreshingly different. He himself wrote: "It has been my habit at the morning service to handle the greater themes of the Christian revelation and then at the evening worship to allow myself a wider scope . . . to win the attention, in honorable ways, of some at least of that vast class of people who today sit so lightly to the Church."

And he succeeded! During the more than twenty-five years he pastored the Wellington United Free Church in Glasgow, great crowds would queue up in anticipation of the evening service, while at other churches the evening congregations were meager if not totally absent. It was not Morrison's fiery eloquence or oratory that drew and held his congregation. His voice was rather weak and his presentation anything but dramatic. Following one service, a lady turned to the famous A. J. Gossip and said, "Didn't Dr. Morrison preach a wonderful sermon?"

"Madam," Gossip replied, "I did not hear half of what he was saying."

"Neither did I," said the woman, "but wasn't it a wonderful sermon!"

Morrison's preaching strength lay in his knowledge of the Bible, his knowledge of his people and their needs, and his ability to put both together in an imaginative way that reached the heart.

In this day of "telling it like it is," Morrison's sermons and some of his sermon titles might be dismissed as sentimental and poetical. Such titles as "The Fault of Over-Prudence," "The Religious Use of Holidays," and "The Higher Ministries of Sleep" would not excite congregations today. But what about "Wasted Gains" (on Prov. 12:27—look it up!), "The Deceptions of God" (Jer. 20:7), "Unobserved Sins" (Exod. 2:12), and "The Intolerance of Jesus" (Matt. 12:30)?

His sermon on Isaiah 27:8 is a masterpiece. The text says, "He stayeth his rough wind in the day of the east wind." Morrison's points are: (1) our trials are timed; (2) our sufferings are measured; and (3) our lives are compensated. This sermon reveals both the pastor's heart and the scholar's mind. Or consider his message on Matthew 14:30,

"Beginning to Sink." He brought out these lessons from Peter's experience: Peter began to sink in familiar waters, he began to sink after loyal discipleship, he began to sink on a permitted path, he began to sink when he began to fear, and when he began to sink his Savior was not far away. That is preaching! Some of Morrison's sermons would give today's preachers ideas for a whole series of messages. "The Refusals of Christ" is one example, and another is "The Lonely People of the Gospel" (Mary—the loneliness of love; Thomas—the loneliness of doubt; Judas—the loneliness of sin; etc.).

As you read Morrison's sermons, you discover a man acquainted with the Bible, alert to the news and problems of the day, sympathetic with suffering (he lost his wife while pastoring in Dundee, and he lost a son in the war), and able to say the most profound truths in a remarkably simple way. In fact, the simplicity of his preaching is utterly disarming. He never used too many words but always seemed to use the right words, making truth glow in an imaginative way. For example: "One of the saddest stories ever written is just the story of our mismanaged triumphs." Or, "Faith is expectant, eager, childlike, buoyant. Its opposite is not doubt, but death." Or, "Christ will have nothing of the culture of the brain, at the expense of the culture of the character."

George Herbert Morrison was born in Glasgow, Scotland, on October 2, 1866. After completing his university studies, he was not sure of his vocation. He became an assistant to Sir James Murray at Oxford, helping with the *New English Dictionary* while trying to "find himself." No doubt this experience helped make him such an accurate writer and give him a love for words. It is worth noting that G. Campbell Morgan, J. H. Jowett, and Alexander Whyte were all, like Morrison, great students of words and readers of dictionaries.

While working at Oxford, Morrison felt the call to preach. He entered the Free Church College in Glasgow and graduated in 1893. At that time a second providential event occurred in his training: he was chosen to assist the famous Alexander Whyte at Free St. George's in Edinburgh. Morrison's responsibility was to conduct the then-new evening service, a challenge he accepted with confidence. He remained with Whyte only a year, but that one year with the gifted preacher gave him spiritual values which controlled his ministry for the rest of his life. His diligent study, his concern for his people, his sanctified imagination, his love of books (he had a library of over six thousand volumes)—all were strengthened and stimulated during that year at Edinburgh. We wonder what would happen to younger preachers today if they spent a year as understudy to some successful pastor. We might have fewer ministerial dropouts.

Morrison pastored at Thurso in northern Scotland, and after four years moved to Dundee. Later he accepted the call to the Wellington United Free Church in Glasgow and became known as "Morrison of Wellington." Until his unexpected death in 1928, Morrison gave his best to his people, both as pastor and preacher. With clock-like regularity he spent his mornings in the study, his afternoons with his people in their homes, and his evenings either at church meetings or at home studying and writing. Like Whyte, he took long holidays, using the summer months for additional study, meditation, and rest. "The only piece of advice Whyte gave me when I was with him," said Morrison, "was to take long holidays!" To this Whyte later replied, "And did you or your people ever regret it?" Although today's overworked pastors might not be able to take two months off each summer, an occasional interruption for incubation would no doubt improve the minister and the ministry.

Morrison did not wrestle with biblical criticism or seek to explain the great questions of his day, even though he was a scholar and a voracious reader. Morrison felt his responsibility was to encourage his people with the truths of Christ that he had proved in his own life, not to discourage them with academic questions. He faced and solved these important questions in his study, but he always stepped into the pulpit with exclamation points, not question marks.

Preaching in a church located directly across from the university, Morrison had a special concern for the youth. He kept up with the honor list and always sent a personal note to students who made it. He did not preach what we would call youth messages, but the students flocked to hear him. He organized "The Round Table" and met with students following the evening service to discuss questions that troubled them. At the open forum the pastor did not permit himself pulpit privileges. It was Morrison unfrocked who won their hearts and helped direct their lives. This personal interchange helped to make the students better Christians and Morrison a better preacher and pastor.

The preacher who reads *The Wings of the Morning* probably will not be satisfied until he secures everything else Morrison wrote. He will want to get *The Wind on the Heath*, *The Ever Open Door*, *The Afterglow of God*, *Flood-Tide*, *The Unlighted Lustre*, *The Weaving of Glory*, *The Footsteps of the Flock* (a remarkable devotional book for each Sunday of the year, taking the reader through the key passages of the Bible—a gold mine of sermonic material!), *The World-wide Gospel*, *The Return of the Angels*, *Sun-Rise*, and others. The wise preacher will index these great sermons. If he is wiser still, he will read each message carefully, first for his own heart and then to improve his ministry. Morrison himself read one sermon a day from a different preacher. Morrison's sermons would be a good place for us to start today!

As he lay dying, Morrison's final words were: "It's an ever open door, never closed to anyone. It's open for me now and I'm going through!" By means of his reprinted sermons (and, we trust, additional volumes will follow), Morrison helps today's preachers point others to that "ever open door," which is Jesus Christ.

40

Amy Carmichael
1867–1951

Let me describe some of the things she did, and then allow you to answer the question: "If she were a missionary from your church, would you support Amy Carmichael?"

She spent nearly sixty years in the field and never once came home to report to her board or to the people who supported her.

While she went to the field under the authority of one board, she pretty much did her own thing and eventually started an organization of her own.

She went to the field to carry on one kind of ministry, but within a few years was carrying on an entirely different ministry that often got her into trouble with the law. At one time, she was in danger of serving seven years in prison for "assisting in the kidnapping of a child."

The reports that she sent out were often not believed by the people who read them. "Such things simply can't be!" they argued, but they were—and she proved it.

She did not ask for financial support, yet she saw every need met right on time. When people offered to sponsor part of her ministry, she suggested they support a different mission.

During the last twenty years of her ministry, she was practically an invalid, directing the work from her room.

My guess is that the average church would never have supported this kind of a missionary. She was too unpredictable and too independent. And perhaps the average mission board would have dropped her from their ranks after her first term. We like ministry work to be carried out in such a predictable way that there can be no surprises, no changes, no unexpected decisions that pioneer new territory for the gospel. It might upset the donors.

But Amy Carmichael was not put together that way. She simply did not fit into our modern world of interchangeable parts, because she was unique. She knew what God wanted her to do, and she did it. She was not a rebel; her board and co-laborers were full partners in the ministry. But she was one of the Lord's special servants, and he used her to accomplish a miracle ministry in southern India.

Amy Carmichael was born on December 16, 1867, in County Down, Northern Ireland. Her father, along with her uncle, owned and managed several flour mills, so the family was fairly comfortable. They came from Covenanter stock and took the things of the Lord seriously. Amy had a happy childhood, and, while a student at a Wesleyan Methodist school in 1883, she trusted Christ.

Changes in the milling business forced the family to move to Belfast. Amy's father died in 1885, and this greatly altered both the finances and the future of the family. Mrs. Carmichael was a woman of strong faith; in fact, much of her "apostolic spirit" rubbed off on her daughter. One particular incident illustrates this.

It was Sunday morning, and Mrs. Carmichael and the children were returning home from church. They met "a poor pathetic old woman" who was burdened with a heavy bundle. Instantly, Amy and her two brothers relieved the woman of her bundle, took her arms, and helped her along. At first the icy stares of the "proper Presbyterians" embarrassed them, but then the Lord moved in and the whole scene changed.

Into Amy's mind flashed Paul's words from 1 Corinthians 3 about "gold, silver, precious stones, wood, hay, stubble; . . . the fire shall try every man's work of what sort it is" (vv. 12, 13). In later years Amy wrote, "We went on. I said nothing to anyone, but I knew that something had happened that had changed life's values. Nothing could ever matter again but the things that were eternal."

In September 1886, some friends invited Amy to Glasgow, where she attended meetings along the lines of the Keswick Convention. For many months, she had been struggling with the problem of how to live a holy life, and she found the answer at the Glasgow meetings. It was not the message of the two speakers that got through to her but the closing prayer of the chairman. He paraphrased Jude 1:24: "O Lord, we know that Thou art able to keep us from falling!" Those words brought light into the darkness, and Amy Carmichael entered into a life of faith and victory.

But holy living was not a luxury to her: it meant sacrifice and ministry. She had no time for Christians who went from meeting to meeting and soaked up Bible truth but never reached out to share Christ with others. Amy was burdened for the girls who worked in the mills, and she had already started a ministry for them at one of the local churches. But the work was growing and in some ways interfering with the church's program (Amy always was one to raise dust).

She decided that, if God wanted her to start a special work, he alone could provide the funds and the laborers; so she began to pray. Little did she realize that this experience with The Welcome (the hall that she built) would prepare her for years of ministry by faith alone. God did provide the funds, and a building was put up just for ministry to the girls at the mills. Many came to know Christ, and many were protected from lives of sin because of the influence of the ministry. This would be Amy Carmichael's emphasis for the rest of her life—to reach out to the downcast and rejected, to love them, win them to Christ, and build them up to help others.

In later years, Amy said that there were three crises in her early life: her conversion, her entrance into the life of faith, and her call to be a missionary. That third crisis took place on January 13, 1892, not in some dramatic way, but simply as she waited quietly before the Lord. He made it clear to her that she was to give her life to him as a missionary and permit him to direct her just as he pleased.

There were obstacles, not the least of which was her commitment to help care for elderly Robert Wilson, an old friend of the family and the chairman of the British Keswick movement. She shared these concerns with her mother and Mr. Wilson, and step by step, the Lord began to open the way. On March 3, 1893, she sailed for Japan, the first missionary sent out by the Keswick Convention.

She had some remarkable experiences in Japan, ministering through an interpreter; but Japan was not to be her permanent field. A serious illness forced her to go to China for rest, and then to Ceylon (now Sri Lanka). Can you imagine a church foreign missions committee discussing her situation and wondering if she could be trusted? By the end of 1894, she was back in England; but a year later, on November 9, 1895, she landed in India, and there she remained until her death on January 18, 1951.

Amy was under the authority of the Church of England Zenana Missionary Society, so she entered into their ministry with zeal. But she noted that many of the missionaries reported no converts—in fact, *expected* none. She also noticed that the missionary community was separated in every way from the people they were trying to reach.

While in Japan, Amy had adopted native dress (as Hudson Taylor did in China) and had sought to identify with the people. But she had not come to India to create problems; so she went on with her work, always seeking the mind of Christ in her decisions.

Then something happened that dramatically changed Amy Carmichael's life and ministry. On March 6, 1901, little Preena, a seven-year-old girl, fled from one of the temples into the mission compound and begged to be protected. It was then that Amy uncovered one of the ugliest hidden sores on "Mother India's" body, the secret traffic in temple girls. She learned how fathers and mothers sold their daughters to different gods, turning the precious girls into temple prostitutes.

Infuriated by what Satan was doing to these dear girls, Amy declared war. How many battles she fought on her knees, wrestling for the bodies and souls of these helpless children! How many times she and her associates risked their lives, and faced arrest and imprisonment, in order to snatch some pleading child from the jaws of defilement and destruction. One by one, other girls found their way to *Amma* (the Tamil word for "mother"), and she courageously protected them. By 1904 there were seventeen children under her care, and then the Lord opened the way for her to receive and minister to babies. In 1918 they opened the boy's work, for the money-hungry idolaters sold boys to the temple gods just as they sold girls.

If you want to enter into the excitement of pioneer missions, then read Amy Carmichael's *Gold Cord*, the story of the Dohnavur Fellowship. Frank Houghton's excellent biography, *Amy Carmichael of Dohnavur*, contains many of the exciting stories that grew out of the new ministry of saving temple children. Both books have been reprinted by Christian Literature Crusade; in fact, many of Amy Carmichael's books are available from that publisher.

Amma greatly admired the work of the China Inland Mission, and, in many ways, patterned herself after Hudson Taylor. She did not solicit funds. When people asked to have the privilege of sponsoring a child, she refused their help. All funds went into the mission account to be dispensed as the Lord directed. The many workers God brought to her side were not paid salaries, and the mission never borrowed money or went into debt. While Amy did not criticize ministries that had other policies, she preferred to work as the Lord had led her.

She was especially careful about selecting workers. That was one reason for the no-salary policy. Many Indians would have gladly been baptized and worked for the mission in order to make a living. "Guard your gate" was one of her favorite warnings, and she heeded it herself. Some of her friends and supporters often were surprised when she rejected applicants who, to them, seemed ideally suited for the ministry; but later events always proved her right. She prayed men and women into places of service, trusting the Lord to prepare them, provide for them, and protect them.

Protection was especially important, not only because of the Indian climate and unsanitary conditions, but even more because of the idolatry and demonism. Satan and his armies attacked the people and the ministry at Dohnavur in ways that make these experiences read like events from the book of Acts. The secret of victory? The Word of God and prayer!

Amma and her associates practiced John 15:7, trusting God to guide them by the Word and provide for their needs one day at a time. I think it would be good for some of us to get acquainted with Amy Carmichael's principles for prayer:

(1) We don't need to explain to our Father things that are known to him.

(2) We don't need to press him, as if we had to deal with an unwilling God.

(3) We don't need to suggest to him what to do, for he himself knows what to do.

If all of us took these principles to heart, think of the religious speeches that would be silenced in many prayer meetings.

Amy Carmichael cautioned her helpers to "leave a margin" in their lives. We have all been reminded to "beware of the barrenness of a busy life." As I read Amy Carmichael's books, I am amazed at the broad scope of her reading, not only in many translations of the Bible, but in the mystics, the church fathers, even the Greek philosophers. To her, reading was an enriching experience, a time for relaxation and renewal and not just escape.

On October 24, 1931, Amy Carmichael suffered a serious fall. Other complications set in, and she had to end her usual activity. She was physically limited to her room and an occasional veranda stroll, but that did not limit her ministry. In the next twenty years she wrote thirteen books and many letters, and she directed the work of the mission through her capable associates.

In 1948 she experienced a second fall, and from then until her Homegoing she was confined to her bed. But she was constantly at the throne of grace, and God answered her prayers. God is still answering those prayers, for the Dohnavur Fellowship continues to minister effectively in southern India.

Amy Carmichael wrote thirty-five books of various kinds—the story of the Fellowship, poems, stories about the children who were rescued, devotionals, and messages for those who suffer. Many of them have been republished by Christian Literature Crusade and should be available in your local Christian bookstore. Not everyone takes to Miss Carmichael's writing; in fact, I must confess that it took me many years to learn to appreciate her style and message (*I* was the one who had to grow.).

His Thoughts Said . . . His Father Said is excellent for times of meditative pondering. *Thou Givest . . . They Gather* is another fine devotional book, compiled from her writings after her death. Two encouraging books for suffering people are *Candles in the Dark* and *Rose from Brier*. When *God's Missionary* was published, it upset many people because of its emphasis on devotion and personal discipline. It still upsets readers—but perhaps they need to be upset. Books about Indian women reached through the Dohnavur ministry include *Mimosa, Ponnammal, Kohila,* and *Ploughed Under. Edges of His Ways* is a daily devotional book that is intellectually stimulating and spiritually rewarding.

"We were committed to things that we must not expect everyone to understand" was the way *Amma* explained her ministry and was also the reason why some devout evangelicals kept at a distance. "The work will never go deeper than we have gone ourselves" was her explanation of why some workers did not remain and why others refused to come. She did not try to please everybody or solicit anybody's support. The work was God's work, and he alone could prosper it. No high-powered machinery, no Madison Avenue promotion, no attempts to compete with other ministries either for funds or personnel.

Amy Carmichael depended on God for day-by-day and hour-by-hour dirrection. God spoke to her through the Word, through the pages of her dog-eared *Daily Light*, through the impulses of the heart; yes, on occasion, even through dreams. Seminary professors who write learned books about how to interpret the Bible would probably call her use of Bible texts or parts of texts superstitious, but they would have to confess that she was a woman led by God and blessed by God. She exercised a simple-hearted faith in God, nurtured by a wholehearted love for God, and her Father saw to it that she was cared for.

Here is a "Confession of Love" that she drew up for a group of Indian girls who banded together to serve Christ. Perhaps it best says to us just what Amy Carmichael believed about Christian life and service.

My Vow: Whatsoever Thou sayest unto me, by Thy grace I will do it.

My Constraint: Thy love, O Christ, my Lord.

My Confidence: Thou art able to keep that which I have committed unto thee.

My Joy: To do Thy will, O God.

My Discipline: That which I would not choose, but which Thy love appoints.

My Prayer: Conform my will to Thine.

My Motto: Love to live—live to love.

My Portion: The Lord is the portion of mine inheritance.

With that kind of devotion and dedication, is it any wonder that Amy Carmichael was misunderstood by believers, persecuted by unbelievers, attacked by Satan, and blessed by the Lord?

Unpredictable? Yes—*but not unblessable!* We could use a few more like her in Christian service today.

41

Frank W. Boreham
1871–1959

It amazes me that my favorite biographical handbook, *Who Was Who in Church History*, mentions Caesar Borgia and William Briconnet, but contains not one line about Frank W. Boreham. I can easily conceive of a preacher getting along in his ministry knowing nothing about Borgia's sensuous intrigues or Briconnet's cowardly defections; but how he could get along knowing nothing about Boreham's *A Bunch of Everlastings,* or his beloved flock at Mosgiel, New Zealand, or his hundreds of delightful essays is really more than I can understand. I trust that a generation ignorant of Frank W. Boreham has not arisen. If this be the case, however, let me remedy it immediately by devoting a chapter to this world-famous British preacher and essayist. The moderator of the Church of Scotland once introduced Boreham as "the man whose name is on all our lips, whose books are on all our shelves and whose illustrations are in all our sermons." Fortunate is the pastor who gets to know and love the writings of Boreham.

"Salvoes of artillery and peals of bells echoed across Europe on the morning of my birth," wrote Boreham in the first paragraph of his delightful autobiography, *My Pilgrimage.* It was Friday, March

3, 1871, the day the Franco-Prussian War ended. When he was four months old, he was on an outing with his nurse when a gypsy caravan passed by and an old gypsy woman, noticing the child, came over to them. She looked at the little boy's hand and said to the nurse, "Tell his mother to put a pen in his hand and he'll never want for a living." The prophecy proved true: Boreham became one of the world's most prolific religious writers, with more than fifty books to his credit, not to speak of hundreds of newspaper and magazine articles and essays.

As the boy grew up, he was introduced to both the things of the Spirit and the things of the mind. Faithful Christian parents saw to it that he was trained in the Word of God and also that he learned to appreciate good reading (children learn to appreciate good books by contagion, not compulsion). Frank's father, noticing that Frank was reading some shallow novels, introduced him to the vast treasures of biography, and the boy was "hooked for life." At sixteen Frank decided to go to London and get a job; this proved to be the first of several turning points in his life. He had trained himself in shorthand, at which he was very competent, and he had beautiful copperplate script, so landing a job was no great problem. After a short stay with a real estate firm, he worked for a London railroad.

London in 1887 was an exciting place. Charles H. Spurgeon was preaching (when not incapacitated by gout) at the Metropolitan Tabernacle; Joseph Parker was electrifying congregations at the City Temple; J. Hudson Taylor was challenging Christians with the needs of China; and F. B. Meyer was teaching believers the joys and victories of the Christian life.

"Honesty compels me to confess," Boreham wrote, "not without shame, that Mr. Spurgeon never really appealed to me. It was, of course, my fault. . . . I enjoyed every sermon that I heard Mr. Spurgeon preach; I marveled at his power to attract the multitudes; I was thankful for his enormous influence. But he never gripped me as some other preachers did."[1] The great preacher's poor health those closing years may help to explain Boreham's evaluation. It was F. B. Meyer who attracted and held the young man from Tunbridge Wells.

Boreham attended Meyer's church in Regent's Park and also the famous Saturday afternoon Bible classes at Aldersgate Street, directed especially to the young men of the city. "I really think that we lived for those Saturday afternoons," Boreham said in his autobiography. "We counted the hours till they came; and, when they came, they never failed to minister to us such hope and faith and courage as sent us back to our tasks with higher spirits and with braver hearts."[2]

There is no doubt that Meyer's positive ministry of encouragement helped to mold Boreham's own ministry, for, like Barnabas, Frank Boreham was "a son of encouragement" (Acts 4:36). Meyer was a Baptist and Boreham had been raised an Anglican, but Boreham's own study of the Bible had convinced him that he should be immersed. So on Easter Tuesday evening, 1890, he was immersed at the Stockwell Old Baptist Church. Little did he realize that his Baptist associations would play an important role in his life and ministry.

In 1891 he united with Kenyon Baptist Church in Brixton, whose pastor, James Douglas, was a good friend of Spurgeon. When the pastor discovered that Boreham was considering the ministry, he naturally urged him to apply to Spurgeon's Pastors' College. Boreham did, and he was the last student that Spurgeon personally selected before his lamented death on January 31, 1892. The Spurgeon family would be used of God to direct Boreham's ministry in ways that he never dreamed of, but all of which were part of God's plan.

In 1894, Thomas Spurgeon returned to London after ministering in New Zealand, and he brought with him from a new church at Mosgiel a request for a pastor. Founded by Scottish immigrants, the Mosgiel church was ten years old and gave promise of being an effective work for the Lord. The college staff decided that Boreham was their man. After a conference with Thomas Spurgeon and with Boreham's parents, the student (who still had one year's training before him) decided it was the Lord's will that he terminate his work at the college and sail for New Zealand. At the farewell service, held at the tabernacle, Boreham made a prophecy of his own that, in the providence of God, came true: "And it is my hope that in the course of my ministry I shall hold three pastorates, and then be free to travel in many lands preaching the everlasting gospel among all denominations."

He served in Mosgiel, New Zealand; Hobart, Tasmania; and Armadale, Australia; and then he traveled to many lands and preached to vast congregations. When he was unable to travel personally, his books carried his messages; and it is these that I want to discuss. If you are interested in the story of his life—and you ought to be—then secure *My Pilgrimage*, published in the United States by Judson Press; and also *The Story of F. W. Boreham*, written by T. Howard Crago.

Boreham had begun writing while a youth in London, but his newspaper articles, plus a devotional booklet, had caused little stir. He knew the gift was there; it would simply take time to develop and discipline it. His first love was preaching, but there was no reason why he could not also write. After all, his spiritual mentor, F. B. Meyer, was the author of dozens of books; even Spurgeon made good use of his pen.

After settling down in Mosgiel, Boreham hit upon the idea of publishing a sermon each week in the local newspaper, an idea that the editor approved with enthusiasm. Many readers were unable to travel to church every Sunday, and the printed sermon would meet their needs. In the beginning Boreham solicited sermons from other pastors, but their contributions gradually fell off, leaving it to Boreham to fill up the two columns each week. He enjoyed the discipline of writing out a message, and the publication of his messages in the newspaper helped to fill his church. In time, other newspapers "down under" were reprinting his material, and several editors asked him for original material for their publications. In the years to come, most of his essays would first be shared by several periodicals and then published in book form.

His first book, *The Luggage of Life*, was turned down by Hodder and Stoughton, but Epworth Press accepted it and launched him into his phenomenal literary career.[3] At one time during his ministry, Boreham was publishing two books a year, with no diminishing of sales. Needless to say, Hodder and Stoughton was embarrassed at the loss of such a successful writer; in later years it tried to capture him for its list, but without success.

I think the best of Boreham to read first is the first volume of his *Texts That Made History* series (reprinted by Judson Press), *A Bunch of Everlastings*. The story behind this unique five-volume series is this: Boreham was about to begin a Sunday evening series on "The Specters of the Mind," when it dawned on him that a series on alternate Sunday evenings would encourage the congregation to return week after week. As if by inspiration, it came to him to preach on "Texts That Made History"; and thus he announced that the next Sunday evening he would preach on "Martin Luther's Text." Subsequent sermons were "John Bunyan's Text," "Oliver Cromwell's Text," "John Wesley's Text," etc., putting to practical use Boreham's interest in biography. Little did he realize that these sermons would continue for 125 Sunday evenings and attract more interest and win more people to Christ than any other series he preached.

Every preacher ought to secure these five volumes, read them, and index them—and beware of stealing Boreham's sermons! Following *A Bunch of Everlastings*, look for *A Handful of Stars*, *A Temple of Topaz*, *A Casket of Cameos*, and *A Faggot of Torches*. Turn next to his essays; you have over forty volumes to choose from! By all means secure the first book he published, *The Luggage of Life*, and I would also suggest *The Other Side of the Hill and Home Again*, *The Silver Shadow*, *The Last Milestone* (which contains many of his pithy biographical essays on famous people and events), *The Passing of John Broadbanks*, and *Mushrooms on the Moor*. But selecting a Boreham book is like choosing a beautiful rose from a large bouquet, or selecting a dessert from a tray of French pastries—you can never make a mistake.

To be sure, the essays in each book are of uneven quality and some will strike your fancy more than others, but all of them will do you good. I personally prefer his autobiographical essays dealing with the church at Mosgiel or with his good friend "John Broadbanks." Once you have met "Tammas" and "Wullie" and "Gavin," you will fall in love with them, and no doubt identify them with people you have met in your own church. And it will not take you long to discover who

"John Broadbanks" really is. It does my soul good to reach across the miles and the years to "fellowship" with the Mosgiel congregation and to share their joys and sorrows, their disagreements, and their "love affair" with their pastor.

Let me warn you: Frank Boreham will not tell you how to double attendance at the evening service, increase the budget, or expand the youth ministry. But he will put you in touch with the essentials of life.

Everything he saw, heard, and experienced became a part of his treasury from which, in later years, he brought out "things new and old." Can you imagine writing an essay on "The Man in the Moon," or "Maxims of the Mud," or "Wet Paint"? It is this kind of imaginative writing that can teach and encourage the preacher to be alert to life and to make sure that his messages take hold of reality. Boreham said: "We shall never attract or arrest our hearers by an elaborate display of theology. . . . Theology is to a sermon what a skeleton is to the body: it gives shape and support to the preacher's utterance without itself being visible." Boreham was not an expositor of the Scriptures in the manner of Spurgeon or Maclaren, but he was a biblical preacher and writer who reached many people who perhaps would have turned away from the conventional sermonic approach. I am not suggesting that you imitate his style; I am suggesting that you get excited about the potential in the common things around you.

Boreham was a disciplined reader. Early in his ministry he determined to read at least one book a week, and often he exceeded his quota. While he especially enjoyed biography and autobiography, he did not limit himself. Whenever he had an idea for an essay or a sermon, he immediately wrote it down and filed it away. (Whenever he went on vacation, he buried his precious notes and manuscripts in the backyard, lest the house burn down and they be lost.) By constantly adding to his treasury, he was never at a loss for new ideas; not until late in his life was the treasury exhausted. After he had retired from the pastoral ministry, he was still getting literary dividends from ideas he had noted years before. "Write it down!" was a basic rule of life, and he even kept pen and paper next to his bed in case a night visitor should come and otherwise be lost by morning. By the way, I should mention that Boreham wrote all his material by hand. At one stage he tried using a typewriter, but his muse was not mechanical.

Pastors will be interested in three convictions that Boreham held. First, he was sure that nobody wanted to be visited immediately after the noon meal; so he went to bed every afternoon and slept for one hour. This helps to explain why he lived such a long life—eighty-eight years (he died on May 18, 1959). Second, he was always punctual, and was unhappy with anybody who was not. While never in a hurry, he was always busy. He disciplined himself to do the important things and wasted no time on the trivial. Third, he was convinced that no pastor could preach two entirely new sermons each Lord's Day and do his best; so he always revised an old sermon for one of the Sunday services. He did not simply re-preach it. He revised a sermon and tried to give it a fresh approach based on experience gained since the first time it was preached. He wrote:

> Dr. Parker taught me—as also did Dr. Meyer—the high art of repeating myself. I heard Dr. Meyer say identically the same thing on half a dozen different occasions. But he displayed such craftsmanship in his repetition that, unless you had previously heard him say it, you would never have suspected him of having said the same thing before.[4]

Alas, many pastors do not work at revising their messages. They find it easier to change churches and use the same material over again.

One of the penalties of effectiveness in writing and preaching is plagiarism, and Frank Boreham was plagiarized much of his life. One American preacher told an Australian friend that he would hate to meet Boreham: "I've plagiarized so many of his sermons, I couldn't bear to look him in the eye!" One London preacher even dared to preach one of Boreham's sermons over the BBC. Unfortunately for him, Boreham's father was listening. He recognized the sermon, identified it in one of his son's books, and wrote the preacher a rather pointed letter. The man sent his apology and even wrote Dr. Boreham, but sad to say, he felt that since the sermon was already in print, it was worth sharing with others. (This brings to mind the fact that G. Campbell Morgan was often plagiarized. When it was announced that he was to preach in various places, he would often receive anonymous letters begging him not to preach certain sermons because they had already been preached there—by others!) I wonder at the effectiveness, not to speak of the character, of a man who must steal material in order to minister. If we do borrow, at least we should give credit.

If at first Boreham does not excite you, give him time. He grows on you. He has a way of touching the nerve centers of life and getting to that level of reality that we too often miss. Some may consider him sentimental; others may feel he is a relic of a vanished era. They are welcome to their opinions. But before you pass judgment, read him for yourself, and read enough to give him a fair trial. If you are preaching from Luke 15, read *The Prodigal* and marvel at Boreham's new insights into this old story. *The Heavenly Octave* deals with the beatitudes. There is something for everybody in a Boreham book, because his writing touches on the unchanging essentials of life, not the passing accidentals; we need this emphasis today.

42

Joseph W. Kemp
1872–1933

God pity the man who comes here!" said Joseph W. Kemp at a committee meeting in the famous Charlotte Baptist Chapel, Edinburgh. The Baptist church in Hawick, of which Kemp was pastor, was enjoying remarkable blessing; Charlotte Chapel was in sad shape. Then Charlotte Chapel called Kemp. "Don't go!" his friends warned. Why exchange a successful work for a derelict one? Kemp prayed, and then he accepted the call. His ministry in Edinburgh not only restored a great church, but also brought salvation and revival to thousands.

Joseph W. Kemp was born in 1872 in Hull, Yorkshire. He was only seven when his father died; two years later his mother died. The six little children were scattered. Joseph, with only eighteen months of schooling, had to go to work. When he was twelve, he went to Bridlington to work as a pageboy, but he soon returned to Hull, where he lived with a devoted Christian named J. H. Russell. Russell helped train the lad and witnessed to him lovingly about Jesus Christ.

Kemp was converted in September 1886. He was chatting with an old sailor, who suddenly asked, "Lad, when are you going to accept Christ?" Kemp arose from his chair, walked across the room, took the sailor by the hand, and said: "I'll do it now!" His own salvation experience no doubt contributed to his later boldness and decisiveness in evangelism. Two years later he was asked to lead a Bible-study class. About the same time he began attending meetings conducted by J. M. Scroggie, uncle of W. Graham Scroggie. These meetings revealed to him some of the wealth in the Word of God. He determined to study his Bible and appropriate its wealth for himself—and then share it. A generous friend sent Kemp to Glasgow Bible Training Institute, from which he graduated in 1894. While studying his Bible, he concluded that immersion was the scriptural form of baptism, a painful decision since he was at the Prospect Street Presbyterian Church. (The pastor was W. P. Mackay, author of the classic *Grace and Truth*.)

During his student days and for a year after graduation, Kemp conducted evangelistic meetings for the Ayrshire Christian Union. He could have become an itinerant soul-winner, but on April 4, 1897, he accepted a call from the Baptist church in Kelso. Horatius Bonar had ministered in that town for many years. Like Bonar, Kemp preached the doctrine of Christ's second coming and he practiced evangelism.

The Baptist church in Hawick called him in July 1898; he ministered there until he moved to Edinburgh in February 1902. Before leaving Kelso, he married a daughter of a key church family. Kemp found a divided church at Hawick and left it united and growing. The young pastor spent his mornings in study and prayer. (As a student, he read every book he could find on prayer. After hearing an address by Andrew Murray, he determined to be a man of prayer.) He used afternoons for visitation and evenings for Bible classes and training sessions for church workers. Evangelism, Bible teaching, and prayer were the main elements in his ministry at Hawick, and they remained so throughout his life.

On Kemp's first Sunday at Charlotte Chapel, only thirty-five members came. But he was not discouraged: God had called him, and God would honor his Word. Kemp began by cleaning and remodeling the chapel. "Worldly places are bright and attractive," he said, alluding to the nineteen pubs in the neighborhood. "Why should God's house be dingy and musty?" Church members removed from their building thirteen cartloads of rubbish. But the spiritual changes at Charlotte Chapel were the most important. The new pastor started two Sunday prayer meetings, one beginning at 7 a.m., the other at 10 a.m. At every public meeting he gave solid, biblical teaching with an evangelistic fervor that eventually caught fire in the church. Kemp and his congregation often "took to the streets" and conducted open-air meetings. Before long, the crowds were going to Charlotte Chapel and not the pubs!

Early in 1905 an evangelist held meetings in the church, but nothing exceptional happened. The officers wisely agreed to have the church continue in prayer until God sent the needed blessing. About this time the great Welsh revival broke out; Kemp went to seek some of the blessing for himself and his people. He urged the people to continue praying for revival. Night after night throughout 1905 multitudes met in different prayer meetings. The blessing came on January 22, 1906, at a special church conference. All that year attendance increased, souls were saved in unusual numbers, and the church felt the power of God. People confessed sin, and broken fellowship was restored. The blessing continued into 1907, when the pastor celebrated his fifth anniversary.

A new church building, designed to accommodate the congregation's increased size, formally opened on October 6, 1912. During its construction the church met in the two-thousand-seat Synod Hall, with the blessing of God continuing unabated. During the dedication services Andrew Urquhart, secretary of Charlotte Chapel, explained the reasons for God's blessing during Kemp's ministry: first was "a firm and unchangeable belief in the power of prayer"; second, the preaching of the gospel; third, "hearty cooperation among as loyal and devoted a band of workers as ever any church possessed"; fourth was "an unfaltering faith in the promises of God."

Kemp's ministry in Edinburgh ended on September 5, 1915, when he left to pastor Calvary Baptist Church in New York City. During the farewell service, John Henry Jowett, then pastoring in New

York, unexpectedly showed up. And when the Kemp family was sailing out of Liverpool, they heard a voice calling from another ship: "Goodbye, Kemp! Goodbye, Kemp!" They discovered it was A. C. Dixon, then pastor of the Metropolitan Tabernacle in London. Calvary in New York resembled Charlotte Chapel in many respects when Joseph Kemp arrived. One of the first things he did was remove a thousand names from the church roll. He called it "ecclesiastical hypocrisy" to advertise inflated statistics. Unfortunately, Kemp's health began to break, and he resigned from Calvary in February 1917. He ministered a short time at the new Metropolitan Tabernacle in New York City, but a complete breakdown forced him to leave the work in 1919.

In the spring of 1920, he accepted a call to the Baptist Tabernacle founded by Thomas Spurgeon in Auckland, New Zealand. God miraculously restored Kemp's health, and he entered the new ministry with great expectations. So popular were his Bible classes that many of the bookstores ran out of Bibles. One byproduct of his ministry was the founding of the New Zealand Bible Training Institute. Again Kemp organized daily prayer meetings for revival, but he did not see the results he had seen in Edinburgh. He wrote a friend:

> We often wonder why revival tarries. For over eighteen months a daily prayer meeting has been held in the Tabernacle, in addition to two or three prayer meetings of the regular order—the burden of all of which has been, "Wilt Thou not revive us again?" Still the revival tarries. People do not respond so readily now to the appeals as they did twenty-five years ago.

Kemp paid his last visit to Great Britain in 1926. He preached at Keswick, and ministered in the United States and Canada on the return trip. Back in Auckland he took up his work with characteristic zeal, but in 1932 his health again began to fail. He died on September 4, 1933, after seven months of serious illness. He was buried the next day in the Hillsborough Cemetery, with six thousand people lining the streets to pay tribute to a great preacher-evangelist who is almost forgotten today.

Joseph Kemp was a Spirit-taught man, spending hours searching the Bible. He did not borrow other men's sermons; he got his messages from God and always preached the Word. He was a man of prayer. *Bounds on Prayer* (now in print as *Power Through Prayer*) by E. M. Bounds was one of his favorite books. Like the apostles of old, he gave himself to prayer and the ministry of the Word (Acts 6:4).

Kemp was not content to minister in a comfortable church; he went after lost souls and preached the gospel to them. He refused to be controlled by what he called "the tyranny of statistics." He taught the Word of God. He saw that new Christians studied the Bible and served the Lord in the church. To Kemp the church was not a field to work in; it was a force to work with. He expected and received the cooperation of his church officers, and God blessed their work together.

His ministry at Charlotte Chapel was no passing thing. His successor, W. Graham Scroggie, ministered for seventeen years with great blessing. The work then prospered under Scroggie's successor, J. Sidlow Baxter. When I visited Charlotte Chapel a few years ago, I gave thanks to God for the ministry of Joseph Kemp.

Kemp was influenced greatly by the life of George Whitefield and the sermons of Charles H. Spurgeon. Charles G. Finney's *Lectures on Revivals* also made an impact on his life. "I have frequently been asked, 'What is the secret of Mr. Kemp's success?'" said one of his church officers. "It is this: he believes in the gospel which he preaches, because he knows what it has done for himself, and what he has seen it do for others. . . . He believes in prayer. In other words, he preaches the gospel in faith, and expects and waits for the results. God honors his faith, and he gets the answer he expects." Prayer, Bible teaching, and evangelism—there is no reason why the formula should not work today.

43

Oswald Chambers
1874 – 1917

I feel I shall be buried for a time, hidden away in obscurity; then suddenly I shall flame out, do my work, and be gone."

Those words were spoken by Oswald Chambers, author of *My Utmost for His Highest* and more than thirty other books that never seem to grow old. His statement was prophetic—except that the flame God lit is still burning brightly, thanks to the printed page.

When you review the life of Oswald Chambers, you can well understand why a friend once introduced him as "the apostle of the haphazard." Like the wind Jesus spoke of in John 3:8, Chambers came and went in a seemingly erratic fashion; yet there was a definite plan in his life, and he was greatly used of God. He is a good reminder to boxed-in Christians that God sometimes bypasses our date-books and management-by-objectives and does the surprising, even the unexpected, in our lives.

Oswald Chambers was born in Aberdeen, Scotland, on July 24, 1874. His parents had been baptized by Charles Spurgeon, who had also ordained Chambers' father into Baptist ministry. While the family was living in London, teenage Oswald gave his heart to Christ.

He and his father were walking home from a meeting conducted by Spurgeon, and Oswald admitted that he would have given himself to the Lord had the opportunity been given. "You can do it now, my boy!" said his father, and right there, the boy trusted Christ and was born again. He was baptized by Rev. J. T. Briscoe and became a member of the Rye Lane Baptist Church in London.

A gifted artist, Chambers entered art school in 1892 and three years later went to Edinburgh to continue his studies. In 1896, he felt a definite call to the ministry, and the following year he entered the Dunoon Training College in Scotland. Not only did he have an outstanding record as a student, but he remained after graduation to teach. He had a special interest in philosophy and psychology, and taught those courses.

But in November 1901, Chambers had a deep experience with the Lord that transformed his life. He called it a baptism of the Holy Spirit, a term I prefer to apply only to the believer's experience at conversion (see 1 Cor. 12:13). This special filling of the Spirit gave him new insights into both the Christian life and the courses he was then teaching. In his ministry of the Word, he reveals both the philosopher and the psychologist.

He left school in 1905 and began an itinerant ministry in Britain, the United States, and Japan. He taught at the Oriental Missionary Society Bible School in Tokyo, and then he became a "missioner" for the League of Prayer that had been founded by Reader Harris. He was married on May 25, 1910, to Gertrude Hobbs, a devoted woman who was also an expert stenographer, a fact that would mean much in the years to come.

Chambers felt there was a need for a Bible college in Britain that would emphasize personal Christian living and not just education and practical training. With the help of some friends, he founded the Bible Training College at Clapham. The school operated on faith and prayer. When a friend offered to endow the school, Chambers refused the offer saying, "No, if you do that it will probably go on longer than God means it to."

He felt led to offer himself as a military chaplain during World War I, and on October 9, 1915, he sailed with the troops for Zeitoun, Egypt, where he ministered until his untimely death on November 15, 1917. He had appendicitis and did not know it; peritonitis set in and his life could not be saved.

At this point his wife Gertrude (whom everybody called Biddy) and his daughter Kathleen enter the picture and become very important. Biddy remained at their home in Zeitoun and ministered for about a year. Then she and her daughter returned to England. Over the years, she had taken stenographic reports of her husband's messages and, at the request of many friends, began to edit and publish them. Oswald Chambers never actually wrote any of his books, although his name is on them. He spoke every word, but it was his wife, and later his daughter, who prepared the manuscripts and mothered each book through the presses. How grateful we are to God that Chambers married an expert stenographer!

His most famous book is *My Utmost for His Highest*, a daily devotional book that not every Christian can immediately appreciate. I recall telling a mature Christian friend many years ago that I was getting nothing out of the book. "Set it aside for a time," she counseled. "It's something you have to grow into." She was right: the problem was not the complexity of the book but the spiritual immaturity of the reader. In later years, I have come to appreciate this classic devotional book, and I learn more from it as the years go by.

Too many devotional books are finished with one reading, because they do not get down to the fundamental truths that keep expanding into more truth. A good book is like a seed: it produces fruit that has in it seed for more fruit. It is not a picture on the wall; it is a window that invites us to wider horizons.

Each time I read a page from *My Utmost for His Highest*, I am reminded of a forgotten nugget, or I see something new that previously had eluded me. It is a book to grow with and, as such, it is unique.

All the writings of Oswald Chambers have their value. I must confess that I get a bit tired of his alliteration, some of which seems forced, but I have learned to look beyond it. I have especially appreciated his book on Abraham, *Not Knowing Whither*. *The Philosophy of Sin* has some penetrating insights in it. Chambers was similar to F. B. Meyer in his ability to diagnose spiritual problems and give biblical solutions. *Biblical Psychology* reveals Chambers the amateur psychologist, but the emphasis is on the Bible and not the psychology. His studies in Job, *Baffled to Fight Better*, are brief but rich, and very rewarding.

The official biography, *Oswald Chambers: His Life and Work*, was compiled and edited by his wife. She quoted from his journals, added her own comments, and quoted from material given her by his many friends and associates in ministry. Like Chambers himself, this book is a bit haphazard, and the reader can easily lose the chronological trail. But the many quotations from Chambers, and the revelation of his personality, make its reading worthwhile. It was published in London in 1933 by Simpkin Marshall, Ltd.

What kind of a man was Oswald Chambers? For one thing, he was not a brittle and pious "saint" who lived aloof from the world and the people around him. He was very much alive, and he had a marvelous sense of humor. One man wrote to Mrs. Chambers that he had been "shocked at what I then considered his undue levity. He was the most irreverent Reverend I had ever met!"

But Chambers gave himself totally to the Lord, and this included his sense of humor. He once wrote in his journal, "Lord, keep me radiantly and joyously Thine." En route to Egypt, he conducted services on the ship and brought his humor into the messages.

"Ah, I see," said one of the men, "your jokes and lightheartedness plough the land, then you put in the seed." You could not find a better philosophy of humor in the pulpit than that.

Chambers emphasized holy living, but he did not divorce it from the practical affairs of life. "I am realizing more and more the futility of separating a life into secular and sacred. It is all His." Those words summarize his position perfectly. He wrote to a friend, "You can be much more for Him than ever you know by just being yourself and relying on Him. . . . Keep praying and playing and being yourself." He felt that his own greatest ministry was that of intercessory prayer.

A gifted teacher, he was careful that the truths he taught were meaningful in his own life. "Views from propagandist teaching are borrowed plumes," he said. "Teaching is meant to stir up thinking, not to store with goods from the outside." That is good counsel in this age when many teachers and preachers manufacture their lessons and sermons out of borrowed nuggets instead of mining their own gold and refining it in experience.

Chambers sought to present truth in ways that would excite new interest in his listeners. One listener said, "I wondered, as I drank in his message, whether I had the same Bible as he had. The written Word became a Living Word, and as I obeyed it my whole life was altered."

He would have agreed with A. W. Tozer that the only *real* world is the world of truth found in the Bible. He wrote: "The Actual world of things and the Real world of Truth have to be made into one in personal experience." Too many Christians try to avoid this creative tension by going either to extreme isolation from the world or to extreme preoccupation with the world.

Oswald Chambers loved books and read widely. The biography contains references to many authors of different theological positions, from Alexander Maclaren and John Henry Jowett to Emmanuel Swedenborg and Ralph Waldo Emerson. "My books!" he wrote to a friend. "I cannot tell you what they are to me—silent, wealthy, loyal lovers. . . . I do thank God for my books with every fiber of my being. Friends that are ever true and ever your own." He always integrated his wide reading with the Word of God, which he considered the only test for spiritual truth.

In many respects, Chambers was not in tune with the general spirit of evangelical Christianity in his day. On his way to Egypt, he wrote in his journal: "How unproselytizing God is! I feel the 'soul winning campaign' is often at heart the apotheosis [glorification] of commercialism, the desire to see so much result from so much expenditure. The ordinary evangelical spirit is less and less congenial to my own soul." His writings are a good antidote to the success philosophy that has invaded the church in our own day. He said that "the 'soul saving passion' as an aim must cease and merge into the passion for Christ, revealing itself in holiness in all human relationships." In other words, soul-winning is not something we *do*, it is something we *are*, twenty-four hours a day, and we live for souls because we love Christ. No counting trophies in his ministry.

He was not afraid to accept truth no matter what channel God might use to give it to him. He told students to "*soak, soak, soak* in philosophy and psychology. . . . It is ignorance of the subjects on the part of ministers and workers that has brought our evangelical theology to such a sorry plight."[1] Both in the pulpit and classroom, and as a personal counselor, Chambers revealed his keen understanding of the Bible, the human heart and mind, and the world of thought. He was able to blend these disciplines into a total ministry that God greatly used.

Let me share a few quotations from Oswald Chambers that, I trust, will whet your appetite for more.

> You can never give another person that which you have found, but you can make him homesick for what you have.
>
> If we are saved and sanctified, God guides us by our ordinary choices, and if we are going to choose what He does not want, He will check, and we must heed.
>
> Every doctrine that is not imbedded in the Cross of Jesus will lead astray.
>
> Stop having a measuring rod for other people. There is always one fact more in every man's case about which we know nothing.
>
> It takes a long time to realize the danger of being an amateur providence, that is, interfering with God's order for others.
>
> Our Lord's first obedience was to the will of His Father, not to the needs of men; the saving of men was the natural outcome of His obedience to the Father.[2]

One of his sayings that is underlined in my copy of *My Utmost for His Highest* has been especially meaningful to me.

> The snare in Christian work is to rejoice in successful service, to rejoice in the fact that God has used you. . . . If you make usefulness the test,

then Jesus Christ was the greatest failure that ever lived. The lodestar of the saint is God Himself, not estimated usefulness. It is the work that God does through us that counts, not what we do for Him.[3]

Mrs. Chambers died in 1966, just after she had begun to prepare the thirty-second volume for the publishers, and her daughter completed the book. How grateful to God we should be for Biddy and Kathleen's unselfish labor of love over the years, in sharing the ministry of Oswald Chambers with us. His body is buried in the cemetery in Old Cairo, his spirit is rejoicing in the presence of God, and his ministry goes on triumphantly.

Perhaps one final quotation will sum up his philosophy of the Christian life. "Never make a principle out of your own experience; let God be as original with other people as He is with you."

He may have been the apostle of the haphazard, but Oswald Chambers can assist any sincere Christian in ordering his life according to the will of God.

44

H. A. Ironside
1876–1951

The last time I heard H. A. Ironside preach was in the late 1940s at Winona Lake, Indiana. His text was from chapter 32 of his beloved Isaiah (which he pronounced "I-SIGH-ah"). In his own quiet way, Ironside exalted Jesus Christ as man's only refuge from the coming wrath of God. I still remember a story he told that day, based on his experiences with the American Indians, of hurrying into the shelter of a huge rock to escape a sudden storm. I also remember that when he read from his big Bible, he held it close to his eyes, for by that time he was almost blind. One more memory remains: that of Ironside sitting on a bench in the Billy Sunday Tabernacle, watching young Billy Graham, who was preaching a dramatic message on the temptation of Christ. Ironside's facial expression was one of appreciation as his younger brother preached the gospel of Jesus Christ. October 14, 1976, marked the centenary of the birth of Henry Allan Ironside. The official biography, *H. A. Ironside* by E. Schuyler English, has been revised and updated by the author. The new edition is published by Loizeaux, publisher of most of Ironside's books.

When Ironside was born, the attending physician thought the baby was dead. Since the mother desperately needed attention, the doctor concentrated on her. Nearly an hour later, a nurse detected the child's pulse. Immediately they plunged the baby into a hot bath, and he began to cry. It seemed evident to the godly parents that the Lord had marked their son for something special.

When Henry, nicknamed Harry, was about two and his brother only three weeks old, his father died. Harry's mother taught him to trust God for everyday needs. Some of the family's experiences read like miracles from the life of Elijah or Paul. Sophia Ironside asked God to make her children preachers of the Word and winners of souls. Under his mother's guidance, Harry began to memorize Scripture when he was three. By age fourteen, he had read through the Bible fourteen times, "once for each year." During the rest of his life he read the Bible through at least once a year. A pastor friend told me of a Bible conference at which he and Ironside were two of the speakers. During the conference the speakers discussed their approaches to personal devotions. Each man shared what he had read from the Word that morning. When it was Ironside's turn, he hesitated, then said, "I read the book of Isaiah." He was saturated with the Word of God.

Sophia decided in 1886 to move her family to California. Even though he was not yet converted, young Harry started a Sunday school, which about sixty neighborhood children attended. When he was twelve, Harry went to Hazzard's Pavilion to hear Dwight L. Moody and was deeply stirred by the message. He prayed that evening, "Lord, help me some day to preach to crowds like these, and to lead souls to Christ." Four decades later he became the pastor of Moody Church in Chicago. In several respects Ironside's sermons were similar to Moody's. They were always directed to the common man and free of theological jargon. They were not long and were filled with the Word of God. Like Moody, Ironside was a master of illustrating truths with personal experiences. From the illustrations in his published expositions, one could almost produce an autobiography.

Ironside finally gave his heart to Christ in February 1890, and almost immediately he identified with the Salvation Army. The Army represented just what he wanted in Christian fellowship and service: separation from sin, courage to witness, a burden for souls, and willingness to live by faith. Two years later he was a respected officer. But disillusionment with the Army's position on sanctification resulted in his resigning his commission in 1895. The full story is given in his book *Holiness: The False and the True*, one of the best books available on practical holiness in the Christian life. The next year Ironside identified himself with the Brethren in San Francisco, and the Brethren remained his "ecclesiastical fellowship" until his death.

Several things about Ironside will amaze you as you read English's excellent biography. First is Ironside's faith. God often provided for his needs in miraculous ways, especially in the early days of his ministry. Reading about such instances will greatly encourage you to trust God daily. One is tempted to add to Hebrews 11: "By faith Harry Ironside, needing a new suit of clothes. . ." Second is Ironside's willingness to go where God sent him and do what God wished. He never promoted himself or played politics to "get meetings." Whether preaching to small crowds on street corners or to large congregations, he always did his best. Third is his constant study of the Word of God. To compensate for his academic limitations, Ironside studied the Bible faithfully. (As a hobby, he taught himself Chinese!) His ministry was one of Bible exposition, simply opening the Word of God and allowing the Spirit to speak for himself. And finally, Ironside always went for souls. To him, Bible exposition was a means to glorify Christ and to call sinners to trust him.

Ironside first visited Moody Church in Chicago in 1925, just two months after P. W. Philpott had moved his congregation into their new 4,000-seat auditorium. Ironside was to conduct a two-week conference, but when Philpott was called out of town, Ironside stayed over another week. Philpott invited him back each year, and his ministry was always appreciated. After Pastor Philpott resigned, the congregation inevitably turned to Ironside. The Brethren, with whom Ironside was associated, believed that local assemblies should have several pastor-teachers and that none should be paid. Ironside had agreed with this conviction. Some of the Chicago Brethren talked of breaking fellowship with him if he accepted the call from Moody Church. But when Ironside was unanimously called to the church on February 24, 1930, and he accepted, even his Brethren friends promised to pray for and support him.

Today it is still impossible to think of Moody Church without thinking of Ironside. Those of us who lived in the Chicago area during his long pastorate (1930–48) thank God for his ministry of the Word. He would select a book of the Bible and preach through it on successive Sundays; most of these series have found their way into print.

Ironside's preaching was the despair of every homiletics professor. I can still hear students arguing with our seminary professor: "But Dr. Ironside doesn't preach with an outline like you're asking us to make." And I can hear the professor's reply: "If you are as good as Dr. Ironside, you don't belong in this class!" While Ironside's messages did not usually follow an obvious outline, they were always organized. He knew where he was going, and he got there. To the casual listener it seemed like the preacher was merely going from verse to verse, making a few comments and explanations and perhaps adding a story. But the careful listener always found a thread of doctrine woven throughout the message. Ironside knew how to compare spiritual things with spiritual. He used the Bible to illustrate and interpret itself. The thing that impressed me most about his preaching was what I call its "personal practicality." He had a message for you, and he wanted you to get it. Usually you did.

Ironside did not "run" Moody Church. He was often away at conferences during the week and left the day-to-day organizational matters with the staff and church officers. Ironside was the preacher. Everybody knew it, and nobody wanted it any other way. I recall seeing a letter from the elders to Ironside, however, requesting that he limit his summer conference ministry so that he would be at the church when many visitors came. It would be interesting to calculate exactly how many days he was gone during those eighteen years of fruitful ministry. One thing is certain: hardly a Lord's Day went by without one or more persons responding to the invitation at the close of the service and trusting Christ.

Some have criticized Ironside for preaching through Bible books instead of preaching "more contemporary messages" in such a strategic pulpit. But time, I think, has vindicated his ministry. His expositions are as fresh and meaningful today as when they were preached. I have many books of "contemporary sermons" in my library, and they read like old newspapers in comparison. Not every preacher is called to be an expositor, but I encourage every preacher to strive to be one. People everywhere are hungry for the Word of God, and the best way to give them a balanced diet is to preach Bible books, week by week.

On Sunday, January 14, 1951, Moody Church was joyfully installing their new pastor, S. Franklin Logsdon, when the cablegram arrived from Mrs. Ironside in New Zealand: "Dr. Ironside died in his sleep this morning after short illness." He had been sick less than a week when, on January 15 (the date in New Zealand), he died. At his request he was buried in New Zealand. A great memorial service was held at Moody Church on Sunday afternoon, February 4, with pastors Logsdon and Howard A. Hermansen officiating, assisted by Ironside's good friend Alex H. Stewart, his biographer E. Schuyler English, Carl Armerding, William Culbertson, and Homer Hammontree. The blessed influence of Ironside still hovers over Moody Church. His ministry has strengthened me and encouraged me to do my best.

A Christian bookseller said to me, "There has arisen a generation that knows not Ironside." If that be true—and I am not sure it is—then it says nothing about Ironside. But it does say a great deal about the new generation! Ironside was not a dazzling preacher; he did not aim to be sensational. He stepped into the pulpit with exclamation points, not question marks. A generation of preachers that has tried every gimmick available to get people's attention would do well to become acquainted with Harry Ironside and to learn afresh the meaning of living by faith and preaching the Word of God in simplicity and love.

45

Clarence Edward Macartney
1879–1957

Traditionally, almost every Scottish ministry couple wanted one of their sons to become a preacher, and John and Catherine Macartney were no exception. God answered their prayers "exceedingly abundantly," because three of their sons were called into the ministry, and the fourth and youngest is known to Christian preachers and teachers around the world.

Clarence Edward Macartney was born on September 18, 1879, in Northwood, Ohio, into a Reformed Presbyterian family. His parents came to America from Scotland. Peter Marshall, chaplain of the United States Senate (1947–49), used to say, "If you want to become a great preacher, you must arrange to be born in Scotland." (Campbell Morgan and Martyn Lloyd-Jones opted for Wales.) Clarence's father was not only a minister, but also an educator, and served as principal of a high school and then professor of mathematics at the college in New Concord, Ohio. When Clarence was nine months old, the college relocated to Beaver Falls, Pennsylvania, and the family moved into "Fern Cliffe," a commodious house that was just right for raising a large family. All his life, Macartney remembered those delightful Fern Cliffe years and thanked God for them.

Clarence's mother was the strongest influence in his life. She was from sturdy Covenanter stock, and everyone who spoke of her called her "a remarkable woman." Not only did she faithfully care for her own family, but she also sought out and helped people who needed special encouragement and care, a trait that appeared years later in her youngest son's pastoral ministry. Unlike some pastors in his own day (and certainly in our day), each week he invested two or three evenings and three or four afternoons in visiting his people. Mention visitation to most preachers today, and they will smile and say, "We're not into that." But like Robert Murray McCheyne and Phillips Brooks, Macartney never married, so he was free from the "many troubles" Paul wrote about in 1 Corinthians 7:28 and could devote more time to church responsibilities.

John Macartney's health declined, and their doctor recommended that the family move to California. They lived there for two years and Clarence attended Pomona College. There he developed a passion for baseball and even became captain of the team. But there was also a strong religious influence on campus. He heard singer George C. Stebbins, who composed "Saved By Grace," and also D. L. Moody's associate Ira D. Sankey, who sang "The Ninety and Nine" for the students. His second year at college, a fellow student died and Clarence was one of the pallbearers. He confessed that it was "a very solemn occasion." God uses a variety of experiences to mold and make his servants, but at the time, we may not realize it.

Clarence never forgot the inscription on the memorial gateway at the entrance of the campus: "Let only the eager, thoughtful and reverent enter here." Years later he quoted the statement in his sermon "Horses to Those who Can Ride" and commented, "Perhaps the time will come when less attention will be paid to the scholarly qualifications of a graduate, and more to the qualifications of character, for entrance and matriculation."[1] Nor did he forget the words inscribed on the other side of the gateway: "They only are loyal to this college who, departing, bear their added riches in trust for mankind." Thanks to his published sermons, Clarence Edward Macartney is still adding riches to God's church.

The California climate didn't help John Macartney's health as much as they had hoped, so he decided the family would move to Denver. Clarence stayed in California to complete his courses at Pomona College and to prepare for university, but he still wasn't certain about his life's vocation. At the suggestion of two of his brothers, he enrolled in the University of Wisconsin, receiving his BA in 1901. We aren't sure how much young Clarence was thinking about the ministry during those early years, but his mother constantly had the matter on her heart and in her prayers.

After graduating from the University of Wisconsin, Clarence took a year off to work as a reporter for a county newspaper. He called the job "a most important chapter in my training for the work of my life," for it taught him to gather facts, organize them, and write them clearly and concisely. About that time, his mother wrote to one of his brothers, "I never knew anyone who was so clearly marked for the pulpit as Clarence, if only the Lord would put grace into his heart."

The Lord did put that grace into his heart, and after his year at the newspaper he headed for Princeton University, where he received his MA in 1904. The next step was Princeton Theological Seminary, where he entered as a member of the junior class and graduated in 1905 with his Bachelor of Divinity degree. The seminary had a stellar faculty, including noted Old Testament scholar Dr. Robert Dick Wilson, who was proficient in over twenty languages. Dr. Wilson was a stalwart defender of the faith, and in 1929 he left Princeton Seminary and joined J. Gresham Machen in founding Westminster Seminary.

But let's backtrack a bit. The summer following his first year at seminary, Clarence was invited to be the summer minister of the Presbyterian Church in the little town of Prairie du Sac, Wisconsin. He would be paid fifty dollars a month, and during those summer months would have numerous pastoral opportunities to help prepare him for his final year at seminary. He accepted the invitation and was determined to follow the two precepts given to the students by Dr. David J. Burrell, celebrated pastor of Marble Collegiate Church on Fifth Avenue in New York City: always have a clear outline, and never preach with notes or from a manuscript. During his more than fifty years of ministry, Dr. Macartney never departed from those guidelines; in fact, years later he wrote a book called *Preaching without Notes*, first published in 1946 and reprinted in 1976 by Baker Books. Only one chapter deals with the theme of the title, but the other five chapters build toward that theme and contain valuable counsel for every preacher.

Serving the church that summer was indeed a challenge. He had few books with him, there was no library in the little town, and he was determined, with God's help, to serve as though he would remain there the rest of his life. He was not on vacation. He had two sermons with him, one on Judas Iscariot and the other on John 12:24, and he confessed that "had it not been for the Old Testament characters, I would have gone into pulpit bankruptcy." Once again, God was equipping him for his future ministry, for the name Clarence Edward Macartney should immediately remind the well-read pastor or layman of biblical biographical preaching.

Shortly after graduation from seminary in 1905, Macartney accepted a call from First Presbyterian Church in Paterson, New Jersey, where he served for nine years. From 1914 to 1927, he served Arch Street Presbyterian Church in Philadelphia, and it was during that pastorate that he became involved in the "Fundamentalist/Modernist Controversy" triggered by the preaching of Harry Emerson Fosdick at First Presbyterian Church in New York City. Fosdick was known for his liberal theology and persuasive preaching. In his autobiography *The Living of These Days*, Fosdick said that Macartney's "theological position was in my judgment incredible," but that Macartney himself was "decent and dignified in his attitude . . . fair-minded and courteous."[2] Fosdick had been attacked viciously from the pulpit and in print by certain Fundamentalist leaders who had not been entirely Christian in their approach, and Macartney's candor and courtesy impressed him.

Fosdick had preached a sermon entitled "Shall the Fundamentalists Win?" which denied many of the cardinal doctrines of the Christian faith. The sermon was printed and distributed widely. In his autobiography, Fosdick claimed that the sermon was "a plea for goodwill,"[3] but how could devout Christians see "goodwill" in the preacher's denial of the virgin birth of Christ and the blood atonement? Macartney preached a sermon entitled "Shall Unbelief Win?" which was also printed and widely circulated. (One of Macartney's friends said, "He is not a contentious man, but he is a conscientious man.") In October 1922, at the meeting of the Philadelphia Presbytery, Macartney presented an address to the Presbytery of New York from the Presbytery of Philadelphia, graciously requesting that the preaching at First Presbyterian Church of New York City conform to the doctrinal standards of the Presbyterian Church. Fosdick was an ordained Baptist minister serving as "stated pulpit supply" in a Presbyterian church, and he ought to respect the fact that he was a guest in the pulpit.

But Dr. Fosdick wasn't disturbed by these negative reactions. "I am profoundly sorry that the sermon has been misinterpreted," he wrote to a friend; "I am profoundly sorry that it has caused a disturbance; but I cannot honestly be sorry at all that I preached the sermon. When I get to heaven I expect it to be one of the stars in my crown."[4]

A great deal of public debate and denominational discussion followed. Fosdick did resign from his ministry at First Presbyterian Church and in 1924 Macartney was elected moderator of the Presbyterian General Assembly, but the differences between the modernists and the fundamentalists had not really been faced or solved. J. Gresham Machen led the conservatives in establishing Westminster Theological Seminary in Philadelphia, as well as The Independent Board for Presbyterian Foreign Missions, and was in danger of being tried as a schismatic. Macartney offered his services as counsel but Machen graciously refused on the grounds that he did not want to be acquitted. He seceded from the denomination and founded the Orthodox Presbyterian Church. At Westminster Seminary, Machen helped to train many ministers, and his two masterpieces, *The Virgin Birth of Christ* and *The Origin of Paul's Religion,* still instruct thinking believers today.

In 1927, Macartney accepted the call to the strategic First Presbyterian Church in Pittsburgh, Pennsylvania, where he remained until 1953. There he followed the same pattern that had been so successful in Paterson and Philadelphia, preaching sermon series on biblical doctrines and personalities and also preaching what he called "sermons from life." He was a master of what we today call "narrative preaching," and knew how to relate biblical events and persons to contemporary life.

In spite of his Scottish heritage, he was not an expository preacher, although his sermons were based solidly on Scripture and he did his homework well. He was more of a topical-textual preacher, using biblical events and characters as the framework for the message. No matter what the text or the topic, Macartney was always evangelistic and declared the good news of the gospel week after week. Billy Sunday's music director, Homer Rodeheaver, told Macartney that if he would devote all his time to evangelism, he could be the greatest evangelist of the century.

There were occasions when he preached against social evils such as liquor advertising, Sabbath desecration, vice, political corruption, and indecent movies. These messages were always based on Scripture. In his sermons, he aimed for simplicity, a clearly stated theme and outline, memorable illustrations, and application to life. One of his rules was, "Put all the Bible into it that you can."

This is a good place for a story that comes out of his visitation ministry while in Pittsburgh. He and an assistant had visited in perhaps a dozen homes one afternoon before stopping to see a British lady who attended First Presbyterian Church. They were sitting comfortably by the fireside chatting when Macartney fell fast asleep in his chair. The lady of the house addressed a question to him and there was no answer. The assistant called out, "Doctor!" Macartney opened his eyes and said to his assistant, "How many, Jimmy?" referring to the number of calls they had made. This had nothing to do with the lady's question, but she was unperturbed, and Macartney hid his laughter by bending over and petting the cat.

Even if he did fall asleep during one visit, Macartney's philosophy of pastoral visitation was a sound one: "I feel that before I preach, I must irrigate my soul with the joys and sorrows of my people." I might add that he had a good sense of humor, but rarely used it in the pulpit. To his Scottish soul, preaching was serious business, and a preacher never knew when he would give his last sermon.

Although he ministered to everyone, Macartney was recognized as a man's preacher. In 1930 he started the "Tuesday Noon Club for Businessmen" with only twelve men, and it grew to a total membership of two thousand, with an average weekly attendance of eight hundred. The men gathered at the church at 11:30 for lunch, and at 12:25 were led in a spirited hymn-sing for ten minutes. The male chorus then sang, and at 12:40 Macartney would speak for ten minutes. He said that those addresses were "straight-forward gospel and scriptural messages, but always adapted to the daily battle of the soul." He could have invited guest preachers to speak, but he wanted to get to know the men and make sure they had opportunities to trust Jesus Christ. Macartney preached five times a week and was rarely away from his own pulpit, and he especially sought to make the Sunday evening services special. Several of his sermon books grew out of the Sunday evening series.

Apart from his ministry, one of his interests was American history in general and Abraham Lincoln in particular. Though he was never recognized as a professional historian, he was highly respected for his knowledge and for the books he wrote in those fields, the first of which was *Lincoln and His Generals.* He also wrote *Lincoln and His Cabinet* and *Lincoln and His Bible.* He made what he called "pilgrimages" to Civil War battlefields, and the result was *Highways and Byways of the Civil War.* He wrote biographies of generals McClellan and Grant. He frequently used Civil War events as illustrations in his sermons.

During his busy ministerial career, Macartney published fifty-seven books, most of them collections of his sermons. While at Arch Street Presbyterian Church in Philadelphia, on October 10, 1915, he first preached the sermon "Come Before Winter." Based on 2 Timothy

4:9 and 21, the sermon calls for the wise use of opportunities and has a strong evangelistic emphasis. The sermon was received with such enthusiasm that he preached it annually at both Arch Street and First Presbyterian, Pittsburgh, and gave it frequently when he was a guest preacher elsewhere. The record shows that he preached the message more than forty times. In his book *Preaching without Notes*, he encouraged ministers not to "throw away" their efforts but to reuse messages that the Lord had especially blessed—but never, of course, as an excuse for laziness.

During his ministerial career, Macartney was offered professorial chairs in preaching, but he said that he would rather preach himself than try to tell others how to preach. He did deliver lectures in various schools, but his own example in the pulpit was his best instruction. In his autobiography *The Making of a Minister*, he wrote: "If I had my ministry to commence over again, I would devote more time to prayer, meditation, and the study of the Bible, although my preaching has been entirely on the Bible. I would take more time off, too, and not run the risk to health which I have run through too-long hours of work by day and by night."[5] Blessed are the balanced!

One of my uncles was vice president of a steel foundry in the Chicago area and an officer in the National Foundryman's Association, and he often had to go to Pittsburgh for meetings. He always arranged to be free on Sundays so he could attend First Presbyterian Church and hear Clarence Edward Macartney preach. His reports to us were exciting. "Dr. Macartney just stands there on the platform, Bible in hand, no notes, no manuscript, and talks to us like a friend. Hearing him preach is the best part of my trip."

How I wish I had been there!

46

William Whiting Borden
1887–1913

One Sunday at the Chicago Avenue Church (which later became Moody Church), Dr. R. A. Torrey challenged believers to surrender their lives in total consecration to Jesus Christ. Many stood to their feet, among them a seven-year-old lad in a sailor-suit. No doubt some of the adults near him smiled at his action, but the boy was deadly serious. In fact, that step of dedication controlled his life until, eighteen short years later, he died in Egypt, preparing to go to China as a missionary.

That lad was William Whiting Borden, the subject of Mrs. Howard Taylor's classic biography, *Borden of Yale '09*. Since there has arisen a generation that knows not Borden, I think it is time they got acquainted.

Borden was born November 1, 1887, with blue blood in his veins and a silver spoon in his mouth. Both the Bordens and the Whitings (his mother's family) came from distinguished English families noted for character and achievement. Bordens fought beside Duke William of Normandy at the Battle of Hastings. The first child born of European parents in Rhode Island was Matthew Borden; the year was 1638. Colonel William Whiting helped to found Hartford, Connecticut. Charles Whiting married Elizabeth Bradford, a descendant of Governor William Bradford of Plymouth Colony. William Bradford Whiting had a distinguished career during the Revolutionary War.

Borden's father was prominent in Chicago. He had made his money in silver mining in Colorado, a venture that was backed by Chicago merchant Marshall Field. But it was his mother who had the stronger influence on her son, for she was a devoted Christian. The fellowship and ministry at the Chicago Avenue Church meant much to her, and she had little interest in the city's society life. The fact that her ancestors came over on the *Mayflower* mattered little to Mrs. Borden. The fact that she was a Christian going to heaven was of far greater value.

William received the standard grade-school education in Chicago, and then went to Hill School in Pottsdown, Pennsylvania, for his high school training. There was a strong Christian influence on the campus, and famous preachers often spoke in chapel. "Campbell Morgan was there," William wrote his mother in 1903, "and preached a fine sermon in the morning, which was said to be the best ever given here. . . . Some of the fellows thought it was a little long, but I did not and wanted more."

The fact that William was the son of a millionaire did not interfere with his normal activities as a boy. He never tried to impress anyone; he was active in student sporting events, and he kept careful account of his money. He even sent his mother a monthly report of his spending. He served as chairman of the Missionary Study Band, and he listened carefully whenever Dr. Robert Speer, missionary statesman, came to speak to the students. William never forgot that act of consecration that he made when he was seven years old.

He graduated from Hill School in 1904, fourth in a class of forty-eight boys. He was only sixteen years old, endowed with unusual physical and mental ability, and too young to start university. It was decided that he should take a trip around the world. His traveling companion was Walter Erdman, a graduate of Princeton University and Seminary. They sailed from San Francisco on September 20, 1904, on the *S.S. Korea*. A number of missionary couples were on board, and William said that meeting them influenced him. In fact, the entire trip only strengthened his determination to be a missionary. "When I look ahead a few years," he wrote his parents, "it seems as though the only thing to do is to prepare for the foreign field."

William was moved by what he saw in Japan and China, and he was impressed by the work of the China Inland Mission. The sights in India stirred his heart, particularly the sacred city of Benares on the Ganges. A few years later, when a friend told William that he was "throwing his life away as a missionary," William calmly replied, "*You* have never seen heathenism."

But the trip involved more than sightseeing. "Walt and I have Bible study together every day when possible," William wrote his mother, "and I enjoy it very much. . . . I pray every day for all my dear family. I also pray that God will take my life into his hands and use it for the furtherance of His kingdom as He sees best." Then he added this significant sentence: "I have so much of everything in this life, and there are so many millions who have nothing and live in darkness!"

Back home in Chicago, Mrs. Borden shared with her husband William's desire to be a missionary. I get the impression that Mr. Borden was not as spiritually minded as his wife, and no doubt his son's decision greatly disturbed him. Had William Whiting Borden devoted his life to business interests, there is little question that he would have become a multimillionaire. But, as a missionary? That was quite something else!

"I am glad that you have told Father about my desire to be a missionary," William confided in his mother, writing from Rome. "I am thinking about it all the time, and looking forward to it with a good deal of anticipation. I know that I am not at all fitted or prepared yet, but in the next four or five years I ought to be able to prepare myself." A book on missions by Robert Speer especially touched him. "When I got through reading," he wrote his mother, "I knelt right down and prayed more earnestly than I have for some time for the mission work and for God's plan for my life. . . . Pray that I may be guided in everything, small and great!"

Dr. Torrey was preaching in London when William and Walt arrived there, and they attended some of his meetings. At the close of one of the meetings, William stood again to reaffirm the commitment he had made to Christ more than ten years before. This new step of dedication seemed to give him a greater burden for the lost and a new freedom in personal witness.

William would have preferred to attend Moody Bible Institute and then go to college, but his parents decided he should go to Yale University instead. He entered the freshman class in 1905 and discovered that, in spite of the school's historic Christian background, there was a lack of spiritual life on campus. "The great majority [of students] smoke, go to the theatre Saturday night and do their studying on Sunday," he wrote home. "Rather a hopeless state of affairs! However, there are some fine Christian men in College and in my own class too, I believe. And I hope to be able to do something, by the grace of God, to help in the right direction."

And he did. He refused to join any secret societies or fraternities, and he chose friends whose spiritual interests were akin to his own. He boldly witnessed for Christ and backed up that witness with such a consistent life that even the unbelievers had to admit he was a Christian. He chose two texts as his mottos for his college years: "Wherewithal shall a young man cleanse his way? By taking heed thereto according to thy word. . . . Thy word have I hid in mine heart that I might not sin against thee" (Ps. 119:9, 11).

William became burdened for the indigent people in the seaport town of New Haven where Yale was located. The result was the founding of the Yale Hope Mission, where William often went to witness for Christ and to help those whose lives had been battered by sin. "What has impressed you most since you came to America?" Dr. Henry Frost, China Inland Mission executive, asked a visitor. The reply: "The sight of that young millionaire kneeling with his arm around a 'bum' in the Yale Hope Mission." Hundreds of lives were dramatically changed through the gospel witness at the mission.

While at Yale, William served as a delegate to the Student Volunteer Movement conference at Nashville, Tennessee. The one speaker who stood out to the young missionary candidate was Dr. Samuel Zwemer, noted missionary to the Muslims. When William learned that there were fifteen million Muslims in China, without a single missionary, his interest was aroused; and he committed himself to that ministry "should the Lord confirm the call." Four years later, as a delegate to the historic Edinburgh Missionary Conference, when introduced Borden stated publicly that he planned to minister to the Muslims of northwest China.

He graduated from Yale in 1909 and that same year entered Princeton Seminary. He was also named a trustee of Moody Bible Institute. The next year, he became a member of the North American Council of the China Inland Mission. William's father had died in 1906, and his mother moved to Princeton, New Jersey, to be near her son during those important years of preparation. Two interesting facts should be noted about his seminary years: he taught a Sunday school class in an African Methodist Episcopal Church, and he gave away $70,000 to various Christian causes.

The story now draws to a rapid close. He graduated from seminary in 1912 and, on September 9, was ordained at Moody Church in Chicago. Dr. James M. Gray preached the ordination sermon, and Dr. John Timothy Stone, pastor of Chicago's Fourth Presbyterian Church, gave the charge to the candidate. The newspapers gave great publicity to the event—so strange it was that a young millionaire would bury himself in China as a missionary. William wrote to his school friends: "I am sorry that there was such unnecessary publicity, and hope you fellows will discount what was said very liberally."

Borden spent the next three months speaking in various colleges, representing the cause of world missions. On December 17, 1912, he sailed for Egypt, where he planned to study with Dr. Zwemer and get a grasp of the Muslim religion and culture. He threw himself into literature distribution and whatever ministry would help to reach the lost. But just at Easter season, 1913, he became ill with cerebral meningitis and died on April 9. The news of his death was reported around the world, with memorial services held in many schools and churches. In his will, Borden left his fortune to various Christian ministries. In his life and death he left to all of us an example of true devotion to Christ and to the things that matter most.

Why should such a gifted life be cut short? Perhaps the best answer was given by Sherwood Day, one of Borden's missionary friends. "I have absolutely no feeling of a life cut short," Day wrote. "A life abandoned to Christ cannot be cut short." From many parts of the world Mrs. Borden received letters telling of the impact of her son's life and death on Christian students and missionaries. Dr. Zwemer, in the funeral message, summarized the meaning of Borden's testimony: "By some, the victory has to be won over poverty . . . but Borden won the victory over an environment of wealth. He felt that life consisted not in 'the abundance of things that a man possesseth,' but in the abundance of things which possess the man."

After all, it is not the length of a person's life that matters, but the strength of one's influence for God. A Judas would read Borden's life and sneer, "Why this waste!" but our Lord would evaluate it differently. William Whiting Borden never got to minister to the Muslims in China, but God knew the intent of his heart and rewarded him accordingly. Borden's desire was to magnify Christ "whether it be by life, or by death," and God gave him his desire.

One lesson is clear: never underestimate the decisions made by a child or a young man. At the age of seven, Borden consecrated himself to Christ. When a freshman at Yale, he wrote in his notebook: "Lord Jesus, I take hands off, as far as my life is concerned. I put Thee on the throne in my heart. Change, cleanse, use me as Thou shalt choose. I take the full power of Thy Holy Spirit. I thank Thee." Then he added this revealing sentence: "May never know a tithe of the result until Morning."

The words of martyred Jim Elliot come to mind: "He is no fool to give what he cannot keep, to gain what he cannot lose."[1]

And the words of our Savior: "He that loveth his life shall lose it; and he that hateth his life in this world shall keep it unto life eternal" (John 12:25).

47

Alva Jay McClain
1888–1968

Here is our preacher!" That's what farmer and Church of the Brethren preacher Walter Scott McClain joyfully announced on April 11, 1888, in Aurelia, Iowa, when his wife Mary presented him with their first son, and he wrote in the family Bible "Alva Jay McClain." Bible-reading relatives supposed that "Alva" came from the "Alvah" in Genesis 36:40, one of Esau's descendants, but they didn't understand the "Jay." In fact, for years, most people thought Alva J. McClain had only a single initial for a middle name, like Harry S. Truman. Why his father chose that name is still a mystery.

Hearing that there was good land in the Arizona Territory, the McClains moved there with their four children in 1898, only to discover that it wasn't exactly the Garden of Eden. Irrigation, of course, was the major problem and would be until the government built a dam. In 1899 they relocated to Los Angeles, where Walter rented a house for his family and sublet rooms to guests. Alva enjoyed the big city with its public library, stores, streetcars, and train station, but the family's California sojourn wouldn't last long. Walter read about a Christian cooperative some Church of the Brethren leaders had formed at Sunnyside, Washington, and he decided it was better to raise the children among Christians than in the big city. Just to be sure, he took a train to Washington to see for himself.

Shortly before Christmas in 1900, Mary got the anticipated summons from Walter, packed, and took the train to Mabton, Washington, the closest stop to Sunnyside. There Walter met his family with a horse and wagon and they drove to their new home. When they arrived at Sunnyside, they saw sand, unpainted wooden shacks, and not much green vegetation; but Walter assured his wife that one day that desert would "blossom like the rose." He was right. It took time, but thanks to irrigation, eventually that area became a fruitful land of orchards and truck gardens.

The children were enrolled in school and also did their share of work on the farm, but when Alva turned sixteen he dropped out of church and devoted himself to sports, dancing, playing cards, smoking, enjoying life with his school friends, and quarterbacking the high school football team. His parents wisely didn't preach or nag but simply prayed and maintained their personal and family devotions at home. Alva was to be their preacher, and God in his time would save him and call him into his service.

Alva bluffed his way through his senior year in high school and almost had to repeat the year, but he was permitted to take a special test that, if he passed, would earn him his diploma. He read the assigned books, easily passed the test, and graduated with his class in 1908. He went to the University of Washington where he again got involved in athletics and excelled. A serious accident while playing baseball sent him to the hospital and then home to recuperate. His father and a friend had founded the Sunnyside Nursery Company, and while home from college, Alva joined the business and became a skillful nurseryman among the famous Yakima Valley apple trees.

He also started thinking about marriage. One day a new resident arrived in town, Josephine Gingrich from Iowa, and Alva claimed her as his girl. She wasn't a professed Christian, but neither was Alva. Friendship turned to love and they were engaged in August 1910 and married the next year on June 7. Their marriage lasted fifty-seven years, until Alva's death in 1968.

In August 1912, they were both converted to faith in Christ at a prophetic conference led by popular Church of the Brethren preacher Louis S. Bauman. Alva's father suggested he take the afternoon off and go to Sunnyside Brethren Church with Josephine to hear the guest preacher. Their arrival at the church raised some eyebrows, but God began to deal with the young couple and they returned for the evening meeting. When the preacher gave the invitation, Alva said to his wife, "I'm going down there." She asked, "Can I go with you?" Both were soundly converted.

Their new life in Christ brought changes in their ambitions, and Alva decided not to return to the University of Washington. More than anything else, he wanted to study God's Word. He had heard God's call and wanted to obey. In 1913 they moved to Long Beach, California, where Louis Bauman was pastoring First Brethren Church, and they listened to the Word expounded and grew in their Christian life. Sensing they had a call to ministry, Bauman suggested that the young couple attend the Bible Institute of Los Angeles, which they did for one year. Then he advised Alva to study at Xenia Theological Seminary in Xenia, Ohio, where he earned a Master of Theology degree. Alva also studied at nearby Antioch College and at Occidental College, graduating from the latter school with a BA, "with highest honors."

He served as pastor of First Brethren Church in Philadelphia from 1918 to 1923, and during that time was Professor of Apologetics at the Philadelphia School of the Bible. The next two years he was Professor of Theology at Ashland College in Ashland, Ohio, and then returned for two years of teaching at the Bible Institute of Los Angeles. When Ashland College founded a seminary, he was called to be Professor of Theology and Apologetics (1930–37). During those years, liberalism crept into the school in spite of the protests and opposition of the orthodox members of the faculty. It was a sad time for Alva and Josephine McClain and the friends who stood with them, but denominational politics and board compromise precipitated a board vote on June 1, 1937, that meant the end of Ashland Seminary.

Believing the Lord was on their side, the conservative minority met that night for prayer and discussion relative to starting a new seminary. Providentially, Dr. Bauman was in town and he joined them. The Lord directed them to begin a new school where Brethren young people could train for Christian service, and Grace Theological Seminary was born. Dr. Bauman wrote a check as the first contribution. When the news got out, the men were accused of dividing the denomination and failing to submit to authority, but like the apostles, they replied, "We ought to obey God rather than men" (Acts 5:29).

The school opened on October 4, 1937, in a church in Akron, Ohio, but the facilities were too confining. Dr. William E. Biederwolf, Director of the Winona Lake (Ind.) Christian Assembly and Bible Conference, invited them to relocate. They accepted his invitation, and in 1939 Winona Lake became their permanent address. Classes initially met in a church, until 1951, when McClain Hall was dedicated on the school's own campus. Over the years, God has provided buildings, faculty, and staff for the growing seminary, and in 1953, Grace College of Liberal Arts opened with Dr. McClain as president.

Any student who attended his classes would say that Dr. McClain was a gifted teacher. However, he didn't suffer fools gladly, but was all business when it came to studying God's Word. In class one day, a student asked, "If God already knows whether or not I'm going to pass my theology exam, why should I study?" Dr. McClain replied, "Young man, if you don't study for this exam, you are predestined to fail!"

His class on Romans was a foundational course in which Dr. McClain taught "all the counsel of God." The lectures had originally been delivered to his congregation at First Brethren Church in Philadelphia, and one of the members had made a stenographic report. This formed the basis for his book *The Gospel of God's Grace: Romans*, originally published in 1973 by Moody Press and reprinted today by BMH Books. Dr. McClain's successor, Dr. Herman A. Hoyt, heard the lectures when he was a student at Grace Seminary and assisted in editing the manuscript. This book is one of the finest overviews of Romans I have read. Before you tackle the detailed commentaries, carefully read this book.

Daniel's Prophecy of the Seventy Weeks was published by Zondervan in 1940, with a new edition released in 1969. It is an excellent discussion of that important Messianic prophecy. *Law and Grace: A Study of New Testament Concepts as They Relate to the Christian Life* is also published by BMH Books and is a balanced discussion of the subject. Dr. McClain didn't divorce theology from practical Christian living.

But I think his finest book is *The Greatness of the Kingdom: An Inductive Study of the Kingdom of God*. It was originally published jointly in 1968 by Moody Press and BMH Books, but today BMH Books is the publisher. I treasure my copy for three reasons. First, the book is biblical and untangles much of the confused "kingdom theology" that still remains from the liberal era in American theology. Second, Dr. McClain autographed the book. Third, he handed the book to me personally, with a smile. I was the junior member of a three-man preaching team at a Grace Seminary conference, and each of us received a copy. The other two men were Dr. Torrey Johnson, one of the founders of Youth for Christ, and Dr. John Walvoord, president of Dallas Seminary. Why I was there was a mystery to me, but I'm glad I was.

McClain was also a member of the Editorial Committee of the *New Scofield Reference Bible*, published in 1967. He was dispensational in his approach to Scripture, and said "Christianity is not a philosophy. But Christianity has a philosophy—the best and the brightest of all philosophies"[1]

He was not a robust man, but battled poor health most of his life and experienced six major surgeries. Apart from the grace of God, he could not have accomplished as much as he did—when you consider his responsibilities in teaching and administration, as well as his participation in denominational activities and ministries to the church at large. For fifty years he was a trustee and Candidate Secretary for the Foreign Mission Society of the Brethren Church, and twice he served as Moderator of the General Assembly. He was a founding member of the Evangelical Theological Society and a member of the Board of Directors of the Winona Lake Christian Assembly—and for nearly ten years secretary of the board.

He retired from Grace College and Seminary in May 1962, and in 1968 moved with his wife, Josephine, to a retirement facility in Iowa, where on November 11 of that same year he was called to Glory. In his final chapel message as president, "Remember Jesus Christ," his text was 2 Timothy 2:8. "You may forget me, what I have said, and what I have done. I shall not complain. I ask of you but one thing: that you will always 'remember Jesus Christ.'" He added, "Remember who He is, and you will never be ashamed to confess Him before men. Remember who He is and you will never have any doubts about your eternal salvation."

We should remember Dr. Alva J. McClain, and in remembering him, remember Jesus Christ, the Savior and Lord he loved and served so faithfully.

48

A. W. Tozer

1897–1963

From 1928 to 1959, A. W. Tozer pastored Southside Alliance Church in Chicago and functioned as the conscience of evangelicalism at large. I heard him preach many times—always with profit—and waited for his books to be published as impatiently as a detective-story addict waits for the next installment of the current serial. I still reread his books regularly, and always find in them something new to think about. This does not mean I always agreed with Tozer. There were times when I felt he was leading a parade of one down a dead-end street, such as when he vigorously opposed Christian movies. His sometimes acid criticisms of new Bible translations and of churches that "majored in counting noses" were but small defects in an otherwise straight and sturdy wall. There was an intensity about his preaching, as there is about his writing. Tozer walked with God and knew him intimately. To listen to Tozer preach was as safe as opening the door of a blast furnace!

To prevent a generation arising that knows not Tozer, I want to devote the first half of this chapter to the man and his books, then I want to consider some other Christian mystics.

The official biography of Tozer is written by David J. Fant Jr. and is entitled *A. W. Tozer: A Twentieth-Century Prophet.* Unfortunately, the book does not tell too much about the man, and what it does tell might have been written for a press release or for page one of an appreciation booklet. The first chapter takes us from his birth (April 21, 1897) to his death (May 12, 1963), and the remaining eleven chapters concentrate on Tozer's writing, summarizing what he believed and why he believed it. If I understand Tozer's philosophy of books and writing, he would disagree with Fant's approach. "Read the man himself!" he would say. "Don't read *about* the man, or what some writer says about the man. Read the man himself!" While I appreciate the excellent quotations Fant selected and agree with his analysis of Tozer's thinking, I still feel that getting acquainted with this vibrant writer via a biographer is like going to a flower show over the telephone. I suggest you read Tozer's books first, then read Fant's biography.

Begin with *The Pursuit of God*, one of the best devotional books ever written by an American pastor. As your grandmother used to say about her home medicines, "It's good for what ails you!" *The Pursuit of God* polishes the lenses of my soul and helps me see better. It cures the fever that often makes a man mistake activity for ministry. It rebukes my lack of worship. For these reasons (and many more), I try to read the book at least once a year. Follow with *The Divine Conquest*, then with *The Knowledge of the Holy*, a book that, to me, is the finest modern devotional treatment of the attributes of God. Once you have read these three volumes, you will have a grasp of the essentials of Tozer's thinking about God, Christ, the Holy Spirit, the church, the Bible, and the responsibility of the believer in today's world. You are then prepared to launch into his books of spiritual essays, such as *The Root of the Righteous, Born After Midnight, Of God and Men, That Incredible Christian, Man: The Dwelling Place of God*, and (if you enjoy poetry and hymnody) *The Christian Book of Mystical Verse*. All of his books are published by Christian Publications, with the exception of *The Knowledge of the Holy*, which is published by Harper. Nearly all of these essays originally appeared as editorials in *The Alliance Witness*, which Tozer edited for many years and which was perhaps the only evangelical publication people read primarily for the editorials!

Let me suggest that you *not* read these books the way you read other books—attempting to finish them quickly, perhaps in one sitting (a phrase Tozer despised). Read Tozer leisurely, meditatively, almost as a worship experience. Read each essay slowly, as though the writer were chatting with you personally, in front of the friendly fireplace in his living room. Read with your heart; keep your ear tuned to that "other voice" that will surely speak to you and remind you of the truths of God's Word. My experience has been that, when reading a book by Tozer, some passage will cause me to put down the book, pick up my Bible, and then start thinking about some truth on my own. And this is exactly what Tozer would want! "The best book is not one that informs merely," he wrote, "but one that stirs the reader up to inform himself."[1] I try to keep a notebook at hand when I read any book, but especially when I read Tozer.

After becoming acquainted with his devotional essays, read the two biographies he wrote: *Wingspread*, the life of A. B. Simpson, founder of the Christian and Missionary Alliance, and *Let My People Go!* the life of missionary Robert A. Jaffray. Then investigate the volumes of sermons that have recently appeared, edited by Gerald B. Smith. Frankly, this series does not excite me. I can hear Tozer *in* these messages, but I believe he would have edited this material differently. I fear this may be prejudice on my part, but I prefer the incisiveness of the essays to the expansiveness of the sermons. But, since they are "genuine Tozer," I have them on my shelf and I read them.

Aiden Wilson Tozer (he preferred his initials, and who can blame him) considered himself an "evangelical mystic." Unfortunately the word *mystic* has never been a popular word in the evangelical vocabulary, especially in this day of activism and statistics. To most evangelicals, a mystic is an odd person who sees visions and hears voices and is about as useful to the church as a spare tire on a bobsled. If that were what mysticism is, I would want no part of it. But that is *not* mysticism; it is only a caricature of it. A mystic is simply a person who: (1) sees a real spiritual world beyond the world of sense, (2) seeks to please God rather than the crowd, (3) cultivates a close fellowship with God, sensing his presence everywhere, and (4) relates his experience to the practical things of life.

In his preface to *The Christian Book of Mystical Verse*, Tozer put it this way:

> I refer to the evangelical mystic who has been brought by the gospel into intimate fellowship with the Godhead. His theology is no less and no more than is taught in the Christian Scriptures. . . . He differs from the ordinary orthodox Christian only because he experiences his faith down in the depths of his sentient being while the other does not. He exists in a world of spiritual reality. He is quietly, deeply and sometimes almost ecstatically aware of the presence of God in his own nature and in the world around him. His religious experience is something elemental, as old as time and the creation. It is immediate acquaintance with God by union with the eternal son.[2]

Tozer's essay "Bible Taught or Spirit Taught?" is a good summary of his views on practical mysticism: "It is altogether possible to be instructed in the rudiments of the faith and still have no real understanding of the whole thing," he wrote. "And it is possible to go on to become expert in Bible doctrine and not have spiritual illumination, with the result that a veil remains over the mind, preventing it from apprehending the truth in its spiritual essence."[3] Tozer's sermons often confront us with these questions: Is God *real* to you? Is your Christian experience a set of definitions, a list of orthodox doctrines, or a living relationship with God? Do you have a firsthand experience with him, or a secondhand experience through others? Is your heart hungering and thirsting after personal holiness? These questions are applicable today, perhaps more than we dare to admit.

Fant, at the end of his biography, listed the books and authors that most influenced Tozer, and this list is something of a basic bibliography on the mystics. I am sure that many evangelical pastors today have either never been exposed to this wealth of devotional writing or have purposely avoided it, so I recommend the list to you. However, before you spend your book budget in securing these volumes, I suggest that you sample them in a manner that is quite easy and (best of all) inexpensive. The Upper Room (Nashville, Tennessee) publishes a series of attractive, pocket-size booklets called "The Great Devotional Classics." I believe there are thirty titles in the series, ranging from William Law (who strongly influenced the Wesleys) to William Temple (archbishop of Canterbury until his death in 1944). I suggest you carry one of these booklets with you to read in spare minutes. Each booklet contains from thirty to forty pages; there is a biographical introduction and a brief discussion of the influence of the writer (or the book) in church history. The thirty or more writers (or titles, where the writers are anonymous) cover a wide spectrum of theological and ecclesiastical groups.

You will find John Knox, prophet of the Reformation in Scotland; François Fenelon, close friend to Madame Guyon; George Fox, founder of the Quakers; John Wesley and Francis Asbury, the great Methodist leaders; Henry Scougal, whose *Life of God in the Soul of Man* is easily the greatest devotional work to come out of Scotland; Søren Kierkegaard, the melancholy Danish philosopher; Dietrich Bonhoeffer, the German theologian; and even Thomas Kelly, the young Quaker writer whose untimely death halted an exciting career. There are selections from anonymous works: *Theologia Germanica*, which Luther put alongside the Bible and Augustine's writings, and *Cloud of Unknowing*, which Tozer loved to quote.

If you profit from this excursion into the land of Christian mysticism, then search for another volume that must be on your devotional shelf. Unfortunately, like many fine books, it is out of print. Abingdon Press ought to reissue this book and make it available to this generation of preachers. I refer to *The Fellowship of the Saints*, an anthology of devotional writings edited by Thomas S. Kepler, for many years professor at Oberlin College. Kepler was an ardent student of the mystics, and in this large (800-page) volume he gives the best of their writings in a chronological sequence that enables the reader to trace the influence of one writer on the next. He starts with Clement of Rome and ends with selections from twentieth-century writers. To be sure, there is some chaff here; but there is so much fine wheat that the chaff does not upset me. Look for a copy in used-book stores; I hope you find one!

Kepler compiled another anthology that you may want to secure: *The Evelyn Underhill Reader.* Evelyn Underhill was a well-known British mystic who died in 1941. Her books, *Mysticism, Practical Mysticism,* and *Worship* are almost standard texts on these subjects. Unfortunately she was never quite sure of her theology, and it is here she parts company with Tozer. She confessed to being "a modernist on many points." But some of her personal insights are helpful, and therefore she should be read. Like poison, these matters should be "handled" but not permitted into one's system!

Harper and Row has published two basic books that should be in your library: *Christian Perfection,* written by François Fenelon and published in 1947, and *Treatises and Sermons of Meister Eckhart,* published in 1958. Fenelon's book is priceless for devotional reading—a chapter a day. Here is a man who conducted "spiritual conferences" in the court of Louis XIV! Chapter 1 is "On the Use of Time" and is one of the finest treatments of this elusive subject, from a spiritual point of view, that you will find anywhere. Chapter 2 deals with "Recreation." Chapter 8 considers "Fidelity in Little Things." Every pastor will want to read chapter 14, "Dryness and Distraction." These chapters are not long, but they are deep and profoundly practical. I cannot recommend this book too highly. Eckhart was a German mystic (1260–1327) whose purity of life gave great power to his preaching. Selections from his many writings are available in different editions, the most popular of which is probably *After Supper in the Refectory: A Series of Instructions,* published in 1917. Tozer recommended this book. The volume referred to above contains selections from *Talks of Instruction* as well as material from other writings.

If you wish to purchase a copy of *Cloud of Unknowing,* the edition edited by Evelyn Underhill is perhaps the best. The introduction by the editor and the glossary of terms are both very helpful to those not conversant with mystical writings. However, I must confess that, so far, this book has failed to reach me, although here and there some statements have struck fire. The repeated phrase "O Ghostly friend in God" still makes me chuckle. Out of respect for the anonymous author, I try to chuckle in a mystical way, but I fear I do not always succeed. As I grow spiritually, I am sure I will better appreciate this book.

The mystics wrote to cultivate the inner man, and certainly this is a neglected activity in our churches today. We have more Marthas than Marys! But, in the long run, the ideal Christian will not be one or the other: he will be a balance of both. Worship and work will not compete; they will cooperate. This is the contribution the evangelical mystics can make to our lives, and I trust you will sincerely give them the opportunity to do so.

Martyn Lloyd-Jones and I were discussing the mystics over dinner one evening, and he related an interesting experience. With his permission I repeat it here.

"Dr. Tozer and I shared a conference years ago," he said, "and I appreciated his ministry and his fellowship very much. One day he said to me, 'Lloyd-Jones, you and I hold just about the same position on spiritual matters, but we have come to this position by different routes.'

" 'How do you mean?' I asked.

" 'Well,' Tozer replied, 'you came by way of the Puritans and I came by way of the mystics.' And, you know, he was right!"

Which perhaps goes to prove that doctrine and devotion have been joined together by God and that no man dare put them asunder. Our understanding of doctrine ought to lead us into greater devotion to Christ, and our deeper devotion ought to make us better servants and soul-winners. Jesus beautifully joined both together when he said: "Abide in me and I in you . . . for without me, ye can do nothing." This is the message of the evangelical mystics, a message we desperately need to hear today.

49

W. E. Sangster
1900–1960

When you visit Westminster Abbey in London, be sure to also visit the nearby Methodist house of worship known as Westminster Central Hall. For sixteen years, from 1939 to 1955, William Edwin Sangster pastored the flock that met in that house of worship—and he not only pastored the flock but, during World War II, managed an air raid shelter in the basement of the building. For 1,688 nights he ministered to the physical, emotional, and spiritual needs of all kinds of people, and at the same time he wrote and preached exciting sermons, earned a PhD, led hundreds of people to faith in Christ, and established himself as a worthy successor to John Wesley as one of Methodism's great leaders.

Sangster was born in London on June 5, 1900. He was nine years old when he identified himself with the Radnor Street Mission in his neighborhood, one of the branch ministries of the Wesley Chapel on City Road. In October 1913, the superintendent of the mission, Frank Wimpory, led Sangster to the Lord, and in a short time the lad became active in soul-winning activities.

The Radnor Street Mission was not only the scene of Sangster's conversion, but also the place where he met Margaret Conway in

1916 and fell in love with her. Ten years later they were married. He preached his first sermon at the mission on February 11, 1917. His father wanted him to become an accountant, but his Sunday school teacher, Robert Flenly, urged him to consider the ministry. He did. God called him, and he surrendered.

After spending time in the army, he entered college and worked hard to prepare himself for the ministry. One of his problems was his accent, which smacked of his London upbringing. He took private lessons in elocution and often spent hours reading sermons aloud or practicing recitations. In his fine biography of his father, *Doctor Sangster*, Paul E. Sangster related that these elocution lessons were very trying to students in adjacent rooms. One day, when Sangster had repeated for the tenth time "Who shall deliver me from the body of this death?" a student knocked at the door and asked, "Will *I* do?" But the practice paid dividends, and Sangster mastered the art of public speaking.

He was probationary minister in the Bognor Circuit from 1923 to 1926, ministering in several Methodist churches. On July 27, 1926, he was ordained at the Wesley Chapel in York; two weeks later he married his childhood sweetheart. He made it very clear to her that he would not be a handyman around the house (he was very unhandy!) or a gardener or a dishwasher, but that he would love her and make her happy—and he kept his word. His book *He Is Able* he dedicated "to Margaret, my wife, with whom it is as easy to keep in love as to fall in love." But his growing ministry often took him away from home, and it is probable that his death on May 24, 1960, was brought on partly by overwork. "I just can't do enough!" was the motto of his life. Yet, on his 1957 Christmas greeting he wrote, "Slow me down, Lord!" Alexander Whyte always advised pastors to "take long holidays," but Sangster was not made in that mold.

His first official charge after ordination was at Conway in North Wales. I have visited this beautiful town on Colwyn Bay, walked across its famous suspension bridge, and investigated the ruins of its historic Conway Castle. What a place for a young man to begin his ministry! He pastored two Methodist churches there, yet he said that he felt as if he were "perpetually on a holiday." Before long the congregations were filling the churches and his reputation as a preacher was growing. His sanctified sense of humor at first upset some of the Welsh saints, but in time they grew to love him and to appreciate his balanced approach to Christian living. In 1929 he moved to Liverpool, where again he pastored two churches, and again the churches were filled. It was at Liverpool that Sangster went through a deep spiritual crisis, the details of which are unknown. "Not even my mother knew exactly what was wrong," his son wrote. "She only knew something *was* wrong."[1]

After his father's death, his son Paul found a handwritten "spiritual analysis" buried in the bottom drawer of the desk. It was dated "18.9.30" and was clearly the record of the spiritual conflict that Sangster had gone through at that time—in spite of large congregations and obvious success in his ministry. It begins, "I am a minister of God and yet my private life is a failure in these ways. . . . " Then he listed eight areas of defeat. He concluded: "I have lost grace. . . . I have lost joy. . . . I have lost taste for my work. . . . I feel a failure." What was the answer? "Pray. Pray. Pray. Strive after holiness like an athlete prepares for a race. The secret is in prayer." He ultimately found victory, although at times his depression was so acute that he considered resigning from the ministry. No doubt this valley experience helped him in later years, especially during the war when he had to encourage so many brokenhearted people.

In 1932, the Sangsters moved to Scarborough, and at first the decision seemed to be a mistake. The church was "run" by four powerful men, three of whom were very wealthy, and they handed down their decisions as the will of God. One of their decisions was that "famous guest preachers" occupy the pulpit ten Sundays during the year, but they soon discovered that the "big names" drew smaller congregations than did their own pastor! The four generals, realizing their error, then offered Sangster a bonus for preaching in his own pulpit! In the end, pastoral leadership prevailed, but there were several skirmishes and not a few battles.

I cannot help but pass along a story about one of the members of Queen Street Church in Scarborough, who happened to be a bit "backward," because almost every church has its eccentric member—someone who is both loved and laughed at, scolded and sheltered. The man in Queen Street was a barber who felt it was his duty to witness to his customers, but often he was not careful in his approach. After lathering a man for a shave, the concerned barber picked up his razor and said, "Sir, are you prepared to meet your God?" Needless to say, the customer fled with the lather still on his face. This same brother was as eccentric in his praying as he was in his witnessing. Once he opened his prayer with "O Lord, Thou wilt have noticed in the evening paper." I can just see Sangster chuckling to himself and praying for his odd friend.

In 1936 Sangster was asked to take the Brunswick Church in Leeds and thus follow the well-known preacher and psychologist Leslie Weatherhead. Every pastor ought to read Sangster's soul-searching analysis of this call. It begins: "A ferment of thought in my mind in these days—a shrinking from the task."[2] What faithful minister of the Word has not felt that way at one time or another! But it was during this time of self-searching that Sangster felt his call to summon Methodism back to evangelism and revival. "Something else has come too," he wrote. "A sense of certainty that God does not want me only for a preacher. He wants me also for a leader—a leader in Methodism."[3] And a leader he did become, not only during his three years in Leeds but more during those sixteen remarkable years at Westminster Central Hall in London.

On September 3, 1939, William Sangster began his ministry at Westminster, and one of his first tasks during that morning worship service was to announce that Britain and Germany were officially at war. A year later the devastating air raids began, and Sangster turned the church basement into a shelter; night after night he lived with the people, encouraged them, and ultimately led many of them to Christ. The Sunday services continued, and the sanctuary was usually full. One Easter Sunday a lady visitor arrived too late to get a seat and was offered by the steward a seat on one of the stone steps in the choir. Of course this was an insult, and she stalked away, muttering, "If that's the way you treat visitors, no wonder the churches are empty!"

So successful was Sangster as a preacher-evangelist that in 1955 he was appointed general secretary of the Home Mission Department, and under his leadership personal evangelism, prayer, and personal holiness became important matters in Methodist churches across the country. His sermons, books, articles, and personal contacts were used of God to awaken not only his own denomination, but other groups, to the importance of winning the lost to Christ. He conducted preaching seminars, evangelism clinics, and other meetings in scores of cities, always hoping to rekindle in the hearts of Methodist preachers and lay leaders the fire that had burned in Wesley's heart. But in 1957 physical problems definitely slowed him down, and in 1958 the diagnosis was made: progressive muscular atrophy—cause, unknown; cure, unknown.

When Sangster found out he was slowly dying, he made four resolutions: "I will never complain. I will keep the home bright. I will count my blessings. I will try to turn it to gain." Later he wrote: "There have been great gains already from my sickness. I live in the present. I am grateful for little things. I have more time—and use it—for prayer." For the next thirty months he experienced the slow paralysis of his muscles, finally being able to move only two fingers. With them he communicated with others by writing, but ultimately even that became illegible. On May 24, 1960, he died. It was Wesley Day, a providential occurrence that must have pleased Sangster no end. More than 1,500 people attended the memorial service at Westminster Central Hall on June 3. Sangster's close friend Professor H. Cecil Pawson gave the address. You will find it, plus a brief biographical sketch and three sermons, in the book *Sangster of Westminster*.

Fortunately, Sangster left us at least fifteen books and many articles and pamphlets. There are two volumes of *Westminster Sermons*. *Sangster's Special Day Sermons* was the last volume he wrote, and in this country it was published by Abingdon. He left over a thousand sermon manuscripts when he died, but he wanted none of them published. His first book was *Why Jesus Never Wrote a Book* (1932). Other titles include: *God Does Guide Us, He Is Able, These Things Abide, Let Me Commend,* and two excellent studies in Christian holiness: *The Path to Perfection* (his doctoral thesis) and *The Pure in Heart.* But Sangster's books on preaching are, to me, more valuable than his sermons, although the sermons clearly show us how he applied his homiletical principles. Secure and read *The Approach to Preaching, The Craft of Sermon Construction,* and *The Craft of Sermon Illustration.*

Sangster's sermons have three characteristics: simplicity, clarity, and intensity. You can understand him! Early in his ministry he formed the habit of reading his messages to his wife and deleting or revising anything she did not clearly understand. He constantly sought the clearest way to express Bible truth, and nobody could describe his messages as one man described P. T. Forsythe's—"fireworks in a fog!" Furthermore, Sangster was a master of illustrations, and his book on the subject is one of the best in the field. I fear that those who have criticized him in this area have not seriously read him. Sangster did not advocate "artificial illustrations" or "sky-scraper sermons—one story on top of another." He used illustrations, and he did it well!

His messages throb with intensity. They reveal a preacher who loved people and who was desperately concerned with helping them spiritually. I once heard a famous Bible teacher, now deceased, boast that he "preached only to the four square feet in front of his face!" Sangster preached to people, to both the mind and the heart, and he prepared his messages with the listener in view. His sermons were not the cold, academic productions of the learned professor (although he *was* learned); they were the warm, pastoral pleadings of a man who pursued personal holiness and who sought to make the gospel of Christ meaningful to the man on the street. In one of his lectures, Sangster suggested that the secret of "unction" in preaching is "personal holiness and . . . a passionate love of souls."[4]

No matter how you measure him, William Sangster was a big man. He had a big heart for lost souls and for all true Christians everywhere. He had a big vision of revival in his denomination and in all the churches, a vision of a nation stirred for Jesus Christ. He was happy to hear of any man's success in the ministry and never criticized a fellow pastor or envied his successes. He once prayed at a meeting of some two thousand ministers, "Lord, we don't mind who is second as long as Thou art first!" He left behind a big store of homiletical wealth for us to use. I suggest you start investigating it very soon.

50

William Culbertson
1905–1971

I n whatever man does without God, he must fail miserably—or succeed miserably."[1] So wrote saintly George MacDonald, and his counsel is desperately needed by Christian leaders and organizations today. An evil idea is abroad in the land that spiritual life is not important to spiritual leadership. So long as the leader projects a "successful image" and manifests "dynamic," he will be successful. Holiness of life, spiritual growth, and obedience to the Word of God have been replaced by promotion, public relations, and obedience to the latest conclusions of the Madison Avenue geniuses.

I do not want to be misunderstood. Christian organizations ought to learn all they can about business methods and leadership principles. Our Lord reminds us that "the children of this world are in their generation wiser than the children of light" (Luke 16:8), and we ought to borrow their wisdom (shortsighted as it is) and put it to work for God. But we dare not undermine the spiritual foundations on which God's work is built. Alas, there are Christian organizations today that have a "form of godliness" (so as not to upset the donors), but in which godliness *as a force* is sadly lacking. Not that there are chinks in the armor; sad to say, the armor was taken off long ago and the organization left naked and ashamed before her enemies. To change the picture, the veneer on the building will peel off little by little, and the foundation of sand will crumble. One day the whole edifice will fall, and a great fall it will be.

In my own ministry, I have met several Christian leaders who knew how to exercise spiritual leadership without sacrificing good business principles. To borrow the old Youth for Christ slogan, they were "geared to the times but anchored to the Rock." One such man was William Culbertson, bishop of the Reformed Episcopal Church, dean of education at Moody Bible Institute (1942–48), and president of that school for twenty-three fruitful years. Wilbur M. Smith stated it perfectly: "My first impression and the lasting one is that he is a man of God."

William Culbertson was born on November 18, 1905, into a very godly home in Philadelphia. He was an only child but not of the "spoiled" variety. He trusted Christ as Savior at age nine, and the experience was so real to him that shortly afterward he led his uncle to the Lord. He graduated from West Philadelphia High School in 1924 (where he had taken four years of Greek!), and that same year entered the Reformed Episcopal Seminary in Philadelphia. The Reformed Episcopal Church had been founded by G. D. Cummins in 1873, mainly because of doctrinal "deterioration" in the American Episcopal church. The group was opposed to the "ritualism and sacerdotalism" of the parent body. James M. Gray, another president of Moody Bible Institute, also belonged to this denomination.

After Culbertson graduated from seminary in 1924, he became pastor of Grace Reformed Episcopal Church, Collingdale, Pennsylvania. He studied at Temple University in Philadelphia and taught at Philadelphia School of the Bible (now Philadelphia Bible College) and at his alma mater. In 1939 he graduated from Temple and was granted an honorary DD from Reformed Episcopal Seminary. He pastored St. John's-by-the-Sea, Ventnor, New Jersey, and the Church of the Atonement, Germantown, Philadelphia, before moving to Chicago in 1942 to become dean of education at Moody Bible Institute.

Will H. Houghton was president of the school at that time, and he was excited about the new dean God had provided, a man who blended deep spirituality with solid education and common sense. Culbertson's years as a bishop in his denomination (he had been elected in 1937) gave him wide experience in "managing spiritual business," and his academic credentials gave him acceptance in the field of education. Preaching and teaching were his first loves, and he especially enjoyed teaching the Pauline epistles and Bible geography. It was an open secret on campus that when Culbertson was bored with a speaker or a meeting, he would study the maps at the back of his Bible! Houghton died on June 14, 1947, and five days later Culbertson was appointed acting president. He never moved into Houghton's office, nor did he exercise any "evangelical politics" to succeed Houghton. Members of the administrative staff urged him to seek the position of president, but he quietly refused. Then on February 4, 1948, the trustees named him president of the school, and he accepted.

According to S. Maxwell Coder, who succeeded Culbertson as dean of education, "William Culbertson moved the Moody Bible Institute out of the nineteenth century and into the twentieth century." Some of the new president's associates did not think he moved things fast enough. One of his favorite expressions was, "Well, let's sleep on it." But when you examine the progress report for his years of administration, you cannot help but conclude that God used him and many things were accomplished. The physical campus was greatly improved, the curriculum updated, and the spiritual life of the campus family strengthened. Old ministries were expanded (or quietly buried), and new ministries inaugurated. All of this was accomplished during a turbulent era in American church history, when more than one Christian organization either compromised the faith or went out of business. God "called home" Culbertson on November 16, 1971. His last words summarized the deep spiritual passion of his entire life: "God—God—yes!"

It was my privilege to know Dr. Culbertson, and it was my further privilege to be chosen to write his biography, *William Culbertson: A*

Man of God (1974). During months of research, I found a few people who disagreed with his program, and some who were impatient with his deliberate style of management, but I found no one who questioned his character or attacked his reputation. Even his enemies (and he had a few) had to admit he was a man of God.

So much for his life and ministry. Now let us go deeper and explore the spiritual principles that operated in his life. Above all else, Culbertson walked with God. He spent time in the Word and in prayer. He looked at the practical decisions of life with the eyes of a man who first looked to God. He did not call committee meetings, make decisions, and then ask God to bless them. He prayed about matters, pondered them long and hard, and brought to bear upon his decisions every experience with God, every truth God had taught him from the Word. You could not be with him very long before saying to yourself, "This is a man of God." This does not mean Culbertson was solemn and ultra-spiritual, a fragile saint only to be admired from a distance. He had a great sense of humor, and he lived in contact with people. He did not waste his time "building a public image." He was what he was whether preaching in a church or playing handball with men on the staff. He practiced a healthy kind of holiness that convinced you it was a joyful, robust thing to be a Christian.

I am impressed by the way God prepared him for his strategic ministry. His years of study (and they were difficult years), his experience as a teacher, his work as a bishop: all contributed to his ministry at Moody Bible Institute. He did not seek any office, and to "politic" for position would have been utterly foreign to him. He was content to do the work God had given him until the Master called him to another ministry. I suppose every organization has its "pyramid climbers" who jockey for promotion and position. Culbertson would not be in their company. A Christian leader recently lamented to me about the small number of younger men and women who are prepared to move into positions of greater leadership. "Where are the replacements?" he asked me. "Isn't God preparing people today as he did in Bible days?" My answer may not be the correct or only one, but it is worth considering: many Christians today will not permit God to prepare them. They go too fast, too soon. When they get "to the top," they soon discover the shoes are too big for their pygmy feet. The applause of the crowd is not always the approval of the Lord.

Culbertson was a lifelong student of the Word and of related subjects. Stephen Olford's evaluation of Culbertson's preaching is apt: "You sense reality in his preaching." Culbertson did not depend on other people for either his sermons or the articles he wrote. What he produced came from God and was (as Robert Murray McCheyne used to say) "oil, beaten oil for the sanctuary." His Monday morning chapel addresses at the institute were filled with solid spiritual food, some of which the students did not completely digest until years later. I have read scores of letters from former students at the institute who had become pastors and missionaries and who wrote something like this: "We did not always fully understand what you taught us in chapel, but now that we are in the heat of the battle, your messages come back to us with new power and blessing."

I have always felt that Culbertson lived under the shadow of Houghton, his predecessor. Houghton was a dynamic leader and eloquent pulpiteer; Culbertson was a quiet leader who preferred to work through organizational channels, and a preacher who depended more on depth of character and thought than on heights of oratory. Each man had to be true to his own gifts and calling, and we must not say that one was better than the other. Each made his contribution to the work and then was "called home." Certainly Culbertson had no reason to doubt his abilities or question his competence because his style of leadership was different from Houghton's.

I get the impression that some Christian leaders are too busy to meditate on the Word, pray, and wait for God to speak to them personally. I have heard many sermons and read many books that merely recycle old material; they are the shallow products of a busy life. Whenever you heard Culbertson speak (or pray), you knew he had just come from the throne with a live coal ready to burst into flame. Christian leaders must realize that if they suffer from shallowness, the malady will spread throughout their entire organization.

I have touched on three factors that contributed to Culbertson's ministry: a deep devotion to Christ, a period of God-directed preparation, and a disciplined effort to "take time to be holy." Let me add a fourth: a loving conviction about biblical separation. Culbertson believed in separation, but not in the pharisaical sort that separates true believers. "There is a schismatic separation," he said in an early sermon, "when *our notions* separate us from true believers, when we separate ourselves unto men or mere opinions. There is no cause for separation when men differ in minor details but not in the great doctrines of Scripture." It was not easy to maintain the school's steady course during those stormy days of the 1950s and 1960s when evangelical groups were debating and dividing over the matter of separation. Because Culbertson feared God, he feared no man; but he was always gracious and kind when he disagreed. He held to his position courageously, but he did not require you to stand with him. He respected your right to disagree, but he expected you to give him the same right.

Not only are some Christian leaders neglecting spiritual and intellectual growth, but they tend to cater to the constituency, especially if they depend on the constituency for support. I have seen Christian organizations completely reverse a policy or abandon a principle because of a few letters of criticism. While it is true we must listen to the counsel and even the criticism of others, it is also true that we dare not be "reeds shaken in the wind." Culbertson listened, pondered, and prayed; he did not impulsively make radical changes just to please people. "For if I yet pleased men, I should not be the servant of Christ" (Gal. 1:10). I suppose the word that best describes his leadership is *integrity*. In a letter to Culbertson in 1939, Houghton said: "With modernism as dead as ever . . . with the worldly churches dying of dry rot, and with so much of Fundamentalism impotent through various causes, there is surely a place of tremendous need for an institution of integrity, loyalty, faith, and power." Integrity is the opposite of duplicity; it speaks of wholeness of character. Like David, William Culbertson "fed them according to the integrity of his heart, and guided them by the skillfulness of his hands" (Ps. 78:72). And like David he was a "man after God's own heart"—a man of God.

Unfortunately, not many of Culbertson's messages have been published. Only three volumes have appeared: *God's Provision for Holy Living*, his Bible readings at British Keswick in 1957; *The Faith Once Delivered*, his keynote addresses for the institute's annual Founder's Week; and *For Times Like These*, his editorials in *Moody Monthly*. A book of his "man to man" addresses to pastors would be valuable, as would a book of his chapel talks.

In time there arises "a generation that knows not Joseph," and we must not complain if yesterday's spiritual heroes become but memories. But there are many of us who give thanks for the privilege of living in the same century as William Culbertson, and we trust we will not forget the lessons he taught us.

Notes

Chapter 3   Matthew Henry

1. C. H. Spurgeon, *Commenting and Commentaries* (London: Banner of Truth Trust, 1969), 3.

Chapter 4   Jonathan Edwards

1. Jonathan Edwards, *Works of Jonathan Edwards*, vol. 1 (London: Banner of Truth Trust, 1976), 237.

Chapter 5   George Whitefield

1. George Whitefield, *Journals* (London: Banner of Truth Trust, 1960).
2. Arnold A. Dallimore, *George Whitefield*, vol. 2 (Westchester, Ill.: Cornerstone Books, 1980), 257–58.
3. Whitefield, *Journals*.
4. C. H. Spurgeon, *The Early Years* (London: Banner of Truth Trust, 1962), 348.

Chapter 6   Charles Simeon

1. Hugh Evan Hopkins, *Charles Simeon of Cambridge* (Grand Rapids: Eerdmans, 1977), 57.
2. Ibid., 174–75.
3. Originally published as *Horae Homileticae* (London: H. C. Bolm, 1847); reprinted as *Expository Outlines on the Whole Bible* (Grand Rapids: Zondervan, 1956).

Chapter 7   Christmas Evans

1. Paxton Hood, *Christmas Evans* (London: Hodder and Stoughton, 1888), 277–80.
2. Ibid., 144–46.
3. Ibid., 133.

Chapter 8   John Henry Newman

1. W. Robertson Nicoll, *Princes of the Church* (London: Hodder and Stoughton, 1921), 29.

2. Alexander Whyte, *Newman: An Appreciation in Two Lectures, with the Choicest Passages of His Writings* (Edinburgh: Oliphant, 1901), 122.

3. Ibid., 90–92, 97.

4. R. W. Church, *The Oxford Movement, Twelve Years, 1833–1845* (London: Macmillan, 1891; repr., New York: Archon, 1966), 15.

5. John Henry Newman, *Lectures and Essays on University Subjects* (London: Longman, Brown, Green, Longmans, and Roberts, 1859), 218.

Chapter 9   Richard Trench

1. John Bromley, *The Man of Ten Talents* (London: SPCK, 1959), 18.

2. Ibid., 152.

Chapter 10   Andrew Bonar

1. Marjorie Bonar, ed., *Andrew Bonar: Diary and Life* (London: Banner of Truth Trust, 1960).

Chapter 11   Robert Murray McCheyne

1. Bonar, *Andrew Bonar*, 154.

Chapter 12   F. W. Robertson

1. Stopford Brooke, ed., *Life and Letters of Frederick W. Robertson* (New York: Harper and Bros., 1865), 86.

2. A. W. W. Dale, *The Life of R. W. Dale* (London: Hodder and Stoughton, 1898), 705.

3. Edwin C. Dargan, *A History of Preaching*, 2 vols. (New York: Armstrong, 1905–12), 2:520.

Chapter 14   Fanny Crosby

1. Edith L. Blumhofer, *Her Heart Can See* (Grand Rapids: Eerdmans, 2005), 170, 358–60.

Chapter 15   Alexander Maclaren

1. John C. Carlile, *Alexander Maclaren D.D.: The Man and His Message* (London: S. W. Partridge Co., 1901; New York: Funk and Wagnalls, 1902), 51.

2. Arthur Porritt, *The Best I Remember* (London: Cassell, 1922), 75.

Chapter 16   J. B. Lightfoot

1. W. Robertson Nicoll, *The Victorian Church*, 2 vols. (London: Black, 1966), 2:49.

2. Nicoll, *Princes of the Church*, 22.

3. Ibid., 23.

Chapter 17   R. W. Dale

1. A. W. W. Dale, *The Life of R. W. Dale of Birmingham* (London: Hodder and Stoughton, 1902), 706.

Chapter 18   Joseph Parker

1. Joseph Parker, *Studies in Texts* (New York: Funk and Wagnalls, 1898–1900; repr., Grand Rapids: Baker, 1973), 1:vi.

2. Nicoll, *Princes of the Church*, 169.

3. Arthur Porritt, *The Best I Remember* (London: Cassell, 1922), 66.

4. J. D. Jones, *Three Score Years and Ten* (London: Hodder and Stoughton, 1940), 68.

5. Alexander Gammie, *Preachers I Have Heard* (London: Pickering and Inglis, 1945), 40.

6. Helen C. A. Dixon and A. C. Dixon: *A Romance of Preaching* (New York: Putnam, 1931), 106–7.

7. Clyde E. Fant Jr. and William M. Pinson, eds., *20 Centuries of Great Preaching*, 13 vols. (Waco: Word, 1971), 5:244.

8. Joseph Parker, *The People's Bible* (London: Hazell and Watson, 1886ff.), 25:449.

9. Parker, *Studies in Texts*, 1:viii–ix.

Chapter 19   J. Hudson Taylor

1. Howard Taylor and Mary Taylor, *Hudson Taylor in Early Years: The Growth of a Soul* (London: Morgan and Scott, 1911), xvii.

2. John Charles Pollock, *Hudson Taylor and Maria* (New York: McGraw-Hill, 1962), 101.

3. Ibid., 202–3.

4. Howard Taylor and Mary Taylor, *Hudson Taylor and the China Inland Mission* (London: Morgan and Scott, 1918), 42.

5. Ibid., 54–55.

6. Ibid., 53.

7. Ibid., 461.

Chapter 20   Charles H. Spurgeon

1. Charles H. Spurgeon, *The Metropolitan Tabernacle Pulpit*, 56 vols. (London: Passmore and Alabaster, 1863ff), 10:573ff.

2. W. Y. Fullerton, *C. H. Spurgeon* (London: Williams and Norgate, 1920; repr., Chicago: Moody, 1966), 255.

3. Bramwell Booth, *Echoes and Memories* (New York: Doran, 1925), 34.

4. Lewis A. Drummond, *Spurgeon: Prince of Preachers* (Grand Rapids: Kregel, 1992), 675, 733–37. See also Fullerton, *C. H. Spurgeon*, 243–47.

Chapter 21   Phillips Brooks

1. Phillips Brooks, *Lectures on Preaching* (Grand Rapids: Baker, 1969), 8–9.
2. Ibid.
3. Ibid., 4, 11, 97, 106.

Chapter 22   Frances Ridley Havergal

1. Maria F. Havergal and G. Havergal, *Memorials of Frances Ridley Havergal* (London: James Nisbet and Co., 1885), 66.

2. Frances Ridley Havergal, *Kept for the Master's Use* (Grand Rapids: Baker, 1979), 12, 35.

Chapter 23   Alexander Whyte

1. G. F. Barbour, *The Life of Alexander Whyte* (London: Hodder and Stoughton, 1923), 160–61.

2. Ibid., 284–85.

3. Alexander Whyte, *Bunyan Characters*, 4 vols. (Edinburgh: Oliphant, Anderson, and Ferrier, 1893–1908), 1:263.

4. Barbour, *Alexander Whyte*, 299.

5. John Dickson Carr, *The Life of Sir Arthur Conan Doyle* (New York: Harper, 1949), 23.

6. Ibid., 44.

7. Barbour, *Alexander Whyte*, 233.

8. Ibid., 252.

9. Gustavus Swift Paine, *The Learned Men* (New York: Crowell, 1959).

Chapter 24   Dwight L. Moody

1. L. T. Remlap, ed., *The Gospel Awakening* (Chicago: J. Fairbanks and Co., n.d.), 90–91.

2. Sarah A. Cooke, *Wayside Sketches* (Grand Rapids: Shaw Publishing Co., n.d.), 50.

3. Stanley N. Gundry, *Love Them In* (Chicago: Moody, 1976), 153–54.

Chapter 25   George Matheson

1. Donald Macmillan, *The Life of George Matheson* (London: Hodder and Stoughton, 1907), 181.

2. Ibid., 172–73.

Chapter 27   F. B. Meyer

1. F. B. Meyer, *The Bells of Is; or, Voices of Human Need and Sorrow* (London: Morgan and Scott, 1894), 17.

2. Ibid., 32–33.

3. F. B. Meyer, *Reveries and Realities; or, Life and Work in London* (London: Morgan and Scott, 1896), 41.

4. W. Y. Fullerton, *At the Sixtieth Milestone: Incidents of the Journey* (London: Marshall, 1917), 80–81.

5. Abraham, Jacob, Joseph, Moses, Joshua, Samuel, David, Elijah, Jeremiah, Jonah, John the Baptist, Peter, and Paul.

Chapter 29   Henry Drummond

1. Nicoll, *Princes of the Church*, 100.

2. Ibid., 101.

3. Gundry, *Love Them In*, 198–201.

Chapter 30   R. A. Torrey

1. Roger Martin, *R. A. Torrey: Apostle of Certainty* (Murfreesboro, Tenn.: Sword of the Lord Publishers, 1976), 34.
2. Ibid., 42.

Chapter 31   Thomas Spurgeon

1. Fullerton, *Sixtieth Milestone*, 151.

Chapter 33   Charles E. Jefferson

1. Charles E. Jefferson, *The Minister as Shepherd* (New York: Crowell, 1912; repr., Grand Rapids: Zondervan, 1933), 36.
2. Ibid., 42.
3. Charles E. Jefferson, *The Building of the Church* (New York: Macmillan, 1910; repr. Grand Rapids: Baker, 1969), 11.
4. Ibid., 19.
5. Ibid., 5.
6. Ibid., 14.
7. Ibid., 15.
8. Ibid., 17.
9. Ibid., 19.
10. Ibid., 21.
11. Ibid., 86.
12. Ibid., 119.
13. Ibid., 171.
14. Ibid., 193.
15. Ibid., 235.
16. Ibid., 298.
17. Jefferson, *Minister as Shepherd*, 21.
18. Ibid., 61.
19. Edgar De Witt Jones, *American Preachers of To-day* (Indianapolis: Bobbs-Merrill, 1933; repr., Freeport, N.Y.: Books for Libraries, 1971), 59.
20. Charles E. Jefferson, *Quiet Hints to Growing Preachers* (New York: Crowell, 1901), 7.
21. Ibid., 19.
22. Ibid., 44.
23. Ibid., 59.
24. Ibid., 133.
25. Jefferson, *Building of the Church*, 256.
26. Ibid., 277.
27. Jones, *American Preachers of To-day*, 60.

Chapter 36   G. Campbell Morgan

1. G. Campbell Morgan, *The Study and Teaching of the English Bible* (New York: Revell, 1910), 74.
2. Ernest H. Jeffs, *Princes of the Modern Pulpit* (London: Low, 1931), 184.
3. Jill Morgan, ed., *This Was His Faith* (Westwood, N.J.: Revell, 1952), 244.

Chapter 37 John Henry Jowett

1. John Henry Jowett, *The Preacher: His Life and Work* (New York: Hodder and Stoughton, 1912), 9.

Chapter 38 J. D. Jones

1. J. D. Jones, *Three Score Years and Ten: The Autobiography of J. D. Jones* (London: Hodder and Stoughton, 1940), 40–41.
2. Jeffs, *Princes of the Modern Pulpit*, 127.
3. Arthur Porritt, *J. D. Jones of Bournemouth* (London: Independent, 1942).

Chapter 41 Frank W. Boreham

1. F. W. Boreham, *My Privilege* (Philadelphia: Judson Press, 1950), 64.
2. Ibid., 65–66.
3. The publishing arm of the Wesleyan Conference did not, however, adopt the name "Epworth Press" until 1918, six years after *The Luggage of Life* had appeared. Before that, books published by the Conference were imprinted with the name of "Conference Book Steward C. H. Kelly."
4. Boreham, *Privilege*, 98–99.

Chapter 43 Oswald Chambers

1. Gertrude Chambers, *Oswald Chambers: His Life and Work* (London: Simpkin Marshall, Ltd., 1933), 132.
2. Harry Verploegh, ed., *The Oswald Chambers Devotional Reader* (Nashville: Thomas Nelson, 1990). See also *Faith, A Holy Walk* compiled by Julie Ackerman Link (Grand Rapids: Discovery House, 1999).
3. David McCasland, ed., *The Quotable Oswald Chambers* (Grand Rapids: Discovery House, 2008).

Chapter 45 Clarence Edward Macartney

1. Clarence Edward Macartney, *Strange Texts but Grand Truths* (Grand Rapids: Kregel, 1994), 121.
2. Harry Emerson Fosdick, *The Living of These Days* (New York: Harper, 1956), 146.
3. Ibid., 145.
4. Robert Moats Miller, *Harry Emerson Fosdick: Preacher, Pastor, Prophet* (New York: Oxford University Press, 1985), 117.
5. Clarence Edward Macartney, *The Making of a Minister* (New York: Channel Press, 1961), 223.

Chapter 46 William Whiting Borden

1. Elisabeth Elliot, ed., *The Journals of Jim Elliot* (Grand Rapids: Revell, 2002), 174.

Chapter 47 Alva Jay McClain

1. Alva Jay McClain, *The Greatness of the Kingdom* (Winona Lake, Ind.: BMH Books, 1968), 527.

Chapter 48   A. W. Tozer

1. A. W. Tozer, "Some Thoughts on Books and Reading," in *Man: The Dwelling Place of God* (Harrisburg, Pa.: Christian Publications, 1966), 149.

2. A. W. Tozer, ed. *The Christian Book of Mystical Verse* (Harrisburg, Pa.: Christian Publications, 1963), vi.

3. A. W. Tozer, *In The Root of the Righteous* (Harrisburg, Pa.: Christian Publications, 1955), 34–37.

Chapter 49   W. E. Sangster

1. Paul E. Sangster, *Doctor Sangster* (London: Epworth, 1962), 89.

2. Ibid., 109–10.

3. Ibid., 109.

4. W. E. Sangster. *The Approach to Preaching* (London: Epworth, 1951; repr., Grand Rapids: Baker, 1974), 32.

Chapter 50   William Culbertson

1. C. S. Lewis, *George MacDonald: An Anthology* (New York: MacMillan, 1947), 71.

Further Reading

Katherine von Bora

Dallmann, William. *Kate Luther: "She is worthy to be loved."* Milwaukee: Northwestern Publishing House, 1941.

Dentler, Clara Louise. *Katherine Luther of the Wittenberg Parsonage.* Philadelphia: United Lutheran Publication House, 1924.

Samuel Rutherford

Coffey, John. *Politics, Religion, and the British Revolutions: The Mind of Samuel Rutherford.* Cambridge: Cambridge University Press, 2002.

Innes, A. Taylor. *Samuel Rutherford. The Evangelical Succession,* series 2. Edinburgh: MacNiven and Wallace, 1883.

Loane, Marcus L. *Makers of Religious Freedom in the Seventeenth Century.* Grand Rapids: Eerdmans, 1961.

Macpherson, John. *The Westminster Confession of Faith.* Edinburgh: Clark, 1882.

Rutherford, Samuel. *An Apology for Divine Grace.* 1636.

———. *Extracts from the Letters of Samuel Rutherford.* Compiled by Hamilton Smith. Crewe, Cheshire: Scripture Truth Publications, 2008.

———. *Joshua Redivivus, or, Mr. Rutherfoord's Letters.* 1664.

———. *Letters.* Edited by Andrew A. Bonar. 2 vols. Edinburgh: Kennedy, 1863.

———. *Lex Rex: The Law and the Prince.* London: Field, 1644.

Smellie, Alexander. *Men of the Covenant.* London: Marshall, Morgan, and Scott, 1924. Reprint, Edinburgh: Banner of Truth Trust, 1975.

Whyte, Alexander. *Samuel Rutherford and Some of His Correspondents.* Edinburgh: Oliphant, Anderson, and Ferrier, 1894.

Matthew Henry

Henry, Matthew. *Matthew Henry's Commentary on the Whole Bible: Complete and Unabridged.* Peabody, Mass.: Hendrickson Publishers, 2005.

Williams, J. B. *The Life of Matthew Henry and the Concise Commentary on the Gospels.* Alachua, Fla.: Bridge-Logos Publishers, 2004.

———. *The Lives of Philip and Matthew Henry*. London: Banner of Truth Trust, 1974.

Jonathan Edwards

Dwight, Sereno E. "Memoirs of Jonathan Edwards" in *The Works of Jonathan Edwards*, vol. 1. Edinburgh: Banner of Truth Trust, 1974.

Marsden, George M. *Jonathan Edwards: A Life*. New Haven: Yale University Press, 2004.

Murray, Iain. *Jonathan Edwards: A New Biography*. Edinburgh: Banner of Truth Trust, 1987.

Nichols, Stephen J. *Jonathan Edwards: A Guided Tour of His Life and Thought*. Phillipsburg, N.J.: P & R Press, 2001.

Stein, Stephen J. *The Cambridge Companion to Jonathan Edwards*. Cambridge: Cambridge University Press, 2006.

George Whitefield

Dallimore, Arnold A. *George Whitefield: The Life and Times of the Great Evangelist of the Eighteenth-Century Revival*. 2 vols. Westchester, Ill: Cornerstone Books, 1970, 1980.

Gillies, John. *Memoirs of Rev. George Whitefield*. Middletown, Conn.: Hunt and Noyes, 1837.

Gledstone, James Paterson. *George Whitefield, M.A., Field-Preacher*. London: Hodder and Stoughton, 1901.

Lambert, Frank. *"Pedlar in Divinity": George Whitefield and the Transatlantic Revivals, 1737–1770*. Princeton, N.J.: Princeton University Press, 2002.

Mansfield, Stephen. *Forgotten Founding Father: The Heroic Legacy of George Whitefield*. Nashville, Tenn.: Cumberland House Publishing, 2001.

Pollock, John. *George Whitefield and the Great Awakening*. London: Hodder and Stoughton, 1973.

Stout, Harry S. *The Divine Dramatist: George Whitefield and the Rise of Modern Evangelicalism*. Grand Rapids: Eerdmans, 1991.

Whitefield, George. *Journals*. London: Banner of Truth Trust, 1960.

Charles Simeon

Hopkins, Hugh Evan. *Charles Simeon of Cambridge*. Grand Rapids: Eerdmans, 1977.

Pollard, Arthur, and Michael Hennell, eds. *Charles Simeon (1759–1836)*. London: SPCK, 1959.

Simeon, Charles. *Evangelical Preaching: An Anthology of Sermons by Charles Simeon*. Edited by James M. Houston. Vancouver: Regent College Publishing, 2003.

Christmas Evans

Hood, Paxton. *Christmas Evans: The Preacher of Wild Wales*. London: Hodder and Stoughton, 1888.

Ramsbottom, B. A. *Christmas Evans*. Luton, England: Bunyan Press, 1985.

Stephen, David Rhys. *Memoirs of the Late Christmas Evans, of Wales*. Reprint, Whitefish, Mont.: Kessinger Publishing, 2007.

John Henry Newman

Church, R. W. *The Oxford Movement, Twelve Years, 1833–1845*. London: Macmillan, 1891. Reprint, New York: Archon, 1966.

Newman, John Henry. *Apologia pro vita sua*. London: Longmans, 1864. Reprint edited by David J. DeLaura. New York: Norton, 1968.

———. *Discourses Addressed to Mixed Congregations*. London: Longmans, 1849. Reprint, Westminster, Md.: Christian Classics, 1966.

———. *Lectures and Essays on University Subjects*. London: Longman, Brown, Green, Longmans, and Roberts, 1859.

———. *A Newman Reader: An Anthology of the Writings of John Henry Cardinal Newman*. Edited by Francis X. Connolly. Garden City, N.Y.: Doubleday, 1964.

———. *Parochial and Plain Sermons*. Edited by W. J. Copeland. 8 vols. London: Rivingtons, 1868. Reprint, Westminster, Md.: Christian Classics, 1968.

———. *The Preaching of John Henry Newman*. Edited by W. D. White. Philadelphia: Fortress, 1969.

———. *Sermons Bearing on Subjects of the Day*. London: Rivingtons, 1843. Reprint, Westminster, Md.: Christian Classics, 1968.

———. *Sermons, Chiefly on the Theory of Religious Belief, Preached Before the University of Oxford*. London: Rivingtons, 1843. Reprinted as *Fifteen Sermons Preached Before the University of Oxford, Between A.D. 1826 and 1843*. Westminster, Md.: Christian Classics, 1970.

———. *Sermons Preached on Various Occasions*. London: Burns and Lambert, 1857. Reprint, Westminster, Md.: Christian Classics, 1968.

———. *Tract Ninety; or, Remarks on Certain Passages in the Thirty-Nine Articles*. Edited by A. W. Evans. London: Constable, 1933.

Nicoll, W. Robertson. *Princes of the Church*. London: Hodder and Stoughton, 1921.

O'Connell, Marvin R. *The Oxford Conspirators: A History of the Oxford Movement, 1833–45*. New York: Macmillan, 1969.

Trevor, Meriol. *Newman*. 2 vols.: *The Pillar of the Cloud* and *Light in Winter*. New York: Macmillan, 1962–63.

———. *Newman's Journey*. Cleveland: Collins and World, 1977.

Turner, Frank M., and Frank Turner. *John Henry Newman: The Challenge to Evangelical Religion*. New Haven: Yale University Press, 2002.

Whyte, Alexander. *Newman: An Appreciation in Two Lectures, with the Choicest Passages of His Writings*. Edinburgh: Oliphant, 1901.

Richard Trench

Bromley, John. *The Man of Ten Talents: A Portrait of Richard Chenevix Trench, 1807–1886, Philologist, Poet, Theologian, Archbishop*. London: SPCK, 1959.

Trench, Richard. *English, Past and Present: Five Lectures*. London: Parker, 1855.

———. *Notes on the Miracles of Our Lord*. London, 1846. Reprint, Grand Rapids: Baker, 1949.

———. *Notes on the Parables of Our Lord*. London, 1841. Reprint, Ann Arbor: Scholarly Publishing Office, University of Michigan Library, 2005.

———. *On the Study of Words: Five Lectures*. London: Parker, 1851.

———. *Sermons New and Old*. London: Kegan Paul, 1886.

———. *Synonyms of the New Testament*. Cambridge: Macmillan, 1854. Reprint, New York: Cosimo Classics, 2007.

Andrew A. Bonar

Bonar, Andrew A. *Commentary on the Book of Leviticus.* Reprint, Ann Arbor: Scholarly Publishing Office, University of Michigan Library, 2005.

Bonar, Marjory. *Andrew A. Bonar: Diary and Life.* London: Banner of Truth Trust, 1960.

———. *Andrew Bonar: The Good Pastor.* Greenville, S.C.: Ambassador-Emerald International, 1999.

Nicoll, Robertson, et al. *Memories of Dr. Horatius Bonar.* Edinburgh: Oliphant, Anderson & Ferrier, 1909.

Robert Murray McCheyne

Bonar, Andrew A., ed. *Additional Remains of the Rev. Robert Murray McCheyne.* Edinburgh: William Oliphant and Co., 1846. Reprinted as *From the Preacher's Heart.* Ross-shire, Scotland: Christian Focus Publications, 1993.

Bonar, Andrew A. *The Memoirs and Remains of the Rev. Robert Murray McCheyne.* Edinburgh: William Oliphant and Co., 1844. Reprint, London: Banner of Truth Trust, 1966.

Bonar, Andrew A., and Robert Murray McCheyne. *Narrative of a Visit to the Holy Land and Mission of Inquiry to the Jews.* Edinburgh: William Oliphant and Company, 1878.

McCheyne, Robert Murray. *A Basket of Fragments.* Aberdeen: James Murray, 1848.

Miller, Basil. *Robert Murray McCheyne.* Christian Life Books, 2003.

Robertson, David. *Awakening: The Life and Ministry of Robert Murray McCheyne.* Carlisle, UK: Paternoster, 2004.

F. W. Robertson

Blackwood, James R. *The Soul of Frederick W. Robertson.* New York: Harper, 1947.

Brastow, Lewis O. *Representative Modern Preachers.* London: Hodder and Stoughton, 1904. Reprint, Plainview, N.Y.: Books for Libraries, 1975.

Faulkenberg, Marilyn Thomas. *Victorian Conscience: F.W. Robertson.* New York: Peter Lang Publishing, 2005.

Robertson, F. W. *Life and Letters of Frederick W. Robertson.* Edited by Stopford A. Brooke. 2 vols. Boston: Ticknor and Fields, 1865. Reprint, 1 vol. New York: Harper, 1903.

———. *The Preaching of F. W. Robertson.* Edited by Gilbert E. Doan Jr. Philadelphia: Fortress, 1964.

———. *Sermons on St. Paul's Epistles to the Corinthians.* Reprint, Ann Arbor: Scholarly Publishing Office, University of Michigan Library, 2005.

John Charles Ryle

Ryle, John Charles. *Churches Beware!* Reprint, Darlington, UK: Evangelical Press, 1998.

———. *Daily Readings from All Four Gospels: For Morning and Evening.* Compiled by Robert Sheehan. Darlington, UK: Evangelical Press, 1998.

Toon, Peter, and Michael Smout. *John Charles Ryle: Evangelical Bishop.* Swengel, Penn: Reiner Publications, 1976.

Fanny Crosby

Blumhofer, Edith L. *Her Heart Can See: The Life and Hymns of Fanny J. Crosby.* Grand Rapids: Eerdmans, 2005.

Crosby, Fanny. *Fanny Crosby's Life Story.* New York: Every Where Publishing Company, 1901.

———. *Fanny J. Crosby: An Autobiography.* Peabody, Mass.: Hendrickson Publishers, 2008.

Harvey, Bonnie. *Fanny Crosby.* Bloomington: Bethany House Publishers, 1999.

Hustad, Donald P., ed. *Fanny Crosby Speaks Again.* Carol Stream, Ill.: Hope Publishing Co., 1977.

Rees, Jean A. *Singing the Story: Fanny Crosby and Her Hymns.* London: Lutterworth Press, 1958.

Ruffin, Bernard. *Fanny Crosby.* Cleveland: Pilgrim Press, 1976.

Alexander Maclaren

Carlile, John Charles. *Alexander Maclaren, D.D.: The Man and His Message.* New York: Funk and Wagnalls, 1902.

Maclaren, Alexander. *The Best of Alexander Maclaren.* Edited by Gaius Glenn Atkins. New York: Harper, 1949.

———. *Expositions of Holy Scripture.* 32 vols. London: Hodder and Stoughton, 1904–10. Reprint, 17 vols. Grand Rapids: Baker, 1974.

———. *The God of the Amen.* London: Alexander and Shepheard, 1891.

———. *The Secret of Power.* London: Snow, 1870.

———. *Sermons Preached in Manchester.* 3 vols. London: Cambridge, 1865.

———. *Triumphant Certainties.* London: Christian Commonwealth, 1897.

———. *The Wearied Christ.* London: Alexander and Shepheard, 1893.

———. *Week-day Evening Addresses.* London: Macmillan, 1877.

———. *A Year's Ministry.* New York: Funk and Wagnalls, 1902.

McLaren, E. T. *Dr. McLaren of Manchester: A Sketch.* London: Hodder and Stoughton, 1912.

Nicoll, W. Robertson. *Princes of the Church.* London: Hodder and Stoughton, 1921.

Porritt, Arthur. *The Best I Remember.* London: Cassell, 1922.

Williamson, David. *The Life of Alexander Maclaren.* London: Clarke, 1910.

J. B. Lightfoot

Bishop Lightfoot. London: Macmillan, 1894.

Eden, George R., and F. C. Macdonald, eds. *Lightfoot of Durham: Memories and Appreciations.* Cambridge: Cambridge University, 1932.

Lightfoot, J. B. *The Apostolic Fathers.* Edited by J. R. Harmer. London: Macmillan, 1891. Reprint, Grand Rapids: Baker, 1956.

———. *Cambridge Sermons.* London: Macmillan, 1890.

———. *Commentary on the Epistles of St. Paul.* 43 vols. London: Macmillan, 1865–75. Reprint, Peabody, Mass.: Hendrickson Publishers, 1993.

———. *Historical Essays.* London: Macmillan, 1895.

———. *Leaders in the Northern Church.* Edited by J. R. Harmer. London: Macmillan, 1890.

———. *On a Fresh Revision of the English New Testament.* London: Cambridge, 1871.

———. *Ordination Addresses and Counsels to Clergy.* London: Macmillan, 1890.

———. *Sermons Preached in St. Paul's Cathedral.* London: Macmillan, 1891.

———. *Sermons Preached on Special Occasions.* London: Macmillan, 1891.

Nicoll, W. Robertson. *Princes of the Church.* London: Hodder and Stoughton, 1921.

R. W. Dale

Dale, A. W. W. *The Life of R. W. Dale.* London: Hodder and Stoughton, 1902.

Dale, R. W. *The Atonement.* London: Hodder and Stoughton, 1875.

———. *Christ and the Future Life.* London: Hodder and Stoughton, 1895.

———. *Christian Doctrine.* New York: Armstrong, 1895.

———. *The Epistle of James and Other Discourses.* Eugene, Ore.: Wipf and Stock Publishers, 2006.

———. *The Living Christ and the Four Gospels.* New York: Armstrong, 1890.

———. *Nine Lectures on Preaching.* New York: Barnes, 1878. Reprint, New York: Doran, n.d.

Joseph Parker

Adamson, William. *The Life of Jospeh Parker, Pastor of City Temple, London.* Reprint, Whitefish, Mont.: Kessinger Publishing, 2008.

Gammie, Alexander. *Preachers I Have Heard.* London: Pickering and Inglis, 1945.

Nicoll, W. Robertson. *Princes of the Church.* London: Hodder and Stoughton, 1921.

Parker, Joseph. *The People's Bible.* 25 vols. London: Hazell and Watson, 1886ff. Reprinted as *Preaching Through the Bible.* 14 vols. Grand Rapids: Baker, 1971.

———. *A Preacher's Life.* London: Hodder and Stoughton, 1899.

———. *Studies in Texts.* 6 vols. New York: Funk and Wagnalls, 1898–1900. Reprint, 3 vols. Grand Rapids: Baker, 1973.

Porritt, Arthur. *The Best I Remember.* London: Cassell, 1922.

J. Hudson Taylor

Cromarty, Jim. *The Pigtail and Chopsticks Man: The Story of J. Hudson Taylor and the China Inland Mission.* Darlington, UK: Evangelical Press, 2002.

Pollock, John Charles. *Hudson Taylor and Maria.* New York: McGraw-Hill, 1962.

Steer, Roger. *J. Hudson Taylor: A Man in Christ.* Carlisle, UK: Authentic, 1969.

———. *Hudson Taylor.* Bloomington: Bethany House Publishers, 1987.

Taylor, Howard, and Mary Taylor. *Biography of James Hudson Taylor.* London: China Inland Mission, 1965. Reprinted as *J. Hudson Taylor: God's Man in China.* Chicago: Moody, 1971.

———. *Hudson Taylor and the China Inland Mission: The Growth of a Work of God.* London: Morgan and Scott, 1918.

———. *Hudson Taylor in Early Years: The Growth of a Soul.* London: Morgan and Scott, 1911.

Taylor, J. Hudson. *Hudson Taylor's Legacy.* Edited by Marshall Broomhall. London: China Inland Mission, 1931.

———. *A Retrospect.* London: Morgan, 1894.

———. *Union and Communion.* London: Morgan and Scott, 1894. Reprint, Minneapolis: Bethany Fellowship, 1971.

Charles H. Spurgeon

Bacon, Ernest W. *Spurgeon: Heir of the Puritans.* Grand Rapids: Eerdmans, 1968.

Booth, Bramwell. *Echoes and Memories.* New York: Doran, 1925.

Fullerton, W. Y. *C. H. Spurgeon.* London: Williams and Norgate, 1920. Reprint, Chicago: Moody, 1966.

Hayden, Eric W. *A History of Spurgeon's Tabernacle.* 2nd ed. Pasadena, Tex.: Pilgrim, 1971.

Murray, Iain. *The Forgotten Spurgeon.* 2nd ed. London: Banner of Truth Trust, 1973.

Spurgeon, Charles H. *All of Grace.* Christian Heritage, 2008.

———. *An All-Round Ministry.* London: Passmore and Alabaster, 1900. Reprint, Pasadena, Tex.: Pilgrim Ministry.

———. *Autobiography.* Edited by Susannah Spurgeon and Joseph Harrald. 4 vols. London: Passmore and Alabaster, 1897–1900. Reprinted as *Spurgeon.* 2 vols. Edinburgh: Banner of Truth Trust, 1962–73.

———. *Commenting and Commentaries.* London: Passmore and Alabaster, 1876. Reprint, London: Banner of Truth Trust, 1969.

———. *Lectures to My Students.* 3 vols. London: Passmore and Alabaster, 1875–94. Reprint, 1 vol. London: Marshall, Morgan, and Scott, 1954.

———. *The Metropolitan Tabernacle Pulpit.* 56 vols. London: Passmore and Alabaster, 1863ff. Reprint, Pasadena, Tex.: Pilgrim Ministry.

———. *Morning and Evening: A New Edition of the Classic Devotional.* Revised and updated edition. Wheaton: Crossway Books, 2003.

Thielicke, Helmut. *Encounter with Spurgeon.* Philadelphia: Fortress, 1963. Reprint, Grand Rapids: Baker, 1975.

Phillips Brooks

Albright, Raymond W. *Focus on Infinity: A Life of Phillips Brooks.* New York: Macmillan, 1961.

Allen, Alexander V. G. *Life and Letters of Phillips Brooks.* 2 vols. New York: Dutton, 1900.

———. *Phillips Brooks, 1835–1893: Memories of His Life.* New York: Dutton, 1907.

Brastow, Lewis O. *Representative Modern Preachers.* London: Hodder and Stoughton, 1904. Reprint, Plainview, N.Y.: Books for Libraries, 1975.

Brooks, Phillips. *The Consolations of God: Great Sermons by Phillips Brooks.* Edited by Ellen Wilbur. Grand Rapids: Eerdmans, 2003.

———. *Essays and Addresses.* Edited by John Cotton Brooks. New York: Dutton, 1894.

———. *Lectures on Preaching.* New York: Dutton, 1877. Reprint, Grand Rapids: Baker, 1969.

———. *Selected Sermons.* Edited by William Scarlett. New York: Dutton, 1949.

Woolverton, John F. *The Education of Phillips Brooks.* Champaign, Ill: University of Illinois Press, 1995.

Frances Ridley Havergal

Havergal, Frances Ridley. *Kept for the Master's Use.* Grand Rapids: Baker, 1979.

———. *The Last Week: Being a Record of the Last Days of Frances Ridley Havergal.* London: James Nisbet and Co., n.d.

Havergal, Maria F. and G. Havergal. *Memorials of Frances Ridley Havergal.* London: James Nisbet and Co., 1885.

Alexander Whyte

Barbour, G. F. *The Life of Alexander Whyte*. London: Hodder and Stoughton, 1923.

Whyte, Alexander. *Bible Characters*. 6 vols. Edinburgh: Oliphant, Anderson, and Ferrier, 1898–1902.

———. *Bunyan Characters*, 4 vols. Edinburgh: Oliphant, Anderson, and Ferrier, 1893–1908.

———. *In Remembrance of Me*. Grand Rapids: Baker, 1970.

———. *Lancelot Andrewes and His "Private Devotions."* Edinburgh: Oliphant, Anderson, and Ferrier, 1896.

———. *Lord, Teach Us to Pray*. New York: Hodder and Stoughton, 1922. Reprint, Vancouver: Regent College Publishing, 1998.

———. *The Nature of Angels*. London: Hodder and Stoughton, 1930. Reprint, Grand Rapids: Baker, 1976.

———. *The Spiritual Life: The Teaching of Thomas Goodwin*. London: Oliphant, 1918.

———. *The Treasury of Alexander Whyte*. Edited by Ralph Turnbull. London: Oliphant, 1957. Reprint, Grand Rapids: Baker, 1968.

———. *The Walk, Conversation, and Character of Jesus Christ Our Lord*. Edinburgh: Oliphant, 1905. Reprint, Grand Rapids: Baker, 1975.

———. *With Mercy and Judgment*. London: Hodder and Stoughton, 1924.

Dwight L. Moody

Curtis, Richard K. *They Called Him Mr. Moody*. Grand Rapids: Eerdmans, 1962.

Day, Richard Ellsworth. *Bush Aglow*. Philadelphia: The Judson Press, 1936.

Findlay, James F., Jr. *Dwight L. Moody; American Evangelist*. Reprint, Grand Rapids: Baker, 1973.

Fitt, Arthur Percy. *Moody Still Lives*. New York: Revell, 1936.

Gundry, Stanley N. *Love Them In: The Proclamation Theology of D. L. Moody*. Chicago: Moody, 1976.

Moody, William R. *The Life of Dwight L. Moody*. New York: Revell, 1900.

Pollock, J. C. *Moody without Sankey*. London: Hodder and Stoughton, 1963.

Smith, Wilbur M. *An Annotated Bibliography of D. L. Moody*. Chicago: Moody, 1948.

Williams, A. W. *Life and Work of Dwight L. Moody*. New York: Cosimo Classics, 2006.

George Matheson

Macmillan, Donald. *The Life of George Matheson*. London: Hodder and Stoughton, 1907.

Matheson, George. *Aids to the Study of German Theology*. Edinburgh: Clark, 1874.

———. *Growth of the Spirit of Christianity, from the First Century to the Dawn of the Lutheran Era*. 2 vols. Edinburgh: Clark, 1877.

———. *Leaves for Quiet Hours*. London: Clarke, 1904.

———. *Moments on the Mount: A Series of Devotional Meditations*. London: Nisbet, 1884.

———. *My Aspirations*. Heart Chords. London: Cassell, 1883.

———. *Natural Elements of Revealed Theology*. London: Nisbet, 1881.

———. *The Representative Men of the Bible*. (O.T.) 2 vols. London: Hodder and Stoughton, 1902–03.

———. *The Representative Men of the New Testament*. London: Hodder and Stoughton, 1905.

———. *The Representative Women of the Bible*. Edited by William Smith. London: Hodder and Stoughton, 1907.

———. *Rests by the River: Devotional Meditations*. London: Hodder and Stoughton, 1906.

———. *Sidelights from Patmos: Thoughts Suggested by the Book of Revelation*. London: Hodder and Stoughton, 1897.

———. *Spiritual Development of St. Paul*. London: Blackwood, 1890.

———. *Studies of the Portrait of Christ*. 2 vols. London: Hodder and Stoughton, 1899–1900.

———. *Times of Retirement: Devotional Meditations*. London: Nisbet, 1901.

———. *Words by the Wayside. Small Books on Great Subjects*, vol. 1. London: Clarke, 1896.

C. I. Scofield

Gaebelein, A. C. *The History of the Scofield Reference Bible*. New York: Our Hope, 1943.

Scofield, C. I. *Addresses on Prophecy*. New York: Gaebelein, 1910.

———. *In Many Pulpits with Dr. C. I. Scofield*. New York: Oxford University, 1922. Reprint, Grand Rapids: Baker, 1966.

———. *Plain Papers on the Doctrine of the Holy Spirit*. New York: Revell, 1899. Reprinted as *A Mighty Wind: Plain Papers on the Doctrines of the Holy Spirit*. Grand Rapids: Baker, 1973.

———, ed. *The Scofield Reference Bible*. New York: Oxford University, 1909.

Trumbull, Charles G. *The Life Story of C. I. Scofield*. New York: Oxford University, 1920. Reprint, Eugene, Ore.: Wipf & Stock Publishers, 2007.

F. B. Meyer

Fullerton, W. Y. *F. B Meyer: A Biography*. London: Marshall, 1929.

Meyer, F. B. *Back to Bethel: Separation from Sin and Fellowship with God*. Chicago: Bible Institute Colportage Association, 1901.

———. *The Bells of Is; or, Voices of Human Need and Sorrow*. London: Morgan and Scott, 1894.

———. *The Call and Challenge of the Unseen*. London: Morgan and Scott, 1928.

———. *Christ in Isaiah*. London: Morgan and Scott, 1895. Reprint, Fort Washington, Pa.: Christian Literature Crusade, 1970.

———. *The Directory of the Devout Life: Meditations on the Sermon on the Mount*. London: Morgan and Scott, 1904. Reprint, Grand Rapids: Baker, 1954.

———. *Exodus*. 2 vols. *A Devotional Commentary*. Edited by A. R. Buckland. London: RTS, 1911–13.

———. *Expository Preaching: Plans and Methods*. London: Hodder and Stoughton, 1912.

———. *Joseph: Loved, Despised, Exalted*. Greenville, S.C.: Ambassador-Emerald International, 2003.

———. *The Life and Light of Men: Expositions of John 1–12*. London: Morgan and Scott, 1891.

———. *Light on Life's Duties*. Chicago: Bible Institute Colportage Association, 1895.

———. *Love to the Uttermost: Expositions of John 13–21*. London: Morgan and Scott, 1898.

———. *Our Daily Homily.* 5 vols. London: Morgan and Scott, 1898–99.

———. *Reveries and Realities; or, Life and Work in London.* London: Morgan and Scott, 1896.

———. *Tried by Fire: Expositions of the First Epistle of Peter.* London: Morgan and Scott, 1895. Reprint, Fort Washington, Pa.: Christian Literature Crusade, 1970.

———. *The Way into the Holiest: Expositions of the Epistle to the Hebrews.* London: Morgan and Scott, 1893.

Sorenson, Stephen W. *The Best of F. B. Meyer: 120 Daily Devotions to Nurture Your Spirit and Refresh Your Soul.* Colorado Springs: Honor Books, 2006.

W. Robertson Nicoll

Darlow, T. H. *William Robertson Nicoll: Life and Letters.* London: Hodder and Stoughton, 1925.

Nicoll, W. Robertson, ed. *The Expositor's Bible.* 50 vols. London: Hodder and Stoughton, 1888–1905. Reprint, 6 vols. Grand Rapids: Eerdmans, 1943.

———, ed. *The Expositor's Greek New Testament.* 5 vols. London: Hodder and Stoughton, 1897–1910. Reprint, Grand Rapids: Eerdmans, 1956.

———. *My Father.* London: Hodder and Stoughton, 1908.

———. *Princes of the Church.* London: Hodder and Stoughton, 1921.

———, ed. *The Sermon Bible.* 12 vols. London: Hodder and Stoughton, 1888–93. Reprinted as *The Sermon-Outline Bible.* 6 vols. Grand Rapids: Baker, 1972.

Stoddart, Jane T. *W. Robertson Nicoll, LL.D., Editor and Preacher.* London: Partridge, 1903.

Henry Drummond

Drummond, Henry. *Dwight L. Moody: Impressions and Facts.* New York: McClure and Phillips, 1900.

———. *The Greatest Thing in the World: An Address.* London: Hodder and Stoughton, 1890. Reprint, Old Tappan, N. J.: Revell, 1968.

———. *Henry Drummond: An Anthology.* Edited by James W. Kennedy. New York: Harper, 1953.

———. *"The Ideal Life" and Other Unpublished Addresses.* London: Hodder and Stoughton, 1897.

———. *Natural Law in the Spiritual World.* London: Hodder and Stoughton, 1883.

Nicoll, W. Robertson. *Princes of the Church.* London: Hodder and Stoughton, 1921.

Shanks, T. J., ed. *A College of Colleges: Led by D. L. Moody and Taught by Henry Drummond, Joseph Cook, John A. Broadus, L. T. Townsend, A. T. Pierson, and Jacob Chamberlain, with Others.* New York: Revell, 1887.

Smith, George Adam. *The Life of Henry Drummond.* London: Hodder and Stoughton, 1899.

R. A. Torrey

Martin, Roger. *R. A. Torrey: Apostle of Certainty.* Murfreesboro, Tenn: Sword of the Lord Publishers, 1976.

Torrey, R. A. *The Holy Spirit: Who He Is and What He Does.* Alachua, Fla.: Bridge-Logos Publishers, 2008.

———. *The Power of Prayer and the Prayer of Power.* New York: Cosimo Classics, 2007.

———. *What the Bible Teaches: The Truths of the Bible Made Plain, Simple, and Understandable.* Peabody, Mass.: Hendrickson Publishers, 2008.

Thomas Spurgeon

Fullerton, W. Y. *Thomas Spurgeon: A Biography.* London: Hodder and Stoughton, 1919.

Hayden, Eric W. *A History of Spurgeon's Tabernacle.* Pasadena, Tex.: Pilgrim, 1971.

Spurgeon, Thomas. *Down to the Sea: Sixteen Sea Sermons.* London: Passmore and Alabaster, 1895.

———. *"God Save the King!" Addresses Concerning King Jesus.* London: Passmore and Alabaster, 1902.

———. *The Gospel of the Grace of God.* London: Passmore and Alabaster, 1884.

———. *Light and Love: A Series of Sermons.* London: Stockwell, 1897.

———. *"My Gospel": Twelve Addresses.* The Baptist Pulpit, vol. 23. London: Stockwell, 1902.

———. *Sermons Preached in the Metropolitan Tabernacle.* London: Stockwell, 1897–1902.

Samuel Chadwick

Chadwick, Samuel. *The Path of Prayer.* Fort Washington, Pa.: Christian Literature Crusade, 2001.

———. *The Way to Pentecost.* Fort Washington, Pa.: Christian Literature Crusade, 2001.

Dunning, Norman G. *Samuel Chadwick.* London: Hodder and Stoughton, 1933.

Charles E. Jefferson

Jefferson, Charles E. *The Building of the Church.* New York: Macmillan, 1910. Reprint, Grand Rapids: Baker, 1969.

———. *Cardinal Ideas of Isaiah.* New York: Macmillan, 1925.

———. *Cardinal Ideas of Jeremiah.* New York: Macmillan, 1928.

———. *The Minister as Shepherd.* New York: Crowell, 1912. Reprint, Grand Rapids: Zondervan, 1933.

———. *Quiet Hints to Growing Preachers.* New York: Crowell, 1901.

Jones, Edgar De Witt. *American Preachers of To-day.* Indianapolis: Bobbs-Merrill, 1933. Reprint, Freeport, N.Y.: Books for Libraries, 1971.

W. H. Griffith Thomas

Clark, M. Guthrie. *William Henry Griffith Thomas.* London: Church Book Room, 1949.

Stevenson, Herbert F., ed. *Keswick's Authentic Voice: 65 Dynamic Addresses Delivered at the Keswick Convention, 1875–1957.* Grand Rapids: Zondervan, 1959.

Thomas, W. H. Griffith. *The Apostle John: Studies in His Life and Writings.* Philadelphia: Sunday School Times, 1923. Reprint, Grand Rapids: Eerdmans, 1953.

———. *The Apostle Peter: Outline Studies in His Life, Character, and Writings.* New York: Revell, 1904. Reprint, Grand Rapids: Eerdmans, 1946.

———. *The Catholic Faith: A Manual of Instruction for Members of the Church of England.* London: Hodder and Stoughton, 1905. Reprint, London: Church Book Room, 1952.

———. *Christianity Is Christ, The Anglican Church Handbooks.* Edited by W. H. Griffith Thomas. London: Longmans, 1909. Reprint, Grand Rapids: Eerdmans, 1955.

———. *Commentary on Romans.* Grand Rapids: Kregel, 1996.

———. *Genesis.* 3 vols. *A Devotional Commentary.* Edited by A. R. Buckland. London: RTS, 1907–08. Reprint, Grand Rapids: Eerdmans, 1946.

———. *Grace and Power: Some Aspects of the Spiritual Life.* New York: Revell, 1916. Reprint, Grand Rapids: Eerdmans, 1949.

———. *The Holy Spirit of God.* London: Longmans, 1913. Reprint, Grand Rapids: Eerdmans, 1955.

———. *"Let Us Go On": The Secret of Christian Progress in the Epistle to the Hebrews.* London: Morgan and Scott, 1923. Reprinted as *Hebrews: A Devotional Commentary.* Grand Rapids: Eerdmans, n.d.

———. *Methods of Bible Study.* London: Marshall, 1902. Reprint, rev. ed. Chicago: Moody, 1975.

———. *Outline Studies in the Acts of the Apostles.* Edited by Winifred G. T. Gillespie. Grand Rapids: Eerdmans, 1956.

———. *Outline Studies in the Gospel of Luke.* Edited by Winifred G. T. Gillespie. Grand Rapids: Eerdmans, 1950.

———. *Outline Studies in the Gospel of Matthew.* Edited by Winifred G. T. Gillespie. Grand Rapids: Eerdmans, 1961.

———. *The Prayers of St. Paul. The Short Course Series.* Edited by John Adams. Edinburgh: Clark, 1914.

———. *The Principles of Theology: An Introduction to the Thirty-Nine Articles.* London: Longmans, 1930. Reprint, Grand Rapids: Baker, 1979.

———. *St. Paul's Epistle to the Romans: A Devotional Commentary.* Grand Rapids: Eerdmans, 1946.

———. *Studies in Colossians and Philemon.* Edited by Winifred G. T. Gillespie. Grand Rapids: Baker, 1973.

———. *Through the Pentateuch Chapter by Chapter.* Edited by Winifred G. T. Gillespie. Grand Rapids: Eerdmans, 1957.

———. *The Work of the Ministry.* London: Hodder and Stoughton, 1911. Reprinted as *Ministerial Life and Work.* Grand Rapids: Baker, 1976.

A. C. Gaebelein and B. H. Carroll

Carroll, B. H. *An Interpretation of the English Bible.* Edited by J. B. Cranfill. 13 vols. New York: Revell, 1916. Reprint, 6 vols. Grand Rapids: Baker, 1973.

Carroll, J. M., et al. *Dr. B. H. Carroll: The Colossus of Baptist History.* Fort Worth: Crowder, 1946.

Gaebelein, A. C. *The Acts of the Apostles.* New York: Our Hope, 1912. Reprint, Neptune, N.J.: Loizeaux, 1965.

———. *The Annotated Bible.* 9 vols. New York: Our Hope, 1913–24. Reprint, 4 vols. Chicago: Moody, 1970.

———. *The Book of Psalms.* New York: Our Hope, 1939.

———. *The Gospel of John.* New York: Our Hope, 1925. Reprint, Neptune, N.J.: Loizeaux, 1965.

———. *Half a Century: The Autobiography of a Servant.* New York: Our Hope, 1930.

———. *The Jewish Question.* New York: Our Hope, 1912.

———. *The Prophet Daniel.* New York: Our Hope, 1911. Reprint, Grand Rapids: Kregel, 1955.

————. *Studies in Zechariah*. New York: Fitch, 1905.

Scofield, C. I., ed. *The Scofield Reference Bible*. New York: Oxford University, 1909.

G. Campbell Morgan

Jeffs, Ernest H. *Princes of the Modern Pulpit*. London: Low, 1931.

Morgan, G. Campbell. *The Crises of the Christ*. New York: Revell, 1903.

————. *The Epistle of Paul the Apostle to the Romans*. Reprint, Eugene, Ore.: Wipf & Stock Publishers, 2001.

————. *Preaching*. New York: Revell, 1937. Reprint, Grand Rapids: Baker, 1974.

————. *The Study and Teaching of the English Bible*. New York: Revell, 1910.

————. *This Was His Faith: The Expository Letters of G. Campbell Morgan*. Edited by Jill Morgan. Westwood, N.J.: Revell, 1952.

Morgan, Jill. *A Man of the Word: Life of G. Campbell Morgan*. London: Pickering and Inglis, 1951. Reprint, Grand Rapids: Baker, 1972.

Morgan, Richard, Howard Morgan, and John Morgan, eds. *In the Shadow of Grace: The Life and Meditations of G. Campbell Morgan*. Grand Rapids: Baker, 2007.

Wagner, Don M. *The Expository Method of G. Campbell Morgan*. Westwood, N.J.: Revell, 1957.

John Henry Jowett

Jowett, John Henry. *"Apostolic Optimism" and Other Sermons*. London: Hodder and Stoughton, 1901.

————. *"The Eagle Life" and Other Studies in the Old Testament*. London: Hodder and Stoughton, 1921. Reprint, Grand Rapids: Baker, 1976.

————. *God—Our Contemporary: Sermons for the Times*. London: Clarke, 1922.

————. *J. H. Jowett*. Edited by Elmer G. Homrighausen. *Great Pulpit Masters*. New York: Revell, 1950. Reprint, Grand Rapids: Baker, 1972.

————. *Life in the Heights: Studies in the Epistles*. London: Hodder and Stoughton, 1924. Reprint, Grand Rapids: Baker, 1973.

————. *My Daily Meditation for the Circling Year*. London: Clarke, 1914.

————. *The Passion for Souls*. London: Clarke, 1905.

————. *The Preacher: His Life and Work*. New York: Hodder and Stoughton, 1912. Reprint, Grand Rapids: Baker, 1968.

————. *The Silver Lining*. London: Melrose, 1907.

————. *Springs in the Desert: Studies in the Psalms*. London: Hodder and Stoughton, 1924. Reprint, Grand Rapids: Baker, 1976.

————. *Things That Matter Most: Short Devotional Readings*. London: Clarke, 1913.

Porritt, Arthur. *John Henry Jowett*. London: Hodder and Stoughton, 1924.

J. D. Jones

Jeffs, Ernest H. *Princes of the Modern Pulpit*. London: Low, 1931.

Jones, J. D. *The Glorious Company of the Apostles*. London: Clarke, 1904.

————. *The Gospel According to St. Mark: A Devotional Commentary*. 4 vols. London: Religious Tract Society, n.d.

———. *The Greatest of These: Addresses on 1 Corinthians 13*. London: Hodder and Stoughton, 1925.

———. *The Hope of the Gospel: Expository Sermons on Christian Encouragement*. Grand Rapids: Kregel, 1995.

———. *If a Man Die*. London: Hodder and Stoughton, 1917.

———. *The Lord of Life and Death*. London: Hodder and Stoughton, 1919. Reprint, Grand Rapids: Baker, 1972.

———. *The Model Prayer*. London: Clarke, n.d.

———. *Richmond Hill Sermons*. London: Hodder and Stoughton, 1932.

———. *Three Score Years and Ten: The Autobiography of J. D. Jones*. London: Hodder and Stoughton, 1940.

———. *The Way into the Kingdom*. London: Religious Tract Society, 1900.

Porritt, Arthur. *J. D. Jones of Bournemouth*. London: Independent, 1942.

George H. Morrison

Gammie, Alexander. *Dr. George H. Morrison: The Man and His Work*. London: Clarke, 1928.

Morrison, Christine M. *Morrison of Wellington*. London: Hodder and Stoughton, 1930.

Morrison, George H. *The Afterglow of God*. New York: Hodder and Stoughton, 1912.

———. *The Ever Open Door*. London: Hodder and Stoughton, 1929.

———. *Flood-Tide*. London: Hodder and Stoughton, 1901. Reprint, Grand Rapids: Baker, 1971.

———. *The Footsteps of the Flock*. London: Hodder and Stoughton, 1904.

———. *The Return of the Angels*. London: Hodder and Stoughton, 1909.

———. *Sun-Rise*. London: Hodder and Stoughton, 1903. Reprint, Grand Rapids: Baker, 1971.

———. *The Unlighted Lustre*. London: Hodder and Stoughton, 1905. Reprint, Grand Rapids: Baker, 1971.

———. *The Weaving of Glory*. London: Hodder and Stoughton, 1913. Reprint, Grand Rapids: Kregel, 1995.

———. *The Wind on the Heath*. London: Hodder and Stoughton, 1915. Reprint, Grand Rapids: Baker, 1971.

———. *The Wings of the Morning*. London: Hodder and Stoughton, 1907. Reprint, Grand Rapids: Baker, 1970.

———. *The World-wide Gospel*. London: Hodder and Stoughton, 1933.

Amy Carmichael

Benge, Janet and Geoff Benge. *Amy Carmichael: Rescuer of Precious Gems*. Seattle: YWAM, 1998.

Carmichael, Amy. *I Come Quietly to Meet You: An Intimate Journey in God's Presence*. Bloomington: Bethany House Publishers, 2005.

Eliot, Elisabeth. *A Chance To Die: The Life and Legacy of Amy Carmichael*. Old Tappan, N.J.: Revell, 1987. Reprint, Grand Rapids: Revell, 2005.

Houghton, Frank. *Amy Carmichael of Dohnavur*. London: SPCK, 1953. Reprint, Fort Washington, Pa.: Christian Literature Crusade, 1988.

Frank W. Boreham

Boreham, Frank W. *A Bunch of Everlastings*. London: Epworth, 1920. Reprint, Philadelphia: Judson, 1942.

———. *A Casket of Cameos*. London: Epworth, 1924. Reprint, Philadelphia: Judson, 1950.

———. *A Faggot of Torches.* London: Epworth, 1926. Reprint, Philadelphia: Judson, 1951.

———. *A Handful of Stars.* London: Epworth, 1922. Reprint, Philadelphia: Judson, 1950.

———. *The Heavenly Octave: A Study of the Beatitudes.* London: Epworth, 1935. Reprint, Grand Rapids: Baker, 1968.

———. *The Last Milestone.* London: Epworth, 1961.

———. *The Luggage of Life.* London: Kelly, 1912.

———. *Mushrooms on the Moor.* London: Kelly, 1915.

———. *My Pilgrimage: An Autobiography.* London: Epworth, 1940.

———. *The Other Side of the Hill and Home Again.* London: Kelly, 1917.

———. *The Passing of John Broadbanks.* London: Epworth, 1936.

———. *The Prodigal.* London: Epworth, 1941.

———. *The Silver Shadow and Other Day-Dreams.* London: Kelly, 1918.

———. *A Temple of Topaz.* London: Epworth, 1928. Reprint, Philadelphia: Judson, 1951.

Crago, T. Howard. *The Story of F. W. Boreham.* London: Marshall, Morgan, and Scott, 1961.

Joseph W. Kemp

De Plata, William R. *Tell It from Calvary: The Record of a Sustained Gospel Witness from Calvary Baptist Church of New York City Since 1847.* New York: Calvary Baptist Church, 1972.

Kemp, Joseph W. *Outline Studies in the Book of Revelation.* New York: The Book Stall, 1917.

———. *Outline Studies on the Tabernacle in the Wilderness.* London: Marshall, 1913.

———. *The Soul-Winner and Soul-Winning.* New York: Doran, 1916.

Kemp, Winnie. *Joseph W. Kemp: The Record of a Spirit-Filled Life.* London: Marshall, Morgan, and Scott, 1936.

Oswald Chambers

Chambers, Gertrude H. *Oswald Chambers: His Life and Work.* London: Simpkin Marshall, Ltd., 1933.

Chambers, Oswald. *The Complete Works of Oswald Chambers.* Compiled by Biddy Chambers. Grand Rapids: Discovery House, 2000.

———. *If You Will Ask.* Grand Rapids: Discovery House, 1994.

———. *Love: A Holy Command.* Grand Rapids: Discovery House, 2008.

McCasland, David. *Oswald Chambers: Abandoned to God.* Grand Rapids: Discovery House, 1993.

Verploegh, Harry, ed. *Oswald Chambers: The Best from All the Books.* 2 vols. Nashville: Thomas Nelson, 1987, 1989.

H. A. Ironside

English, E. Schuyler. *H. A. Ironside: Ordained of the Lord.* Grand Rapids: Zondervan, 1946. Reprinted as *Ordained of the Lord. H. A. Ironside: A Biography.* Rev. ed. Neptune, N.J.: Loizeaux, 1976.

Ironside, H. A. *Addresses on the Gospel of John.* New York: Loizeaux, 1942.

———. *"Charge That to My Account" and Other Gospel Messages.* Chicago: Bible Colportage Association, 1931.

———. *Expository Messages on the Epistle to the Galatians.* New York: Loizeaux, 1940.

———. *Expository Notes on the Prophet Isaiah.* New York: Loizeaux, 1952.

———. *Holiness: The False and the True.* New York: Loizeaux, 1939.

———. *In the Heavenlies: Practical Expository Addresses on the Epistle to the Ephesians.* New York: Loizeaux, 1949.

———. *Ironside Expository Commentaries.* Grand Rapids: Kregel, 2005.

———. *Lectures on Daniel the Prophet.* New York: Loizeaux, 1920.

———. *Lectures on the Book of Revelation.* New York: Loizeaux, 1919.

———. *Lectures on the Epistle to the Romans.* New York: Loizeaux, 1951.

———. *Random Reminiscences from Fifty Years of Ministry.* New York: Loizeaux, 1939.

———. *Studies in the Epistle to the Hebrews . . . Lectures on the Epistle to Titus.* New York: Loizeaux, 1942.

Clarence Edward Macartney

Macartney, Clarence Edward. *Bible Epitaphs.* Grand Rapids: Baker, 1974.

———. *Chariots of Fire.* Grand Rapids: Kregel, 1994.

———. *Great Interviews of Jesus.* Grand Rapids: Baker, 1974.

———. *Great Nights of The Bible.* New York: Abingdon, 1943.

———. *Great Women of the Bible.* Grand Rapids: Baker, 1974.

———. *The Greatest Men of the Bible.* New York: Abingdon, 1941.

———. *The Greatest Texts of the Bible.* New York: Abingdon, 1947.

———. *The Greatest Words in the Bible and In Human Speech.* Whitmore and Smith, 1938.

———. *He Chose Twelve.* Grand Rapids: Kregel, 1993.

———. *The Lamb of God.* Grand Rapids: Kregel, 1994.

———. *The Making of A Minister.* New York: Channel Press, 1961.

———. *The Man Who Forgot, and Other Sermons on Bible Characters.* 1956.

———. *Peter and His Lord.* 1937.

———. *Preaching Without Notes.* Grand Rapids: Baker, 1976.

———. *Salute Thy Soul.* New York: Abingdon, 1957.

———. *Sermons on Old Testament Heroes.* 1935.

———. *Strange Texts but Grand Truths.* Grand Rapids: Kregel, 1994.

———. *Trials of Great Men of the Bible.* New York: Abingdon, 1946.

———. *12 Great Questions About Christ.* Grand Rapids: Kregel, 1993.

———. *The Way of a Man with a Maid.* Grand Rapids: Baker, 1974.

———. *The Wisest Fool and Other Men of the Bible.* New York: Abingdon, 1949.

———. *The Woman of Tekoah.* Grand Rapids: Baker, 1977.

———. *You Can Conquer.* New York: Abingdon, 1954.

William Whiting Borden

Taylor, Mrs. Howard. *Borden of Yale '09—"The Life that Counts."* China Inland Mission, 1926.

———. *William Borden: An Overseas Missionary Fellowship Book.* Chicago: Moody, 1980.

Alva Jay McClain

McClain, Alva J. *Bible Truths*. Winona Lake, Ind.: BMH Books, 1979.

———. *Daniel's Prophecy of the Seventy Weeks*. Winona Lake, Ind.: BMH Books, 2007.

———. *The Gospel of God's Grace: Romans*. Winona Lake, Ind.: BMH Books, 1989.

———. *The Greatness of the Kingdom*. Winona Lake, Ind.: BMH Books, 1968.

———. *Law and Grace: A Study of New Testament Concepts as They Relate to the Christian Life*. Winona Lake, Ind.: BMH Books, 2001.

Rohr, Norman B. *A Saint in Glory Stands: The Story of Alva J. McClain*. Winona Lake, Ind.: BMH Books, 1986.

A. W. Tozer

Anonymous. *Cloud of Unknowing: A Book of Contemplation*. Edited by Evelyn Underhill. London: Watkins, 1970.

Dorsett, Lyle. *A Passion for God: The Spiritual Journey of A.W. Tozer*. Chicago: Moody, 2008.

Eckhart, Meister. *After Supper in the Refectory: A Series of Instructions*. Translated by N. Leeson. London: Mowbray, 1917.

———. *Treatises and Sermons*. Edited and translated by James M. Clark and John V. Skinner. New York: Harper, 1958.

Fant, David J., Jr. *A. W. Tozer: A Twentieth-Century Prophet*. Harrisburg, Pa.: Christian Publications, 1964.

Fenelon, François. *Christian Perfection*. Edited by Charles F. Whiston. Translated by Mildred Whitney Stillman. New York: Harper, 1947.

Kepler, Thomas S., ed. *The Fellowship of the Saints*. New York: Abingdon, 1948.

Snyder, James L. *The Life of A.W. Tozer: In Pursuit of God*. Ventura, Calif.: Regal Books, 2009.

Tozer, A. W. *Born After Midnight*. Harrisburg, Pa.: Christian Publications, 1964.

———, ed. *The Christian Book of Mystical Verse*. Harrisburg, Pa.: Christian Publications, 1963.

———. *The Divine Conquest*. Harrisburg, Pa.: Christian Publications, 1950.

———. *The Root of the Righteous*. Harrisburg, Pa.: Christian Publications, 1955.

———. *The Knowledge of the Holy: The Attributes of God*. New York: Harper, 1961.

———. *Let My People Go! The Life of Robert A. Jaffray*. Harrisburg, Pa.: Christian Publications, 1947.

———. *Man: The Dwelling Place of God*. Harrisburg, Pa.: Christian Publications, 1966.

———. *Of God and Men*. Harrisburg, Pa.: Christian Publications, 1960.

———. *The Pursuit of God*. Harrisburg, Pa.: Christian Publications, 1948.

———. *That Incredible Christian*. Harrisburg, Pa.: Christian Publications, 1964.

———. *Tozer on Worship and Entertainment*. Camp Hill, Pa.: WingSpread Publishers, 2006.

———. *The Tozer Pulpit*. Edited by Gerald B. Smith. Harrisburg, Pa.: Christian Publications, 1967.

———. *Wingspread: Albert B. Simpson*. Harrisburg, Pa.: Christian Publications, 1943.

Underhill, Evelyn. *The Evelyn Underhill Reader*. Edited by Thomas S. Kepler. New York: Abingdon, 1962.

W. E. Sangster

Sangster, Paul E. *Doctor Sangster.* London: Epworth, 1962.

Sangster, W. E. *The Approach to Preaching.* London: Epworth, 1951. Reprint, Grand Rapids: Baker, 1974.

———. *The Craft of Sermon Construction.* London: Epworth, 1949. Reprint, Grand Rapids: Baker, 1972.

———. *The Craft of Sermon Illustration.* London: Epworth, 1946. Reprint, Grand Rapids: Baker, 1973.

———. *God Does Guide Us.* London: Hodder and Stoughton, 1934.

———. *He Is Able.* London: Epworth, 1949. Reprint, Grand Rapids: Baker, 1975.

———. *Let Me Commend: Realistic Evangelism.* New York: Abingdon-Cokesbury, 1948.

———. *The Path to Perfection.* London: Hodder and Stoughton, 1943.

———. *The Pure in Heart.* London: Epworth, 1954.

———. *Questions People Ask About Religion.* New York: Abingdon, 1980.

———. *Sangster of Westminster.* London: Marshall, Morgan, and Scott, 1960.

———. *Special Day Sermons.* New York: Abingdon, 1960.

———. *Teach Me to Pray.* Nashville, Tenn.: Upper Room Books, 2000.

———. *These Things Abide.* London: Hodder and Stoughton, 1939.

———. *Westminster Sermons.* 2 vols. London: Epworth, 1960–61.

———. *Why Jesus Never Wrote a Book.* London: Epworth, 1932.

William Culbertson

Culbertson, William. *The Faith Once Delivered: Keynote Messages from Moody Founder's Week.* Chicago: Moody, 1972.

———. *For Times Like These.* Chicago: Moody, 1972.

———. *God's Provision for Holy Living.* Chicago: Moody, 1957.

Stevenson, Herbert F., ed. *Keswick's Triumphant Voice: Forty-eight Outstanding Addresses Delivered at the Keswick Convention, 1882–1962.* Grand Rapids: Zondervan, 1963.

Wiersbe, Warren W. *William Culbertson: A Man of God.* Chicago: Moody, 1974.

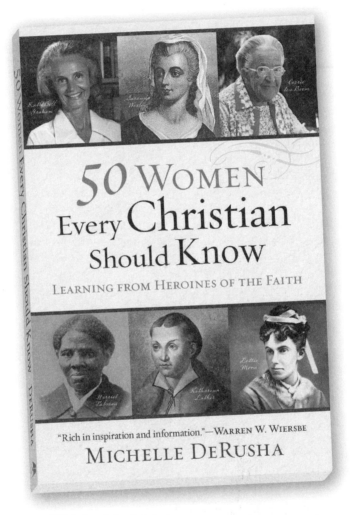